DATE DUE

INNOVATION
HAPPENS ELSEWHERE

INNOVATION HAPPENS ELSEWHERE

Open Source as Business Strategy

RON GOLDMAN

RICHARD P. GABRIEL

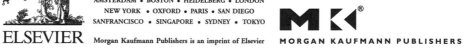

ELSEVIER

AMSTERDAM • BOSTON • HEIDELBERG • LONDON
NEW YORK • OXFORD • PARIS • SAN DIEGO
SANFRANCISCO • SINGAPORE • SYDNEY • TOKYO

Morgan Kaufmann Publishers is an imprint of Elsevier

MORGAN KAUFMANN PUBLISHERS

Senior Editor	Tim Cox
Assistant Editor	Richard Camp
Publishing Services Manager	Simon Crump
Senior Production Editor	Paul Gottehrer
Cover Design Manager	Cate Rickard Barr
Cover Design	Yvo Riezebos Design
Text Design	Rebecca Evans
Composition	Cepha
Technical Illustration	Dartmouth
Copyeditor	Julie Nemer
Proofreader	Pamela Andrada
Indexer	Steve Rath
Interior printer	The Maple-Vail Book Manufacturing Group
Cover printer	Phoenix Color Corporation

Morgan Kaufmann Publishers is an imprint of Elsevier.
500 Sansome Street, Suite 400, San Francisco, CA 94111

This book is printed on acid-free paper.

Library of Congress Cataloging-in-Publication Data

ISBN: 1-55860-889-3

For information on all Morgan Kaufmann publications,
visit our website at www.mkp.com or www.books.elsevier.com

Printed in the United States of America
05 06 07 08 09   5 4 3 2 1

Working together to grow
libraries in developing countries

www.elsevier.com | www.bookaid.org | www.sabre.org

ELSEVIER   BOOK AID International   Sabre Foundation

To all the people volunteering on open source projects

Ron Goldman

For Jo, Mika, Joseph, John, and Helen

Richard P. Gabriel

ABOUT THE AUTHORS

Ron Goldman is a researcher at Sun Microsystems Laboratories in California working on alternative software development methodologies and new software architectures inspired by biology. He has been working with open source since hacking on GDB at Lucid, Inc. back in 1992. Since 1998 he has been helping groups at Sun Microsystems understand open source and advising them on how to build successful communities around their open-source projects.

Prior to Sun he developed a program to generate and manipulate visual representations of complex data for use by social scientists as part of a collaboration between NYNEX Science & Technology and the Institute for Research on Learning. He has worked on programming language design, programming environments, user interface design, and data visualization. He has a PhD in Computer Science from Stanford University where he was a member of the robotics group.

Richard P. Gabriel received a PhD in Computer Science from Stanford University in 1981, and an MFA in Poetry from Warren Wilson College in 1998. He has been a researcher at Stanford University, company president and Chief Technical Officer at Lucid, Inc., vice president of development at ParcPlace-Digitalk, a management consultant for several startups and Sun Microsystems, and Consulting Professor of Computer Science at Stanford University.

He currently is a Distinguished Engineer and principal investigator of a small research group at Sun Laboratories, researching the architecture, design, and implementation of extraordinarily large, self-sustaining systems as well as development techniques for building them. He is one of Sun's open source experts, advising the company on community-based strategies. He is also President of the Hillside Group, a nonprofit that nurtures the software patterns community by holding conferences, publishing books, and awarding scholarships.

He is an ACM Fellow, has been a finalist in several poetry manuscript contests, including the National Poetry Series book prize, and has won the Texas Instruments Excellence in Technical Communications Award, the Northeastern University Outstanding Alumni Award, the ACM SIGPLAN Distinguished Service Award, and the ACM/AAAI Allen Newell Award.

From the press release for the 2004 Allen Newell award from the Association of Computing Machinery (ACM):

A man of remarkable breadth and challenging intellect, Richard Gabriel has had a remarkable influence not only on fundamental issues in programming languages and software design but also on the interaction between computer science and other disciplines, notably architecture and poetry. Dr. Gabriel's background spans industry and academia, technology and humanities, introspection and application. He stretches the imagination of computer scientists with ideas and innovations from other fields and thus his role in shaping the growth and impact of object technology and its followers has been profound.

CONTENTS

APPENDIX C *Contributor Agreements*   361

APPENDIX D *Codename Spinnaker*   377

FOREWORD

The most important innovation of the Industrial Revolution wasn't the steam engine or the Bessemer furnace or any technological breakthrough, it was limited liability, because that mobilized the flow of capital.

—William A. Sahlman[1]

At first glance, this book appears to be about developing software more effectively. If you're not in the business of creating, acquiring, or depending on software—surely there is someone left in this category—why pay attention?

Because today, the software community is pioneering the changes arising in our society from the transformation from industrial to informational economy. The case of open source software presents the richest example available of the changes underway in the structure of our economic institutions.

These changes reflect the shift in the nature of capital and the meaning of ownership. When money replaced land as the main store of economic value, the corporation and the financial services industry developed. Open source points the way to the innovations arising from the shift from financial to knowledge-based capital.

The industrial economy required access to unprecedented amounts of financial capital. In the 18th century the financial system was called upon to support commerce on the scale of a ship full of cargo; by the middle of the 19th century, Carnegie was building steel mills, Rockefeller refineries, and Gould railroads. John D. Rockefeller wrote that the financial engineering of Trusts—the forerunner of the limited liability corporation—was as great an achievement as the technology to extract and refine petroleum.

Limited liability was vital because this new scale of financial risk had become too great for entrepreneurs to bear. It brought with it a variety of institutional changes—bankruptcy court replaced debtors' prison as the outcome of financial failure—and a rebalancing of economic power favoring capital over land and labor, later readjusted by the development of antitrust law and the labor movement. Then, since the 1930s, these new relationships among capital, labor, and consumers remained broadly unchanged in the industrialized world.

But they are changing now.

Today, financial capital is no longer scarce: human and intellectual capital are. Once again, a pattern of changing relationships among holders of the new and old

---

[1] Associate Professor, Harvard Business School, in an unpublished lecture.

forms of capital is unfolding, as the information economy begins to mature. Financial capital is no longer scarce—venture capitalists have lately been giving money back to investors because they lack sufficient opportunities that combine good ideas with proven people. And so we should expect to see institutional innovations that mobilize these newly scarce resources. *Corporations and financial institutions will see their roles wane as landowners did in the 19th century; owners of human and intellectual capital will grow in power as financiers did before them.*

"Human and intellectual capital" is not a metaphor—talent and knowledge are capital goods in the same sense as milling machines and delivery vans: they represent productive capacity, they require investment, they depreciate, and they can be bought, leased, or rented.

These forms of capital present unique features that do not fit our management models for financial and physical capital. Thus, the network-based innovations that are making most markets more liquid and efficient—ECNs in the financial world, CNET, Amazon, and the like in the world of goods—have made only limited inroads in the human capital markets. Thus far, Monster.com and MyRichUncle.com are interesting developments, but have not transformed markets for human capital.[2]

There are two challenges facing efficient human capital markets. First, most individual capabilities are difficult to characterize, so that trades are difficult; money is by definition fungible, human capabilities are not. Second, the social trend is away from standard forms of employment and toward free agency. Formerly only available to stars like Charlie Chaplin or Curt Flood, free agency and other more self-organized forms of employment are increasingly popular.[3] Each corporate downsizing, job offshoring, and economic downturn teaches more people how to be free agents.

The challenge of markets for intellectual property is even more daunting. Information has unique economic characteristics: it can be shared at very low marginal cost; and often reducing its scarcity *increases* its value. The more people who use AOL software, the more content is available to AOL users. The distribution of enormous quantities of AOL CDs is *not* equivalent to giving away razors to sell blades. Because many AOL users come to meet others in the AOL community, it's as if giving away razors made blades work better. Seth Godin, author of *Viral Marketing*, has offered his books free for downloading— making his content un-scarce—and then self-published hardcover "mementos" for $40. He summed up a key idea of marketing intellectual capital: "You give it away until you charge for it."

---

[2] For more about the future of markets for human capital, see *Future Wealth*, by Stan Davis and Christopher Meyer.

[3] These developments are described in Dan Pink's *Free Agent Nation*.

Creating, rewarding, distributing, and pricing information is the tectonic hotspot of our current economic evolution, where the industrial plate is diving beneath the new information landmass. Above it, we can see an archipelago, formed of islands of innovation, often marked by conflict. For example:

- In the world of entertainment, Napster's (original) exploitation of the economics of information has been contending with industrial-era pricing models as if the value were in the CD, not the content. A new field, "Digital Rights Management," has surfaced in law, to help—maybe— work through these issues across all media and other forms of IP.

- The early work to sequence the human genome pitted Celera, with the ambition to make the information proprietary, against the efforts of government-sponsored programs aiming to make this intellectual property freely available;

- MIT has made its course materials available free on the Internet;

- Creative Commons, a "non-profit organization working to re-establish the balance between public and private gain in the proprietary control and use of creative work," was launched in 2002 in part to counterbalance the push by copyright and patent owners to extend the lifetime of these restrictions indefinitely. Creative Commons has defined "some rights reserved" licenses that creators of intellectual property can use when they contribute their work to the Commons; they acknowledge that they take inspiration from the Free Software Foundation's GNU General Public License, discussed in detail in this book. This is open source in the literacy domain.

- iTunes, Apple's online music store, has succeeded by defining "ownership" of music as the right to copy it onto unlimited CDs and five computers. This is a version of open source for music.

- Sun Microsystems, with several other companies with a stake in the success of the programming language Java, created the Java Fund to invest in startups that built Java-based software. Their purpose was to accelerate the visibility and acceptance of Java as a standard. In effect, they were trading proprietary ownership to attract the human and intellectual capital required for their success.

The elephant in the room not yet mentioned is, of course, the development of the Linux operating system, and the Open Source software activities for which it serves as avatar. Because Linux has achieved such success in terms of the size of its community, the quality of its product, and above all its commercial importance— not just as a competitor to Microsoft but as the basis of new companies like Red

Hat and new activities at, for example, IBM, it is the most visible and persuasive evidence that surprising innovations are taking place.

The open source community points the way to new concepts of property because it occupies the crossroads of the two streams of novelty: first, it engages self-organizing free agents as its labor force, mobilizing human capital. Second, open source relies upon the very low cost of reusability and distribution of software code for its economic effectiveness, mobilizing intellectual capital.

Thus, *Innovation Happens Elsewhere* is at least as important for those who have no interest in software as for those who do, because in the details of the history and practice of the open source community lie clues to the institutional adaptations of the information economy; in the clauses of the software licenses presented here lie the case law that will come to define property in the information age. There are other books that have a great deal to say about this evolution[4], but Ron Goldman and Richard Gabriel offer the unique inside-out insight gained in flesh-and-blood open source projects and personal roles developing the structures that have supported them.

And it is the flesh and blood that will be affected. Life in the "gift economy" associated with open source activities is lived by a different set of legal rules, values, and norms than those in the zero-sum industrial world. Ultimately, this will prove a powerful platform for economic growth, and may even accelerate the equalization of incomes around the world. A recent example: the Chinese government had established a requirement that Intel and others conform to a technological standard, whose patents were held solely by Chinese companies, to gain the right to sell WiFi chips in China. Intel responded that the value of a single worldwide WiFi standard was undeniable and large, and that they would forego the Chinese market rather than conform. China backed down.

The importance of this example is not just that Intel was upholding the open standard business model against the desire for proprietary profits; it's that China, which has for decades disregarded the importance of intellectual property rights, has come to see upholding these property rights as *in their own interest* as they play with the rest of the developed world.

The basis of property is not immutable—in the agricultural economy, land itself spawned a set of rules for how its value could be shared—this Dirt Rights Management approach was called "usufruct." We are in the midst of another reinvention of property, and the best clues to its nature available can be found in the world of open source software. Read on.

Christopher Meyer
Chief Executive, Monitor Networks
March, 2005

---

[4] See, for example, *The Success of Open Source,* by Steven Weber, or *The Wisdom of Crowds*, by James Surowiecky.

PREFACE

In the fall of 1998 Bill Joy and Mike Clary asked us to help establish a community of developers and companies around Sun's then-new Jini network technology. Jini is a simple distributed computing model based on the Java programming language that enables services running on different computer systems to spontaneously interact with each other over the network with minimal pre-planning for such interactions. For Jini to succeed, it was clear that the underlying Jini protocols and infrastructure would need to become pervasive, and to accomplish that would require a strong community of participants and partners. Moreover Sun did not have the expertise to define Jini services in areas like printing, digital photography, storage, white goods, or the many other potential markets for products that would benefit from being network enabled.

As a preliminary step the Sun Community Source License (SCSL) had been developed to provide a framework where the source code for Jini could be safely shared. SCSL is not true open source, but has many of the same characteristics. However a license and providing the source code were not enough—there had to be more to motivate people to participate. We worked with the Jini engineering and marketing teams to apply the lessons we had learned from being involved in various open source and community development projects and from our studies of complexity science to create a true Jini Community.

We worked hard to help establish an identity for the community. To build identity and culture requires face-to-face interaction, so we organized community meetings that were held in interesting places and featuring non-traditional speakers. The first Jini Community meeting was at the Aspen Institute in Aspen, Colorado. We played team-building games, we engaged a recording graphic artist, we broke into groups in unusual ways.[1] We encouraged nonstandard thinking and speaking as individuals rather than as representatives of companies at times. The keynote speakers included Robert Dahl, a political scientist, talking

---

[1] For example, we used a team-building exercise in which people sort themselves into a line where one end represents January 1 and the other December 31, and each person's place in the line corresponds to their birthday. No talking, writing, or showing documents is allowed, so the idea is for people to establish how to communicate silently while communicating silently. The result is tested by having people call off their birthdate in the order they are standing in the line. Then we would select groups by counting off in this ordering.

"On Democracy," and Thomas Petzinger, a *Wall Street Journal* columnist, speaking about new business models based on cooperation.

We also helped create a website for the project (http://www.jini.org) as a meeting place, a newspaper, a repository of shared documents, a totem, and a place to share work and projects. Most of the shared assets of the community could be accessed there. The website had a public part that advertised the community, and private parts for members only to help foster community identity.

Common vocabulary leads to shared stories and then to shared beliefs. We created a pattern language on how the Jini Community could work, which has served to create a shared vocabulary—terms like *dangerous waterhole, cut & run*, and *microcosm* that serve as linguistic markers for the uniqueness of the community and culture. The pattern language was designed to teach how to build (self-) governance structures and procedures on the fly which have proven to be comfortable and delightful in the past but which were to be tailored to the specific on-the-spot needs of the community.

We also worked with the community on developing a formal decision-making process and a "community process" for the purpose of ratifying definitions for Jini services. The former was to make it clear how community-wide decisions are made—how are proposals created, how are they voted on, how are appeals made—and the latter was to specify how the community can officially bless or endorse a service definition.

The request to help build a community around a technology for business purposes led us to research and think about business in the commons. How do open-source projects work? How can a company participate? Why would a company engage in an activity centered around giving things away? How and why could such a thing work?

Since the spring of 2000 we have done similar work with other Sun-sponsored open-source projects such as NetBeans, OpenOffice, Project JXTA, and java.net. We have worked with each of those teams to help them to define their open source strategy along with how to implement it.

This book contains not only the lessons we have learned from helping to create and nurture communities around these Sun-sponsored and other open source and community development projects, but the fruit of years of participation in innovative communities of many sorts. Specifically, one of us[2] was the originator of the Common Lisp Group, which is the first, large-scale, email-based design effort; this group worked from 1981 until the early 1990s. The same author[2] founded Lucid, Inc, one of whose products—designed and implemented in the late 1980s—used a suite of free-software tools tied together by a proprietary,

---

[2] RPG.

database-centered coordination layer. The tools included GCC, GDB, and a window-based version of Emacs originally called Lucid Emacs and now called Xemacs. The interaction of the suite of tools with the coordination layer was through an open set of protocols, and several compilers were modified to support these protocols. Lucid was one of the first companies to do significant work on open-source code (in this case, Free Software Foundation code) as part of a business strategy, and in fact, the existence of LGPL is partly due to this early commercial use of GPLed code.

This book also includes insights from studying other open-source projects such as Linux, Apache, Emacs, Xemacs, GCC, GDB, and Mozilla.

We have had experience with projects and companies that were trying to achieve something creative in the context of a passionate user, developer, and partner landscape where the knowledge, expertise, and innovation in that landscape needed to be part of the creativity.

Ron Goldman
Richard P. Gabriel
March, 2005

This book is a work in progress and we welcome comments on how to improve it. Please send your suggestions to IHE@dreamsongs.com. An online version of it can be found at: http://www.dreamsongs.com/IHE

ACKNOWLEDGMENTS

The authors wish to acknowledge everyone who has talked with us or written about their experiences with open source; we have heavily mined those works to produce this book.

We wish to thank Bill Joy and Mike Clary who initiated this work by asking us to help create a vibrant community of developers using Sun's Jini Technology. We also want to acknowledge the strong support we received from Emily Suter and Ingrid Van Den Hoogen. We also thank the members of the Jini development team, especially Ken Arnold, Mark Hodapp, Jim Hurley, Charles Lamb, and Jimmy Torres. We also acknowledge some of the Jini Community members that helped us such as Cees de Groot, Alan Kaminsky, Michael Ogg, Aleta Ricciardi, Sylvia Tidwell Scheuring, Jerome Scheuring, and Bill Venners.

Thanks to Rob Gingell and Bonnie Toy for asking us to advise other groups at Sun who were considering using open source and for supporting us while we completed this book.

The members of Sun's Open Source Program Office, Danese Cooper, James Duncan Davidson, and Eric Renaud, were very helpful in spreading the open source message at Sun. Danese, in particular, helped shape this book in its early stages.

We thank Brian Behlendorf and Mitchell Baker for sharing with us the lessons they had learned from the Apache and Mozilla projects, and also Tim O'Reilly for sharing his insights about open source.

Sonali Shah provided us with key insights into why individuals participate in open source, and how outsiders participate in a company's innovative activities.

We have benefited from comments on early versions of this book from a number of readers including Bob Sproull, Emily Suter, Danese Cooper, Lawrence Lee, Ed Burns, Steven Rubin, Philippe Lalande, Duncan Findlater, Michael Davey, Rod Evans, and Tony Graham.

Anders Hejlsberg and Dave Thomas provided valuable information about some of the historical points noted in this book.

We also want to thank the various Sun groups that have let us experiment on them as they have explored using open source. The NetBeans team has been especially helpful, particularly Evan Adams, Kartik Mithal, Dirk Ruiz, and David

Taber. From StarOffice/OpenOffice we want to thank Alan Templeton, John Heard, and Marissa Bishop. The whole JXTA team has been great to work with, thanks to Juan Carlos Soto, Emily Suter, and Ingrid Van Den Hoogen. Also John Tollefsrud of the Sun GridEngine project. The java.net team—though they didn't realize it at the time—permitted us the most freedom we've ever had to try to create a community around open source and the open source ethos that was informed by our experiences before and during writing this book. Ingrid Van Den Hoogen was gracious enough to put her reputation in our hands once more, and we were joined again by Emily Suter. Daniel Steinberg of Dim Sum Thinking taught us about how journalism fit into community building, and Cathy Guthrie, Micheline Nijmeh, John Bobowicz, Ken Ostereich, and Chris Cheline helped keep the rubber off the sky (mostly).

Also thanks for their help to Guy L. Steele Jr., Jan Hauser, Jennifer Umstattd, John Ravella, Thomas Petzinger Jr., Robert Dahl, Kathy Knutsen, Bill Lard, Clifford Allen, Mike Schilling, Douglas Begle, Thomas Benthin, Pankag Garg, Peter G. Capek, and Steve Graham.

We thank Tim Cox, Richard Camp, and Stacie Pierce, and Paul Gottehrer of Morgan Kaufmann for their help in publishing this book, and also our external reviewers, Lara Fabans, Harold E. Gottschalk Jr., and Ted Leung, for their comments, which helped us improve the presentation.

Ron Goldman extends his special thanks to Mary Alexander for editorial assistance and writing advice.

Richard Gabriel thanks Jo Lawless for enduring yet another writing project, and the Lisp community for providing him with the opportunity to help create one of the first online design communities—the Common Lisp community.

CHAPTER 1

Introduction

BUSINESS IS CHANGING after the expansive thinking of the late 1990s followed by the lessons learned in the early 2000s: It no longer makes sense for every company to make and own every aspect of its business. Many companies—perhaps all of them—require software, and many create software as an integral part of running their businesses; and some even produce software as part of their offerings. Every such company knows deeply that producing software is not a cakewalk and that the pace of creating final, usable software is slow. A naïve promise of open source is that it is somehow free of cost. But the real opportunities of open source come from many directions.

In fact, there are so many business and strategic reasons for a company heavily invested in creating software to adopt open-source activities that a company that does not can be considered to be out of touch with its own destiny. Even if a company decides that public (or pure, all-volunteer) open source is not for it, using open source within its firewalls could be a smart decision for pure software development methodology reasons.

Open Source: A Different Way of Doing Business

When businesspeople first encounter the idea of public open-source software, they are usually attracted by the fact that it is cost-free and that they get access to the underlying source code—open-source software is like coming across a blueberry bush bursting with fat ripe blueberries. But then it hits them that open-source software comes on an as-is basis with no warranty, no indemnification, and no support. No one is officially responsible—there is no one to contract with and no one to sue for liability.

Also confusing is the open-source development process. Who is in charge? How are decisions made? What is the development schedule? Finally, the idea of giving work done by their developers away to anyone—possibly including their business competitors—seems to violate common sense.

All in all this is not how they are used to doing business. But open source does make sense.

Innovation Happens Elsewhere

Companies who wish to create wealth are always interested in productivity. Productivity includes being able to innovate effectively. Effective innovation is not merely being able to invent and improve, but also being able to determine what to invent and how to improve. High productivity requires doing less to produce as much or more—a company that requires its own employees to labor hard and long to make its products or perform its services will be less profitable, in general, than one that can take advantage of the efforts of others. In most cases, this means that a company wishing to innovate productively must recognize that valuable work and talent exist outside the confines of the company and that it must find ways of using that outside material and expertise while still maintaining a competitive edge.

Until now, the most effective way of accomplishing this has been to purchase a company that has a technology or product of interest to the buyer along with the personnel who can maintain and move it forward. One of the best-known examples of this was Turbo Pascal, one of Borland International's most successful products—one that helped put Borland on the map.

Turbo Pascal started out as Blue Label Software (BLS) Pascal, developed and marketed by a company called PolyData based in Copenhagen, Denmark, and written primarily by Anders Hejlsberg. It was a subset of the full Pascal language along with an editor, compiler, and run-time libraries. BLS Pascal evolved into a complete Pascal implementation, changing its name to COMPAS and then PolyPascal as it moved to other platforms and further evolved. In 1983 PolyData entered into a license agreement with Borland. Borland wrote a new editor and menu system for PolyPascal, and the resulting product became Turbo Pascal. PolyPascal and Turbo Pascal were marketed in parallel for a few years, but thereafter PolyPascal was discontinued. When Anders Hejlsberg moved to the United States in 1987, he became a full-time employee of Borland.

One of Borland's most significant innovations with PolyPascal was to take a product that had previously sold for about $500 and sell it for $49.95. At that time, fully professional-grade development environments including a language compiler sold for around $3000, and Turbo Pascal was of similar quality. Therefore, this price innovation had a dramatic effect on the market. Moreover, not only was Borland able to get a top-quality development tool, but it was able to hire a top programming-language designer and implementor. By not having a stake in how hard it had been to develop the product, Borland was able to price the package so that it would sell dramatically well. Few people at that time—the early 1980s—had any idea that software developed for sale could be sold reasonably at commodity prices. And even after Borland entered the scene with Turbo Pascal, the lesson was learned only slowly.

Nevertheless, an important part of the Turbo Pascal story is that intellectual property rights were well defined and protected for both PolyData and Borland. Borland would not have entered into the agreement without the exclusive rights the agreement provided. Deciding whether to incorporate open source as part of a business strategy requires coming to grips with which property rights and control over the technology are important to your company.

The phrase "innovation happens elsewhere" captures the essence of the idea of adding just the smallest amount of innovation necessary for competitive advantage. It is common for people working for a technology company to suffer, at least a little, from the belief that all the really innovative people in their particular technology happen to work at that company. This can cause such a company to work too hard to produce every last bit of related technology, which is often not the best competitive approach. Many advantages accrue when a company adopts the attitude that most innovation happens elsewhere and focuses on choosing the best outside innovations and figuring out the right distinguishing features to make its products competitive.

Traditional open source is one of the best examples of this approach. The Internet started out as the ARPAnet, and many of the underlying technologies powering it—Domain Name Service (DNS via BIND), email transport (sendmail), and various open TCP/IP implementations—were developed in the public domain and remain open-source implementations, even when there are commercial versions available. Working in the public domain in the style of an open university research environment was the norm when the foundations of the Internet were being laid in the 1970s and early 1980s. Although there were software companies and software for sale, software was considered secondary to hardware, which made up the bulk of the purchase price of a computer system. Even in the late 1980s the concept that the software for a system might cost more than the hardware was laughable—the hardware is *real*, after all. Today it is quite common for the software costs to dominate the cost of a desktop computer system, and this trend has paralleled the rise of the software market. Open source is the continuation of this earlier style of software production, and the increase in activity in open-source projects has likewise mirrored the expansion of the commercial software segment, largely as a reaction to it.

Despite their apparent political or philosophical tendencies, the open-source and free-software activities point the way toward harnessing outside innovation for companies. What we mean is that not only is the software produced by open-source projects useful for improving productivity for companies, but so are the open-source practices and the idea of companies participating in and starting open-source projects.

By engaging an outside community, a company can learn which innovations to make and how to make them. All that is required is to play by some rules, give up the commodity part of the product, and skillfully retain the high-value part. In exchange, the community will, in general, act as a co-author of the company's product and innovate in unexpected ways.

Open source is not simply a resource—it is a viable business strategy.

Jumping In

A number of companies have jumped into open source, some of them basing their businesses entirely on it, such as Red Hat, VA Software, and CollabNet, but many more have started open-source projects both inside and outside their corporate firewalls. Among the larger or more widely known companies using open source as part of their business strategies are General Electric (GE), Sun Microsystems, IBM, Apple, Hewlett-Packard (HP), SGI, Oracle, Cisco, Intel, and Symbian.

Apple is an interesting example because it is not generally known as embracing open source but is thought of as being a highly proprietary company from its earlier years. Apple's OS X is based on Darwin, which is an open-source project. Here is what Apple's developer website says about it:

> *Apple's open source projects allow developers to customize and enhance key Apple software. Through the open source model, Apple engineers and the open source community collaborate to create better, faster and more reliable products for our users.*
>
> *Beneath the appealing, easy-to-use interface of Mac OS X is a rock-solid foundation that is engineered for stability, reliability, and performance. This foundation is a core operating system commonly known as Darwin. Darwin integrates a number of technologies, most importantly Mach 3.0, operating-system services based on 4.4BSD (Berkeley Software Distribution), high-performance networking facilities, and support for multiple integrated file systems.[1]*

However, an important part of this strategy is hidden. Because Darwin is one of the Unix family of operating systems, a fair number of other open-source packages happen to work on the platform, which helps Apple dramatically because the

---

1. http://developer.apple.com/darwin/

Macintosh platform is regarded as hosting relatively few applications. Even though the current crop of open-source Unix applications is not especially appealing for businesses per se, they are appealing to the scientific and engineering communities, which are well represented in the business sector, and as Linux makes inroads into the server and client markets, the application base for OS X can only get better.

For example, there is an open-source project called Fink dedicated to bringing some of the open-source Unix programs to Darwin:

> *The Fink project wants to bring the full world of Unix Open Source software to Darwin and Mac OS X. We modify Unix software so that it compiles and runs on Mac OS X ("port" it) and make it available for download as a coherent distribution.*[2]

There are currently about 3500 packages in the Fink project. The packages by and large are not integrated into the full Aqua user interface, but they do provide significant functionality to the platform.

Understanding Open Source

Open source forms a commons where certain types of development take place in the open and the artifacts are available for general use. The primary problem software-related companies face at the beginning of the twenty-first century is how to innovate effectively. Innovation is relatively common and easy, but being able to choose which innovations will make the most business sense and then monetizing them is not easy. There is in general a trade-off between doing things in the commons, where innovation is easy because of the large number of diverse people and unfamiliar ideas, and doing things behind closed doors, where it is easy to keep a competitive advantage through secrecy and intellectual property laws. The first step is understanding innovation and creativity and how a commons can be a good venue for them.

Open source itself seems new and is mysterious in many ways. Why would anyone work for free? Where did these ideas come from? What sorts of software are created using an open-source methodology? Open source seems like it comes from a mob, but in reality it comes from a set of communities. These communities are tied together through culture, vocabulary, customs, practices, values, ethics, and morals. Being able to work with an open-source community requires understanding all these things well enough not to be made a fool of

---

2. http://fink.sourceforge.net/

immediately and then learning how to work effectively within the chosen community. There is an arc of maturation as you enter an open-source community as a newcomer or foreigner and then progress to becoming an inhabitant, then perhaps to leader, and then on to respected elder. Open source works on principles common to gift economies, which are generally more fundamental, or primitive, than free-market economies (which tend to be overly rational in how they treat value and compensation). Perhaps it's best to call gift economies precapitalistic.

Nevertheless there are many business reasons to embrace open source, all the way from just using open-source software such as Linux or Apache to starting and running open-source projects. The reasons to engage with open source include the following:

- Getting high-quality, free software and software design and development help.

- Making your software ubiquitous through participation and low cost.

- Engaging end-users in design and testing.

- Reducing time to market.

- Doing marketing and marketing research.

- Working with partners who prefer a loose relationship.

- Positioning a company.

- Harvesting innovation.

- Making standards.

- Building a brand through ubiquity and positioning vis-à-vis the open-source community.

- Adopting transparent development processes.

- Changing customer and market perceptions.

- Making a vision pervasive.

- Changing the rules.

- Reducing support costs.

- Injecting discipline into the development process.

- Improving integration.

- Satisfying more customers.

- Porting to otherwise unimportant platforms.

- Avoiding lock-in.

- Changing pricing practices.

- Signing up partners and creating consortia.

- Creating markets.

- Making ethical, moral, and political statements.

All-volunteer open source is the purest form. Projects such as Linux and Apache, before they were noticed and embraced by companies, were examples of all-volunteer open source; most of the projects on SourceForge are also examples. When a company joins an open-source project and especially when a company starts an open-source project, it brings to the table experts and processes that are not usually part of open-source projects. These include usability experts, release management, quality assurance, specification writing, documentation writers, and project management. These other process appurtenances can be carried over to varying degrees, but inevitably they alter the all-volunteer nature of open source, and therefore a company needs to know about how open source works in order to bring these other roles and practices to the table effectively. This is the central topic of this book.

An important legal key to open source is licensing. There is a pervasive myth that open-source software is not owned by anyone and that a company doing open source must give up ownership and control of its property. Actually, open source recognizes ownership and generally the primacy of ownership and its concomitant rights. Software licenses can yield many levels of rights because there is a vast gap between having no rights and all rights. Licenses can give the right to distribute and make changes to source code, but also can limit what sorts of distributions and changes are allowed. The license establishes, to an extent, the legal basis for an open-source project and community. There are a variety of licenses ranging from granting the right to view source, to gated communities, to open source, to free software, to public domain.

Engaging in an open-source project requires understanding the community, its culture and customs, its tools, and its way of working. Open-source projects are distributed and work through email, websites, and other written documents. There are standard versioning tools, compilers, bug-tracking tools, and customs for using them. Building, testing, support, and releases are handled in particular ways. There is a sort of hierarchy to the developers centered on module owners and the concept of a meritocracy, where rights are expanded only after abilities have been demonstrated.

In general, a company starting an open-source project needs to expend energy and resources creating a sufficiently large and robust community that will contribute, regardless of the type of contribution expected. Some managers and executives, upon beginning to engage in open source, are surprised that it seems more like a social activity than a development exercise, but this is the reality. To work with an open-source project—especially to start one up—requires an understanding of the culture and customs of the open-source way.

Beyond figuring out the business reasons for doing open source, a company or project needs to look at a variety of issues to determine whether it makes sense to use an open-source approach. These include whether you and your management buy into the open-source lifestyle, whether the source code is suitable and ready for source licensing, whether you have the resources, and whether your resource expectations are reasonable. Then you have to get the source code ready, get the company ready, choose a license, create a development plan and roadmap, make a budget and get funding, educate your developers, and build a website. Beyond these, there are commonsense things to do to build the community and maintain credibility in the open-source community.

After you've started an open-source project, there is a lot of work to do to keep its momentum building: It's not a matter of throwing the source code over a wall and watching a crowd gather. You need to craft and evolve the vision for the project, keep resources applied to the community, actively bring in contributors and users, evolve the website, keep things active and looking active, grow and mature your community members, and communicate transparently.

There are things you need to do to succeed. You really need to understand and buy into the open-source lifestyle. You need to start a relevant and useful project, not one that duplicates an existing effort. You need to get your code in shape and choose a good license—both for the open-source community and for your company. If you don't seem to have a way to make money or other commercial gain, the open-source community may consider you not with-it enough to risk expending effort on your project. And there are things to avoid. The biggest mistakes you can make involve control. The one characteristic of companies that open-source developers despise is overcontrol. It is natural to want to control a project, but the level of control that makes sense for an open-source project may seem too lax for development managers and executives. In many ways, the development processes in open source seem inefficient because they are based on written communication, and it's easy to fall into taking shortcuts, for instance by making important decisions in local, face-to-face meetings. This can cause tensions inside and outside the project in your company.

Moreover, the community will not arise just by itself. There is nurturing to do. And it's easy to buy into this concept intellectually while still failing to understand or appreciate what it means for everyday work. Most open-source communities need to have an email (or push-based) culture in order to seem vigorous and viable. Pull-type websites need to have compelling content for people to visit every day, and an open-source project is unlikely to have that.

Nevertheless, many companies have embraced the use of open source. In 2002, a study by Berlecon Research (*FLOSS—Free/Libre Open Source Software: Survey and Study*) conducted for the European Commission found that eight of the world's 25 largest software companies, including IBM, HP/Compaq, SAP, Hitachi, and Sun Microsystems, had a major involvement with open source and that another three companies engaged in lesser open-source activity. This was based on public announcements by the companies of their involvement, and so the actual use of open source is undoubtedly higher.

Communities

One of the hardest lessons to learn about working in open source is that the work involves community building, politics, citizenship, principles, and governance. An open-source project consists of some shared artifacts—source code, documentation, and so forth and some mailing lists, newsgroups, and perhaps some other social software. That is, there are the things, on the one hand, and the people, on the other. The people form a community, a community that interacts, that forms customs and traditions, that develops friendships and affiliations, and that, in short, creates a culture. Many software developers ignore the social aspects of open source and might even be surprised, in many cases, to hear people talk of open source as a social or community activity. At the first Jini community meeting, one developer remarked, "Is Jini a technology or a sociology experiment?"

For a company to succeed at open source, and more so than for an individual or an established open-source project, it must take community seriously and be explicit about it. This is because there is always some suspicion by outsiders that a company has some hidden, unpleasant agenda.

Community building consists of the activities done to foster a culture and make it pleasant and rewarding to be a member of the community. There must be ways for individuals to visit the community, learn about it, join it as new-comers, become productive members, develop into experts, and finally become respected elders.

Politics enters the scene when companies or other competing interests are involved. How are compromises made? How are the positions of established expertise respected? These are political questions.

Citizenship has to do not only with the ways individuals mature through an arc of roles, but with whether individuals have the opportunity to feel that being a member of the community distinguishes them from others and whether this distinction is a source of pride. Perhaps the community has a significant name (Linux), a logo or other identifiable sign (a penguin), or established customs (yearly community meetings). Perhaps the community is known for its level of technical expertise or its important contributions.

Principles form the backbone of any open-source project. Software developers and engineers are overwhelmingly principled and ethical,[3] so that any open-source project started by a company needs to embrace and make explicit its dedication to principles. Open-source projects started by individuals generally don't have to be explicit about their principles because such principles are so prevalent within the developer community. But a company does not have this luxury.

Governance has to do with how decisions are made about the workings of the community. For the Linux project, Linus Torvalds makes many decisions about what code gets accepted into the source tree and who else has the authority to make such decisions, so he is part of the governance of the project; he decided that he makes such decisions. For companies, governance generally needs to be more explicit and, obviously, equitable and fair. As non-company-based open-source projects mature, they are finding that governance needs to be made explicit.

A good example of the importance of community is the project that designed Common Lisp, which was one of the first large network-based design collaborations, begun in 1981. One of us (RPG) was the originator of the Common Lisp effort. It began in the summer of 1981 as a consolidation effort between descendents of an older dialect of Lisp called MacLisp. After a series of short face-to-face meetings, the bulk of the work shifted to an email-based discussion on the ARPAnet (the predecessor of the Internet). The acknowledged list of contributors contains 62 individuals who exchanged over 2000 email messages over a 2-year period along with two or three face-to-face meetings and four drafts of the specification written primarily by Guy L. Steele Jr. Over its lifetime, the group exchanged well over 10,000 email messages.

The culture of this community was central to how it worked. The community developed an interaction style and a particular online culture in which a person's participation as well as "influence" depended on his or her expertise. Keep in mind that at that time (1981) there were no or very few online communities. Network email was limited to some universities and Department of Defense–related companies. It turned out—as we know only so well today—that people are more prone to be insulting and forthright in email than in person. Many of the discussions carried on over the network were quite spirited, but they had the advantage of being written down. There was no need to rely on dim memory

---

3. Virus writers and crackers notwithstanding.

or pale ink because all the mail was automatically stored in a centralized place, so there was no chance of losing or misplacing it.

The discussions were often in the form of proposals, discussions, and counterproposals for the design of Common Lisp. Code examples from existing software or proposed new syntax were often exchanged. And all was subject to quick review by community members. New members of the community wishing to come up to speed could go to the archives.

This online style had some drawbacks. Foremost, it was not possible to observe the facial and body reactions of other people, to see whether some point angered them, which would mean the point was important to them. There was no immediate way to see that an argument had gone too far or had little support. This meant that time was wasted and that carefully crafted written arguments were required to get anything done.

The leader of the group was Scott Fahlman of Carnegie-Mellon University, and there was an inner circle of decision makers—Scott Fahlman, Guy Steele, David Moon, Daniel Weinreb, and Richard P. Gabriel—called the Quinquevirate or Gang of Five. Just outside this circle was the semi-official Common Lisp Group, which included 33 individuals. This was its governance.

In all, the benefits of the contentious interaction style characteristic of the culture outweighed its problems. Moreover, the expert leadership, the small core of decision makers, the excellent specification-writing talent, and the freedom to work continuously without needing to schedule meeting times meant that the result was quite extraordinary. Despite the diverse and oddball nature of the individuals, a definite culture emerged with strong bonds, a private language, emergent roles, and definite traditions.[4]

The Common Lisp community was based on the principles of openness and the celebration of technical expertise that characterized the MIT AI (Artificial Intelligence) Lab culture. This is the culture that formed and still supports the views of Richard Stallman, who is the founder of the Free Software Foundation— which kicked off the open-source movement—and who was an active member of the Common Lisp community.

Politics was central to the community. One goal was to bring together Lisp machine companies that had developed new and different Lisp language features to distinguish themselves from each other and other Lisp vendors (both hardware

---

4. The transcript of the Common Lisp email interactions was studied by JoAnne Yates and Wanda J. Orlikowski of the MIT Sloan School, resulting in two reports: "Knee-Jerk Anti-LOOPism and Other E-mail Phenomena: Oral, Written, and Electronic Patterns in Computer-Mediated Communication," MIT Sloan School Working Paper #3578-93, and "From Memo to Dialogue: Enacting Genres of Communication in Electronic Mail," MIT Sloan School Working Paper #3525, Sloan School, MIT, Cambridge, MA, July 1993.

and software vendors) to agree on a common standard—if it was successful, this standard would diminish their differentiators.[5] Moreover, software Lisp vendors working on general-purpose computer implementations, academics, and Lisp users were invited into the community, with their conflicting and unusual perspectives and requirements—some commercial, some scientific, some engineering-based, and some just oddball. All these groups were expected to come to a common agreement. This is politics par excellence. Pride of citizenship was conferred by the attentiveness of ARPA to the group and the fame of some of its principals.

Finally, the curious fact about the Common Lisp effort was that even though its apparent product was a specification of Common Lisp in the form of a book, the members of the community never worked on the text of that book. There were no artifacts that formed the center of the community; people, in general, did not contribute code, text, or editing expertise. The writing was done entirely by Guy Steele and the other members of the Quinquevirate. The community was there to make decisions, much as do legislatures and constitutional conventions. A newcomer to the Common Lisp community needed to listen and read the email archives—until Steele's first draft there was no artifact available to study and change; and after, only Steele could change the draft. The day-to-day activity consisted of political and technical debate followed by making specific decisions, which means that the Common Lisp project was essentially all community.

Who This Book Is Intended For

We wrote this book to help business executives understand when and how an open-source strategy can help them to achieve their company's business goals. We also want to provide support for the managers charged with implementing that strategy in their day-to-day work running a project that makes use of open source.

The book is also aimed at the engineers who may need to work on open-source projects. We want to give them an idea of what they will experience and what will be expected of them. We also want to give them the information they will need to educate their managers and co-workers about open source.

Third, the book is for anyone interested in a better understanding of open source—its larger history, its philosophy, and its future prospects.

---

5. And, in fact, some have argued that the eventual success of Common Lisp as a standard language combined with improvements in general-purpose computers and compiler technology dealt all the Lisp machine companies a death blow.

SOFTWARE DEVELOPERS

Since we wrote the first draft of this book, the depth of the recession of the early twenty-first century has made itself felt in the software industry. We don't want to make this book specific to a particular era, but we want to point out to software developers of any time period the educational and experiential advantages of working with open source. It is unlikely that open-source code will disappear. This means that open-source systems will form the basis of a significant portion of our computing infrastructure for many years. An individual who has experience working with open-source software will enjoy a variety of advantages.

Experience with open source can add value to your skill set. Operating systems, web servers, scripting-level languages, wikis, weblogs, email infrastructure, and many other facilities come from the open-source world, and experience with these pieces of software is valuable. Experience working with open-source projects can be of value to companies that have or plan to have open-source projects of their own. Knowing the roles of the members and having a good idea of how the process works is essential for companies to succeed with open source, and knowledge comes more from experience than from books.

Working with an open-source project will give you experience working in a distributed development environment and perhaps working with non-English speakers from different cultural backgrounds. Increasingly companies are locating development groups around the world, both in-sourced and out-sourced, and experience in this sort of environment can be essential.

Open-source projects work using documents and written communications. The documents can be as simple as an emailed specification or design rationale, but they are documents nevertheless. Working through writing is a way to bring more discipline to the development process. Moreover, you can become a better writer by practicing writing, and working on an email-heavy project will give you lots of practice.

In an open-source project, the source code is available for inspection, and the designers and implementors of the software are generally available and willing to answer questions. Reading (and critiquing) source code is one of the best ways to learn about design and implementation. Open-source software is available for continual improvement, so it might be higher quality than commercial code and, thus, a better educational experience.

Before open source became prevalent, self-training in many of these areas was a hit-or-miss affair. Learning software development requires interaction, and it was difficult before Internet-based open-source projects existed to find places to get the sort of interaction needed for training.

Open Source as Business Strategy

Making a public open-source project successful takes more than a press release and putting some code outside the firewall. Open source is a development methodology, but companies whose thinking stops there will find the experience disappointing. Open source is sometimes called a lifestyle, which means that successful open-source projects operate under a set of cultural conventions that may be foreign or difficult for some companies to accept. Public-open source is not a cost-saving mechanism, and it takes a careful business analysis to justify using it.

This book focuses on what a company needs to do to make open source a part of its business. This starts with understanding the business reasons for using open source and goes on to the details of day-to-day project activities. Included are examples of how companies such as Sun, IBM, HP, and Cisco Systems have successfully benefited from their use of open source.

Our examples tend to be drawn from Sun projects. The reason for this is that we have had the opportunity to observe not only the reaction of the community and pundits to company-sponsored open-source projects and the reports of people working on the inside on these projects, but also the internal discussions, pro and con, good and bad, of the decision makers. We were able to see what advice was taken and not taken, and what the results were. Sun is neither the best practitioner of open source as a business strategy nor the worst. Sun's record is spotty with some good successes and several embarrassments; the company embraces some of the fundamental tenets of openness and working with a community that are required for a successful use of open source as a strategy, but it often fails to embrace them thoroughly enough to realize all the benefits.

We do not advocate using open source blindly as a strategy, and we are not die-hard promoters of open source. We hope this book is a balanced look at the pros and cons of open source, along with tested advice on how to succeed once open source has been chosen as a part of a company's strategy.

CHAPTER 2

Innovation Happens Elsewhere

AT THE BEGINNING OF THE TWENTY-FIRST CENTURY the biggest challenge high-tech companies face is how to innovate effectively. Effective innovation is finding the right innovations to invest in to make a good profit. To many, open source is about Linux and a few other software systems and how to use them to make an inexpensive backroom. But open source is also a practice and a tool for encouraging and harvesting innovations. Open source is a way for companies to engage in highly effective marketing—both in the sense of marketing a company, software, and brand, and in the sense of finding out what products and product features to build.

Like any engine, an open-source innovation engine requires design, engineering, tuning, and maintenance. But to do those things requires understanding the science behind the machine. This is called "innovation happens elsewhere."

Open Source Is a Commons

Open source is fundamentally about people volunteering to work on projects in what could be called the *commons;* that is, it is about working on things for the public good. The sort of commons we are talking about is composed of things whose most basic value is not diminished by making a copy—in fact, making a copy in many cases increases its value. For example, if a piece of software is not for sale, then its value is not decreased if someone makes and uses a copy of it. If the software implements a collaborative tool, for example, then the additional copy makes it more valuable by increasing the number of people collaborating. Written works and knowledge are also part of this commons. Taking advantage of such a commons can be as simple as just taking what's there—this is permitted—but learning and applying the rules of engagement for the communities surrounding this commons can enhance the exchange and pave the way for putting works important to you in the commons and eliciting various forms of volunteer effort.

Open source is not a small or niche movement. There are tens of thousands of open-source projects—the largest but not the only openly available open-source hosting site, Sourceforge,[1] in mid-2004 hosted over 80,000 projects and had over 810,000 registered members. Interest in using open-source code residing in the commons by corporations is strong enough that some are starting to adapt their internal product life cycle and development methodologies to accommodate the nature of open source. And during this period of downturn for the technology portions of the economy, open-source projects are a means for software developers and designers not only to hone their skills on real-world projects but to expand their expertise in useful directions. Working on open-source projects, learning the tools and processes, and gaining expertise in various open-source applications and systems is likely to prove valuable, if for no other reason than that seeing other people's code and style expands your own horizons and makes you a better developer and designer.

Can the Commons Make a Difference?

Although the commons we're talking about includes other things, it is largely the commons of source code licensed in such a way that many can work on it at the same time. The best-known software in this commons is Linux, which is a sort of Unix operating system. Linux can be viewed as a narrow technological phenomenon—of importance to some companies in the technology sector, but not affecting regular people in their homes and lives. To understand how the commons can benefit ordinary people, it's easier to look at other things in the commons, such as the World Wide Web. The Web is interesting because it is not only within the commons—built by a group effort—but forms part of the infrastructure of the commons. It's worth looking at the growth of the Web a bit to begin to understand the power of open source for business.

For many, the Web is the first authority—not simply ordinary folks but professionals turn to the Web for information. Nearly all the scientific and technical journals the authors read are available online. Many people and most companies and other organizations put up websites and keep them up to date. Some are as ordinary and prosaic as a man talking about his hobbies and cats, and others are elaborate collections of essays and artwork or opinions and software.

---

1. http://sourceforge.net

Today there are approximately 3 million distinct public websites,[2] and on average each site has about 450 pages, meaning there are nearly 1.5 billion web pages. And this doesn't count web dark matter, which is information stored in databases that is served up using dynamic web page technology.

The Web was built as a volunteer effort—there was no central planning, only a set of simple protocols and tools, and the idea took off on its own. The core of the Web is a protocol called http (HyperText Transfer Protocol), which enables one computer to request of another a particular resource—usually a web page—via the Internet. This protocol (http) works on top of the basic Internet protocols, and it can be considered a peer of other layered protocols such as email (smtp, Simple Mail Transfer Protocol) and file transfer (ftp, File Transfer Protocol). Three more things were needed from the infrastructure. The first was a way to describe web pages that was not based on a proprietary format. The choice here was the HyperText Markup Language (html). This was originally an extremely simple language—it was not capable of displaying precisely typeset material natively, but it was a language easy to learn. The second was a way to locate pages to display that didn't depend on what computer or operating system was being talked to—the Universal Resource Locator (URL). The third was the web browser.

The keys to the remarkable success of this approach lay in the web browser more than in the other components. The first key was that the early web browsers tried their best to display something regardless of how imperfect the html describing the requested page was. The second was that web browsers could display the source html for the page being displayed. Using this feature, amateur web designers could find a page whose layout they liked and then mimic it for a page of their own. Even if they were not too careful in mimicking, the tolerant web browsers would probably show enough of what they intended to get by.

With this tolerance for imperfectly described pages and such gifts as the early websites that the early creators provided, the Web took off in ways that couldn't have been foreseen. People used existing websites and their openly viewable source code to clone (with variations) web page design and put out their own content. People shared their hobbies and expertise. Organizations with special interests educated the public, and clubs spread interest in their club activities. Scientists and engineers started using the Web to disseminate their research results. Term papers, dissertations, and manias started appearing on the web, so that by 2003 there was almost literally no corner of human knowledge that was not at least mentioned on the Web. With the advent of search engines, it's now possible

---

2. These data are from the OCLC Web Characterization Project (http://wcp.oclc.org). A public site is one that is openly available for anyone. There are in addition 2.5 million private sites that are password or payment protected, including about 100,000 adult sites, and another 3 million provisional sites that are under construction.

to find this information easily. It used to take a prodigious and obsessive person to be able to tell you the names of the poem and the poet given only a flawed memory of a line, but now anyone can answer such questions within 5 minutes given a browser and Internet connection.

This growth came predominantly from the individual efforts of volunteerism. In many cases today, individuals pay to put up their websites—in other words, they pay to give something away. The Web has been used for independent news sources, and there are numerous examples in which web-based action has changed the course of history. There is little doubt that the Web has transformed how people work and interact. Weblogs (simple journal mechanisms) are flourishing and gathering enough power to affect politics, and wikis (reader-extendable websites) are being used to construct grassroots dictionaries and encyclopedias.

The Commons and Software

Open-source software—and the closely related variant, free software[3]—is being increasingly used in mainstream computing, meaning in information technology (IT) departments in companies and for consumer websites. Open source is becoming common through the Linux operating system and the Apache web server. In addition, there are open-source databases, compilers, window systems, programming languages, text editors, software development environments, productivity suites, and just about anything you can think of. The Apache web server is currently the one most commonly used for public websites. The use of the Linux operating system in commercial settings is spreading rapidly, poised to one day become predominant.

Many companies beyond the early pioneers are embarking on more and more open-source or open-source-like projects, particularly those that are building platforms and require ubiquity. Moreover, many companies are adopting open source for some of their internal projects, especially those that are working on internal tools and utilities for which sharing across the company makes sense.

Open versus Closed

According to Henry Chesbrough (*Open Innovation: The New Imperative for Creating and Profiting from Technology*), the traditional strategy for

---

3. Free software is software whose source is licensed in such a way to guarantee that the source remains open and to encourage making related software free. The concept of free software comes from Richard Stallman and the Free Software Foundation, and free software licenses include the GPL and LGPL. In this book, the term *open source* is taken to include free software.

creating new technology and profiting from it is based on the old AT&T/Bell Labs model:

- Make sure the best and brightest people work for you.

- Invent new things and get them to market first, which means you'll win.

- Control intellectual property so no one else can get a toehold.

The model is a closed engine in which all innovation is company produced within closed walls. In the past, it not only was possible but common for large companies to corner the market on the smartest people in a technology field. But during the 1990s, this changed. As new companies started up, with the possibility of founders and early employees becoming instantly rich, researchers and advanced developers started moving around instead of staying with the same company for their entire careers. Knowledge was spread and an employee's loyalty to a particular company (and vice versa) became much rarer.

The old model has broken down. As Chesbrough points out, although as recently as 1991 70.7% of industrial research and development (R&D) spending was done by companies with 25,000 employees or more, by 1999 this figure had dropped to 41.3%. Moreover, as we see later, the first-mover advantage, wherein the company with the first product in a new space gains and retains a market-share advantage, is a myth. The newer model is to look for innovations wherever they may pop up and use them carefully by layering on unique value. Proprietary research to innovate still makes sense, but not to the exclusion of looking outside a company's own firewalls.

Use of the Commons: Creativity and Conversations

At the heart of the reasons for a company to use open source is the nature of creativity. Creativity arises from diversity of ideas and viewpoints. Such ideas and viewpoints are spawned from conversations, either through direct dialog with people or through indirect interaction through artifacts such as art, literature, song, and technology.

CREATIVITY

Creativity is regarded by many as a talent that some people are blessed with and others not. Talent, however, is simply what comes easily. For artists, scientists, engineers, and writers, creativity comes from the ability to put together various triggers that they happen on; a *trigger* is anything that causes a thought to come to mind. Imagine a group of people in the distant past trying to figure out how to achieve better workplace collaboration. When the members of this group observed sports teams operating smoothly, they found many triggers there: specifically defined roles, coaching, and game plans. In fact, sports acted as a set of triggers for understanding and operating on workplace collaboration. So powerful were these triggers that we've adopted some of their names into our vocabulary of business teamwork.

The term *trigger* is borrowed from *The Triggering Town* by the twentieth-century poet and writing teacher Richard Hugo, who used it to teach writing poetry:

> *A poem can be said to have two subjects, the initiating or triggering subject, which starts the poem or "causes" the poem to be written, and the real or generated subject, which the poem comes to say or mean, and which is generated or discovered in the poem during the writing. That's not quite right because it suggests that the poet recognizes the real subject. The poet may not be aware of what the real subject is but only [has] some instinctive feeling that the poem is done. (p. 4)*

For Hugo, a trigger is what starts a poet off in a particular direction. That direction can change or the ultimate thrust of the poem can be something else or simply perceived as something else, but the trigger is the creative spark that gets things going. Triggers are in fact ubiquitous in human life. We find them operating in art, engineering, and the sciences.

Looking at literature more broadly we see connections between works—much of our literature is a response to other writings and writers. In art we notice that when one painter started the style later called Impressionism, many others followed the trigger. Where did Impressionism come from? In his essay on the origins of Impressionism, Louis Emile Edmond Duranty quotes a letter from the artist Eugène Fromentin:

> *A sculptor or a painter has a wife or a mistress who is slim, light, and lively, with a turned-up nose and small eyes. He loves these things in her, even with their faults. Perhaps he even went through a passionate affair to win her. Now, this woman—who is the ideal of this artist's heart and mind, who has aroused and revealed his true taste, sensitivity, and imagination because he has discovered and chosen her—is the absolute opposite of the feminine ideal that he insists on putting into his paintings and statues. Instead he keeps returning to Greece, to women who are somber, severe, and strong as horses. In the morning he betrays the turned-up nose that delights him at night, and straightens it. Consequently he either dies of boredom or brings to his work all*

the gaiety and effort of thought *of a box-maker who is skilled at gluing and who wonders where he will go to* have some fun *after he has finished work.*[4]

Or, Duranty goes on to say, the living woman will displace the Greek Venus and we will see instead the slim, light, and lively woman with the turned-up nose. She has become a trigger. And such triggers coming from life—the way light works to form color, the movement and natural poses of ordinary people, and the idea that an actual viewer cannot see everything—gave rise to Impressionism, whose practitioners and works became triggers to other painters and which combined with other triggers to instigate the styles and movements in art we see today.

Brainstorming groups work precisely because the number of diverse triggers available is large and the group is encouraged to make associations that normally would be edited out quickly. For such groups to work well, there have to be three main ingredients: a willingness to contribute ideas with relative abandon, a willingness to surrender ownership and protection of your ideas to the group, and a willingness to accept the responsibility of nurturing and continuously improving any ideas generated by the group as if they were your own. These principles guide not only successful brainstorming groups, but also such diverse activities as writers' workshops, appreciative inquiry, and design charrettes.

Some triggers are legendary. Isaac Newton thought of the laws of gravity after being struck by the idea that an apple would fall from a tree regardless of how high it was while the moon, surely affected by the same force as the apples, remained at a distance. The apple was a trigger to a series of thoughts that led to good science.

In problem solving, triggers include descriptions of characterizations or descriptions of existing knowledge and techniques that cause the problem solver to home in on an approach to try. These descriptions are usually general or abstract, so there is an ability required to see the connection. But additional triggers can appear from anywhere and can have remarkable effects. Many scientists and mathematicians report that the solutions to problems appeared to them while they were engaged in some other activity. Things happening in their lives acted as triggers.

Companies in a particular market use one another as triggers, looking at how the others approach the market and making both small and large improvements, making products where the market has left holes in the product space, and combining product ideas from other companies. For example, it is well-known that Microsoft used the Apple Macintosh as a trigger for their Windows products. Apple used the Xerox PARC Star as a trigger for the Macintosh window

---

4. "La Nouvelle Peinture," in Charles S. Moffett, Ruth Berson, Barbara Lee Williams, and Fronia E. Wissman, *The New Painting, Impressionism, 1874–1886: An Exhibition Organized by the Fine Arts Museums of San Francisco with the National Gallery of Art, Washington, D.C.*, p. 40.

system. And Xerox PARC used earlier window-like systems as their triggers, such systems as the Stanford AI Lab's DataDisk system, Doug Engelbart's On-Line System (NLS) from his Augmentation of Human Intellect project at Stanford Research Institute (now known as SRI International) in the 1960s, the later windowing work at MIT on Lisp machines, and Ivan Sutherland's Sketchpad system from 1962. And, of course, all such systems were triggered by paper, artists' canvases, and blackboards.

It's easy to think that triggers can't be of much use in the real business world because there is so much evidence that the company that comes up with an idea first is the one that benefits the most. Coupled with strong intellectual property laws, it must be getting even worse now.

The power of triggers and the relative immunity of a company's success to not being first can be found in the work of Gerard J. Tellis and Peter N. Golder. In their book *Will & Vision: How Latecomers Grow to Dominate Markets*, Tellis and Golder carefully define *pioneers* and *markets* and come to what some business theorists consider counterintuitive findings about the first-mover advantage. Traditional wisdom holds that first movers dominate; one market study showed that in the steady state, market pioneers hold a 30% share of their markets, whereas latecomers hold 13%. Another study found that about 70% of current market leaders pioneered the markets they dominate. Tellis and Golder note that these studies actually measure the effect of early leaders, not the true pioneers, with part of the blame for the flawed studies lying at the feet of the current market leaders who, when interviewed, tend to not know the technological history of their market well.

For example, Procter & Gamble claims it created the disposable-diaper market in 1961, the implication being that they invented the disposable diaper and thereby created the market. In fact, they were simply an early leader; Johnson & Johnson developed disposable diapers (called Chux) in the 1930s for hospital use and manufactured them for other uses by 1936 or 1937. Two other quick examples: Gillette entered the safety razor market in 1903, but a company called Star had introduced a safety razor in 1876. HP entered the laser printer market in 1984, but IBM had one on the market in 1975 (the 3800).

Tellis and Golder define a *pioneer* as "the first firm to commercialize [a] product" (p. 32) and a *market* as "a competitive environment in which firms attempt to satisfy some distinct but enduring consumer need" (p. 33). Using these definitions, they found in examining 66 markets that the failure rate for pioneers was almost 65%. In only 9% of the markets were the current market leaders true pioneers—and the average market share of the survivors is now a mere 6%. The real success goes to early leaders—firms that entered the market an average of 19 years after the pioneers and currently have a market share three times the size of the pioneers.

This means that being the first to market is not necessary for success. In the cases Tellis and Golder discuss, a pioneer's inventive efforts form a trigger that the eventual leader picks up on. Improvements are made, often continual improvements as the product matures. But the time span between the introduction of the pioneer's product and the eventual leader's product contains the customer (or user) response to the idea (and technology) and forms its own small commons that the eventual leader uses to gather information and innovation to make the product a success.

Tellis and Golder's point is that a visionary company with enough persistence can come to dominate a market. The vision is usually of the widespread use of a technology product—which implies an acceptably low price—and the persistence is to stick with product development long enough to achieve an acceptable price for an acceptable product.

This brings up another theme important to open source that we explore later—*continuous (re)design.* Continuous (re)design is the way that artifacts in the commons are improved—not only their implementations but their designs—by the acts of people improving small pieces, adapting the technology to other applications, and finding new ideas that might apply.

A nearly perfect example is Sony and the videorecorder. Ampex produced the first videorecorder in 1956, which initially sold for $75,000. It recorded only in black and white on 2-inch tape. It was such a hit that by 1960 a mass-produced version was selling for $50,000 to about 100 customers a year. Also in the 1950s, Sony's cofounder, Masaru Ibuka, had a similar vision, but with an important difference. Ibuka's vision was for a low-cost home version of the videorecorder. In pursuit of this vision, he asked his engineers to come up with a videorecorder, which they did for a selling price of $55,000. Ibuka, believing in a home rather than a professional market for videorecorders, asked them to redesign it to cut the price by 90%, which they did. But then he asked them to redesign it to cut the price by another 90%. It took 20 years for the whole engineering process, but eventually (in 1975) Sony released the Betamax, which sold for under $1000 and over the next 15 years Sony's annual sales grew from $17 million to $2 billion while Ampex's never even reached $500 million. And while this was happening, JVC and Matsushita grew to $5 billion between them. The latecomers were selling $7 billion in recorders, but the pioneer, Ampex, was stuck at 6% of the market.

What this means for open source is that doing secret development in hopes of springing a new product on the marketplace to gain the much-coveted first-mover advantage rarely works. In almost every market, the technology is well known and many pioneers have failed or are failing. It is a race to see which firm can come up with the enduring product for a large market, and an enduring market comes from matching users' needs well with an affordably priced product. Matching users' needs requires interacting with them; affordable pricing requires, for software, primarily low maintenance costs.

If there is no first-mover advantage, then it doesn't matter too much whether the early work is done inside a company's firewalls or in the commons. And it doesn't matter that the early work can serve as a trigger to many companies because that happens already. But we return to this theme shortly.

CONVERSATIONS

The second half of how the commons works for a company is the conversations. These take many forms. The best way to think about this is by analogy to a great city, by which we mean a city where people gather to exchange goods, culture, food, and ideas. Although all cities do these things to a certain degree, the great cities stand out.

Every place great with creativity is a confluence of smaller communities of interest and practice whose proximity serves as triggers for further creation. Renaissance Florence was great not because there were only painters there, but because there were also sculptors, goldsmiths, poets, writers, clerics, architects, builders, and an expectation of great creation. Today in places such as San Francisco, London, Boston, Austin, San Diego, and Prague there is tremendous diversity of thoughts, artists, technologists, chefs, theaters, and workshops. This is why companies and individuals flock to those places; that's why it's invigorating to be in them.

In *The Rise of the Creative Class*, a recent study on the transformation of work, Richard Florida writes about creativity and places like this:

> *Creative people... cluster in places that are centers of creativity and also where they like to live. From classical Athens and Rome, to the Florence of the Medici and Elizabethan London, to Greenwich Village and the San Francisco Bay Area, creativity has always gravitated to specific locations. As the great urbanist Jane Jacobs pointed out a long time ago, successful places are multidimensional and diverse—they don't just cater to a single industry or a single demographic group; they are full of stimulation and creative interplay. (p. 7)*

In a context like this, communities do what they do best—create a wide-ranging portfolio of resources. In doing this, they are mimicking the great cities in history, which were not simply confluences of diverse and creative people but also a source of rich culture, galleries, books, workshops, teachers, students, cafés, cuisines, architectural styles, and building methods. A great city is creative only if things are created there.

A great city concentrates triggers, creating the context for creativity, and it also brings the possibility of important conversations: between poets and sculptors, between businesspeople and painters, and between clerics and composers. If our software commons is also a community, we can expect other sorts of important conversations: between customers and companies, between designers and users, between designers in one company and designers in another, between developers and users, between marketing and customers, and between developers in one company and developers in another. Under the right conditions, these conversations can do important things for a company. First, the company can rapidly learn how to improve its products. The conversations are direct, which means that the cost of having them can be low and the translation to concrete product-based actions can be efficient. Second, by inviting customers and others into the circle of trust, the realities of doing business—such as delays caused by product cycles and rushed quality assurance—will be less likely to be held against the company. The nature of the relationship is entirely different. It is more akin to the gift economy that we experience in our families and religions than to the commodity economy that dominates business. In such gift-based relationships, the goals are collaboration, joint authorship, and appreciative inquiry. We say more about this later; for now, keep in mind that the sorts of open-source projects talked about in this book combine the commodity and gift cultures.

As mentioned earlier, Tellis and Golder attribute enduring market leadership to two qualities: will and vision. They think of these largely as attributes of the leaders of the enduring market-leader companies, but perhaps they need only be traits of the companies. An enduring market leader is a company that dominates and has dominated its market for many years, often dozens. For this definition to make sense, only mass markets make sense, and this is reflected in their definition of a *market* as a competitive arena that satisfies an enduring consumer need. *Consumer*, of course, is not a pretty word and is considered by many to be insulting[5]—a company has one major interaction with consumers: It sells to them.

Vision, to Tellis and Golder, has to do with how a person or company envisions the consumers or mass market for a product. For example, the true vision of Sony's cofounder was not the videorecorder but a videorecorder for the masses priced at $500. What he envisioned was not making copies of broadcast material, but millions of faces sitting in front of TVs playing back recorded material broadcast earlier. The trigger of all research aimed at implementing such visions is not the thing itself or its technology but its price. Because achieving a vision requires an almost absurd amount of research and development,

---

5. http://www.investorwords.com defines *consumer* as "an individual who buys products or services for personal use and not for manufacture or resale." This excludes anyone who might be a collaborator or with whom you might want to have a conversation.

companies and their visionaries require an almost absurd amount of willpower and persistence to keep at it until the technical and manufacturing breakthroughs can be made that enable the mass market (pricing) vision to be realized.

If we were to stop here, the lesson would not be important; the lesson would be that it pays to be lucky enough to have the resources to keep working until you get it right. But keep in mind that you need to do the refinements, but it's a lot easier if you have resources from some other source.

An important characteristic of enduring market leaders is that they usually initially deliver a fairly low-quality product that is just good enough for the consumer, followed by a lengthy conversation with the consumer to determine what sorts of features and level of quality are actually required. After this, the enduring market leader's products often eventually outstrip the niche high-quality-product companies' products. In other words, the will or persistence that Tellis and Golder speak of is not akin to stubbornness; it is a form of continuous (re)design.

The pattern is to start modestly and improve according to the dictates of the users, to get something of acceptable quality into the largest marketplace you can and then later improve or add a narrower focus with higher-quality, more inventive products. This pattern has come to be known as "worse is better,"[6] and its key is the conversation that takes place between the users of a product or technology and its designers and builders. Unfortunately, the primary exemplars of this pattern are within the technology-for-technologists sector.[7] That is, the users are developers and artifacts that fall into this category include operating systems (Unix), programming languages (C), and text editors (Emacs). The idea is that the users of a technology are provided with an early version of it, which they can extend and improve over time. The early version should be complete enough to be useful, but should not be particularly fully featured, and ideally the usage patterns should not be nailed down completely so that a wide range of possible design and implementation features is feasible. Then by conversing with the users—through email, code exchanges, and design discussions—the technology can be moved forward according to the most dominant and interesting uses.

This approach is called "worse is better" for two reasons: to indicate that the initial release is not what would normally be considered product quality or complete and to emphasize that it is acceptable to stop short of a perfect design. When you can afford the discipline of allowing the users of a technology to help design it and be part of its future, the result is usually designed as well or better

---

6. Gabriel, http://dreamsongs.com/WorseIsBetter.html

7. We would prefer them to be conversations between end-users and designers, but this loop, although it exists, is more tenuous and harder to demonstrate than it should be.

than the original designers could have done and is almost always better suited or adapted to its users.

"Worse is better" works by taking advantage of conversations with users, but the key is to listen and design with discrimination—not every suggestion should be followed. In most cases, there will be a handful of surprising ideas that should be grabbed for follow-up. Coming up with new ideas is not as difficult as selecting which ones to implement—the more ideas on the table, the more likely a good one is there ready to be found. The choice is sometimes more reliably made when there are several minds looking at the question, and that's what "worse is better" promotes.

When we put this approach together with the observation by Tellis and Golder that being first with a previously unknown product is not very important, we can see that there is little risk in using the commons for collaborative design and implementation.

DIVERSITY AND SELECTION VERSUS CONTINUOUS (RE)DESIGN

There are actually two ways to achieve excellence in design and execution: (1) diversity followed by selection and (2) continuous (re)design. In the diversity and selection approach lots of artifacts are produced and the best are picked. For example, when we visit the Musée d'Orsay in Paris to view the Impressionist paintings, we notice that they're all quite good. Partly this is because the painters were good and they were exploring the beginnings of a new way of painting, but partly this is because we are seeing only the best Impressionist work. When we read the great poems of William Butler Yeats, we are reading only a selection of his work. When we harvest triggers, we are selecting from a diversity.

On the other hand, continuous (re)design takes a good starting place and revises and revises until that starting artifact has become as good as it can be. When a great poet revises heavily, we often see very good work—certainly it demonstrates deep knowledge and practiced craft.

In fact, the best work is always the result of a combination of the two approaches. And both approaches and their implied practices apply to open source and how it moves forward.

Innovation Happens Elsewhere

Innovation happens everywhere, but there is simply more elsewhere than here. Silly as it sounds, this is the brutal truth: Regardless of how smart, creative, and innovative you believe your organization is, there are more smart, creative, and innovative people outside your organization than inside. In addition, the majority of elsewhere doesn't particularly care to make products in your space. But customers already using a product for real work are in a good position to offer suggestions about the directions in which that product should evolve. Even if such users don't have concrete suggestions, the ways that they use the product can provide hints about how to improve it. Remember, innovation comes from triggers, and the trigger does not have to be aware of what it is triggering. Just as a palm tree near the beach at sunset can trigger a poet's masterpiece without any thought whatsoever, a user using a product or mentioning a circumstance of its use can trigger a major product direction in a designer prepared to receive such a trigger.

As Henry Chesbrough points out, R&D spending profiles suggest that it is less and less common for innovative people to be found at large companies with virtual monopolies in specific technology areas. Not all the smart people work for you, you cannot afford to try to create all the innovations yourself, and you cannot provide enough triggers internally to find the stunning new product idea.

More and more the game is about being connected rather than about domination. The worst thing that you could do would be to allow "innovation happens elsewhere" to become "revenue happens elsewhere."

To succeed, companies need to find ways to use outside innovations and to become part of a distributed fabric of innovation through a combination of licensing and well-chosen gifts. Although the concept of a gift may not at first seem to fit well with free-market capitalism, it might when thought of in the context of collaborating with others to build common commodity-like infrastructure. If it makes business sense in that context, then perhaps it makes business sense in others.

This is what open source is all about: harnessing engines of innovation in software.

CHAPTER 3

What Is Open Source?

THERE IS AN EXISTING LARGE OPEN-SOURCE COMMUNITY with established practices and culture. Companies and others wishing to start or join an existing open-source project need to understand the ground rules and established practices for this larger community because the term *open source* sets expectations that need to be either met or explained. A good way to conceptualize this is to think of the open-source community as a foreign country with its own culture and every open-source project as existing in that country. Although it might be possible to impose different cultural rules on that project, it is more likely to be easier to adopt existing customs. Therefore, understanding open source as it exists is crucial to success.

There are many definitions of what constitutes open source. The basic idea is very simple: By making the source code for a piece of software available to all, any programmer can modify it to better suit his or her needs and redistribute the improved version to other users. By working together, a community of both users and developers can improve the functionality and quality of the software.

Thus to be open source requires that anyone can get and modify the source code and that they can freely redistribute any derived works they create from it. The different licenses have various wrinkles on whether modifications must also be made into open source or if they can be kept proprietary.

Later in this book we also discuss cases that do not meet the full definition of open source but do involve some form of collaborative development of the source code, for example, Java.

Open Source in Brief

In practice, a typical open-source project uses a web or other Internet site as the repository for the source code, documentation, discussions, design documents, bug and issue lists, and other artifacts associated with the project. A particular person or group is the copyright owner for the source, at least initially, and this owner grants permission for individuals or other groups to make modifications to the source mediated through a version control system such as CVS (Concurrent Versions System). Periodic builds are automatically produced, and there are usually several versions of varying stability and age compiled and prebuilt for a number of platforms that anyone can download and try out.

Although the owners of the source essentially have total control of the project, they generally will enlist the advice of the community about its direction. Sometimes contributors retain copyright of their own contributions while licensing them under the same or compatible license, and other times the contributors assign copyright to the owners of the project.

Ownership versus licensing is an important distinction to grasp. Even when rights are broadly granted through a license with considerable freedom about what an outside party can do with the source, the source code is still owned by the copyright holders who can do whatever they wish with it, including selling it, granting other licenses to it, or changing the direction of its development.

Often a project will be broken into modules, which can be thought of as logical or conceptual wholes, and a *module owner* is assigned to each. The module owner is in charge of inspecting proposed source changes and deciding whether to accept them or not. The module owner can also grant check-in privileges to developers who have earned his or her trust so that they can also modify the official source code. In many open-source projects, the overall owner and the module owners are the primary contributors while others contribute a small percentage of the work. In general, debugging through use is the significant source of contributions from the larger community.

Some open-source projects, especially those whose source is owned by companies, establish a governance mechanism that ensures that the community has a recognized voice in decision making, which in turn makes the playing field more level than it otherwise might be.

A QUICK HISTORY OF OPEN SOURCE

In 1984, Richard Stallman formed the Free Software Foundation[1] and started the GNU project (GNU is an acronym for "GNU's Not Unix"). He did so in response to seeing the collapse of the software-sharing community at the MIT AI Lab as everyone left to join companies making proprietary software. Stallman coined the term *free software* to express his philosophy that programmers should be allowed access to the source code so they could modify it to suit their needs. He developed the GNU General Public License (GPL) to assure that he would always be able to see and modify the source code for any software he wrote, along with

---

1. http://www.gnu.org

the modifications made by anyone else who might work on it. A number of important Unix tools and utilities have been developed as part of the GNU project, including the GNU GCC compiler and GNU Emacs.

In 1989 the University of California at Berkeley released its networking code and supporting utilities as Networking Release 1, the first freely redistributable Berkeley Software Distribution (BSD). This was followed in 1991 with Networking Release 2, which contained almost all the source code for BSD Unix (all but six files were included).

In 1991 Linus Torvalds started work on the Linux kernel under the GNU GPL and around 1992 combined it with the not-quite-complete GNU system to produce a complete free operating system. In 1995 Red Hat Software was formed to sell CD-ROMs and to offer support and services for the users of Red Hat Linux.

In 1995 a group of webmasters created the Apache project, based on the NCSA web server. Apache 1.0 was released later that year. According to the February 2004 Netcraft web-server survey, the Apache web server is more widely used than all other web servers combined and currently has over 67% of the web-server market.

In 1998 Netscape announced they would release the source code to their Navigator browser and 3 months later did so. Partly in response to the Netscape announcement, a group of leaders in the free software community, including Sam Ockman, John "maddog" Hall, Eric Raymond, and Larry Augustin, met to discuss how to better market the ideas of free software. They decided to use the term *open source* and, working with others, created the Open Source Definition,[2] which is based on the *Debian Free Software Guidelines* written by Bruce Perens for the Debian Linux distribution. They created an organization, the Open Source Initiative, to further the ideas of open source and to certify licenses as being true open source. There is a continuing tension between those who support *free software* and those who favor *open source* due to different philosophical outlooks.

More details on the history of open source are available online and in such books as *Open Sources: Voices from the Open Source Revolution* edited by Chris DiBona, Sam Ockman, and Mark Stone or *Rebel Code: Inside Linux and the Open Source Revolution* by Glyn Moody.

HYBRID OPEN SOURCE

In pure open-source projects, all the workers are volunteers. There are rarely if ever formal processes that are followed or formal specifications produced.

---

2. http://www.opensource.org/docs/definition.html

The team may or may not have usability experts, documentation writers, testers, or project management of any variety. In some circles, this form of open source is called "all-volunteer open source." Basically, whoever shows up is the team.

When companies start open-source projects, it is typical for those projects to be part of (or all of) a company initiative being done for strategic purposes and aims. Because many companies use a more traditional or conventional development process, such companies starting open-source projects are likely to want to engage the open-source community with some of their traditional tools and in-house experts. When this happens, we call it a "hybrid open-source project."

For example, GE started its Visualization Toolkit open-source project,[3] but they wanted to establish a strong cultural value around testing and quality. Based on some ideas from Extreme Programming, they instituted a distributed, automatic testing system that kicks in every night on the changes submitted to the project that day.

Another example is NetBeans where from the beginning Sun assigned human-computer interaction (HCI) experts, documentation writers, product managers, release engineers, and quality assurance people to work on it. These folks were trained in what open-source development was like and the ways that they would need to adapt, but nevertheless these other functions and some of the ways they normally operated within Sun were carried over into the project.

In large part, this book is about hybrid open source.

Philosophical Tenets of Open Source

Understanding the philosophical tenets of open source is simpler once you know a little about its cultural history, which is about as ancient as anything in electronic computing.

HISTORICAL ROOTS OF OPEN SOURCE

The open-source philosophy has its roots in the era of timesharing at large research universities such as MIT, Stanford, and CMU. In the 1960s and 1970s, these schools had research laboratories whose researchers and projects produced software—this included basic platforms such as operating systems and programming languages as well as higher-level, application-type software. This was necessary because either the research work itself was in the area of operating

---

3. This project is described in detail later in this chapter.

systems and programming languages or there were no suitable commercial or "professionally" created systems filling these roles.

The computers these labs used were almost exclusively timeshared machines, with a limited number of terminals connected to them. During the day, the machine was heavily used not only for research but also for writing papers and for administrative and clerical purposes. Yes, there was email in the 1960s. Imagine a 1 MIP machine with about a megabyte of memory shared by 100–200 people. A lot of real work was done at night.

In a typical corporate office at that time, doors were normally locked at night and the only people wandering the halls were the janitors, who had keys to every office. Terminals were usually in offices, and if those offices were locked, the terminals were not available for use by anyone without a key. Almost certainly there were fewer terminals than people, and so the physical resources were shared as well as the computational ones. It was assumed that work took place during business hours and that the computational resources either sat idle at night or were running under the control of specific authorized individuals. After all, the computers were expensive and were required for the proper operation of the company.

Imagine if this were also true of university research labs. People could start large computations and head home, experimental operating systems might crash, experimental computations might crash the operating system—in short, things could get wedged easily. Moreover, there could be more people wishing to work than available terminals in unlocked areas and offices.

Suppose it's the 1960s and the terminal controlling an out-of-control computation is behind a locked door and the problem is sufficient to hamper other people working at 2 AM. What can you do? Suppose there is no way to kill or suspend the computation except by accessing the controlling terminal? Must everyone go home until the one person returns the next day? Time is too valuable, and there might be 50 people who would have to go home because one person has locked his or her door. Or suppose the operating system has crashed in such a way that even rebooting wouldn't fix it—the permanent context has been changed enough that the operating system software needs to be fixed (perhaps a new peripheral has been added, such as a robot arm). Do you wait until you can talk to the programmer in charge to make the change when you yourself are sufficiently expert to fix things?

No, you institute three changes from normal procedures:

- You do not allow offices to be locked.

- You create mechanisms for attaching a different terminal to an existing session.

- You permit anyone to work on any of the source files.

This would be horrifying by some standards, but it worked just fine and created a culture that had very high productivity. First, rather than having a single or several system administrators (sys admins), such labs developed quite a few homegrown sys admins, perhaps a few dozen for a 200-person lab. These folks could do most anything sys admins do today, and in addition they were pretty darn good system programmers—typically for each part of the operating system or other system software there would be one or two experts who had created it and another three to six who were competent enough to maintain and improve it. People who joined the lab had all the source code available to look at how things were done and, in fact, to learn how to program well. What better way to learn about programming than by studying the working code of master programmers?

The result was that the machines were productively used 24 hours a day, 365 (or 366) days a year, with support. Operating systems, programming languages, and a lot of the software we take for granted today were developed incrementally over a few years' time with the full-time or part-time help of hundreds of programmers.

Social pressure and a kind of hierarchy of merit was used as a filter on who could work on what. Vandalism, bad behavior, and harmful mischievousness rarely, if ever, took place, such was the strength of the code of ethics that developed in such installations.

Here's a story we heard from the old days—it may not be true in its details, but its essence is accurate:

> *A new faculty member joined one of the "open-source-like" labs and had a terminal in his office. Used to a more traditional environment, he started a job, locked the door, and went home for the night. The job ran away and locked up the system in such a way it needed to be killed from the terminal or the system would need to be rebooted. One of the system programmers had to break open the door, pulling the hinges out of the door jamb. The next morning the new faculty member found his door leaning against the wall, splinters all over the floor, a note on his seat explaining what happened, and another note from the director of the lab informing him that his unrestricted funds account would be charged to have the door and jamb repaired.*

This is the culture from which the open-source movement emerged. The attitude is that people will behave well and that there is a common good being promoted. Source code is part of a shared experience that builds and supports the culture.

WARNING

Therefore, if as you read the following tenets you feel that they don't match how you work, how you feel, and how you could work, then you will not be able to fit into the culture required to make a successful open-source project. In that case, you should not pursue open-sourcing your project: Your project will not succeed, your project will embarrass your company in the public eye, and you will have mangled your project in such a way that you will have to abandon it.

Harsh, yes, but open source is not for everyone or for every project—at least not yet.

Let's look at some of the tenets of open source.

EVERYONE TOGETHER IS SMARTER THAN YOUR GROUP ALONE

When a producer puts on a play, audience members have no choice but to assume the role of critic: either you like the play or you don't, and you tell your friends what you think. But if the playwright were to turn to potential audience members at some point while writing the play and ask for help, these potential audience members would probably try their best to help and at some point might assume (in their own minds) a co-author role. It's harder for a co-author to be as harshly critical as a critic.

Inviting people to look at source code puts them in a frame of mind to help out. Not only will you gain a lot of testers, but these testers will have the source code and many of them will be able to locate the source of a problem in the code itself. The sum total of people running the software will encompass a wide variety of experience and expertise, and it is not unreasonable to assume that every type of bug in your code has been seen by someone in the pool at one time or another. It's like having a thousand people proofread a book for spelling and typographic errors.

You will mostly get highly informed and dedicated testers. The fact that the source code is available means that many of them will be at least able to develop their own workarounds to problems, and so they will stick with the software longer. But just as important, you will get a number of people who will want to contribute, often substantially, to the core source code.

A very common reaction to the idea of someone outside the organization contributing to the code base is that you don't want "a bunch of losers messing things up." Our experience is the opposite. First, there is no requirement in open source that every change proposed by someone must be taken back into the main source branch. So, you can select what you take, and you can modify or improve it if you wish. Second, it is your decision whether someone is trusted enough to check things directly into the source tree. You will have developed a relationship with all these people, looked at their work, and worked with them to improve their skills and use the style you want and, in most cases you will wish you could hire them. Third, there will not be that many of them anyway. For Linux, which is the biggest open-source project, there are on the order of 100 people who are permitted to check code into the source tree without supervision. Many of these people "own" parts of the code or modules, and they supervise other contributors. Fourth, almost all of the people who have access to the source code will be able to identify and perhaps isolate problems, and this will make things easier on the developers. In fact, most people will hesitate to mess things up and will simply report problems.

The phrase "innovation happens elsewhere" is based on the observation that not all the smart people work for you. But suppose they do: Suppose that *all* the people out there are losers when it comes to your project and its software. What will you do if one of your developers becomes ill or leaves your company? Any replacement will have to come from this pool of losers. Do you really believe you are in this position? Better have excellent health benefits, fabulous compensation packages, and bodyguards for your developers.

OPEN SOURCE REQUIRES AN OPEN DEVELOPMENT PROCESS—STARTING WITH THE DESIGN

It might be tempting to think that open source is really just about making the source code available for viewing. If you drop code into a public location and continue development on a private copy inside your company, you are not doing open source. You are running a source access program or simply providing extra documentation. To develop the right level of trust, the code out there must be the real source code that your developers are working on. You might have various modules checked out while the code is being worked on, but that must be true on a module-by-module basis not the entire source base.

Moreover, your developers are simply part of the larger pool of developers. They are perhaps better focused, they might work together better, or they might have goals of importance to your company, but they are otherwise in exactly the same boat as all the outside developers.

This means also that many, if not all, of what would otherwise be internal development mailing lists need to be public. All design and implementation decisions that affect the public source code must be done in the open. There can be no distinction between us and them.

In exchange for this, you build incredible loyalty and an intense desire to move the code forward with a shared vision. You get immediate and totally relevant feedback from the market. If you are short of resources, perhaps they will be supplied from the outside. The highly influential book on people management *Peopleware* (by Tom DeMarco and Timothy Lister) suggests that a good way to build a team is to have an introductory shared project, where the project itself comes to symbolize the group. Perhaps it's getting your newly assembled team together to cook an impromptu meal, but in the end it's working a shared artifact that does the trick. It's the same trick here. But it's no trick, it is part of the social nature of people.

THE BUSINESS MODEL MUST REINFORCE THE OPEN-SOURCE EFFORTS

You cannot charge people to use code that they are writing or have written. That means that you cannot simply take the code and charge money directly for it. You need to choose a business model that supports open source. The following are some classic open-source business models:

- Bundle open-source software with perhaps some other software and with support, charging for the bundle and for additional testing and quality.

- Add value in the form of additional modules or surrounding software and sell that additional software bundled with the open-source software.

- Provide a service based on the open-source software, such as a subscription service that updates customers' sites with tested and assured code.

- Sell consulting services that leverage the open-source software.

- Sell ancillary things such as books, T-shirts, and mugs.

- Sell hardware that runs the open-source software particularly well.

- Sell software that uses the open-source software as a platform.

There are two more business models that apply if you own the copyright to all of the source code and expect mostly minimal contributions from outside developers.

- Release the software as open source, but license the software to companies that wish to use it in a proprietary product.

- Sell the newest version, but release the previous version as open source.

Ubiquity, winning over hearts, thousands of eyes looking over the code, better platform security, and getting additional outside help are some of the reasons to do open source. The classic case is that you need to make a platform ubiquitous for some other business reason, and so you use open source as the conduit to ubiquity.

CREATING AND INVOLVING OUTSIDE DEVELOPERS REQUIRES INTERNAL RESOURCES

Many people think doing open source is a no-brainer: You can add developers to your team and don't need to pay them. However, you do need to attract, foster, and support those outside developers, and that does require internal resources. First and foremost, it requires that your internal developers take the time to participate on the public mailing lists, answer questions from outside developers, and promptly respond to bug fixes and code contributions. Your developers also need to document the system architecture so outside folks can find their way around in the source code. You may even need to rewrite the source code to be more modular, especially if it is currently one big monolithic mess.

Another cost is setting up and maintaining the infrastructure needed for an open-source project: a CVS code archive, a bug database, various mailing lists, and a website for the project. For large projects, these can each require a full-time person.

OPEN SOURCE IS A GIFT ECONOMY

To understand open source, it helps to make a distinction between a *commodity economy*, to which we are accustomed in a capitalist society, and a *gift economy*. In a gift economy, gifts are exchanged, forming a bond based on mutual obligation: In the simplest form of gift exchange, when one person gives a gift to another, the receiver becomes obligated to the giver, but not in a purely mercenary way—rather, the recipient becomes very much like a member of the giver's family where mutual obligations are many, varied, and long lasting. A person may give a gift with the realistic expectation that someday a gift of equal or greater use value will be received or that the recipient will pass on a further gift. In an open-source project, the gift of source code is reciprocated by suggestions, bug reports, debugging, hard work, praise, and more source code.

The commodity economy depends on scarcity. Its most famous law is that of "diminishing returns," whose working requires a fixed supply. Scarcity of material or scarcity of competitors creates high profit margins. It works through competition.

The gift economy is an economy of abundance—the gifts exchanged are inexhaustible. Gift economies are embedded within noneconomic institutions such as kinship, marriage, hospitality, artistic patronage, and ritual friendship. A healthy Western family operates on a gift economy. In an open-source project, the status and reputation of individuals depend on the quality of the gifts they contribute.

For open source to succeed in communities that include corporations, the source-code gift-based economy needs to thrive alongside the commodity economy just beyond its boundaries.

THE WORK-IN-PROGRESS EFFECT

The concept of the gift economy is related to what we call the *work-in-progress* effect. This effect is one of the primary reasons that writers' workshops in the literary and software-patterns worlds work as well as they do. The act of opening the curtain early when there is still time to affect the outcome seems to elicit a profound response from the audience, and the response is heightened when the invitation is to be, essentially, co-authors. Harsh criticism is replaced by constructive criticism. Responsibility becomes jointly held. The co-authors align in their regard for the work, although their individual opinions about what to do may differ quite a bit. The concern becomes how to make the work the best it can be rather than commenting on the work or the author.

Open source depends on this response.

OPEN SOURCE IS NOT BUSINESS AS USUAL

In summary, deciding to make a project open source means that it will be very different from your normal proprietary project. All decisions and design will need to be done in the open. Schedules will depend on people outside your company whom you cannot control. The community that emerges will take on a life of its own, possibly taking the project in directions you neither anticipated nor desire.

Your business model and processes must be different or else you won't succeed. You don't do open source as an add-on to your usual process. Deciding to do open source is like deciding to get married and start a family: It takes a commitment, and once you start down that path it will change how you live.

Open Source and Agile Methodologies

During the last 5 years, a set of methodologies have become popular, called *agile methodologies*. An agile methodology is, in general, one that emphasizes incremental development and small design steps guided by frequent interactions with customers. The customer and developers get together and agree on the next set of features and capabilities for the software. Ideally, the work should take at most a few weeks. The developers then make the additions and the software is released to the customers, who react to it, perhaps making corrective suggestions.

Agile methodologies and open source would seem, at first glance, to be radically different: Agile methodologies are thought of as being about small, collocated teams and open source as being about large, distributed ones. A company might expect that the benefits of one are pretty different from the benefits of the other. Agile methodologies arose, largely, from the ranks of paid consultants, whereas open source seems like a hippie phenomenon. A company might, therefore, believe there is a sharp choice to be made between them, but the choice has more to do with the conversations, the diversity of participants, and the transparency of the process to the outside world than it does with the philosophy of design and development: The two approaches share many principles and values.

Some agile methodologies have special practices that set them apart from others—for example, extreme programming uses pair programming and test-driven development. Pair programming is the practice of two people sitting at the same computer screen with one person typing and the other observing and commenting. Instead of one person sitting alone with his or her thoughts, pair programmers engage in a conversation while working, which serves as a real-time continuous design and code review. Test-driven development is the practice of defining and implementing testing code before the actual product code is implemented. The following are the agile development principles taken from the Agile Manifesto website[4]—most of these principles also apply to open source, except as noted.

- *"Our highest priority is to satisfy the customer through early and continuous delivery of valuable software."*

  Open source does not talk about the customer, but in general, open-source projects do nightly builds and frequent named releases, mostly for the purpose of in-situ testing.

- *"Welcome changing requirements, even late in development. Agile processes harness change for the customer's competitive advantage."*

  Open-source projects resist major changes as time goes on, but there is always the possibility of forking a project if such changes strike enough developers as worthwhile.

---

4. http://agilemanifesto.org/principles.html

- *"Deliver working software frequently, from a couple of weeks to a couple of months, with a preference to the shorter time scale."*

  Open source delivers working code every night, usually, and an open-source motto is "release early, release often."

- *"Business people and developers must work together daily throughout the project."*

  Open-source projects don't have a concept of a businessperson with whom they work, but users who participate in the project serve the same role.

- *"Build projects around motivated individuals. Give them the environment and support they need, and trust them to get the job done."*

  All open-source projects do this, almost by definition. If there is no motivation to work on a project, a developer won't. That is, open-source projects are purely voluntary, which means that motivation is guaranteed. Open-source projects use a set of agreed-on tools for version control, compilation, debugging, bug and issue tracking, and discussion.

- *"The most efficient and effective method of conveying information to and within a development team is face-to-face conversation."*

  Open source differs most from agile methodologies here. Open-source projects value written communication over face-to-face communication. On the other hand, open-source projects can be widely distributed, and don't require collocation.

- *"Working software is the primary measure of progress."*

  This is in perfect agreement with open source.

- *"Agile processes promote sustainable development. The sponsors, developers, and users should be able to maintain a constant pace indefinitely."*

  Although this uses vocabulary that open-source developers would not use, the spirit of the principle is embraced by open source.

- *"Continuous attention to technical excellence and good design enhances agility."*

  Open source is predicated on technical excellence and good design.

- *"Simplicity—the art of maximizing the amount of work not done—is essential."*

  Open-source developers would agree that simplicity is essential, but open-source projects also don't have to worry quite as much about scarcity as agile projects do. There are rarely contractually committed people on open-source projects—certainly not the purely voluntary ones—so the amount of work to be done depends on the beliefs of the individual developers.

- *"The best architectures, requirements, and designs emerge from self-organizing teams."*

  Possibly open-source developers would not state things this way, but the nature of open-source projects depends on this being true.

- *"At regular intervals, the team reflects on how to become more effective, and then tunes and adjusts its behavior accordingly."*

  This is probably not done much in open-source projects, although as open-source projects mature, they tend to develop a richer set of governance mechanisms. For example, Apache started with a very simple governance structure similar to that of Linux and now there is the Apache Software Foundation with management, directors, and officers. This represents a sort of reflection, and almost all community projects evolve their mechanisms over time.

In short, both the agile and open-source methodologies embrace a number of principles and values, which share the ideas of trying to build software suited especially to a class of users, interacting with those users during the design and implementation phases, blending design and implementation, working in groups, respecting technical excellence, doing the job with motivated people, and generally engaging in continuous (re)design.

A good example of a company-related open-source project that embraces both open-source and agile values is the Visualization ToolKit (VTK), which is partly sponsored by GE. VTK is a software system for 3D computer graphics, image processing, and visualization, and portions of it are subject to patents held by GE and a smaller company called Kitware. As its website states:

> *VTK supports a wide variety of visualization algorithms including scalar, vector, tensor, texture, and volumetric methods; and advanced modeling techniques such as implicit modelling, polygon reduction, mesh smoothing, cutting, contouring, and Delaunay triangulation. In addition, dozens of imaging algorithms have been directly integrated to allow the user to mix 2D imaging/3D graphics algorithms and data. The design and implementation of the library has been strongly influenced by object oriented principles. VTK has been installed and tested on nearly every Unix-based platform, PCs (Windows 98/ME/NT/2000/ XP), and Mac OS X Jaguar or later.*[5]

The kit is substantial, encompassing over 600 C++ classes and around half a million lines of code. There are over 2000 people on the VTK mailing list.

---

5. http://www.vtk.org/index.php

GE's stance regarding VTK as a commercial advantage is summed up in the following statement: "We don't sell VTK, we sell what we do with VTK."[6] GE has a number of internal and external customers of the toolkit—it is used in a variety of projects GE is involved with. Kitware provides professional services associated with VTK.

As an open-source project, VTK is a bit unusual, and this is the result of some of its principals being involved with GE, which is the prime supporter of a design and implementation methodology called *six sigma*. Six sigma refers to a statistic that states that a manufactured artifact is 99.99966% defect-free, and it also refers to a process in which factors important to the customers' perception of quality are identified and systematically addressed during a design and implementation cycle whose steps are Define, Measure, Analyze, Improve, Control (DMAIC). Open source involves the possibility of diverse innovations and also provides opportunities for interacting with customers in a direct way, which is appealing to an organization focused on customers, but there is also the possibility of erratic results when there is not a strong, explicit emphasis on quality that can be enforced. Therefore, open source went only part of the way to satisfying GE's goals for quality.

Moreover, the original VTK implementation team was small and dispersed within GE, and its members were admittedly not software engineers. The open-source component added to this the need to find a way to handle quality. The solution was to adopt some of the practices of Extreme Programming, which is one of the agile methodologies. Extreme Programming (or XP) emphasizes testing and advocates a practice called test-driven design in which tests are written at the same time as, or before, the code is designed and written.[7] Writing tests first has the effect of providing a sort of formal specification—the test code—as well as a set of tests to be used for regression and integration testing. XP calls for frequent (tested) releases, and VTK combines this with the open-source practice of "release early, release often" to do nightly, fully tested builds.

The VTK developers implemented a regimen in which submitted code is tested overnight using a large corpus of regression tests, image regression tests (comparing program output to a gold standard), statistical performance comparisons, style checks, compilation, error log analyses, and memory leak and bounds-check analyses; the software's documentation is automatically produced; and the result is a quality dashboard that is displayed every day on the website. The dashboard is similar to those produced by the Mozilla project,[8]

---

6. http://www.crd.ge.com/~lorensen/ExtremeTesting/ExtremeTestingTalk.pdf, p. 5.

7. There is considerably more to Extreme Programming. Kent Beck's book, *Extreme Programming Explained: Embrace Change* is a good place to learn about it, as is the website http://www.extremeprogramming.org.

8. http://tinderbox.mozilla.org/showbuilds.cgi

but considerably more detailed. The tests are run on around 50 different builds on a variety of platforms across the Internet, and distributions are made for all the platforms.

The reasons for this approach, as stated by the original team, are as follows:

- To shorten the software engineering life cycle of design/implement/test to a granularity of 1 day.

- To make software that always works.

- To find and fix defects in hours not weeks by bringing quality assurance inside the development cycle and by breaking the cycle of letting users find bugs.

- To automate everything.

- To make all developers responsible for testing (developers are expected to fix their bugs immediately).

Among the values expressed by the original development team are the following:

- Test early and often; this is critical to high-quality software.

- Retain measurements to assess progress and measure productivity.

- Present results in concise informative ways.

- Know and show the status of the system at any time.

This is not all. The VTK website provides excellent documentation and a coding style guide with examples. Most of the details of the mechanics of the code are spelled out in detail. Moreover, there are several textbooks available on VTK.

In short, the VTK open-source project has integrated open-source and extreme-programming practices to satisfy GE's need to express to customers its commitment to quality, even in projects only partially controlled by GE. Furthermore, GE has tapped into a larger development community to assist its own small team, so that its customers get the benefits of a high-functionality, high-quality system infused with GE values.

CONTINUOUS (RE)DESIGN

The primary source of similarities between open-source and the agile methodologies is their shared emphasis on continuous (re)design. Continuous design is the idea that design and building are intertwined and that changes to a design should be made as more is learned about the true requirements for the software. This is why both camps agree with the mantra, "release early, release often."

Continuous design is an approach that is predicated on recognizing that it is rarely possible to design perfectly upfront. The realization is that design is often the result of slowly dawning insights rather than of knowing everything at the start of the project and that, like most projects, the activities are progressive and uncertain. Specifications of software function, usability, and structure, for example, cannot be fully known before software is designed and implemented. In continuous design, software source code, bug databases, and archived online discussions capture and track the preferences and realities of co-emerging software systems and their user/developer communities in a continuous cycle of innovation, change, and design. Explicit and formal specifications and formal design processes rarely exist: The code itself along with the archived discussions are the specification.

Some open-source projects, especially hybrid company/volunteer projects, use more formal processes and produce more formal artifacts such as specifications, but even these projects accept the idea that the design should change as the requirements are better understood. In fact, we could argue that even software produced using the current principles of software design, software engineering, and software evolution are often discretized versions of continuous design—imposing the idea of formal design and specifications done largely upfront, but (unconsciously) allowing the effect of continuous design over a series of infrequent major releases rather than through small, essentially daily ones.

Common Open-Source Myths, Misconceptions, and Questions

The picture of open-source software painted by the popular media tends to be superficial and simplistic. Open source is touted as a miraculous way to produce software at no cost. For anyone developing software professionally, all this open-source hype no doubt seems pretty farfetched. Let's take a closer look and try to shed some light on what open source is really all about.

MYTH 1: OPEN-SOURCE DEVELOPMENT IS SOMETHING NEW

If you read the newspaper, open source seems to have started with the Linux operating system back in 1991 (or more likely, in 1997 or 1998 when whoever wrote the article finally heard about Linux). The actual facts are a bit different: Open source is as old as computer programming. If you had wandered into places such as MIT or Stanford in the 1960s, you would have seen that sharing software source code was assumed. Early development of the ARPAnet was helped by freely available source code, a practice that continued as it grew into today's Internet. The Berkeley version of Unix dates from the mid-1970s. All in all quite a distinguished lineage.

The creation of software by a loosely coupled group of volunteers seems a thoroughly contemporary phenomenon, based on the free outlook of the 1960s— a kind of fallout of free love and hippiedom—but the concept of distributed group development is hardly new.

On Guy Fawkes Day, 1857, Richard Chenevix Trench, addressing the Philological Society, proposed the production of a new, complete English dictionary based on finding the earliest occurrences of each of the English words ever in printed use. That is, the dictionary would be constructed by reading every book ever written and noting down exactly where in each book a significant use of every word occurred; these citations would be used to write definitions and short histories of the words' uses. In order to do this, Trench proposed enlisting the volunteer assistance of individuals throughout English-speaking countries by advertising for their assistance.

Over a period of 70 years, many hundreds of people sent in over 6 million slips with words and their interesting occurrences in thousands of books. This resulted in the *Oxford English Dictionary*, the ultimate authority on English, with 300,000 words, about 2.5 million citations, and 8.3 citations per entry in 20 volumes.

Compare this with the best effort by an individual—Samuel Johnson, over a 9-year period, using the same methodology and a handful of assistants called *amanuenses*, produced a two-volume dictionary with about 40,000 words and in most cases one citation per entry. As we look at these two works, Johnson's dictionary is a monument to individual effort and a work of art, revealing as much about Johnson as about the language he perceived around him, while the OED is the standard benchmark for dictionaries, the final arbiter of meaning and etymology.

MYTH 2: OPEN-SOURCE DEVELOPMENT IS DONE BY HOBBYISTS AND STUDENTS

The stereotype for the sort of person who contributes to an open-source project is that of a hobbyist or student, someone you perhaps wouldn't take too seriously. After all, full-time professional programmers don't have time for such things. Well, first, students and hobbyists can often write very good code. Next, lots of professionals do like to program on their own time. A study done by the Boston Consulting Group[9] found that over 45% of those participating in open-source projects were experienced, professional programmers, with another 20% being sys admins, IT managers, or academics. The same study found that over 30% of these professionals were paid by their day job to develop open-source software. Both Sun and IBM have engineering teams contributing to various parts of the Apache web server. Most companies building PC peripherals now write the needed device drivers for Linux as well as Windows. In fact, the open-source process encourages the replacement of contributions from less capable programmers with code from more capable ones.

MYTH 3: OPEN-SOURCE SOFTWARE IS LOW QUALITY

How can a bunch of random programmers, with no quality assurance (QA) folks, produce code with any degree of quality? Isn't open-source software full of bugs? Well, there may initially be as many bugs in open source as in proprietary code, but because it's open more developers will actually look at the code, catching many bugs in the process. Also everyone using the code is essentially doing QA; they report on any bugs that they find, and because they have access to the source code, they often also fix the bugs themselves.

In 2003, Reasoning, Inc., performed a defect analysis[10] of the Apache web server and Tomcat, which is a mechanism for extending Apache with Java servlets, by using their defect discovery tool. For Apache, the tool found 31 defects in 58,944 source lines, a defect density of 0.53 defects per thousand lines of source code (KSLC). In a sampling of 200 projects totaling 35 million lines of code, 33% had a defect density below 0.36 defects/KSLC, 33% had a defect density between 0.36 and 0.71 defects/KSLC, and the remaining 33% had a defect density above 0.71 defects/KSLC. This puts Apache squarely in the middle of the studied quality distribution. For Tomcat, the tool found 17 software defects in 70,988 lines of Tomcat source code. The defect density of the Tomcat code inspected was 0.24 defects/KSLC. This puts Tomcat in the upper half of quality.

If you still don't believe that open-source software is of similar quality to most commercial software, just take a look at some open-source software you use every day. Assuming you make any use of the Internet, you are relying on open-source code such as BIND, which is at the heart of the Domain Name Service (DNS); or sendmail, which probably transports most email; and Apache, which as of

---

9. *The Boston Consulting Group Hacker Survey,* Release 0.73, 2002.

10. http://www.reasoning.com/downloads.html

February 2004 was the software running on over 67% of the world's web servers. Then there's Linux, which has won several awards for quality and has a notably longer mean time between reboots than some other major PC operating systems.

MYTH 4: LARGE-SCALE DEVELOPMENT ISN'T EFFICIENT

Having thousands of people fixing bugs might work, but how can you possibly coordinate the work of that number of developers? Without central control how can it possibly be an efficient process? Well, that's correct, but why does it need to be efficient? When you have limited resources, efficiency is important, but in an open-source effort with lots of developers, if some go off and write a module that eventually is rejected, it doesn't matter. Open-source efforts often progress in small steps. If several people are working on different solutions to a problem, as long as one eventually produces a solution, you are making forward progress. If two solutions are produced, that's even better: just pick the best one. Also, with the ease of email and news groups, the various people working on the problem will probably find each other and spontaneously self-organize to work together to produce a result that is better than any of them alone could have produced—all without any central control.

MYTH 5: IF THE SOFTWARE IS FREE, THEN WHO'S GOING TO PAY YOU TO WRITE IT?

Why should your company pay you to write free software? Well, your company may already be doing that. Are you working on a product that is sold or distributed for free? Are you working on something only used internally? Is the income generated from selling the software you write greater than the cost to produce it? The profit may come from other activities. Likewise for free software. Your company will continue to make its money from selling hardware (e.g., servers, storage, and workstations); proprietary software; books; and consulting, training, and support.

For example, O'Reilly and Associates sells enough Perl books to pay the main Perl developers to work on new Perl features. Several of the main Linux developers are employed by Red Hat, which makes its money by packaging up free software. Cygnus (now part of Red Hat) sells support for the GNU compiler and debugger, which its employees continue to develop and give away. Sun sells servers, but gives away Java.

Look at the sections "The Business Model Must Reinforce the Open-Source Efforts" and (in Chapter 4) "Business Reasons for Choosing to Open Source

Your Code" for more details about how your company can make money from open-source software development. Keep in mind, however, that roughly 90% of the money spent on software development is for custom software that is never sold; commercial software represents less than 10% of the total investment.

MYTH 6: BY MAKING YOUR SOFTWARE OPEN SOURCE YOU'LL GET THOUSANDS OF DEVELOPERS WORKING ON IT FOR NO COST

That would be nice, but in reality most open-source projects have only a few dozen core developers doing most of the work, with maybe a few hundred other developers contributing occasional bug reports, bug fixes, and possible enhancements. Then there are the thousands of users, who may contribute bug reports and requests for new features. The users also post messages asking how to use the software and, in a healthy project, the more experienced users post answers to those questions. Some users may even help write documentation.

Hewlett-Packard and Intel report a 5:1 or 6:1 ratio of community to corporate developers for open-source projects the two companies have been involved with.[11] Our belief is that this is a little high, but it isn't too far off.

Another source of data is SourceForge, which has about 80,000 projects with 90,000 developers. The distribution of the number of developers to projects there follows a power law with about 60,000 projects with between zero and one active developers, 3000 with three, five with 30, and one with 100. To factor out the large number of inactive or dead projects on SourceForge, a study in May 2002 by Krishnamurthy[12] looked at participation only in mature, active projects and found the average number of developers per project to be four. Only 19 out of the 100 projects studied had more than 10 developers, whereas 22% of the projects had only one developer associated with them.

It's true that you don't need to pay any outside developers who choose to work on your project. However you do need to pay the cost of maintaining the infrastructure necessary for open-source development (e.g., a CVS code server, a bug database, project mailing lists, and project website), along with the people to integrate the contributions you get. You won't get something for nothing, but for a successful open-source project you can get back more than what you put in.

---

11. *The Open Source Software Challenge in 2001*, Stanford University Graduate School of Business Case SM 85.

12. http://www.firstmonday.dk/issues/issue7_6/krishnamurthy

MYTH 7: OPEN SOURCE DOESN'T SCALE

Experience with conventional, proprietary software development teaches that the larger the project, the greater the number of resources needed for coordination and design. For an open-source project where all the discussion is via mailing lists and where there is no formal management structure, it seems that it would be impossible to efficiently organize the developers. Hence, open source might work for small projects, but not for large ones.

In his essay, *The Mythical Man-Month*, Frederick P. Brooks states that adding more developers to a late project will just make it later. In an open-source project, developers can be added at any time with no forewarning. One issue with Brooks' Law and the various studies that have subsequently either supported or qualified it is that there is a tacit assumption about the development process. Although rarely stated, the assumption is that the development team will be made up of individual contributors, each working on a separate part of the software, forming an efficient allocation of developers to the code. As it turns out, neither extreme programming nor open source obeys that assumption. Moreover, these studies assume that developers are a scarce resource, which is not true for open source.

Although it has been difficult to set up proper experiments to test how extreme programming affects Brooks' Law, one preliminary study[13] showed that when a programmer was added to create a pair-programming situation, the added programmer could immediately contribute by observing and pointing out simple errors and by asking probing questions that served to clarify the thought processes of the primary programmer. Thus, the new programmer could be productive immediately, although not as productive as a full-speed developer. The difficulty in experimental methodology is to obtain a valid comparison between an extreme programming project and a traditional one.

In an open-source project, developers are no longer treated as a scarce resource that must be used efficiently. Therefore, a developer added to a project doesn't need to have a separate part carved out. Moreover, a new developer can probably contribute immediately in the same way as in extreme programming by finding (and fixing) simple errors and asking probing questions. In his essay, Brooks points out that new developers must be trained, that larger teams require greater overhead to communicate with each other, and that not every task may be partitioned.

For an open-source project, it is important to distinguish between those developers who make up the *core team*—the module owners and few developers with check-in privileges—and the much larger number of occasional contributors.

---

13. Laurie Williams, North Carolina State University, private communication.

The core team is always going to be too small and all the lessons of conventional software development apply to them, including Brooks' Law. However it is with the larger group of contributors that open source changes the rules: These are the folks who can track down obscure bugs and create fixes for them, help each other to get up to speed on the code, implement features from the project's wishlist, or explore and experiment with more radical modifications—all activities that free up the core team to focus on its own main work.

Instead of controlling and scheduling developers, open source relies on the developers' self-organizing based on their interests and abilities. Instead of a management structure to coordinate everyone's work, open-source development requires resources to evaluate and integrate developer contributions. Moreover, those resources can draw on the total community of developers and are not limited to any core group. To see this, look at the success of some of the large open-source projects such as Apache or Linux.

MYTH 8: A COMPANY DOING OPEN SOURCE GIVES UP OWNERSHIP OF ITS SOURCE CODE AND PATENTS

Your company still owns any source code that it releases under an open-source license because your company still owns the copyright. The open-source license grants others the right to examine and use the source code, but it does not affect your company's ownership of the code. As the copyright owner, your company can release the source code under another license or use it in a proprietary product. Only if the source code were distributed containing an explicit disclaimer of copyright protection by your company would the software pass to the public domain and thereby no longer be owned by your company.[14]

However, source code contributed back to your company by outside developers is owned by the author, who holds the copyright for it. Under some licenses, such as the Sun Community Source License (SCSL), your company would be able to use the contributed code without restrictions. Under an open source license, such as GPL or the Mozilla Public License (MPL), your company would be bound by the terms of the license just like any other developer.

Similarly, your company still owns the patents embodied in any source released under an open-source license, but if your company does not explicitly talk about the uses to which any such patents may be put, others might be free to use those patents.

---

14. Code of Federal Regulations, Title 37, Volume 1 (Patents, Trademarks, and Copyrights) Part 201, Section 201.26, Paragraph i.

MYTH 9: AN OPEN-SOURCE COMMUNITY IS AN OPEN COMMUNITY

An open-source community is a community surrounding an open-source artifact, but it may not be an open community, meaning that it might not be open to anyone at all joining, and that once in the community a member might not know how to move ahead and become a leader. The community can be as closed, idiosyncratic, and undemocratic as it wants to be. The license guarantees that everyone in the community has certain rights with respect to the code, but in general it does not say anything about the community.

Open Source and Community

A successful open-source project is a community effort by people with different needs and skills and includes users, designers, programmers, testers, and others. The word *community* encompasses many meanings and is used by different people to mean many different things. For understanding open source, we find the following definition from *Community Building on the Web* by Amy Jo Kim most useful:

> *A community is a group of people with a shared interest, purpose, or goal, who get to know each other better over time.* (p. 28)

Both aspects are equally important: Conversations around their shared interest in the open-source project cause the participants to learn about each other. A scattered collection of people just using a piece of software is not a community, but can become one by talking with each other to understand how to best use the software. We particularly want to distinguish a true community from a *user group*, where people come mainly to learn about a product or technology but do not interact much with each other—typically the users listen to and ask questions of one or more experts.

If you ask people connected with open source about their community and how it works, many will draw something like Figure 3.1. They will tell you about how people start as just users and how some will become more involved by reporting bugs. Some may become developers who fix bugs or make minor enhancements. A few developers then get more involved and join the ranks of the core developers, being granted the right to check-in changes to the actual project's source code. This is a very code-centric view of the open-source process as a hierarchy that has users at the periphery, occasional developers closer in, core developers even closer in, and the code at the center.

And, in fact, this view makes the hierarchy into a funnel in which the goal is to convert people from one ring in the diagram to people in the next one in—almost as if the goal were to turn people into code in the end, the highest form of existence.

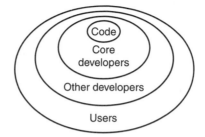

FIGURE 3.1 Single community built around source code.

A direct result of this perspective is that the actual users of the program are marginalized. Although the success of the project is often measured by the number of people that use the computer program being developed, only those people who are willing and able to talk about the code can participate in discussions on the project's mailing lists. Major decisions are made by those writing the code, not by those who will only use it.

If we step back a bit, we can see that the people involved in an open-source project take on various roles. Over time they may act as users, designers, or coders. So a better diagram looks like Figure 3.2. Here the code is still at the center; users, designers, and coders can look at the code, but only the *core coders* deal directly with the code. We use the term *coder* rather than *developer* to emphasize the roles being played: A coder is someone who manipulates code, either by writing new code to implement some design feature or by inspecting and correcting existing code someone else has written.

The thin solid black lines in Figure 3.2 indicate changes to the source code, the dotted lines indicate viewing the source code and interacting with the program,

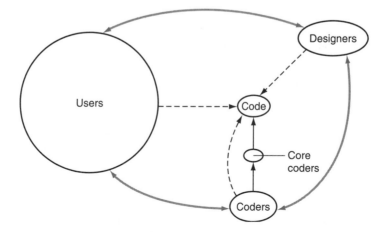

FIGURE 3.2 Different roles, still focused on code.

and the thicker, gray lines indicate communications between people in the different roles. Note that the ovals representing the different roles are not drawn to scale; the users' circle should be much, much bigger for any healthy open-source project.

This is still a view that focuses on the source code, but it brings out that design is separate from coding and that designers need not be coders. It also reflects the fact that people in the community may not simply advance from user to core developer in a linear progression but adopt the roles that make sense for what they are doing at the moment.

If we step back still further and look at all the ways that people interact in the context of an open-source project, we see they do so in many different ways, such as:

- Reading, writing, modifying and debugging the actual source code.

- Reporting and commenting on bugs.

- Reading and writing documents such as user manuals, tutorials, how-tos, system documentation, and project roadmaps.

- Participating in online public discussions via mailing lists, newsgroups, and IRC chat sessions.

- Visiting the project's official website or other related websites.

- Attending meetings and conferences such as user groups, community meetings, working groups, and trade shows.

Many of these do not involve the source code at all: Users can discuss how best to do their jobs, perhaps only just touching on how the project's tools can help them. Other conversations may focus on standards for protocols or application programming interfaces (APIs) that the project uses. Still other conversations may address issues affecting the larger open-source community. Each different conversation involves a different group of people. These groups may range in size from small working groups of fewer than 20 members to full communities of hundreds or thousands of participating individuals. We might represent these multiple communities as in Figure 3.3. Some people will participate in different discussions, making them members of several communities. This overlap helps to create the larger community associated with the open-source project as a whole.

Each of these communities has its own special interests; for example, some communities connected to Linux might include system administrators concerned with installing and configuring the Linux operating system on various types of computers. Another group of people might be concerned with business

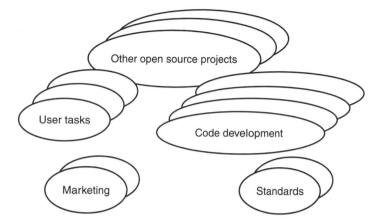

FIGURE 3.3 Communities built around common interests.

productivity tools (such as word processors, spreadsheets, and presentation tools) that are available for Linux—their focus is on what tools exist and how to use them. A third community might form around computer games available for Linux, with a subcommunity around a specific game such as Quake—this group would focus on exchanging tips, rumors of new games, and finding opponents to play with.

Each community will flourish or wither depending on how well its interests are met by the community resources. For example a community of newbies asking basic questions about how to use a piece of software will succeed only if more experienced users who can answer those questions are also part of the community.

In the course of a successful open-source project, different communities will come and go. New ones will spring up, grow, and possibly become dormant or die. As long as there are always some thriving communities, the larger open-source project can be considered alive and well.

Note that death of a community does not equal failure. Consider a community that arises to develop a new standard. After the standard it developed has been accepted by the larger Internet community, the community has achieved its purpose and is no longer necessary. If future revisions to the standard are called for, the community might be resurrected.

EXAMPLES OF MULTIPLE COMMUNITIES

To make this more concrete, let's look in depth at some of the different communities within two Sun-sponsored projects, Jini and NetBeans.

Jini

Jini technology is a simple distributed computing model based on the Java programming language developed by Sun. Among other things, it was intended as a model for services—small bits of functionality—to discover each other dynamically and create a network of interoperating program parts. These services could be housed within devices—physically separate computing platforms as far as Jini is concerned.

For Jini to succeed, it was clear that the underlying Jini protocols and infrastructure would need to become pervasive, and to accomplish that would require a strong community of participants and partners. Moreover, Sun did not have the expertise to define Jini services in areas such as printing, digital photography, storage, white goods, and the many other potential markets for products that would benefit from being network enabled.

Within the Jini Community that has developed since the core code was released, there are many separate communities focused on creating Jini services in different application areas, as shown in Figure 3.4. A small number of developers care about further developing the core Jini code. Others care only about areas such as printing or enterprise applications or building networked appliances that use Jini to connect to services. People working in one application area often have little in common with those working in another area. For example, those people working on creating services for appliances in the home have a very different set of concerns from those using Jini to connect legacy enterprise applications.

A similar situation exists in any large open-source project. In Apache, for example, there are smaller subcommunities focused on the Apache HTTP Server, the Apache Portable Runtime, the Jakarta Project (which includes major efforts such as Tomcat, Struts, and Ant), mod_perl, PHP, TCL, and XML (with subprojects such as Xerces, Xalan, Batik, and Crimson).

In addition to communities focused on developing code, other Jini-related groups have formed around interests such as helping beginners learn Jini, Jini in

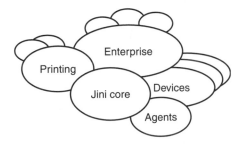

FIGURE 3.4 Different Jini code development interests.

academia, and even Jini marketing and Jini business development. As of spring 2004, there were over 150 projects (although some of them seemed to be no longer active).

A characteristic of the Jini community that is not typical of other open-source communities is its elaborate governance mechanisms. Membership is divided into bodies consisting of individuals and companies, called houses. In the General House each person has one vote, and in the Commercial House each company has one vote; and any major decision requires both houses to agree. There is also an appeals board (Technical Oversight Committee) for which the General House, the Commercial House, and Sun Microsystems each selects three members.

NetBeans

NetBeans is a modular, standards-based *integrated development environment* (IDE) that software developers use to create and modify applications written in Java. An integrated development environment is a software bundle consisting of a text editor (for creating and modifying software source code), code-building automation tools (for combining source code components into a whole application), a compiler (for preparing source code for machine execution), a code execution platform (an interpreter or runtime environment to run the code), and a debugger (for locating and repairing coding errors). NetBeans supports a wide range of features, from JSP development and debugging to integrated CVS support and beyond. All of these pieces of functionality are implemented in the form of modules that plug into the NetBeans core. As an open-source project, the basic version of NetBeans is available free to anyone wishing to use it. Sun's main interest in NetBeans is to bring developers to the Java platform and make them successful.

Figure 3.5 diagrams the various communities involved with the NetBeans project circa 2002. In addition to those directly involved with developing the NetBeans source code, there are three additional groups at Sun working on the various editions of Forte for Java: *Community Edition* (CE), *Internet Edition* (IE), and *Enterprise Edition* (EE). (*Note*: In late 2003, the Forte for Java product line was renamed as Sun Java Studio.) The last two editions are for-sale products that include additional proprietary modules. There are also various third-party companies developing NetBeans modules that are also for sale.

There are several distinct user communities. First, there are those developers using NetBeans as an IDE to create Java applications—their concern is how to best use NetBeans to write Java programs. There is also a geographical information system (GIS) built using the NetBeans framework—users of that application are not involved with any programming; they want to discuss issues

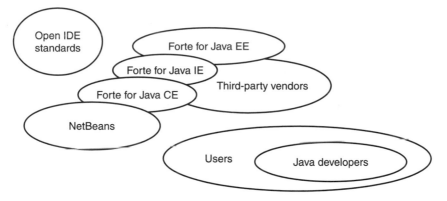

FIGURE 3.5 Multiple NetBeans products and uses.

around using GIS. When the NetBeans IDE is enhanced to handle languages in addition to Java, such as C/C++, then there will be a new user community of C/C++ developers.

Note that in the diagram in Figure 3.5 the oval labeled *Users* should be several orders of magnitude larger than all of the other ovals; the users number in the tens or hundreds of thousands, whereas the people modifying the NetBeans code are in the hundreds.

For NetBeans to be a success, all of these communities need to be successful. Each must grow for NetBeans to prosper.

NetBeans provides another example of how an open-source project can involve multiple communities, in this case three very different cultures:

- NetBeans
- Forte
- Sun

At Sun, the NetBeans open-source project arose from the simultaneous acquisitions of NetBeans, a small startup company in Prague, Czech Republic, and Forte Software, a company based in Oakland, California. These two companies joined Sun's existing Tools organization, bringing together three companies, with three different corporate cultures, sets of values, day-to-day processes, and business goals. This was a challenging acquisition integration task.

Unifying three different corporate cultures and day-to-day processes would be challenging enough; however, the bigger challenge may have been that the Tools organization was now spread across three different sites (Menlo Park, Oakland,

and Prague). Recall that distributed development is fundamental to the open-source methodology. It is simply assumed. So the open-source methodology represented both a natural solution for the Tools organization's physical distribution and a neutral fourth methodology to bridge the differences in corporate cultures and processes.

Other Projects

Note that the users for both Jini and NetBeans are still mainly programmers. If we look at a project such as OpenOffice.org, which is aimed at creating an office suite for anyone to use, then the diversity of the communities becomes even clearer. OpenOffice.org is the open-source project based on Sun's StarOffice product, a multiplatform office productivity suite that includes the key desktop applications, such as a word processor, spreadsheet, presentation manager, and drawing program, with a user interface and feature set similar to those of other office suites. OpenOffice.org has groups focused on creating better user documentation, marketing and promoting OpenOffice, and usability issues. The basic community of people using OpenOffice has split to include (as of March 2004) new groups for native-language discussion forums in over two dozen languages, including Arabic, Chinese, Dutch, French, German, Hindi, Italian, Japanese, Russian, Spanish, and Portuguese.

Hewlett-Packard was the central member of a printing community for Linux.[15] IBM is the primary sponsor of an open source project for a Java-based universal tool platform and IDE called Eclipse,[16] which, as of March 2004, spun off from immediate IBM control to become a nonprofit foundation. Within Eclipse, there are communities for such things as the basic platform, the Java IDE itself, for a variety of tools, for AspectJ, and for numerous other plug-ins and technologies. Each has its own mailing list, and there are a variety of newsgroups. The Eclipse project is discussed in depth in the section "The Eclipse Story" in Chapter 4.

LOOKING BEYOND THE CODE

An open-source project has many different communities, each with a different purpose. For a successful project, each of these communities must be nurtured and helped to grow. In a successful community a vocabulary might spring up that is derived from the project's technology, application area, and existing culture. Such

---

15. Formerly located at: http://hp.sourceforge.net and http://sourceforge.net/foundry/printing

16. http://www.eclipse.org

a community will come to resemble a long-existing club with its own phrases, in-jokes, rituals, and customs—an astute creator of such a community will know this and will help the community grow these aspects. A less astute one will focus on the code, probably leaving out vital potential members of the community.

One way to make the focus go beyond the code is to actively make roles for nondevelopers such as user interface (UI) designers and documentation writers. For example, NetBeans has a communitywide mailing list dedicated to the design and discussion of UI issues. There is also a NetBeans project focusing on UI development and issues, plus a process for other developers to get UI design assistance from the members of the UI project. When the NetBeans project first started, there was a hesitancy to add nondeveloper roles because this wasn't something that the high-profile open-source projects such as Apache or Linux did. Now the community values the work of the UI group. A similar example is the recent addition of a usability group as part of the GNOME project—its work has been welcomed by the larger GNOME community as something long needed.

There are notable examples of communities that work together in an open-source-like way that do not involve software source code. One of the most interesting is Wikipedia.[17] Wikipedia is an encyclopedia contributed entirely by volunteer efforts, using WikiWikiWeb technology at its base. In only 3 years, the online community has written over 230,000 entries. (Wikis are described in the section "The WikiWikiWeb" in Chapter 8.)

Once companies involved with open-source projects realize that all of these other communities exist, they can consider business reasons for interacting with them—informal channels to customers, collaborations, and sources of innovation, for example. By cultivating new communities around user interests, such companies can work to ensure the success and growth of the underlying open-source project.

As you read the next chapter and think about your project's business goals and business model, you need to consider how you will involve the various groups that have an interest in your project, as in Figure 3.6. Your business model must include a community focus.

The Secret of Why Open Source Works

Open source works when a group of people all embrace a set of shared goals and establish a community based on mutual trust. All three factors—enough interested people, shared goals, and trust—are required; if any one is missing, the project will fail.

---

17. http://www.wikipedia.org

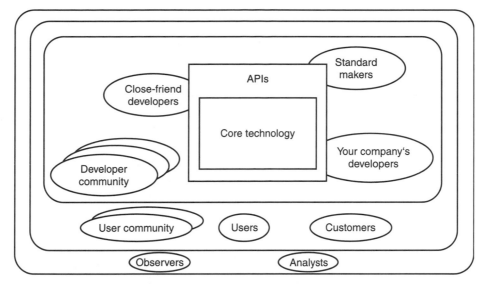

FIGURE 3.6 Possible constituencies.

SELF-ORGANIZATION THROUGH SHARED GOALS

Open-source projects often have hundreds or even thousands of people participating in their development. Yet there is no formal management structure to coordinate their many and varied activities.

The traditional approach to managing a large group of workers has been to establish a strict hierarchy of managers controlling the activities of the people below them. Such large command-and-control organizations have been the norm in business and the military from the Roman legions to General Motors. Such organizations pay a big cost in the number of people needed as managers, the amount of communications they require for coordination, and the rigidity of their response to novel situations. A big problem is that people lower down in the organization rarely have any idea how what they are told to do corresponds to the larger strategy. In fact, according to studies reported in the book *The Strategy-Focused Organization* by Robert Kaplan and David Norton, over 90% of companies fail to implement their strategy largely because the strategy is not communicated properly to the people in the company.

At the second Jini community meeting, Lieutenant General (Retired) Paul Van Riper, the former commanding general of the Marine Corps Combat Development Command, spoke on how the Marine Corps had made a shift from top-down control to policies based on self-organization for use in combat. For example, instead of a platoon being commanded to capture a hilltop, they might now be instructed to set up an observation post on a hilltop in order to view enemy troop movements along an important roadway. If the initial hill is defended or inaccessible, the platoon can choose a neighboring hilltop that also satisfies the goal instead. Including the strategic purpose as part of each order results in a much more flexible and responsive organization. A similar organizational shift in the business world was presented by Tom Petzinger at the first Jini community meeting—and is the topic of his book *The New Pioneers*.

Open source takes this self-organization process several steps further: Rather than someone high up in the organization setting out the goals, the actual people using and developing the software discuss on public mailing lists or newsgroups what improvements are needed. People propose features or capabilities that they want to see added—usually because they want to use them themselves. If enough other users and developers agree that the feature would be useful, then some of them may volunteer to write the code to implement it. However, if interest is too low, nothing may happen.

Sometimes a single developer will care enough about an idea to code up a prototype of it, and, if enough people try the prototype and like it, it may become part of the official project or at least be kept as an option for those who want to use it. Note that this type of exploratory development is a common aspect of open source. It is a way of introducing new goals into the community through demonstration rather than just conversation. Some may complain that this is not efficient—the developer's effort is wasted if the innovation is rejected— but, as with evolution, efficiency is not the point. That developer may have had no interest in working on anything else aside from the innovation that was rejected and would not have worked on other parts of the project. So the work did not take away from existing efforts—although if the work had been adopted it might have meant that some existing modules would have been replaced. Also, even if a particular contribution is not incorporated into the project directly, the ideas behind it may very well find their way into later contributions.

Although the overall open-source project may have hundreds of participants, there always is a basic core team, usually consisting of fewer than 10 developers. With that small a group, informal communication suffices to coordinate development activities. In fact, the team works pretty much like any proprietary software development team does. Two main differences are that the open-source core team members are almost always geographically dispersed—so they communicate mainly via email and chat—and that they get immediate feedback from the rest of the community on their decisions.

For those larger open-source efforts (e.g., Linux, Mozilla, NetBeans, and Apache) that have many more dedicated developers, the work is divided into separate modules, each with its own small core team. This is a good example of Conway's Law—the architecture of the code follows the structure of the organization. This tendency to keep the code modular gives open-source software a flexibility and adaptability that is often lost in the more monolithic code produced by proprietary companies.

This pressure for modularization also can be seen in the evolution of project mailing lists: Whenever the traffic on a list or newsgroup gets too great, the community breaks the discussion into subtopics. The separation of the code and the associated discussions makes it possible for people with limited time to follow and actively participate in the project.

The project mailing lists also show self-organization in how questions get answered. For conventional products, companies employ people whose job is to answer customer questions. Open-source projects do not have such people, and at first glance we might expect that the main developers would be overwhelmed trying to answer questions from the thousands of users. This isn't what happens, however. Instead, the more advanced users answer questions from the intermediate users, who in turn answer questions from the novices, leaving only the extremely sophisticated or difficult queries for the developers to reply to.

Another way open source self-organizes is seen in how bugs are identified and fixed. The entire community is constantly using, and therefore testing, the software. Each member shares the goal of wanting to improve it and so will report problems, often locating the code causing the bug and including a possible fix. This full testing coverage and repair takes place with no coordination required and minimal core-team overhead.

Having common goals brings people into the project and through group discussion these goals are refined and developed. However, as the project goes forward, if part of the community has goals not shared with the rest, then the project may fork. For example, when some members of the NetBSD community decided that security was a major goal that wasn't being given enough emphasis, that group decided to create a new project, OpenBSD, that had as its main goal the building of the most secure Unix-like operating system.

TRUST ENABLES COOPERATION

The sharing of goals creates a reason for people to participate in the open-source project. To create a true community requires trust—trust that your contributions will not be scorned and that you won't be made a fool of or taken advantage of. When participants show each other mutual respect, it becomes possible for them to cooperate. If discussions degenerate into flaming and put-downs, if suggestions and contributions are laughed at, if decisions are made in an arbitrary way, then most folks will go elsewhere and not put any energy into the project.

A classic example of how many open-source projects work to build trust is shown by how a new developer acquires the right to modify the project's source code. When new developers join a project, they need to earn the respect of the current developers. They do this by submitting bug fixes and modifications and by participating in group discussions. Only after demonstrating that they can act responsibly will they be granted check-in privileges. Thus, developers know that the code they write can be modified only by people they trust; their code is safe from anyone who would arbitrarily or ignorantly change it.

Another concern people have is that they be treated fairly. Before investing effort into a project, most people want to be assured that they will have a voice in any major decisions. When decisions flow out of community discussions and represent consensus, that process reinforces the sense of community, people will be invested in carrying out the necessary work. If decisions seem arbitrary or go against their interests, then people have no motivation to participate and are apt to leave. Many open-source developers worry that a company will decide to sponsor an open-source project because it plans to take the community's work, package it up in a proprietary product, and deny the community access to it. If these fears are not laid to rest and the company doesn't earn the community's trust, then it will be hard to attract outside developers to work on the project and it is even likely that a competing open-source project will be created—possibly starting with the very code that the company donated.

It is important to remember that open source is based on a gift economy: Participants trust that the gifts they give to the project will be returned in kind by other community members. It's more like a family than a consortium— individuals create relationships with other participants through continuing interactions; the relationships that hold the project together are person-to-person, not company-to-company.

ACHIEVING CRITICAL MASS VIA THE INTERNET

The Internet is a major enabler of open-source projects. It helps people living all over the globe to find others with common interests. Through email, newsgroups, and the Web, these people can easily communicate, share code, and coordinate their activities. Without the Internet, it would be vastly more difficult, if not impossible, to run a successful open-source project.

An open-source project requires people, both users and developers. Many open-source projects start with a developer or two who have a program that they feel others will find useful. They can advertise their application through newsgroups and mailing lists, and they can make it available on relevant websites.

Through the use of search engines and special-interest lists, people anywhere in the world can then locate and try out programs they might be interested in. People who like a program will spread the word. This makes it possible for groups to form based on very specialized interests—with the whole, networked world to draw on, it's hard to think of a topic that won't draw a quorum.

After finding a program they like, people are able to provide feedback to its creator via email and they can also discuss issues of using it with other users. The ease with which new mailing lists, newsgroups, and websites can be created makes electronic discussions both quick and simple. Email discussions among a large group of people can be easier both to follow and to separate by topics compared to face-to-face discussion. Mailing lists also allow the group to coordinate future development.

While the Internet makes it easy for new individuals to find an open-source project, whether or not they stay and participate will be determined in large part by the project's culture—is there a sense of community and trust, or instead is it cold, cliquish, and unfriendly? Unlike the business world where people assigned to a project are forced to work together, with open source, interested potential contributors who do not engage with the core developers because of having a different vision or due to incompatible work styles—will probably go elsewhere.

OPEN SOURCE IS AN EVOLUTIONARY PROCESS

The open-source process involves small, incremental improvements to some artifact, usually the source code for a computer program. It is essential that the starting point be a useful artifact, such as a working computer program. If the program is incomplete and does not do anything, then a small improvement will result in a similarly incomplete, broken program—so there is little motivation or satisfaction in making a small change to it. To finish the program and make it useful would require a large amount of work and initially only the originator has such a strong commitment.

A direct consequence of this is that an open-source project that starts around a great idea, but with no code written, should not expect the community to create a working application. The community can only be expected to help develop and refine the idea through discussion. If there are one or more developers already committed to writing the initial version, then this feedback on what the application should do can be invaluable—although without a working prototype it can also be ungrounded and too blue sky to be practical. The main point is that if you start an open-source project without a working prototype, do not expect the community to write the initial code for you. It just won't happen.

It may help to think about this in terms of biological evolution: Dead matter does not evolve;[18] only living organisms can evolve. They do so as a result of random small changes. Some of the changes are improvements, whereas others are neutral or harmful to the organism. The environment then selects which of these changes are retained and which are forgotten, and these selections are passed on through reproduction.

For open source, every new idea posted to the project's mailing lists and each contribution of code is a potential change. With new ideas, the community acts to select which are to be discussed further and possibly become part of the project's goals. For code, the module owners are the ones to select which changes are accepted and added to the project's code base. Note that the module owners cannot dictate what other developers work on—in some sense, incoming contributions really are random.

Most changes will be small bug fixes or minor improvements, but occasionally someone will contribute ideas or code that is a major change, possibly taking the project in a new direction. As with biological evolution, these large jumps cannot be predicted. They are also experiments that may or may not succeed. Just like life, open-source projects must embrace these opportunities to remain vibrant.

Evolutionary processes tend to be profligate in their use of resources—they are not what a manager would consider efficient. However, through large-scale parallel exploration of possibilities, evolution discovers wonderful innovative solutions. Open source combines the directed efforts of proprietary software development, in the focused work done by the core team, with the open-ended contributions made by volunteers.

CO-EVOLUTION OF SOFTWARE AND COMMUNITY

In an open-source project, software building and community building are intertwined. As the software matures, the community needs to keep up with it—the principle of slowly dawning insights applies to both activities.

An example is the Apache Incubator Project, which was created in October 2002. It provides an entry path into the Apache Software Foundation for projects and code bases whose owners wish to become part of Apache. The Incubator also provides documentation on how the Foundation works and how to get things done within its framework.

The Incubator is a community structure that was developed after the code base became large, sophisticated, variegated, and widely adopted. This required creating a controlled and self-explanatory mechanism for joining the community.

---

18. Dead matter can change, but because it cannot reproduce, dead matter cannot propagate beneficial changes.

The Apache Software Foundation has apparently discovered the work-in-progress effect and is using it explicitly. At the top of the home page for the Incubator it says the following:

Notice: *This document is a WIP (Work In Progress).*[19]

Variations on Open Source: Gated Communities and Internal Open Source

Sometimes a company is not willing or able to relinquish all control of the source code it has written. It may be that sale of the software is too important a part of its business. Or it is unwilling to give up the intellectual property (IP) used in the software—or it cannot because it uses another company's IP that it only licenses. Whatever the reason, it chooses not to open source its code. There are two important variations on open source that the company can consider in order to get at least some of the benefits of collaborative development. The first is to share only with people or companies that agree to a license that lets them see the source code but that strictly limits what they can do with it. The other alternative is to keep the source code totally within the company, but allow access to it by the company's developers who are working on other projects. Both options reduce the size and scope of the potential community but can still provide additional value.

GATED COMMUNITIES

One of the hallmarks of open source is that anyone can redistribute the code, with or without changes, to anyone else. This is not so when the source requires a special license that restricts the distribution only to other licensees. For example, from 1975 until 1992 anyone wanting to access the source code for the Unix operating system was required to purchase a license from AT&T. Many organizations relied on the Unix sources distributed by the University of California at Berkeley, but they all were supposed to have an official Unix license from AT&T. It was only after 386/BSD was released in 1992, followed by releases by both the NetBSD and FreeBSD projects in 1993, that source code for a full Unix system became freely available as open source.

A source license can be used to create a gated community: Anyone agreeing to it is in the community, and anyone who does not is left outside the gate, unable to see and use the source code. This can be attractive to the company that wrote the source code because it can still sell the software and

---

19. http://incubator.apache.org

retain all of its IP. Whether this is attractive to outside developers depends on the other license terms.

The most restrictive source licenses only allow a licensee to look at the source code—a licensee cannot modify or redistribute it. Even this little access can be useful if you are building other software that must interoperate with the licensed software. The source code essentially provides additional documentation and can aid debugging. This is what Microsoft offers with its Shared Source program for its Windows operating system. Those few companies that qualify can use the source code to help them better understand Windows in order to debug or tune their own hardware or software. A less restrictive source license might allow a company to modify the source and use it internally, but not distribute it to anyone.

Only when the license allows redistribution is an open-source community possible. For example, Sun's former Free Solaris Source License Program allowed anyone who had signed the license to view and modify the Solaris 8 source code. Licensees were allowed to distribute their changes only to other licensees via a Sun secure website that included mailing lists for discussing the source code.[20]

Licenses of this type often make a distinction between commercial and research use. Commercial use is when a company takes the source code and modifies it to create a product it then sells or uses internally for a production system. Such commercial use may require an additional license, possibly including royalty payments to the original author of the source code. Research use involves no sales or other commercial gain, and the distribution of binaries to anyone may be allowed.

The Java community is a good example of a gated community. It is an open organization of international Java developers and licensees whose charter is to develop and revise Java technology specifications, reference implementations, and technology compatibility kits. Java technology was originally created by Sun Microsystems and released under the Sun Community Source License (SCSL). Decisions are made using the Java Community Process (JCP), which has evolved from the informal process that Sun used beginning in 1995 to a formalized process overseen by representatives from many organizations across the Java community. The original reason for using a gated community was to maintain the compatibility of different Java implementations—write once, run anywhere. Now that Java is established and seen as a standard, the JCP is beginning to allow true open-source Java development.

The Jini project is another example of a gated community. It uses a variant of the SCSL that allows free commercial use and has a more democratic governance structure.

In fall 2000 Hewlett-Packard's printing and imaging division launched what it calls the Collaborative Development Program (CDP), a secure web-based

---

20. In January 2005 Sun started a true open-source project around the Solaris 10 source code.

development environment that links HP's worldwide employees, business partners, and customers to collaborate on software development projects. As of early 2002, the program hosted over 350 projects and 3000 users; approximately 10% of the users are external to HP. Forty-five external companies are developing projects with HP using CDP.

Some of the benefits of joining a gated community include using the source code as additional documentation, enhanced ability to find and fix bugs, ability to make local modifications, and ability to obtain and share modifications with others. The disadvantages can include the tainting of your developers by their seeing proprietary code, licenses that do not allow modifying the source code, and licenses that do not allow you to share changes with others.

The company that originally created the software can benefit from additional sales due to the extra value customers perceive from having access to the source code, assistance in finding and fixing bugs, customer porting of the code to additional platforms, improvements that can be distributed to other customers, and receiving better feedback from customers.

INTERNAL OPEN-SOURCE

The source code for most proprietary software is usually seen only by the team of developers assigned to work on it. Some companies limit which employees are even allowed to look at a program's source code, and most companies severely control who can modify source code. Some companies do have code reviews where people not on the team look at the code, but their involvement is generally limited to a critique of the code.

It can be to a company's benefit to open up the source code to everyone within the company. Access to a product's source code provides documentation to those developing other products that must interoperate with it. It can help in testing and fixing bugs. It can facilitate code reuse. In short, all of the same benefits that outside companies can get by being able to see the source code are available with internal open source. Even when sharing totally within a company, proposed changes must still be approved by the project's core team or other people who have earned their trust. We refer to such projects as internal open source, but others sometimes use the term *corporate source*.

Sharing source code within a company is much simpler than sharing it with those outside. Internal use requires no software licenses, just putting the source on some internally accessible file server. Of course, so far we're speaking only of the technical aspects of sharing—it may take a very big shift in mindset to open up a project's code to developers in other parts of the company. In fact, one of the biggest benefits might be increased communication between different parts of the company.

The focus on creating communities is a major difference between internal open source and other programs many companies have to encourage software reuse. Software reuse has at its core the idea of a library of reusable software components maintained by a code librarian. The code is usually seen as being static—contributed by a developer on one project for use on unrelated other projects. Software reuse projects often fail by not addressing social and political issues inside the organization. Internal open source must also overcome similar social and political obstacles, but they are faced more directly in working to build a community of developers and users to collaborate on an application that the community is all interested in moving ahead. If your company has a software reuse program, to make it more successful consider using open-source principles to build communities around the various components and frameworks.

Because internal open source takes place totally inside a company, there is no way to know just how many companies are applying open-source principles to their internal development process. Both VA Software, with their SourceForge product, and CollabNet, with SourceCast, are companies committed to open source that make their living by selling collaborative software development tools to other companies. Although many of their customers may only be seeking assistance for geographically distributed project teams, others are no doubt taking advantage of the ability to involve people outside of a project in its development.

Hewlett-Packard started a Corporate Source Initiative to use open-source practices internally in June 2000. One of the major goals of this program is to increase the technology transfer from HP Labs to the rest of the company. By using the community building aspects of open source, HP hopes to build a stronger community within HP Labs and then extend that community to include other developers in the rest of HP who are working on products, infrastructure, and corporate operations. By early 2002 it had about 1500 registered users working on about 30 projects, all of which were research projects not tied to any HP product. Researchers at HP Labs have written about a variable approach to open source they call *progressive open source* (POS) to describe the range of ways a company can use open-source development methods: traditional open source, gated communities, and internal open source.[21]

IBM uses tools from VA Software—SourceForge Enterprise Edition—to host an internal-project, open-source site called the *Internal IBM Open-Source Bazaar*, where any team can do open-source development within IBM. The tool provides

---

21. Jamie Dinkelacker, Pankaj K. Garg, Rob Miller, and Dean Nelson, *Progressive Open Source*, HP Laboratories, 2001.

a source-code repository, mailing lists, source-code control mechanisms, and license management. The site supports hundreds of projects and thousands of developers working on open-source projects that IBM doesn't want exposed to outside parties. IBM is one of about 50 companies that use SourceForge Enterprise Edition for their internal open-source projects.

Sun Labs set up a very similar program inside Sun called OpenProject, starting in December 2001, with the twin goals of helping with technology transfer from Sun Labs to the rest of Sun and providing a home for small, unsponsored projects to encourage innovation. In May 2002 the scope of OpenProject grew with the addition of a number of groups from Sun's Enterprise Services organization that wanted to build communities around the development and use of internal Sun tools. These tools include the various applications that are used internally by Sun field engineers and customer support to install, test, and maintain Sun computers. The aim is to enable the worldwide shared development of these tools, as well as to create forums where Sun employees can locate the tools they need and discuss how to best use them. By March 2004 there were over 800 registered users of OpenProject working on over 300 hosted projects, most of which were internal tools.

To manage and guide this internal tool development effort, a special Technical Council was created with representatives from organizations throughout Sun. This Technical Council is responsible for locating existing tools and working with their developers to contribute their source code to OpenProject, for identifying gaps in the existing tools and developing new tools to fill them, for pointing the community to what is cool and identifying the best-of-class tools, and for encouraging groups and engineers throughout Sun to work together.

Internal open-source projects need to be nurtured just as all open-source projects do. In fact, they may need even more support from managers and executives because the people involved in them do so as part of their job and, although the project may benefit the company as a whole, their involvement can be seen by their immediate manager as taking too much time from their assigned job.

Done correctly, internal open source allows a company to leverage the work of all of its employees, to eliminate duplicate work, and to encourage innovation. The same open-source principles come into play whether the potential community is the entire Internet or just a single company's intranet.

Open Source: Why Do They Do It?

One of the first questions a dyed-in-the-wool businessperson will ask about open source is why in the world people would volunteer to do something that they could be paid to do. Numerous explanations have been put forward, including the following:

- Need for the product—in order to create, customize, or improve a product or feature. This reason dominates the decision-making process for all early participation in both open-source and gated-source projects, but, as time goes on, continued participation is based on other things for open-source projects whereas a need for the software continues to prevail as motivation for gated-source projects.

- Enjoyment, fun, and desire to create and improve—because they enjoy it and find creating or improving software creative and interesting. This is the primary reason people continue in open-source projects for the long term. Such people tend to scan the email archives, bug reports, and feature-request lists to find things that catch their eye, things that are challenging or represent an area they want to learn about.

- Reputation and status—in order to build or maintain reputation or status within the community.

- Affiliation—in order to socialize or spend time with like-minded individuals.

- Identity—in order to reinforce or build a desired self-image.

- Values and ideology—to promote specific ideals, such as the free software philosophy.

- Training, learning, reputation outside the community, and career concerns—to improve their skills, with the belief that such improvement will lead to a better job or promotion.

- Fairness—to pay off the debt they owe from having used the software or received help from the community. For some, the bargain takes a long time to pay off.

- Hope of making things better—to find or create better solutions than those already in place.

- Feedback—to get comments on the work and how well they are doing as a programmer or designer. As with other creative activities, this is a driving urge. Here is what open-source expert Sonali Shah says,

  > . . . *creative programmers want to associate with one another: only their peers are able to truly appreciate their art. Part of this is that programmers want to earn respect by showing others their talents. But it's*

also important that people want to share the beauty of what they have found. This sharing is another act that helps build community and friendship.[22]

What Is Open Source?

Open source is about software source code, licenses, communities, culture, and distributed software development. Although open-source projects can provide plenty of benefits for companies who use it, open source is not something to do on a whim. Open source is based at least in part on a phenomenon called the gift economy, which on the surface seems at odds with corporate practices.

Nevertheless, marketing and innovation benefits, as well as clearly separating commodity efforts from value-enhancing ones, can make all the difference in a business climate that values carefully thought-out innovation.

---

22. *Community-Based Innovation & Product Development: Findings from Open Source Software and Consumer Sporting Goods*, p. 33.

CHAPTER 4

Why Consider Open Source?

AN OPEN-SOURCE PROJECT WORKS BEST when everyone involved derives some benefit from it. There must be a good reason for a person or group to make its work available and for other people—users, developers, and other interested parties—to want to participate.

One very compelling reason for you to participate in an existing open-source project is if your work can build on it. By joining the project, you avoid needing to redo large amounts of work. Plus, there is an existing community of users and developers who have an interest in what you are adding to their project. An example of this was Sun's contribution of its Java Server Pages technology to the Apache web-server project to create the Jakarta project.[1] By doing this, Sun assured that JSP would become available on the most widely used web server, that the Apache developers would not create a competitor to JSP, that it would be easier to work with other companies such as IBM on JSP technology, and that JSP could build on the work already done for Apache. For the Apache community, adding JSP was a way to add desired functionality and expand the community of Apache developers; it was also a vote of confidence in their work with Apache.

There are many reasons for people to participate in an open-source project. These include the following:

- The software being developed helps them to do their work better.

- They can influence development.

- They can modify the code to suit their needs.

- They can interact with and learn from other users.

- They can be part of a cool project.

---

1. http://jakarta.apache.org

75

These are also reasons why you might choose to join an existing open-source project.

Business Reasons for Choosing to Open Source Your Code

Deciding to manage a development project as an open-source project requires making a careful determination of the project's business goals—an open-source project is generally more expensive to operate than a proprietary project, and there are different scheduling and development processes that need to be adopted and that can affect product delivery.

The following is a list of business reasons to support the use of open source for a project. To illustrate them, we provide concrete examples based on our experiences with various Sun-sponsored projects such as NetBeans, OpenOffice, Project JXTA, Java.net, and Jini.

VISIBILITY

When a project is run using open source, the existence and nature of the project are visible to the outside world and to people in other parts of your company. If the project is visible to a strategically important community— whether it participates in the project or not—your company is better able to present plans, goals, features, and statements of progress. Open source makes available additional communication channels, including more informal ones consulted by the target developer community.

For example, any sort of open, Java-related activity, such as the NetBeans project, enables the Sun developers working on it to use the various Java newsgroups as well as Slashdot and other weblogs to communicate directly with other developers. Although this is a good way to get feedback from the community about technical matters, it is not suited to marketing hype.

TRAINING AND EDUCATION

The best way to learn design and implementation skills is to read and study good designs and source code. This teaching method is rarely used in software development and engineering curricula, so it's often up to companies to do on-the-job training. Whether the open-source project is internal or external, it can supply source code, design documents (or at least archives of design discussions), and provide opportunities to try out ideas and talk to designers and implementors.

In general, this is an advantage with transparency. For example, creative writing, music, art, sculpture, and most engineering disciplines use publicly visible artifacts to educate practitioners. Apprenticeships are a classic form of observational education. In some older crafts, an apprentice would do menial tasks such as cleanup and setup for months or years before actually being instructed and helping with the real work, and this was educational because the apprentice could observe the craftsperson at work, which would help him or her know what practicing the craft was all about.

UBIQUITY

By providing an open-source offering, a project can begin to spread that offering first to the outside users and developers of the project, then out to the broader open-source community, and then perhaps to the larger developer community. Both the no-cost and open nature of the offering and the transparent stance of the project to the users of the offering contribute to the spread of the offering. The transparent stance conveys the message that your company's developers don't consider themselves the ultimate authority on the offering and not only value the contributions of the community but consider other members of the community as equals.

For example, an explicit goal of NetBeans was to create a common IDE platform that would be one of the three most popular Java development environments. This is a ubiquity goal. Jini is another example of a project that has attempted to establish a new, ubiquitous platform for services. Eclipse is also directed at ubiquity.

Another example is StarOffice, for which ubiquity includes creating a large and diverse user base. A person might go to OpenOffice.org to download the latest version, but then stay to participate in the mailing-list discussions of how to best use the OpenOffice application and how it might be improved. Because of the feeling of community that arises from being part of those discussions, the person is much more likely to recommend OpenOffice to others; and a user becomes a community member.

Ubiquity helps a company engage in service businesses. With Eclipse, IBM is creating a plug-in platform that its professional services business can leverage, and similarly GE's involvement with the Visualization Toolkit enables them to have more convincing and substantial engagements, both inside and outside the company.

DESIGN DISCIPLINE

Doing development open-source style requires making almost all decisions on mailing lists open to the public. Design and implementation proposals are made in writing and discussed by the community, and the resulting decisions are summarized in writing. All this written material is archived and available to everyone. By enforcing this level of discipline, the quality of the design and implementation decisions is likely to increase—simply because they are being done deliberately and in writing. The process of writing it all down creates a need to express issues in a clear way, which often forces you to better understand matters. This better understanding then leads to a better design. In many ways, the open-source process resembles the literate programming methods promoted over the years by computer scientists such as Donald Knuth.

BEST STANDARDS DEVELOPMENT

Some projects have as a goal developing a standard—API definitions, language extensions, or tool extensions. Opening up the process to everyone makes it more likely to get the best advice and achieve the greatest adoption.

The best and first example of this is the Common Lisp[2] community, which was created precisely to do standards development. Initially, the goal was a de facto standard embodied in a particular book (*Common Lisp the Language*, by Guy L. Steele Jr.) and a set of informal agreements, but after the artificial intelligence industry and the Department of Defense embraced the language, it became the subject of ANSI standardization.

The NetBeans IDE APIs had been designed in an open way to begin with, so an open-source approach simply maintained this practice. A goal for OpenOffice was to create an XML standard for file formats.

In general, it appears that a standardization effort that is based on an open-source or commons-based community is less likely to suffer from the worst of politics. Open-source and commons-based communities almost always have at least a hint of meritocracy built in, where status and influence are based on achievements within the community rather than on the strength or influence of the organization that the individual represents. Further, the decision-making

---

2. Although the Lisp language is currently not in vogue, in the 1980s it was an important language during the Artificial Intelligence boom. Sun, IBM, DEC, HP, and other manufacturers of general-purpose computers offered Lisp implementations and development environments either developed in-house or by one of several third-party Lisp software companies. In addition, five companies—LMI, Symbolics, Three Rivers, Xerox, and Texas Instruments—produced special-purpose "Lisp machines" specifically for executing Lisp code.

conversations in such a community are much more likely to center around technical and engineering issues than around business and marketing issues.

For example, the Jini Community is partially organized around a standards-granting body. Because the community is made up of both individuals and companies, its organization has two "houses," one in which each individual has one vote and the other in which each company has one vote. Any proposed standard must be approved by both houses to be adopted by this community. The discussions in this community about proposed standards indeed revolve around the technology, and the community has been quite successful at getting companies to work together that traditionally have had a lot of trouble doing so. We believe it is important that the sponsoring company, Sun Microsystems, rarely has a significant stake directly in the application area and thereby can act as an unbiased helper in the discussions—Sun's stake is in the underlying infrastructure that Jini provides, which is provided at no cost.

CONVERSATIONS

A technology company can thrive when it engages in conversations with its customers and potential customers. Such conversations largely take place between a salesperson and a technical customer, but relationships between technical staffs are important.

Open source is a way to engage a broad group of people—fans and foes alike. Some of the conversations are about design and implementation issues directly associated with the source code, but there are many other, indirect opportunities for a company to learn.

It is relatively rare for an outsider to be interested in helping a company with its proprietary products, and frequently outsiders are not in a position to know enough about a company's strategy and dynamics to offer useful advice. But, by listening carefully to the corners of the conversations with outsiders in an open forum such as an open-source project, a company can learn quite a bit that could impact new products and product directions.

By listening to people talking about the challenges and problems they face—particularly with the technology of the open-source project—a company can figure out what new products or directions would help with those problems. When participants talk about how they use some other technology in conjunction with the technology being developed by the open-source project, a company might make plans to integrate this other technology or make it easier to work with by creating or extending the infrastructure. This is not the same as just doing what the customer says because the customer might not know or care enough about the technology behind the solution—it's seeing the problems and trends that matter.

The listening company needs to think and problem solve carefully to come up with a good solution.

Such conversations sometimes are more natural face to face. A sponsoring company can arrange for a community meeting or other event where members of the community are given an opportunity to talk about their projects and work. The wise company will send someone hopelessly curious to find out all about the problems and exciting opportunities facing community members and thereby arrange to bring back valuable ideas for new products.

Naturally, conversations such as these can forge relationships between companies, such relationships being less likely in the more adversarial and isolated world of business. By letting people talk to people, companies can talk to companies.

Design help

By opening up the design process to the community, a project can get not only advice on direction but help on how to design the implementation for that direction. This can come in the form of what is generally considered design, as well as direction regarding features and usability from pure users. We call users who provide good directions and even pure design *user/designers*.

Most developers don't distinguish between development and design, so by aiming for development help, many open-source projects expect design help as well. Getting design help was an important goal for the Jini project, because for Jini success meant defining Jini services for printing and consumer appliances that fall outside of Sun's areas of expertise. Community feedback on the benefits of using NetBeans, not just as an IDE but also as an application run-time platform, resulted in adding a new direction to the NetBeans project. Now NetBeans also supports developers who wish to create applications on top of the NetBeans core framework. This new focus on NetBeans as a platform has also helped to improve the NetBeans IDE.

Of all the business reasons given here, design help may be the most important. Many software products fail because they do not meet the needs of their intended users. An article in *Scientific American* by W. Wyatt Gibbs ("Software's Chronic Crisis," September 1994) stated that "some three quarters of all large systems are *operating failures* that either do not function as intended or are not used at all." Indeed, the 1994 *CHAOS Report* by the Standish Group stated that over 30% of software projects are canceled, with the greatest risk factor being lack of user involvement. User feedback, coupled with the open-source practice of incremental development and frequent releases, helps keep a project in touch with reality and focused on what is most important. Feedback from users includes answering the question of whether the project is even worth doing at all.

GUIDANCE FOR PROPRIETARY PRODUCTS

Some open-source licenses permit proprietary products to be based on an open-source system, sometimes by adding features and sometimes by providing quality and support. The ability to develop the best such product can be improved by commentary and feedback from the community.

Apple's Darwin open-source project, of course, forms the basis for OS X—it is the underlying operating system on top of which the nice Finder-based look-and-feel is implemented.

Guidance for proprietary products was a major goal for NetBeans, with the Forte for Java Internet and Enterprise Editions being for-sale products built on the NetBeans platform. (*Note*: Forte for Java has been renamed Sun Java Studio.)

BUILD A MARKET FOR A PROPRIETARY PRODUCT

When a company has a proprietary product built on top of a free, open-source version, the free version will bring in customers and increase the company's market share. Users of the free version can be persuaded to upgrade to the for-sale version to get new features, better support, training, or consulting services. It also makes it more difficult for competitors to enter the market because they will need to compete with a free product.

Rather than having their proprietary product possibly compete with their open-source version, some companies make them one and the same. However, new features may appear first in the proprietary version and make their way into a later release of the open-source version only after a delay of several months. Customers who want the latest features are often willing to pay for the proprietary version rather than wait for them to be added to the free version. This approach was pioneered by Aladdin Enterprises for GhostScript, probably the world's most widely used second-source PostScript and PDF interpreter, and has also been used by TurboLinux.

Another approach is to release the software as open source—using a license such as the GPL that requires that any larger work based on the open-source code also be made open source—and then license the software to any companies that wish to use it in a proprietary product. This is what Trolltech AS does with its Qt multiplatform application development framework, which is the basis of the open-source KDE graphical desktop for Linux. It is also the strategy used by both MySQL AB and Sleepycat Software for their database products.

Being able to sell or license a proprietary product based on an open-source code base requires that a company own the copyright to all the source code and be doing most of the development of the code. You should expect only minimal contributions from outside developers, who are generally not eager to have a company profit from their work.

DEVELOPMENT HELP

One of the myths of open source is that an open-source project will attract a lot of developers, and therefore the costs of operating a project using open source will be lower than using proprietary processes. This isn't true[3] primarily because most software is still largely monolithic or made of modules that are too large and so most volunteer developers do not have the time or motivation to fully understand the code well enough to want or be able to add significantly to it. However, finding bugs, fixing some bugs, and porting software to other platforms or making it work in new configurations are the sort of help a project can reasonably hope to get.

If the code for your project is relatively modular and doesn't require weeks of study in order to be modified, then you can expect outside developers to contribute code for new features and even entire new modules. But note that these contributions will probably not be for features you had planned on for the next release. Instead they will be whatever the individual outside developers need for their work. Such contributions may appeal to many other community members, broadening the project's scope.

NetBeans is structured as a set of modules communicating through APIs. One goal was to create a community of module developers, which has happened: Outside developers have indeed contributed new modules and continue to work on them. Similarly, the OpenOffice community has been effective in improving its huge code base by adding new modules for spell checking and printing, helping port OpenOffice to Linux, working on a port to Mac OS X, and localizing it to more than two dozen languages.

INTERNAL OPEN SOURCE AND REUSE

A company can use an open-source methodology within its walls for a variety of internal benefits. By organizing development around the commons, the entire organization can be informed about which projects exist, how the project is doing, and who is working on it. Sometimes people can make quick but significant contributions. And sometimes the organization can make use of intermediate releases and participate in quality control. For companies that do alpha and beta

---

3. On SourceForge, only about 1% of all projects have more than 10 developers.

testing, such internal releases can help find and fix problems before—rather instead of—releasing them outside the company.

Detailed internal information such as this can benefit sales, marketing, and sales engineering by providing ways of finding out information without (over)burdening development.

But most important, doing internal open source opens up the possibility of reuse. By reuse we don't mean the planned *use* of libraries and frameworks but the unexpected and serendipitous reuse similar to what happens when you visit the junkyard or scrapheap. There may be pieces of code not designed to be used in multiple contexts that can cannibalized or used in unexpected ways, and an open-source or commons-based development approach can provide visibility into projects, thereby encouraging such reuse.

SUPPORT HELP

One of the hallmarks of a good open-source project is that community members provide support to each other. More experienced developers and users help out folks with less knowledge, and practically everyone answers the questions posted by beginners. Community members assemble and edit lists of *frequently asked questions* (FAQs) and post them to the project's website. Some folks may even write tutorials and articles to help others get started. All of this community support activity is work that you do not need to provide resources to do.

But keep in mind this is not a way to get something for nothing. There must be a reason for knowledgeable folks to want to visit your project's website and participate in discussions. One of the best reasons is that you have one or more employees participating who are even more experienced and who can answer the more difficult questions that are posted to the project's mailing lists. This could be some of your senior developers, or someone slightly less experienced who can refer the question to the appropriate senior developer. It should not be a junior person because community members will quickly perceive this and feel that you consider them second-class citizens.

For the Jini project, Sun's top developers participate on the public mailing lists. This has attracted lots of experienced outside developers to these lists because they know both that they can get their advanced questions answered there and also that they can benefit from seeing the answers to other people's questions. Because of the community feeling that has been created, these outside developers are then willing to answer the less difficult questions, freeing up the Sun core team to do other work.

Although Jini is mostly a community of developers, this sharing of support also works with users, as can be seen on OpenOffice.org. The OpenOffice community has written *How-to* guides giving step-by-step instructions on how to do specific tasks with OpenOffice, has put together lists of FAQs, and has created sample and template files that demonstrate OpenOffice's capabilities and how to accomplish certain tasks. This help has been made available in many languages including Chinese, Dutch, English, French, German, Italian, Portuguese, and Spanish. The website also has a general users' mailing list—plus native language mailing lists in over two dozen languages—where anyone with a problem can post questions that others in the community will answer.

FACILITATE TECHNOLOGY TRANSFER

When you are introducing a new technology and trying to spread it to other developers, creating an open-source project can help. The project provides an attractive place for people to come to learn the new technology by doing things with it and seeing what others are doing with it. The people that originated the technology are available to answer questions and to steer further development based on community feedback.

The Jini project is an example of how a gated-community effort can help to introduce many new developers to a technology. Having Sun's core Jini team working with outside developers that were trying to learn about Jini created a vibrant Jini community that continues to flourish and to help introduce Jini technology to new developers.

This is very different from creating a user group for a technology. User groups tend to be places for novices to go to download tutorials and white papers, to read FAQs, and to ask their questions. Aside from the occasional online chat session, there is no sense of discussing issues with the team developing the technology. As a result, as soon as developers start to master the technology they tend to drift away.

Using corporate source can facilitate technology transfer within your company. When ongoing research is both visible and accessible through an internal open-source effort, developers in other parts of your company can learn about and experiment with new technologies and better relate them to your products and marketplace. Just encouraging more communication between researchers and the rest of your company can be a win. Both HP Labs and Sun Labs have internal open-source efforts to help them to move new technologies into the rest of the company.

LIMITED RESOURCES

Sometimes you just may not have enough resources to do all the work that's needed on your own. We've pointed out several times that you can't expect volunteer help to pick up the slack, but there are several other open-source-related options that might work for you.

The simplest is building on top of an existing open-source project. If the work you want to do adds value to the work already done by the project and fits in with its vision, then the community will welcome your contributions. Depending on the project's license and philosophy, you might be able to create a for-sale product if that is important to your business model.

Sun took this route when deciding how to improve the desktop shipped with Solaris. Rather than investing the effort in upgrading its proprietary Common Desktop Environment (CDE), it made more sense to switch to GNOME and focus Sun's resources on improving certain aspects of GNOME such as accessibility, integration with Java, and documentation—all areas where the GNOME community welcomed additional participation.

If there is no existing project you can join, then creating a new open-source project or a gated community might work, provided that you can recruit other companies and individuals that share your vision and are willing to work to realize it. An open-source project may provide a better framework than trying to set up a more formal consortium. The way Java is developed is an example of this strategy: Through the Java Community Process, new extensions to Java are jointly developed by participating companies that write the necessary specifications, reference implementations, and technology compatibility kits.

You can also use corporate source to pool the efforts of developers and engineers throughout your company that have common needs. For example, within Sun various teams in different parts of the company each needed to develop an internal tool to monitor service requests (trouble tickets) and report various statistics about them. A team in France developed a client-server version of the tool, which they then shared with another team in Germany that had been looking into writing a similar one. The German team had to rewrite part of the tool to work in their particular environment, but that was much easier than starting from scratch. Moreover, their revised version improved on the server component and the French team was able to adopt their changes. Meanwhile, other teams in the United Kingdom and Sweden have joined in the effort and are working on other improvements. Each team now has a better tool with less effort on its part then if it had developed it alone.

Note that all of these options are quite different from putting out a half-done project and hoping someone will come along to help finish it.

IMPROVED QUALITY

When releases are made available to users early in the development process, bugs are more likely to be caught. When the source code is made available to developers outside the core team, those bugs can be located and fixed. The outside developers can also add many of the small features that the core team wants but doesn't have time to get to—making the product more usable. This all results in greatly improved quality in the official release. Moreover, the bugs that bother users the most are the ones that are actually most apt to be fixed.

For example, sendmail is the Internet mail program used in the majority of email systems worldwide. Eric Allman, sendmail's original author and now CTO of Sendmail Inc., which offers a commercial version based on the open-source version, had the following to say on how open source improves product quality:

> *Another thing I've learned big time is that there is no QA department better than the Internet itself. Nobody can afford to simulate the Internet QA lab. By having the open source support, we get this incredible base of people that are willing to be on the bleeding edge, and give great feedback.*[4]

Perhaps the Visualization Toolkit people would dispute this by claiming that adding automated testing to an open-source project achieves an even higher level of quality.

TIME TO MARKET

For open source, there is a time-to-market advantage, but it is a more complicated notion than simply getting a product into a space quickly. By using available open-source code in a project, a company is able to avoid re-inventing it. This can speed up getting to market, but the more important effect is that a company can get to a very good product quickly, especially one with a greater number of already proven features and better quality. That is, the right product is achieved faster. If existing open-source code is available, this could also mean getting a product into the new market space ahead of the competition. If such code isn't available and the idea is to start an open-source project to design and implement a new product, then the company will not get a product out faster than by going it alone, but the initial open-source-based product will probably be a better product than one done with proprietary methodologies. Tellis and Golder argue this is likely a better strategy than simply being first (see the section "Creativity" in Chapter 2).

---

4. From an interview with Boardwatch, formerly located at http://www.boardwatch.com/boardwatchonline/2002/may02/technology-ericallman.htm.

Although open source may sometimes seem slower than proprietary development, it is also more deliberate and informed development because of the extensive design help from the community. The 1.0 release of an open-source project usually compares to the 2.0 or 3.0 release of a proprietary product.

BETTER WAY TO DO RELEASES

The open-source process of doing daily development releases and frequent stable releases in addition to periodic, major, official releases is often better suited to customer needs. Cutting-edge customers immediately have access to the latest features and bug fixes by downloading daily or weekly builds, whereas more conservative customers—customers who adopt change slowly to avoid risk—can wait for major releases that are guaranteed to be more solid and bug-free. In short, customers can choose the level of risk they are comfortable with.

Major releases are possibly done less frequently, but by having an open development process with more communication between users and developers, the development can be done less frantically without everyone feeling that the project has slowed down.

In this and in other ways, open source is like some of the agile methodologies.

BETTER RELATIONS WITH CUSTOMERS

Open source breaks down the barriers between your company and your customers. Being included in the development process makes outside developers and users feel they are a part of the community working on the project. When done correctly, this leads to a better relationship between them and your company.

Many of these developers and users are also key influencers in their own companies, so their having a closer relationship with your company can directly translate into their recommending other products from your company for use by their organization.

By having more direct interactions with your customers, you can get a much better sense of what they need and how you can adapt your products to satisfy those needs. In fact, giving your customers access to the source code lets them assist in fixing the bugs and adding the features that they care most about. Even making the source code available through a gated-community approach, instead of full open source, can still provide additional value to the customer.

BETTER RELATIONS WITH OTHER PARTS OF YOUR COMPANY

Open source can also help break down barriers within your company. In many companies, the formal organization makes it difficult or impossible for two people in separate parts of the company to collaborate. Making the source code part of an open-source project can allow you to more readily share it with other people within your own company. The open-source methodology creates a context where it is both easy and natural for anyone, anywhere in the company, to join the project's public discussions. This can encourage cross-company communications and cooperation, such as between researchers and product engineers, between developers and customer support, or among geographically dispersed parts of the organization.

Corporate source—limiting the scope of an open-source project to keep it within your company—can have a similar effect. An important consideration is whether your development organization requires *transparency* or open development. Transparency means that the plans, roadmap, design documents, and sometimes the source code are visible within your company, but does not require that development follow an open-source development methodology. It may be that your company's development culture wouldn't tolerate such a methodology, but an informal commons-based approach using transparency and informal communications is sufficient. One way to determine this is to ask whether serendipitous development help or reuse is something your company needs; if this is the case, the source code needs to be available and probably an open-source process needs to be in place.

NURTURE INNOVATION

One of the benefits of open-source projects can be the innovative new features and applications that people come up with. These innovations can help your project build momentum or expand to a new audience, move your technology forward, increase the size of the marketplace, generate positive publicity, and generally help you win. Most often, the innovations will come as a surprise. A related benefit to working with open source is to find out what potential customers are doing, which can lead to new products or new features for existing products. By observing the problems other people are having, you can sometimes come up with engineering that can solve, resolve, or alleviate those problems. The nature of innovation and how working in the commons can benefit it is described in Chapter 2.

You can work to make innovation more likely by making your project a safe place for people to experiment. It is important to remove as many barriers to collaboration as possible: social, political, and technical. A good project provides developers with the necessary infrastructure (CVS, mailing lists, etc.) so they can focus on creating novel software.

With the Jini project, we made it very easy for anyone to create a new subproject. Each registered community member could get disk space on the project's website to encourage code sharing. At community meetings and in other ways, developers were encouraged to report on what they were doing with Jini technology. One result of this was to increase the project's momentum by expanding people's ideas about what the Jini technology could be used for.

Nurturing innovation can be important both for traditional open-source projects and for corporate source projects within your company. In both cases, it is important that you recognize innovation when it happens and actively work to harvest it. Innovation can present a golden opportunity if you are able to follow up on it.

COMMUNITY BUILDING FOR SPECULATIVE REASONS

In some cases, your company is interested in getting into a new area where it may have little or only emerging expertise and credibility. Starting an open-source project can bring expertise and contacts from the community concerned with the area.

An example is Project JXTA. Sun engineers are collaborating with many outside experts to explore possibilities of peer-to-peer computing (P2P). By working with a larger community, Sun hopes to better establish expertise in the P2P space and to be able to take early advantage of business opportunities that arise based on P2P.

Another Sun example is the Java.net website,[5] which was created primarily as a community site but also as a sort of central open-source hosting site for Java-related projects—a kind of SourceForge for Java. However, not only were the usual open-source tools provided, but social software tools such as wikis and weblogs were added. The website has a newspaper feel, and there is a site editor, akin to a newspaper's editor-in-chief. The goal is to bring together open-source developers in the hopes that a marketplace might develop.

AVOIDING LOCK-IN

A common strategy for companies is to offer a high-value product and create brand lock-in—making it hard to move to another product—by providing special

------

5. http://java.net

platform-specific capabilities. An open-source community will not tolerate proprietary lock-in and will generally move toward making the offering as portable as possible.

This was a major goal for NetBeans, where the competitors to NetBeans and Forte for Java were seen as promoting lock-in not only to their own IDEs but perhaps also to particular Java implementations.

This could be a goal for Eclipse, as well. IBM is concerned with the dominance of Microsoft in the software development and server markets, and Eclipse certainly could be aimed at providing a popular, open-source alternative to Microsoft's proprietary products in this area.

RISK REDUCTION

Of concern to many companies is the risk they face if a software product they depend on is discontinued. With open-source applications, they know they can continue product development even if the original developers stop working on it. In the past, the primary way of reducing the risk that a producer would abandon software or go out of business was a practice called *software escrow* wherein the source code was held by a third party as if in a vault whose contents were to be released to the consumer of the software upon certain contractually defined events.

The risk that a software product might stop being supported can be acute when the product is offered by a small company. Customers are often wary of buying a product from a small company because the company might go out of business. By making the product open source, a small company can assure customers that even if the company disappears the software will still survive. Rather than making its money from software sales, the small company would instead need to sell support, training, and/or consulting services.

Making an application open source also reduces the risk for the company that initially developed it. For example, Cisco Systems decided to release their Cisco Enterprise Print System software (CEPS) under an open-source license partly to reduce its dependency on in-house programming staff. Cisco wanted to make sure that if the original programmers left the company, the software would continue to be maintained. In fact, one of the two original developers did eventually take a new job elsewhere, but, because it is an open-source project, he has been able to continue to work on it. If a developer really identifies with a project, then you can ensure that person's participation for a long time by making it open source.

Another way that a company reduces its own risk by making a product open source is that the outside developers who work on the project become attractive candidates to hire: They are knowledgeable about the product and have a proven track record. There are numerous examples where a major contributor is later hired by the company that started the open-source project.

APPEAL TO THE COMMUNITY WHOSE NAME IS "THE OPEN-SOURCE COMMUNITY"

Some open-source pundits and leaders talk about "the open-source community" as if it were a clearly identifiable set of people. Some even speak as if this community were homogeneous and universal, making statements such as "the open-source community rejects" some company-sponsored project. This happened to the Jini project when it first appeared.

Jini was one of the first forays by a large company into commons-based software development. (Other small companies, such as Lucid, Inc., in the 1980s, worked on open-source software as part of their product strategies.) Jini was released under a gated-community license called the Sun Community Source License (SCSL), and Sun termed this sort of license a "community source" license, both to distinguish it from open-source licenses and to ensure that there would be no confusion between the two types of development communities. Some of the open-source leaders denounced Sun for hijacking the concept of open source, for confusing the public by introducing a new name, and for introducing a new model. Further, some of these leaders stated to the press that open-source developers were not interested in community source and did not participate in the Jini community. Actually, there were quite a few open-source developers in the Jini community at that time and still are.

Since then, the early leaders of the "open-source community" have grown to accept community source and other gated communities to the extent that they don't go out of their way to criticize them much. And many of those leaders have come to accept that this is a different idea needing a different name to avoid confusion. Moreover, these leaders have assumed a diminished role as open source has been adopted by more companies and people.

But even today there is a benefit to be had by gaining the acceptance of and positive statements from the pundits and leaders of "the open-source community" and of some of the smaller communities within it. For example, the Linux community is a thriving Unix community within the broader open-source community. By doing an open-source project, the organization running the project can get closer to that community.

A prime example of this was releasing the StarOffice source code under the GNU LGPL. Using that license, which is a favorite of many in "the open-source community," improved Sun's reputation.

The open-source community was not a strong Java development community when NetBeans was open sourced in June 2000. In fact, much of this community is not a strong C++ development community, favoring C instead. Further, this community was slow to pick up Java partly because of Sun's ownership of it. By doing a full-up Java project as open source, Sun hoped to improve its standing with that community. Note that since then many successful Java open-source projects have been created and that there is now a very large and vibrant open-source community for Java.

STORYTELLING THROUGH CONNECTED ACTIVITIES

This is a general marketing-based goal. Typically marketing takes place via collateral material, events such as JavaOne and product launches and press releases. There are not very many ways to get small pieces of news into the world. Websites have helped with this. An open-source project has a website, mailing lists, and community events, but they are aimed more at developers and users than at the press and analysts. It is possible to tell these smaller stories within the context of normal open-source communications. For example, a developer could mention in a design consideration something that implies a new strategic direction for your company. Even simply having a developer at your company working hard at making some program or system work well on a competitor's system conveys a story about your company's values that is not possible to tell through normal marketing avenues.

Storytelling was an explicit NetBeans goal, although it is not likely that many outside the inner circle of the NetBeans-community designers were comfortable thinking of it in this way. The Forte for Java product line is marketed partly through the open-source project, and statements about the Forte for Java direction are made indirectly through the actions and discussions by NetBeans developers working in the NetBeans community.

STATEMENT OF VISION AND TERMS OF ENGAGEMENT

Sometimes a company would like to make a statement of vision or establish new terms of engagement. This can be thought of as changing or adding to the conceptual landscape of the field or market. For example, when IBM wanted to establish itself further as a leader in part of the Java landscape, it released Eclipse as open source. Eclipse is "a kind of universal tool platform—an open extensible IDE for anything and nothing in particular."[6] At that time, the only significant open-source Java IDE was NetBeans. IBM had established itself as a supporter of open source through its support for Linux, and it had put out some small open-source projects such as Jikes, but it had yet to make a big statement of its beliefs in open source in the Java arena. Moreover, it didn't have an open-source Java IDE as its competitor, Sun, did. The full Eclipse story is recounted later.

STATEMENT OF VALUES

Doing an open-source project signals your company's belief in open-source principles and acknowledges that the world beyond your company is full of expertise and innovation. It is a statement of humility. Every open-source project achieves this result, at least to some degree.

The previous example about working to enhance the performance of a competitor's product shows that your company cares about its customers and wants to provide them with the best products possible—even if they come from a competitor.

The business goal that is achieved by affirming your company's values is indirect, helping to establish your company's reputation. This, in turn, influences how potential customers and business partners think about your company and what they expect in their dealings with your company.

An important characteristic of a company is its trustworthiness. Trustworthiness is hard to come by—you cannot achieve it with a single act but only with a long sequence of good acts. Trustworthiness is also built by making what you do very transparent so that there are no secrets. Open source is a way to live in a glass house; and when people observe you acting well just as they often do, then your trustworthiness will increase.

GET BRAND LOYALTY FOR YOUR COMPANY'S HARDWARE/SOFTWARE

Creating a community of users and developers around an open-source project earns your company the reputation of being a "good guy," and that can create brand loyalty.

Every company-sponsored open-source project has this goal, whether stated or not. For example, with NetBeans the primary business goal was to increase the

---

6. This is how Eclipse is described on the Eclipse community website (http://www.eclipse.org).

number of Java developers by providing a solid Java IDE, but making it an open-source project helped Sun gain some brand loyalty for both the Sun and Java brands.

GET THE HIT EFFECT WORKING

By studying how movies and popular music become runaway hits, researchers have found that a large network of key influencers can cause a word-of-mouth wildfire to spread rapidly. If the right people speak favorably about a work, those favorable words can spread and the same favorable message bumping into the same person from different directions can cause that person to become a fan. This can happen with an open-source project when key influencers are in the community and are favorable to its projects.

This is an important mechanism for ubiquity.

CREATE A MARKETPLACE

By providing a ubiquitous open-source platform, you can create a marketplace for add-ons, support, and other related products and services. Having an open-source base platform greatly reduces the risk a player in the new marketplace must take on because there is no single owner of the underlying technology to possibly leave the market or go out of business.

Building a marketplace can require a multistep process using at least two distinct approaches. The first is to build an open-source community around a single software project that can have associated, perhaps for-sale software developed by outside parties. NetBeans is an example. NetBeans is an IDE that enables modules conforming to certain APIs to be plugged into it, and these modules are the goods in the marketplace. Sun hopes that it can participate in the marketplace with proprietary software, and that the existence of the marketplace for Java increases the Java programmer population. Eclipse, originally an IBM open-source project and associated IDE, is another example of this approach. Part of this marketplace can be seen at the Eclipse plug-in website,[7] which describes itself as a portal and marketplace.

The other approach is to build an infrastructure for a set of open-source projects centered on the technology around which the company wishes to form a market. Sun has built such an infrastructure and community called Java.net.

---

7. http://www.eclipseplugincentral.com

Java.net is both a set of communities that creates Java software and a website containing infrastructure to host those communities. Groups and companies are encouraged to host their own open-source projects at Java.net at no cost, and, because there is also an active, portal-like community associated with Java.net, ideas and partnerships may spawn as well as source code spreading. Java.net is therefore like a great city attracting creative people into its neighborhoods. A second, loosely affiliated website called Java.com is provided where Java software can be advertised and sold. In each of these examples (NetBeans, Eclipse, and Java.net), an open-source approach was used to anchor a community that creates the desired marketplace.

COMMODITIZE COMPETITION

Providing a no-cost offering can force a competitor to play a commodity game where small advantages and brand loyalty, for example, can play a stronger role than in a high-value game.

OpenOffice is an example of this goal: Its free office-productivity software makes it more difficult for other companies, such as Microsoft, to charge large amounts for proprietary software with similar features. It transforms office-productivity software from a high-value, single-vendor product into a commodity.

PRICING FOR SMALL BUSINESSES

Small companies face problems that larger, more established companies do not. We have already mentioned how making a product open source reduces customer risk because the product can then survive a small company going out of business. Making a product open source can also resolve a potential problem of how to price the product.

When a small company enters an existing market and underprices its product to be competitive, customers will wonder why the price is low. This suspicion may keep customers away from the new product. If the company meets market prices, then it comes up against many other issues that favor large, established companies. Making the product open source makes the question of pricing go away. Customers no longer wonder why the price is so low because this aspect of open source is understood. They are okay with the product being "free" and the small company charging for a nicely packaged version of the software, manuals, support, and training or consulting services.

ACQUISITION AND PARTNERSHIP—PERSONAL AND CORPORATE

In the mid-1990s DOOM was released as open source. DOOM is a first-person shooter (FPS) game. Since then, there has been growth in the development and distribution of *mods*, which are variants or updates to proprietary computer game engines that have game-extension capabilities such as scripting languages. The current range of mods includes new game types, game character models and skins (surface textures), levels (game play arenas or virtual worlds), and artificially intelligent game bots (in-game opponents). Two game companies, id Software and Epic Games, provide tools for creating mods and require essentially open-source licenses for their creation. Half-Life: Counter Strike is among the most popular of the FPS games (fall 2003) and was developed under an open-source license. The two primary developers now have a financial arrangement with Valve, the commercial developers of Half-Life, sharing in the revenue stream for Counter Strike.

This is a business model in which developers create a market with an open-source project based around a commercial product. By increasing the size of the commercial product's market, these developers might be able to arrange a partnership with the commercial company or be bought out by it.

THE ECLIPSE STORY

Eclipse is a good example of a successful business-related open-source project. As with all real success stories, there is no single or simple thread or fact that explains all aspects. That is, Eclipse was done as open source not for one strategic reason but instead for several.

Since the time IBM committed to Java, the company had developed a strong competence and practice in Java. Because IBM values being able to work with customers on their own terms, it wanted to bolster Java in the marketplace so that it would not need to invest excessively in maintaining multiple expertises. Because Microsoft succeeds at least partly by providing good tools for developers, IBM wanted to establish serious competition for Microsoft Visual Studio in the eyes of developers. Further, IBM had had only modest success selling to customers who were not already IBM's. Open source provided legitimacy to appeal to the Linux, C, and Microsoft installed bases without involving much IBM baggage. Eclipse was a way to address these issues.

There was also the issue of effort. For a plug-in technology such as Eclipse, the problems of integrating a variety of pluggable components were bigger than one company could continue to solve while providing sensible investments in the infrastructure, and open source could provide a way to share the costs while providing a broad set of tools.

To accomplish these goals, IBM decided to engage the open-source community.

Where did Eclipse come from? The Eclipse project was the natural follow-up to IBM's VisualAge family of development tools. Many of the substantial contributions to Eclipse came from a Canadian company IBM had acquired called Object Technology International (OTI), headquartered in Ottawa. OTI had previously developed IDEs and virtual machines (VMs)[8] for IBM's VisualAge Smalltalk and VisualAge Java. The early work on a Java-based IDE was part of a broader research effort on multiple language technologies at OTI where the IDE was given the internal name Eclipse.

The goal of the OTI Eclipse project was to provide IBM product developers and key independent software vendors (ISVs) with a common, extensible tool platform competitive with Microsoft's Visual Studio. The first commercial release of Eclipse technology was IBM's VisualAge Micro Edition (later called WebSphere Studio Device Developer), an IDE for embedded Java development where important design constraints come from diminished computing and presentation resources.

The Eclipse team had two primary objectives for the roll-out of the technology:

- Deliver technology to establish a perception of ubiquity—that developers, engineers, and users all use (this is a bottom-up developer-to-developer approach).

- Build an ecosystem or marketplace for companies to build commercial offerings on top of the open-source base; the hope was that this would generate a healthy tension between the paradigm of open source and the commercial need for profitable products.

For many computer companies, a medium- and long-term strategy is to work with researchers and educators who then train their students on that company's products and technology. This translates into future sales and loyalty. This is one of the reasons that Unix and now Linux are as popular as they are—Unix was once a staple of university computer science and engineering departments. However, this requires investment and an understanding of the university and laboratory scene, which were problems for IBM. Eclipse provided technology that researchers could get excited about.

---

8. A virtual machine is software that runs on a real computer and presents an execution environment more amenable to executing code in a particular programming language than the real computer. It is a way to achieve portability of applications over a wide range of computer hardware.

Similarly, IBM had difficulties penetrating non-IBM installed markets despite the existence of both programs and investments in this area. In both these cases, IBM was unable to make headway in markets and communities important to its future. Eclipse provided the perception of independence and provided a forum for competitors and other IBM outsiders to observe and with which to engage.

Eclipse could have been released as a free but proprietary tool, but IBM realized that the platform would see wider acceptance in the broader developer and vendor community if it were made a true open-source project. Furthermore, this would drive home the message that Java and open source could provide a serious challenge to Microsoft. By providing the ability to support platforms and languages other than Java, Eclipse enabled developers with existing languages and tools to benefit from the same IDE framework and tools, providing many of the benefits of Visual Studio Net. This reduced the need for expensive tooling for a wide variety of researchers and tool vendors.

IBM therefore made a concerted effort to engage educators, researchers, vendors, and key influencers to move Eclipse from an IBM internal development to a full open-source project. The internal code name was familiar to developers, so IBM deviated from its normal naming practices and allowed the internal code name Eclipse.org to represent the project. This provided a lightning rod for developers expressing their frustration at Sun's control of Java.

IBM brought some well-known names into the mix: Erich Gamma was the first author of *Design Patterns*, and Kent Beck was a founder of the software patterns community and the father of Extreme Programming. Gamma is now one of the main Eclipse project leaders, and he and Beck wrote a book called *Contributing to Eclipse: Principles, Patterns, and Plugins*, which is part of a new Addison-Wesley series called The Eclipse Series.

IBM played its marketing hand quite well. IBM sponsored Eclipse receptions and workshops at major object-oriented programming conferences, produced the excellent book mentioned above, made research grants to universities, and eventually created an Eclipse conference, called EclipseCon. The Gamma-Beck book was given as a gift to all attendees of OOPSLA 2003 by IBM Research.

This extraordinary marketing effort combined with the technical excellence of Eclipse resulted in the Eclipse project's having 50 corporate members and 18 million downloads by the end of 2003. Further, this success also motivated IBM to spin out Eclipse.org in 2004 as a nonprofit foundation; this new Eclipse.org has a tiered hierarchy of governance and management, with IBM retaining a small but significant degree of control in the form of having a member on the board of directors and a full-time executive director to lead the management team. Three separate councils oversee Eclipse development projects.

As part of the spin-out effort, IBM reached out to other companies such as Sun, which was suspicious about IBM and had a major investment in its own IDE, NetBeans. Sun declined to join Eclipse.org.

The result was that IBM gained the high ground and changed the landscape for competition in Java tools platforms. Eclipse is the exemplar in this area, and the vocabulary and terms of engagement in this arena are largely under IBM's control.

Two facts about Eclipse raise the question of whether part of IBM's strategy was to deliver some tweaks to Sun as part of their cooperative/competitive relationship. First, even though the choice of the name Eclipse might not have been aimed originally at Sun, the fact that it has the meaning of overshadowing the Sun was probably not a negative factor in IBM's decision to use the code name as the external name. Second, IBM had always felt that Sun had been overbearing in its control and expansion of Java, and therefore IBM might have been trying to wrest some control from Sun and criticize it technically by using a different windowing toolkit from the standard one, which is called Swing. The toolkit Eclipse uses, called the Standard Widget Toolkit (SWT), was considered by some to be easier to work with than Swing and performed better on the operating systems platforms to which it was targeted.

The question of the toolkit, however, is complicated, as such things always are. A hallmark of the VisualAge family was portable support for native look and feel; this was carried forward with SWT, which leveraged OTI's peer-layer experience with Smalltalk IDEs. Because SWT already existed for WebSphere Studio Device Developer, time-to-market considerations added to the push to use SWT in Eclipse as a graphical user interface (GUI) for Eclipse-based tools.

The Eclipse story is only one of IBM's engagements with open source, which includes working on Linux—again to create an alternative to the Microsoft platforms. Although IBM's commitment to Eclipse is significant, it spends much more on Linux.

Creating Your Business Model and Following Through with It

Every company is interested in activities that support its business. You must be able to explain how the relevant business goals for your project contribute to your company. Some of the goals we have listed, such as selling a proprietary product based on an open-source project, have a direct connection to revenue. Others have a more indirect connection, such as better relations with customers, making it easier to sell your company's hardware or services into an organization.

For example, Sun makes most of its money by selling hardware, so any software that encourages customers to buy Sun servers or workstations supports Sun's main business model. It can do so directly by providing desired functionality and high quality, as Solaris does. It can do so by offering an alternative to software available on other platforms, such as StarOffice. It can try to level the playing field (or even tilt it in Sun's favor) by establishing new standards, as Java does. It can try to create a new market where Sun can be a major player, such as Jini. It can do so by gaining developer mindshare, so more applications for Sun hardware will become available, such as NetBeans. If shifting to open-source development will make these activities more likely to succeed, then a strong case can be made to do so. As an aside, please note that each of these strategies may be best supported by a different type of license; we discuss licenses in the next chapter.

Your business model justifies your use of open source both to managers within your company and also to outside developers. It is important that you be able to communicate your business model to both groups.

Many outside developers are suspicious of the motives of large companies and will view an open-source project sponsored by such a company as an attempt to pull a fast one. To quell these fears, you must be able to explain how your company plans to benefit from participating in the open-source project. Only when they understand what your company plans to gain will they be comfortable supporting the project. If they don't hear a sensible business reason for why your company is using open source, you can be sure that someone will suggest a variety of sneaky motives, often based on the fears open-source developers have that companies will steal their work and put it into proprietary products. If you are not willing to disclose your main business reasons, then you should rethink making your project open source.

You will also need to explain your business model to other groups within your company that you need to interact with. Other parts of your company will expect your project to be business-as-usual and may not be happy when they find out otherwise. For example, if another group inside your company has a product that depends on yours, then you need to explain to them that the company does not control the release schedule and that your project will not do a release if your community feels the code isn't quite ready. You can expect there to be lots of pressure on your project to act like a normal proprietary project.

Measuring Success

There are fairly standard ways of measuring whether a proprietary project is successful. These include product sales, market share, number of bugs, meeting schedule deadlines, and other familiar assessments. Many of these also apply to open-source projects, but there are additional metrics that are necessary.

Each of the business goals for your project should have an associated measure. Here are some possible metrics for various business goals.

- Ubiquity: number of users, number of mentions by the press, response by competitors

- Standards development: number of participating parties, number of parties adopting the standard

- Design help: number of additional user/designers, amount of email on mailing lists

- Development help: number of outside developers, number of bugs reported/fixed, number/quality of contributions, amount of email on mailing lists

- Appeal to community: quality and number of comments in open-source community

By default your project will be measured the same way a proprietary one is, which will probably result in the open-source activities getting shortchanged. For a successful open-source project you need to get management to agree to a different set of metrics. The performance reviews for any employee participating in an open-source project need to include measures for their open-source-related activities. Note that just adding new metrics in with all the standard existing ones won't work; you cannot expect people to successfully do both their old jobs and take on the new tasks required to create a healthy open-source community.

An Example: The Innovation Happens Elsewhere Strategy

The business reasons for open source as presented tend to have a more tactical focus. Let's now look at an example of how open source might support a larger business strategy.

Most companies are not large enough to influence the direction of their own markets, and few companies are able to design products that truly serve their customers. Most companies find they need to fine-tune designs and products over a series of releases. Some companies use time to introduce products: The Saturn car company started by introducing inexpensive but high-value cars that appealed to young adults just starting out in their careers, and, while learning the tastes and values of that generation, Saturn has introduced new models that reflect the increasing affluence of its core customer base. This is an example of using the world outside the corporation as a source of innovation. Software companies using open source can perhaps exploit this strategy in its most pure form. So, what is the strategy?

To simplify the discussion, let's consider only companies that produce technology products. The Innovation Happens Elsewhere (IHE) strategy begins by recognizing where the company's proprietary value lies. Everything outside this inner circle of protected ideas and technology is available for instigating outside innovation beneficial to the company. The primary goal of the strategy is to increase the number of potential customers—that is, the size of the market available to the company. To do this, the IHE company tries to create more products in the market that either are enablers for the products the IHE company sells or form an aftermarket for them. Rather than trying to accomplish this alone, the IHE company tries to encourage other companies or organizations to do this work—but for their own purposes.

The impetus for companies to do this comes from tools, technology, communities, and prototypes that the IHE company provides. By opening up part of itself to the outside, the IHE company can provide gifts that trigger the gift-economy effect: technology; tools, and prototypes that are of high value to outside companies and organizations and that trigger them to work in areas important to the IHE company; and communities where others can work within a culture that supports the vision of the IHE company (see Figure 4.1). Let's break this down a little.

Giving gifts of technology and tools initially spurs outside individuals to work on or with those gifts for their own benefit—perhaps one of the tools is useful to a software developer for one of his or her home projects. Later, that developer might bring the tool into his or her company, where colleagues start to use it for their own purposes. Because the tool was a gift (and perhaps its source is available), individuals and their companies send bug fixes, extensions, modules, and ideas back to the IHE company. The gift has been picked up—for selfish purposes—but it stimulates a gift in turn of work that is of value to the IHE company directly, which takes those tools, technologies, prototypes, and ideas back and uses them to enhance its own products. In the open-source realm, this is the fundamental expected payback for opening up software source. For the IHE company, this is only the beginning.

Next, an outside company using gifts from the IHE company recognizes that these tools, technologies, and prototypes can be combined with its own technology to produce products at lower cost, at less risk, and of great value to their customer base. Again, this is done for selfish reasons, but such outside

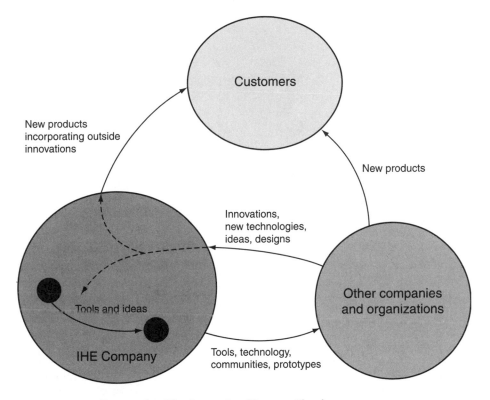

FIGURE 4.1   The Innovation Happens Elsewhere strategy.

companies are, by doing this, contributing to expanding the customer base for the IHE company. Sometimes a company or organization will think of an application or variation of the gift that will open it up to entirely new and unexpected markets. This is the sort of return gift the IHE strategy can provide.

Even further, the IHE company, by creating, building, and maintaining a set of communities around these gifts, can engage in serious conversations with outside companies, organizations, and individuals. Such conversations not only can improve the IHE company's products, designs, and directions, but also provides the IHE company with an opportunity to demonstrate leadership and vision, thereby putting it in a position to strongly influence the direction and structure of the competitive landscape. Because this is done in a context of gift-giving, culture exchange, and conversations, this is leadership and seduction, not control and power. If the IHE company exhibits learning in response to these communities, other members will continue to give gifts, work with the company, and help it maneuver through difficult competitive and market situations.

Communities are also a way to tell stories to the community while minimizing the effects of cynical write-off. When a company puts out white papers, advertising, and other public relations materials, the audience is likely to discount as hype statements made there. But within a community, where developers and engineers are talking to each other, the messages can be both smaller—too small for press releases—and larger: global visions and proposals for new directions couched in design and other engineering statements. By valuing the comments and ideas from outside community members—by showing respect—the IHE company can create a channel unlike any other.

The ability to communicate through communities such as this means that the IHE company can nudge the market in directions that play to its strengths. And by both demonstrating great innovation and respecting the innovation of others and by providing just the right gifts, the company can increase the size of its market and tune itself and its informal "partners" to that market, which is itself tuned through the vision of the company. That is, the market, the IHE company, and companies in the virtuous cycle of innovation co-evolve under the partial direction or influence of the IHE company.

The IHE company takes direct advantage of the returned gifts from others, both by using them in its own products and by using them to help its internal operations. The IHE company puts itself in the best position when it embraces at all levels the philosophy of Innovation Happens Elsewhere with people in the company always looking inside and outside the company for innovation they and their groups can use.

There are several keys to using this strategy. The first key is understanding and isolating the true proprietary value and technologies of the company. The more accurately this is done, the better able the company is to use its gifts and thrive. If what's proprietary and valuable to customers is too small, the company will have a hard time surviving as others crowd into its space. If what's judged proprietary and of value is too large—or too much of what the company makes or works on—then there will be few gifts available to get the cycle of innovation going.

The second key is the confidence that your organization can engineer products well and quickly enough to stay ahead of competition. Microsoft, for example, does not believe it has enough of an engineering edge over competitors to do other than hold all its source code proprietary. Perhaps this is why it tries to combat open source rather than embracing it.

The third key is a company culture that can embrace and celebrate innovations wherever they occur. In a sense, this is confidence and enthusiasm for ideas, but it is also respect and the right balance of pride and humility. Some organizations seem to fear ideas that originate from outside. Such organizations cannot use Innovation Happens Elsewhere.

OPEN SOURCE AND INNOVATION HAPPENS ELSEWHERE

Companies that develop software can use open source as a basis for sharing tools, technology, and prototypes, and communities can be built around open-source projects. In this case, it's important to recognize both that such communities need to succeed as software development efforts and that the goal for such communities is to fuel the IHE feedback cycle.

Sun Microsystems's NetBeans open-source project is a good example of a community built to support the IHE strategy (see Figure 4.2). Recall that NetBeans is an open-source platform for building an IDE specifically for the Java language. Sun gets improvements from the open-source community and builds a proprietary version of NetBeans—called Forte for Java (now Sun Java Studio)—which is a tested version of NetBeans extended with proprietary modules. Other companies use the NetBeans technology in-house and as part of other products. Forte for Java is in addition positioned as a platform on which other companies can sell plug-in modules—that is, Forte for Java is the basis of a marketplace.

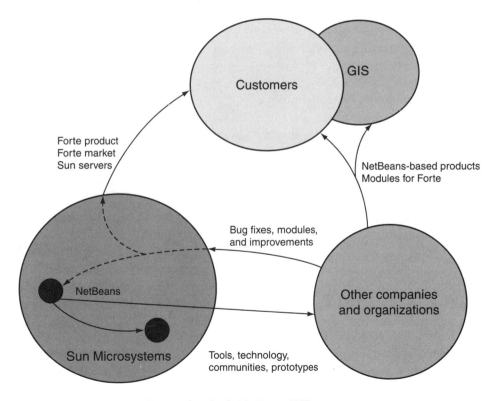

FIGURE 4.2 Sun's NetBeans IHE strategy.

The effect is to increase the population of Java language programmers both by providing tools for those developers directly and through other companies building on the NetBeans platform. This way, not only is Sun Microsystems building the Java community, but so are other companies and individuals in the NetBeans community. Sun sells an IDE derived from NetBeans, but, most important, Sun sells server hardware that runs Java particularly well. Further, Java developers within Sun use NetBeans and Forte for their own work.

An unexpected innovation happened when a group removed the Java-specific modules from the NetBeans IDE and replaced them with mapping, visualization, and analysis modules in order to build a modular environment for spatial analysis and visualization. This potentially opens up a future geographic information systems (GIS) market to Sun, a market not originally contemplated.

LESSONS FROM THE IHE STRATEGY

There are many advantages to using open source, but being able to engage the Innovation Happens Elsewhere strategy is especially compelling. Not only does it build the market size, but the tactics to make it work help companies that use it get to better products faster by directly involving the customer base in their design. Through direct conversations with customers, there is reduced guess-work in gathering market requirements. Moreover, there are some operational efficiencies to be gained through better testing, community-based support, and some significant product contributions.

Sometimes—no, usually—a surprise will happen; an innovation or application of the ideas and technology will come along that you have never dreamed of, never heard of, or couldn't imagine, done by a group or individual you have never heard of. And it could be a pivotal market for your company or could change how you view and develop your original technology.

What is most stunning, however, is the difference in the feel of companies that truly engage with their communities of customers, partners, and competitors. Morale is boosted, progress is constant, and it simply feels like something good is always happening.

Business Reasons for Using Open-Source Products

So far we've talked only about reasons to make one of your proprietary products into an open-source project. There is also the question of when it makes sense for a company to use an existing open-source product. We conclude this chapter by discussing some of the issues that arise from using open-source products in a company setting.

Basically the same concerns arise with open-source software as with proprietary products:

- Will it do what you need?
- What type of support is available?
- What is the total cost of ownership?
- Will the software product continue to be developed?

When purchasing a proprietary product you know how to answer these questions, but these answers don't apply for open source.

MEETING YOUR NEEDS

The first question is pretty much the same for any software under consideration—how do the features of the software match up with your needs? Open-source software is often less polished than commercial products, so you need to decide if extra polish is worth paying more for.

Choosing software also involves looking at what other needs you have that might be met in future releases. Here the transparency of the open-source process makes it easier to get a handle on what new features are planned and when they might be ready—all of the planning happens on public mailing lists and is displayed in the project's roadmap—you can even send an email to the main developers. Most companies are much more guarded about planned release dates of proprietary products and what features will be in future releases.

If a feature you need is missing, open source has an advantage in that you can work with the project to add it. You can lobby with the community about adding the feature, have your own developers write the needed code, or hire consultants to do so.

GETTING SUPPORT

When you buy a product from a company, you expect that the company will stand behind its product by providing both a warranty and product support. If you have a problem, you believe that you can go to the company and legally it is required to fix that problem. Although this may be true for physical products such as automobiles, by far the majority of commercial software products come with very limited warranties and minimal support. If you've ever read the End-User License Agreement (EULA) for a piece of commercial software, then you know that the warranty is basically just a refund of your purchase price. And if you've ever tried to get basic, no-cost support from a large software company, then you know how difficult and frustrating it can be—although some do have lots of good information available through the company's website that more sophisticated users can take advantage of. Most companies do have support plans that you can purchase. Support may also be available from third-party companies.

With open source, there is often no company to deal with. However, there is usually a community and that community exists in large part to support its members in the use of the software. This support takes two forms: online documents and discussion forums. When evaluating an open-source application you need to check both. Go to the project's website and see how much documentation is available, whether a good FAQ for it exists, and whether there are active mailing lists or newsgroups devoted to user questions. Check if the main developers participate in the user forums—tough questions that might stump a customer support person for a commercial product are often answered by the actual developers of an open-source project. Although getting support through a public mailing list may seem very informal, many who have tried it find it gets the job done, often more quickly and better than previous experiences with support for commercial products.

For the more successful open-source applications, there are companies that sell support. For example, rather than downloading a free copy of the Linux operating system, many people choose to buy it from Red Hat because support is included. Other companies, such as Caldera, Linuxcare, and IBM, also offer support for Linux, as do many consultants. Some open-source projects have commercial versions that are supported—StarOffice is a supported commercial product sold by Sun that is based on OpenOffice.

Training is related to support, and, indeed, for popular widespread open-source products it is easy to find training classes and books, both introductory texts and advanced reference material. Some publishers, such as O'Reilly, specialize in providing high-quality books on how to use open-source applications.

TOTAL COST

Open-source software is not always free—sometimes you may have to pay for it, as you do for the basic Red Hat Linux distribution—but what you are paying for usually is the convenience and quality assurance that went into packaging the software. Of course, once you have the software you can install it on as many computers as you wish (although the other installations might not be covered by the support agreement). So, instead of needing to purchase multiple licenses, one for each computer you wish to run the software on, open source immediately saves you money, possibly quite a lot of money. However, keep in mind that your total cost also includes the cost of deployment, training, and support, plus indirect operating costs due to ease of use (or, more appropriately, how difficult it is for your employees to do their jobs using it) and interoperability with other software you use. According to some studies, software and hardware costs account for less than 20% of the total cost.

RISK

Considering the expense involved in switching from one software application to another, you want to evaluate the future prospects of any software you choose: Will it continue to be a supported product, or will it be discontinued? If the company making it goes out of business, what happens?

For open source it is important to assess the health of the project in order to be confident that the software will continue to be developed. To do so, look at the size of the community, check how much documentation is available, see whether a good FAQ for it exists, and browse through the various mailing lists and newsgroups associated with it to determine how active the community is. Also check to see how often there has been a new release of the software. Look at the project's road map to understand the overall vision.

Even a small project with just a few developers may have advantages over a proprietary product. A single developer may be more willing to fix bugs and add features. Also, there is always the possibility of hiring the main developer as a consultant to make the changes you need. Finally, with an open-source project of any size your risk is always reduced because the source code is available to you.

As with any company, an open-source project can disappear, and with it perhaps its source code and community. You may be able to retain rights to use, maintain, and further develop the source code if the license gives you those rights. By judging the health and importance of the project, you can decide whether this is a risk you wish to accept.

There is another way that open source lets you choose the level of risk you are comfortable with. You can minimize your risk by using only the major releases that have undergone thorough testing. Or you can accept more risk if you want access to new features as soon as they have been added to a development build. Or you can choose to be somewhere in the middle by using the stable builds that are known to at least basically work and may have received some testing. Better yet, do your own testing if you have the resources.

One last risk deserves mention if you wish to distribute an open-source application, possibly along with some of your own products, for use by your customers. By definition, open source can be redistributed, but you need to check the license that the software uses to determine if there are additional conditions that you must meet. If you have not made any changes to the software, but are merely redistributing binaries that you got directly from the project, then there should be no problems, although the license may require that you acknowledge the open-source project in your advertising materials or restrict your use of the project's name in product endorsements. If you have made changes to the software, then you may need to make the source code for those changes publicly available, depending on the license. Because open-source software does not include any warranty or support, your customers may expect you to provide both. Finally, some companies have tried to scare others away from using open source by falsely claiming that, if you merely bundle one of your proprietary programs on a CD with an open-source program, you then need to make your proprietary source code public—it's just not true: Your code stays yours.

Why Consider Open Source?

Open source is a commons-based means of doing continuous design, but the business reasons for joining or starting an open-source project go far beyond source code and distributed development. The reasons range over almost the entire spectrum of business-related activities: marketing, strategy, distribution, sales, human resources, and innovation. The last one—innovation—is the one that interests us most because without innovation there is no company, and not much fun either.

CHAPTER 5

Licenses

OPEN SOURCE IS A COMMONS-BASED ACTIVITY in which a community of people work on a shared artifact, in this case source code. Source code is covered by copyright law, which in the United States grants copyright to an author immediately upon completion of the piece. When copyright law in the United States was first written, the duration of protection was 14 years with perhaps an opportunity to renew it once. Now copyright extends until the death of the author plus 70 years.

Software enjoys the same protections as any other literary work. In addition, software may contain the implementations of patented methods—called software patents. Currently, the copyright holder retains the right to strict control of the work, including copying, derived works, distributions, and public performance. Originally, copyright law tried to strike a balance between providing an incentive for creators and allowing other creators to build on works already created. The expansion of copyright protection has been rapid over the last 40 years as institutional "content" creators lobbied for expanded protection.

A key to understanding open source as a business strategy is coming to terms with the idea that there is a middle ground between "all rights reserved" and the public domain. It is possible for a holder of intellectual property to carefully craft a description of rights the holder wishes to retain and freedoms the holder grants to licensees. Think in terms of "some rights reserved" or "most rights reserved." Even when source code is visible and even downloadable on the Internet, the copyright and patent holders retain ownership of the material and, by licensing arrangements, control what they wish to control. In fact, copyright and patents are in place precisely to encourage people to create, invent, and put on display their creations and explain their inventions.

A good, clear example of this is the VTK project. The project provides a simple license as part of the copyright notice—and in fact, the term *copyright* is used the way most open-source projects use the term *license*, and some open-source licenses, such as BSD (discussed later), likewise state their license terms as part of the copyright notice. The VTK directory structure isolates files and classes that contain patented algorithms (they are in special subdirectories), and the license states that any commercial use of those parts requires licenses from the patent holders—and it provides contact information for them. The commercial use could be as part of VTK or as part of other systems. However, individuals, universities, and companies can use the code without special terms as long as there is no commercial benefit derived, and the nonpatented parts can be used commercially without special licenses.

This represents an example of how the rights to intellectual property have been carved up by one group. Other groups might limit the use of patents to software developed as part of the open-source project, while uses of those patents in other, unrelated software would be restricted or prohibited.

Naturally, crafting a too restrictive set of rights granted to others can stifle the success of an open-source project, but there is no need to abandon all property rights. For open source to work, the author or copyright holder basically needs to grant rights to use, modify, and distribute. This is accomplished through licensing, which, although granting rights to others, does not transfer ownership in any way, so that the owner of the source code can change how the source is licensed in the future, can decide not to license it, or can transfer ownership.

A variety of licenses have been created to meet the different needs of open-source projects—the original Berkeley Unix was released under the Berkeley Software Distribution (BSD) license, Linux and Emacs use the GNU General Public License (GPL), and Netscape created the Mozilla Public License (MPL) for its browser. Companies such as IBM and Sun have written a variety of licenses including the Common Public License (CPL), Sun Industry Standards Source License (SISSL), and Sun Community Source License (SCSL). Over 50 different licenses have been certified as meeting the criteria for open source by the Open Source Initiative, a nonprofit corporation dedicated to managing and promoting the Open Source Definition,[1] and additional types of licenses have been created for use by other open-source projects.

This large number of possible licenses creates confusion for people considering starting in an open-source project. When choosing a license for your project, it is best to use one of the existing licenses—preferably one already in widespread use—rather than trying to create a new one.

Creating a new license is a difficult legal process. It is likely that an existing license captures most, if not all, the concerns you might have, and the open-source community has little patience for people and organizations who don't believe in the already working, existing licenses. Moreover, a new license would perhaps

---

1. http://www.opensource.org

need to be certified by the Open Source Initiative to satisfy the business objectives of its creator. Existing licenses—especially those in widespread use—are like brands in that people already are familiar with their terms and how to work with software licensed under them. By choosing a well-known, accepted license, you are also choosing a reduced learning and adoption curve for your community members.

In this chapter we discuss what goes into a typical license and describe some of the most commonly used ones, including which type of projects they are best for. Which license is best for your project depends on your reasons for choosing to do open-source development. Chapter 7 includes a section on "Choosing a License" that presents a list of questions to help you pick which license to use.

Many people equate open source with the various open-source licenses, but the license is only a gate that people pass through. If people are not willing to agree to the terms of the license, then they don't pass through the gate. For those people who do accept, the license doesn't specify how they will work together; it merely defines some very basic ground rules.

What a License Does

A license grants outside developers certain rights that establish what they can and cannot do with the source code. The licenses we consider here grant the developer the right to use and modify the source code. Some licenses also include the right to use any intellectual property (IP), such as patents, that is embodied in the source code. Most licenses do not grant developers the right to take that IP and use it in a different application.

Each license also requires developers to assume certain responsibilities. For example, some licenses require that any bug fixes that a developer makes to the source code must be contributed back to the original author. Another common requirement is that any IP used in the source code that a developer contributes must be made available (usually without fee) to other developers who use that code.

A major area of variation among licenses is what, if anything, the developer must do in order to redistribute executable binaries built from modified versions of the source code. Many open-source licenses require that the modified source code also be made available, at no or nominal cost, to anyone who wants to see and use it—this being the whole point of open source. Some of the Sun-created licenses, SCSL and SISSL, include compatibility requirements in the license.

Some licenses allow the source code to be incorporated into a *larger work* that is not subject to the terms of the license, although the original source code that is being included still is; other licenses consider any additions to be extensions of the original program and subject to all of the license terms. This is a key factor to consider if you plan on combining open-source code with proprietary code.

Finally, all the licenses deal with various legal matters: warranty (typically none), liability (typically limited), termination of the license (if you violate any of its terms), dealing with brands and trademarks (typically not included with the license), and several other boilerplate issues that are also to be found in typical licenses accompanying commercial software (e.g., clauses about governing law, dispute resolution, U.S. government use, international use, and severability).

What a License Does Not Do

It is just as important to realize what a license does not do. A license describes certain boundary conditions, but does not speak about how developers will actually work together. It is up to other documents or traditions to describe the process of contributing code, making a new release, and deciding what to do when disagreements arise. The next chapter looks at the day-to-day functioning of a typical open-source project and how to build up a community of users and developers.

The license may not automatically apply to changes contributed by outside developers. Many open-source projects require people wishing to contribute code to first sign a contributor's agreement before their code is accepted. (This agreement is discussed later in the section "Supplementing the License—Contributor Agreements.")

One other matter that most licenses do not touch on is how to ensure that modifications to the source code maintain compatibility with established standards. One way this can be done is to require that any distributed code pass a compatibility test in order to be granted the right to use a logo or brand. If there is an established brand, then this can be enough of a carrot for developers to keep things compatible. Most often, compatibility is maintained because the community values it and will not accept code contributions that deviate from the standard—anyone who wants to create an incompatible version is thus forced to fork the code and start a new project.

More on Copyright . . .

The author of a piece of software owns the copyright to the code and therefore the right to choose the terms of the license. The copyright owner may license the code to one group under one set of terms and to another group under a different set of terms. For example, the main product of the company Trolltech AS is the Qt library, a toolkit for building graphical user interfaces for applications. Trolltech makes the Qt library available under two very different licenses: the Q Public License (QPL) for use in noncommercial software[2] (used by the KDE open-source project in its work to build a graphical desktop for Linux) and the Professional License for companies wishing to build a commercial product using the Qt library. The QPL version is free. The Professional License version is a commercial product that must be purchased.

Because the copyright holder determines the license terms, there can be a problem if there are multiple copyright owners. People who make changes or additions to the original source code become the copyright owners for the code they have written, even if it is just one line. When these changes are contributed back to the open-source project, their authors usually license them under the same terms as the original source code; indeed, many of the open-source licenses require this. Many open-source projects will not accept a contribution unless it is released under the same license as the original code—having various pieces of the source code under different, possibly incompatible, licenses would be too confusing and difficult.

A further problem arises if a project decides that it wants to change the license being used. For example, the Mozilla project is in the process of changing from the MPL to a triple licensing of the source code under either MPL, GPL, or LGPL. However, to make this happen, every person who has contributed any source code, and hence owns the copyright to it, must agree to the change. Just tracking down all of the copyright holders can be a major task, let alone getting them to agree to the proposed licensing changes. Because of this, some open-source projects request, or even demand, that contributors also assign their copyright to either the original author of the code or some agreed-on third party, such as the Free Software Foundation.

. . . And a Quick Word on Patents

Everything you know about patents from proprietary software development still applies to the world of open-source projects. Because your code is "published" when it is made available to people working on the project, any international patents required to implement the code need to be applied for beforehand and any U.S. patents need to be filed within 1 year. By contributing the source code to the project before a patent has been applied for, you may be giving up your right to

---

2. As of September 2000, the Qt library is also available under the GPL for use by open-source projects.

patent the material, and by contributing it to the project without explicit license terms, you may be granting anyone who distributes a product based on the project the right to use your patent without compensation. Depending on the license you use, others may or may not have the right to use the source code, and the patent, in other work.

It is also possible to make source code freely available, but require people to license your patents from you before they can distribute any software based on the source code. For example, the MPEG4IP project on SourceForge,[3] started by Cisco's Technology Center, provides an end-to-end system to explore MPEG-4 multimedia, but the codecs used by it are subject to patent royalties.

The Licenses

As mentioned earlier, there are several dozen different open-source licenses in use today. Of these, only a few are in widespread use. A check of the world's largest open-source software development website, SourceForge,[4] in March 2004 showed that of the over 53,000 open-source projects hosted there that specified a license about 94% used one of only four basic types of licenses. By far the most popular choices are the GPL and the LGPL, used by almost 79% of the SourceForge projects. The Apache, BSD, and MIT family of licenses is next, accounting for over 10%. Just over 2% use the Artistic License. About 2% use the MPL, SPL, or CPL. The remaining 5% of the projects use three dozen other licenses. An almost identical breakdown of license use was found for the over 23,000 projects hosted on freshmeat,[5] another repository of open-source code.

Before discussing the features and characteristics of these four types of open-source licenses, let us first look at some more-closed options based on proprietary licenses. These licenses allow varying amounts of collaboration but are not open source. We present the proprietary licenses first in order to show the progression from the licenses and contracts familiar to companies, to those common in open-source projects. The spectrum of licenses provides a spectrum of benefits, obligations, and opportunities for companies, and there really is no single perfect place on this spectrum for all projects. Each project has its own business requirements. Successful gated communities, for example, have been established and provided good value for companies, even though some open-source pundits

---

3. http://mpeg4ip.sourceforge.net

4. http://sourceforge.net

5. http://freshmeat.net

have criticized them. Such criticism reflects the fact that, to some, open source is a political movement, while to others, it is primarily a business decision.

Note: This section is only an overview of the various licenses—for the real details you need to read the licenses themselves. The full text of each license discussed is included in Appendix B. Also please see the section "Choosing a License" in Chapter 7 for help in figuring out which license is best for your project.

PROPRIETARY LICENSES—GATED COMMUNITIES

Although not open source, it is possible to do collaboration under a proprietary license. Usually such collaboration is between a few companies rather than being open to anyone. This has been referred to in the open source world as a *gated community.*

Typically a company signs a traditional nondisclosure agreement (NDA) or similar legal contract in order to be permitted to look at source code. The agreement or license specifies what the signer can and cannot do with the source code—for example, whether they can modify it or distribute it. Unlike the click-through licenses used by many open-source projects, the NDA needs to be signed by both parties.

Such collaborations can involve a number of collaborators. For example, Sun's Free Solaris Source License Program allowed anyone who had signed the license to view and modify the Solaris 8 source code. Signatories were allowed to distribute their changes to other licensees only via a Sun secure website and were not allowed to incorporate any Solaris code into other products. Although offering licensees only very limited rights, this was still attractive to outside organizations that had compelling reasons to tailor the source code to their needs.

This type of license can create a strong class system, with the licensees having fewer rights than the organization issuing the license. This can severely limit the size and scope of contributions that licensees will be willing to share. The originating organization might gain few, if any, of the benefits of an open-source project. There are two main reasons to use a proprietary license: if your company does not own all of the source code, so it cannot legally make it available publicly, or if the technology involved is so advanced that it is important to minimize the number of people who are permitted to look at it.

MICROSOFT SHARED SOURCE LICENSE

In May 2001, Microsoft began providing limited access to some of its source code through its newly created Shared Source Program. This access is quite limited for commercial software that is already established in the marketplace, such as its Windows operating system. For products that they are trying to promote, such as Windows CE or the Common Language Infrastructure (CLI) for C#, the access is greater.

For Windows all that is allowed by the license is looking at the code and debugging against it. Making changes to the code is not permitted. Only a few organizations are eligible to see this source code. These include large businesses that have enterprise licenses for Windows, the top systems integrators, governments, many universities, and the big original equipment manufacturers (OEMs). In total, over 4000 organizations in 28 countries qualify. As of June 2004, over 400 of those have signed up for the program.

The CLI license allows the source code to be viewed, modified, and redistributed as long as it is used only for noncommercial purposes. This makes it much more attractive for research purposes—in fact, the CLI program is focused on the academic community. The Windows CE license was updated in June 2004 to allow commercial redistribution of modified versions (under the standard royalty agreement). These programs are available to anyone, worldwide. As of March 2004, there have been over 250,000 downloads of the Windows CE code and 100,000 of the CLI.

The licenses themselves are quite short, just one or two pages page each, and are written in plain English.

Microsoft's Shared Source Program is further described on the Microsoft website.[6]

SUN COMMUNITY SOURCE LICENSE (SCSL)

The Sun Community Source License (SCSL) was created by Sun in late 1998 in an attempt to combine the best of proprietary and open-source development. When the SCSL was written, many people at Sun were familiar with open source but were worried that releasing technologies such as Java under an open-source license would allow business competitors to hijack the technology by extending and embracing it—destroying any possibility of the goal to "write once, run anywhere." Therefore, two major goals of the SCSL were that propriety modifications and extensions (including performance improvements) be allowed, but also that compatibility among deployed versions of the software be required and enforced through testing.

---

6. http://www.microsoft.com/resources/sharedsource/default.mspx

The SCSL defines two types of use: *Research Use* and *Commercial Use*. Research Use means that the source code is to be used only for research, development, educational, or personal use. Commercial Use is when an executable based on the source code is used or distributed for any direct or indirect commercial or strategic gain or advantage. (The original version of the SCSL also included a third type of use, *Internal Deployment Use*, which fell between Research and Commercial Use. In the most recent version of the SCSL, Internal Deployment has been merged with Commercial Use.)

Research Use basically allows you to do anything to the source code except give it to someone who has not also signed the SCSL. The only requirement is that any bug fixes be provided back to Sun.

Commercial Use adds a requirement that any code that is distributed must pass a compatibility test as provided in the appropriate Technology Compatibility Kit (TCK). Commercial Use also requires that an organization must sign separate Commercial Use and trademark licenses. Because those licenses may include royalty payments, the SCSL does not meet the definition of an open-source license. The requirement that any distributed code must maintain compatibility has also caused some open-source leaders to reject the SCSL because they see this as limiting what developers can do with the source code. Of course, Sun never claimed that the SCSL was an open-source license—hence, the term *community source*.

The SCSL grants the right to use any IP associated with the original source code and requires that a developer who contributes source code must also grant rights to any IP that it requires to other developers who wish to use that code.

The SCSL was originally developed as a license for Jini, but was then modified to allow it to be used for providing developers access to Java. Because the needs of Java and Jini were different, the resulting common license became more complex. For example, to use the Java TCK requires signing a separate support agreement with Sun.

The requirements of making the SCSL meet the needs for both Java and Jini, added to the sheer number of issues that the license must cover, resulted in a long and complicated license. Many developers and companies have found this confusing, causing some to refuse to sign the license. A revised version of the SCSL, made available in October 2000, while still complex, is somewhat clearer.

Work on Java by many companies as part of the Java Community Process (JCP) uses the SCSL as the standard license for all reference implementations and TCKs developed. Although initially Sun was the original contributor for all the Java source code released, now other companies that lead development efforts for new Java APIs are the original contributors for those technologies—they are the ones licensing the new technology and specifying any possible royalties. As Java moves forward, Sun is becoming an equal player with no special privileges.

The SCSL is intended for projects that are trying to develop an infrastructure technology, where compatibility and interoperability are crucial and where having a strong committed party guiding the development of the technology is seen as a positive factor. Organizations that sign the SCSL are in a second-class role compared to that of the original contributor, and that may limit the type and number of contributions they are willing to make to improve the licensed technology.

For example, Jini was released under the SCSL in January 1999 and has been successful in creating a large community of developers using and enhancing Jini. As of June 2004, there were over 200,000 developers who had downloaded the source code. Many of the companies working with Jini are very happy to let Sun take the lead on developing the core Jini technology while they devote their efforts to Jini-based products. However, they have also been reluctant to contribute enhancements they have made that would be useful to other Jini community members.

For a good overview of the ideas behind the SCSL, please see the paper "Sun Community Source License Principles" by Richard P. Gabriel and William N. Joy.[7] A copy of the most recent version of the SCSL as used for Jini can be found on the Sun website.[8]

OPEN STANDARD/PROPRIETARY CODE

Not a license per se, this model of collaboration is limited to the joint development of a public standard. Individual organizations then develop their own proprietary code to implement the agreed-on standards, which is pretty much business as usual but it may be all that is required to get the job done. Note that the use of *open* here means that the details of the standard are available for anyone to use or implement. It does not mean that the process that created the standard was open to anyone.

An example of this is the public development of the ADA programming language, which was followed by several companies creating proprietary implementations of ADA compilers. Another example is the IEEE 754 floating-point standard, which was openly developed and then implemented in proprietary hardware by various chip manufacturers.

---

7. http://www.sun.com/software/communitysource/principles.html

8. http://www.sun.com/software/jini/licensing/licenses.html

Here the collaboration is the process of reaching agreement on what the standard should be. Once such a standard exists, proprietary efforts can compete to implement it.

SUN INDUSTRY STANDARDS SOURCE LICENSE (SISSL)

The Sun Industry Standards Source License (SISSL) is an open-source license for providing the source code to implement a specified standard, along with the right to use any IP associated with that source code. Developers can use and modify this source code and distribute executables built from it as they wish, but, if they make any modifications that do not comply with the standard, then they must publish the differences and make available a reference implementation under the same terms as the SISSL—forcing anyone attempting to use embrace-and-extend tactics to publicly document their changes. The SISSL is a true open-source license and has been certified as such by the Open Source Initiative.

Larger works may be created under the SISSL, so it is possible to add proprietary code and not be required to publish it.

The SISSL does not include any provisions for developers to voluntarily contribute source code back to the community. It is up to individual developers to choose a license under which they want to offer their modifications, if at all.

Reasons to use the SISSL include developing momentum for a standard and preventing other companies from hijacking the standard with proprietary extensions. If the code is freely available, it is easier for developers to adopt the standard. If they then modify the code to be incompatible with the standard, the SISSL forces them to announce their changes and to publish the modified source code.

Sun introduced the SISSL in February 2000 when it released the source code for a key component of the Network File System (NFS) protocol—the Transport Independent Remote Procedure Call protocol (TI-RPC). Since then, Sun has also used the SISSL for projects such as OpenOffice (actually under a dual license of SISSL and LGPL) and GridEngine.

A copy of the SISSL can be found on the OpenOffice website.[9]

MOZILLA PUBLIC LICENSE (MPL), SUN PUBLIC LICENSE (SPL), AND IBM COMMON PUBLIC LICENSE (CPL)

The Mozilla Public License (MPL) was created by Netscape in early 1998 as it prepared to release the Netscape Communicator browser source code. Netscape

---

9. http://www.openoffice.org/licenses/sissl_license.html

wanted to allow companies to use the source code to create new proprietary larger works, but at the same time they wanted to ensure that modifications to the existing code would be contributed back to them and the rest of the community. No existing open-source license met those two goals, so they were forced to create a new license.

The license they wrote was the Netscape Public License (NPL). Working in a true open-source manner, they posted a beta version of the license for public comment. They got plenty of feedback, and based on that they made a number of changes to the license and created a second license, the Mozilla Public License. The two licenses are identical, except that the NPL includes several clauses granting Netscape additional rights such as ownership of the Netscape brand and logo, the right to use code covered by the NPL in other Netscape products without those products falling under the NPL, the right to relicense code covered by the NPL to third parties under terms different from the NPL, and the right to include proprietary third-party code in the Netscape version of the browser. All of the source code released by Netscape on March 31, 1998, was initially under the NPL, whereas all new browser code created by Netscape was to be developed under the MPL. Moreover, all of the NPL code was scheduled to transition to the MPL within 2 years.

The MPL explicitly grants the right to use any IP associated with the original source code and requires that when developers contribute source code they must also grant rights to any IP that it requires to other developers who wish to use that code.

Larger works may be created using the MPL, so that it is possible to add proprietary code and not be required to publish it. Note that any changes to files in the original source code are considered modifications that must be made available to the community; they are not considered part of a larger work. This means that, although it is possible to add proprietary modules as part of a larger work, the interfaces in the original code to those modules must be made public.

The Sun Public License (SPL) is practically identical to the Mozilla Public License (MPL). It merely changes all references to Mozilla to Sun and includes documentation as part of the source code. It is also a true open-source license. IBM's Common Public License (CPL) is similar but slightly shorter.

The reason to use the MPL is to create a community of developers who can easily share modifications but who might also want to make proprietary additions to go into products they would sell. For example, Sun released the source code for NetBeans (a Java IDE) under SPL, hoping to create an active community of developers working to improve it but allowing those same developers to sell any proprietary modules they develop.

A copy of the latest version of the MPL can be found on the Mozilla website,[10] the SPL is available on the NetBeans website,[11] and the CPL can be found on the IBM website.[12]

GNU GENERAL PUBLIC LICENSE (GPL) AND GNU LESSER GENERAL PUBLIC LICENSE (LGPL)

The license most associated with open source is the GNU General Public License (GPL). It was created by Richard Stallman for use by the Free Software Foundation to distribute the source code developed for the GNU project. An early version of the license was first used for GNU Emacs in 1985 and version 1.0 of the GPL was published in February 1989. The philosophy behind the license is that, although organizations can sell computer software, the source code should be freely available for developers to learn from and to modify.

Many people do not realize that the Free Software Foundation actually encourages people to charge as much as they wish or can to redistribute free software.[13] When Stallman speaks of *free software*, he is referring to freedom, not price. That is, this is *free* as in *free speech*, not *free beer*—a user is free to run the program, change the program, and redistribute the program with or without changes. The only stipulation on pricing that the GPL makes is that, when a copy of the source code is not distributed with the binaries, anyone who requests the source code can be charged only for the actual cost of making a copy. So it is possible to create or modify a piece of software licensed under the GPL and "sell" it for thousands of dollars, as long as the people who buy it are also given the source code on request. Of course, once they have the source code they in turn can redistribute it to anyone they choose, for whatever price they choose.

The GPL does not allow larger works to be created from the open-source code base. The source code for any modifications or extensions must also be released under the GPL. This is the famous "viral" nature of the GPL. Developers who contribute code to a GPL project are assured that they will always be able to see the source code to any future extensions; no one will be able to take their code and use it in a proprietary product.

---

10. http://www.mozilla.org/MPL

11. http://www.netbeans.org/about/legal/spl.html

12. http://www.ibm.com/developerworks/oss/CPLv1.0.html

13. http://www.gnu.org/philosophy/selling.html

Some people worry that if they were to include a GPLed program on a CD, that any other programs on the CD would become "infected" and they would need to make the source code for those other programs publicly available. This is not the case: The GPL explicitly states that bundling GPLed code with other programs has no effect on the other programs. It is only when source code released under the GPL is incorporated with other source code, compiled, and distributed that the other source code becomes subject to the GPL. All three steps are required for the GPL to take effect.

If you use GPLed code in another program, but do not distribute that program, then there is no requirement for you to make your source code available. It is the act of distributing the binary executables that triggers the requirement to publish the source code. Individuals are welcome to modify GPLed code for their own use. When the GPL was written, this made sense because only the developer could use the resulting program if it was not distributed. With the growing number of programs that are used to support websites, this is no longer the case: Installing the program on a website can make it available to millions without actually distributing it. This is an area where the GPL may be modified in the future.

The GPL ties access to the source code with the right to use any IP in the source code by insisting that any patent associated with contributed code "must be licensed for everyone's free use or not licensed at all." If a company makes a contribution to a GPL project, it must allow any IP it owns that is in the donated code to be freely used by the members of the project. The GPL states that if a patent license does not permit royalty-free redistribution of the program by all those who receive copies of it, then no one can distribute it. This is "to avoid the danger that redistributors of a free program will individually obtain patent licenses, in effect making the program proprietary."

The Free Software Foundation has a second license, the GNU Lesser General Public License (LGPL), which is used for software libraries. Any modifications made to the source code for the library must be made available as with the GPL, but the source code for any program that is only linked with the library does not need to be made available. Thus, a proprietary program can use LGPLed libraries.

The reason to use the GPL or LGPL is to make sure that any modifications to the original source code remain available and cannot be modified and then used privately in proprietary programs. HP licensed its e-speak technology using both types of license. The common core portions of e-speak were under GPL, so any changes must be shared with all; the libraries were under LGPL, so people could use them freely with proprietary code they wrote to create new e-services. Thus, HP assured that the basic technology was shared, but also encouraged developers to write code for new services.

Some people and companies have complained that the GPL deprives them of their rights by forcing them to publish any changes they make to code that has been released under the GPL. This is a bogus argument based on major misconceptions about the ideas in the GPL. Instead of depriving people of rights, the GPL grants additional rights to those who choose to accept its conditions. Typically the source code for a proprietary product cannot be viewed, let alone modified or redistributed. The copyright on publicly available source code permits only reading—that is, all other rights are reserved to the copyright holder. The GPL offers developers a "carrot": If they agree to make available their changes to the licensed software, they are then (and only then) permitted to modify and redistribute the code. No one is forced to accept the license, and anyone who accepts it is granted additional rights in exchange for sharing alike. Those who distort this by complaining about the GPL's limiting them are usually those most protective of their own proprietary work, which they would never even consider sharing.

Copies of the various GNU licenses can be found on the Free Software Foundation website.[14] The FSF also maintains a FAQ page[15] that answers many questions about the use of the GPL and LGPL.

ARTISTIC LICENSE

The Artistic License was created by Larry Wall in 1991 for Perl. An earlier version of Perl was released under the GPL, but Wall felt that the terms were too restrictive and wrote the Artistic License so that Perl could be used in commercial packages. The source code for Perl is currently available under either the GPL or the Artistic License.

The Artistic License is quite different from the other open-source licenses in the number and scope of the alternatives it offers. Most licenses have very specific intents, for example to encourage or require people who make changes to the source to make those changes available to the original copyright holder and thereby to everyone. The Artistic License basically allows you to do anything you want as long as either you publish your changes to the source code along with a description of them or you rename your executables and document the differences—thus giving the original author artistic control over it.

A copy of the Artistic License can be found on the Perl website.[16]

---

14. http://www.gnu.org/copyleft/gpl.html (GPL) and http://www.gnu.org/copyleft/lesser.html (LGPL).

15. http://www.gnu.org/copyleft/gpl-faq.html

16. http://www.perl.com/pub/a/language/misc/Artistic.html

APACHE, BERKELEY SOFTWARE DISTRIBUTION (BSD), AND MIT LICENSES

A number of open-source licenses are variations on the license used by the original Berkeley Software Distribution (BSD) of Unix in June 1989, which is based on simple copyright. Essentially, every file has a copyright notice listing the original author and a requirement that any versions of the source code that are distributed include the original copyright notice. There is also a no-endorsement clause saying that the names of the originators and contributors cannot be used to endorse products derived from the source code. Finally, there is the usual disclaimer of any warranty.

The original BSD license also included an advertising clause stating that any advertisements for derived products must include a statement saying the product was based on work done by the original contributor. This clause was removed from the BSD license in 1999, but still appears in licenses that were derived from the original BSD license.

Variants of the BSD license, such as the one used by the Apache Software Foundation, add a clause saying that any derived products cannot use certain terms in the product name without prior permission. Products derived from the Apache source code cannot have the word *Apache* in their names unless they have permission from the Apache Software Foundation.

The MIT License was written in 1987 for the release of the X Window System source code; it thus predates the BSD license. The two licenses are equivalent except for the BSD's no-endorsement clause. The MIT License is also sometimes called the X License, the MIT/X License, or the X Window System License.

There are essentially no requirements on developers working with source code released under a BSD-style license. They can make any modifications they wish and redistribute the results however they choose. There are no incentives in the license to encourage developers to contribute their modifications back to the community.

The BSD-style license does not include any mention of the right to use the IP in the source code. Just because a company has contributed source code under a BSD-style license does not mean that it has given up its rights to any IP it owns in the donated code. If developers donate code that includes IP they own, then they can require that anyone wishing to use their donation acquire a separate commercial license from them. Most open-source projects would reject such a donation. Likewise, if a company were to claim that some of the project's code infringed on one of its patents, then the response of the open-source project likely would be to remove the offending code and to rewrite it so that it no longer infringed.

Note that in January 2004 the Apache Software Foundation made major changes to the Apache license that included a new requirement regarding patents. In the new 2.0 license, people making a contribution that includes patents they own must agree to grant a no-cost patent license to the project and its users.

The reason to use a BSD-style license is to make the source code as easily available as possible to outside developers, while possibly retaining the right to be credited for the original work. Sun's Project JXTA uses a variant of the Apache version 1.1 license.

A copy of the BSD license can be found on the Open Source Initiative website.[17] A copy of the Apache license can be found at the Apache Software Foundation website.[18] A copy of the X license is included with the latest release of the X Window System.[19]

PUBLIC DOMAIN

Another choice is to use no license or copyright whatsoever and simply put source code into the public domain. From that point on, in theory, people can essentially do anything they like with the code. However, putting something into the public domain can be difficult because most countries of the world consider a work to be copyrighted automatically at the moment it is created—the author need not do anything special, such as registering the work or including a copyright notice in it. The U.S. copyright law was brought into agreement with this automatic copyright policy with the passing of the Berne Convention Implementation Act of 1988.[20]

After the copyright expires the work enters the public domain. With today's long copyright terms, this can be a long wait—in the United States it is currently the author's lifetime plus 70 years. One exception to this is that the federal government cannot hold the copyright to any work it develops itself, so all government works enter the public domain immediately. This can also apply to

---

17. http://www.opensource.org/licenses/bsd-license.html

18. http://www.apache.org/licenses/LICENSE-2.0

19. http://freedesktop.org/~org/X11R6.7.0/doc/LICENSE3.html

20. In the United States the Judicial Improvements Act of 1990 authorized the creation of a national shareware registry, so software copyright owners may donate their software to the public domain by assigning it to the Machine-Readable Collections Reading Room of the Library of Congress. The copy of the public-domain software must contain an explicit disclaimer of copyright protection from the copyright owner [37 Code of Federal Regulations Part 201.26 (1991)].

works created by universities or companies that are funded by the government, depending on the contract terms.

Some folks try to achieve the effect of placing a work in the public domain by including a copyright notice together with a statement saying that people are free to do anything they want with the code. This presents a possible liability issue for the original author, so it is prudent to also include a no-warranty clause, at which point you might as well use the basic BSD license.

A work can be placed in the public domain by making a copyright-only dedication or public domain certification. This is an overt declaration that certifies that the declarer owns all copyrights in the work and is relinquishing all rights under copyright law. Such a dedication should be witnessed and recorded by a third party as evidence of the relinquishment. The Creative Commons offers such a service and dedication language at their website.[21]

You may want to make source code public domain if you had no plans for any further work on it. An example is end-of-life code that you are essentially dumping on the chance that it may be useful to someone, somewhere. Another example is sample code that you provide to help people get started using some technology.

A summary of licenses is provided in Table 5.1.

Dual Licensing

Ideally, any two open-source projects should be able to share their source code with each other. However, if the two projects use incompatible licenses, then this may not be possible. For example, code developed for the Linux operating system, which uses the GPL, cannot be used by the Apache web server project because the GPL specifies additional requirements that are incompatible with the Apache license. To avoid this problem, some open-source projects have chosen to make their source code available under a dual-licensing scheme that gives developers a choice as to which license they will be bound by.

If there are two disjoint developer communities that cannot or will not use the same license, then a dual-licensing scheme to allow both communities to participate can make sense. However, both groups need to benefit. For companies that will not participate under GPL and developers who want to use the code with other GPLed code, only a dual license can bridge the gap. The Mozilla project started with code under a dual license of the Netscape Public License and the

---

21. http://creativecommons.org

Table 5.1 SUMMARY OF LICENSES

	Proprietary	SCSL	SISSL	MPL, SPL, CPL	GPL	LGPL	Artistic License	Apache	BSD, MIT, X	Public Domain
Can be mixed with proprietary software	✔	✔	✔	✔			✔	✔	✔	✔
IP used in contributions must be made available to all developers		✔	1	✔	✔	✔		✔		
Modifications must be published		2,3	4	5	✔	✔	6			
When incorporated into a larger work, license covers all of it					✔					
Includes compatibility requirements		✔	✔				7			
Original developer has special rights	✔	✔								
Can redistribute binaries		✔	✔	✔	✔	✔	✔	✔	✔	✔
Can redistribute source code		8	✔	✔	✔	✔	✔	✔	✔	✔

Notes: 1. Only if the IP is required by a modification that does not comply with the standard.
2. All bug fixes must be published.
3. If a modified or new interface specification (API) is shared with any third party, then the API must be published for all to see.
4. Only changes that do not comply with the standard must be published.
5. Only changes to files containing the original code or community contributions must be published.
6. License includes several alternative conditions that if met do not require modifications to be published.
7. Under some conditions must give nonstandard executables nonstandard names and clearly document the differences in manual pages, together with instructions on where to get the standard version.
8. May be distributed only to those who have signed the SCSL.

Mozilla Public License because Netscape needed to have special access to the code in its proprietary products. Use of the NPL was intended to diminish over time and indeed has done so. Now Mozilla is shifting to a triple license of MPL, GPL, and LGPL in order to work better with other open-source projects that use GPL.

For OpenOffice, Sun has released the source code under a dual license that allows developers to choose to abide by either the LGPL or the rules of the SISSL. This allows companies that will not touch code under the LGPL to still be able to participate, even though the main community are the developers working under the LGPL.

It is important that any code sent back to a dual-licensed project be contributed under the same dual-license structure. Individual developers can take the code, modify it, and redistribute it using only one of the licenses, but if they want to have their changes incorporated into the official source code then they must make them available under the same dual license that the project uses. Otherwise, the project would need to keep track of which contributions were made under which license and it would be impossible to combine them; in effect, the project would fork. In OpenOffice, for example, it is important to avoid having some code that can be used only by LGPL developers and other code only by SISSL developers.

Dual licensing is also used by some companies to allow them to make money from their open-source work. They make the software they develop available under both an open-source license such as the GPL and a commercial license. Open-source developers can choose to use the open-source license, but any companies that wish to incorporate the code in a proprietary product must pay for it under the commercial license. This is the business model used by Trolltech AS for its Qt multiplatform application development framework and by both MySQL AB and Sleepycat Software for their database products.

Supplementing the License—Contributor Agreements

While the license specifies what rights someone has to use the source code, many open-source projects also require that developers wishing to contribute to the project sign an additional form. Developers must state that they have the right to contribute their source code—that is, that they own it and that it does not belong to someone else. If the developer works for a company, the form has the developer state that the company grants the right to use the contributed code to the project. Note that even developers doing open-source work on their own time might still need to get approval from their employers because employee agreements often specify that the company owns anything employees invent.

This is discussed further in the section "Getting Approval as an Individual" in Chapter 7.

The form also usually states that the developer grants to the project the right to freely use any patents and third-party IP used by the contributed code.

Some projects use the form to assign the copyright of the code to the project. Other projects, such as OpenOffice, use a joint copyright assignment so that both the project and the contributor retain full rights to use, modify, and redistribute the copyrighted work.

Developers usually need to sign the form only the first time they contribute code; the form then applies to any subsequent contributions. Note that requiring developers to sign such a form before accepting their contributions goes beyond the scope of the license. Developers are still free to exercise their rights to the code, but, if they want to participate with the specific project code base, they must sign the form. For example, to have a contribution included in the Sun-maintained OpenOffice project requires a joint copyright assignment. So far, several years after the start of the project, developers have been willing to go along with this. If the additional requirements of the contributor agreement form are not acceptable, then a developer may be motivated to join or create a new project, that is, to fork the project.

The actual text of contributor agreements for several open-source projects can be found in Appendix C.

Other project licenses, such as the VTK project license, state that by contributing to the project the outside developers give as a gift to the three copyright holders of VTK their contributed code and intellectual property. This is an implicit contributor agreement.

Licenses for Documentation

An open-source project consists of more than just the source code. There is also associated documentation. Some of this is internal documentation used only by the project's developers that can be covered by the same licensing as the code it describes. Other documentation, however, such as user guides, tutorials, and reference manuals that are intended for widespread distribution, have different licensing needs than the source code, especially if they will be published as books.

The point of using an open-source model for documentation is both to make it freely available to as many people as possible and to make it as good and up-to-date as possible by having many people write and review it. Both the freedom to distribute a document and the freedom to modify it are essential. Note that there are many documents that can be freely downloaded for personal use but that are protected by copyright and cannot be modified except by the original authors.

Documentation is different from source code in many important ways. Although both can be downloaded for online use, people often want the convenience of a printed version of documentation, and a commercially published book is usually of better quality than a copy you print for yourself. There are major costs involved in writing and publishing a book, so potential authors and publishers have concerns about how many people will actually buy the book—as opposed to reading it online or printing their own copy—and also about other publishers reprinting the book and selling it. Any documentation license needs to address these concerns. Note that whereas code is usually developed to solve a problem for its writer ("scratch your own itch"), books are written mainly to earn money for the author and to solve the readers' problems.

There is also the question of the author's reputation. When you read a book, you directly experience the author's words. This is unlike software, where a user never sees the source code, only the effect of running it. Often a book has a single author, and if there are problems because the text has errors or is difficult to read, then the reader will rightly blame the author. Likewise, the reader will give the author credit for clear writing and good information. If anyone can modify the text and distribute a new version, then the author might be blamed for errors someone else introduced, and the author's reputation could suffer. So making sure that any third-party modifications are clearly marked as such may be important to the author.

Documentation licenses need to specify whether commercial redistribution is permitted, what types of modifications are allowed and how they are to be identified, whether translations are allowed, whether the source text must be made available (and, if so, whether it must be in a nonproprietary format), and how to credit the original author and publisher. Like source licenses, documentation licenses usually specify that there is no warranty and that aggregation with other documents doesn't cause the license to apply to them.

Some licenses mention good practices for showing common courtesy to authors, such as contacting the authors well before redistributing any large number of copies, to give them a chance to provide an updated version of the document, and offering them a free copy of any published book or CD-ROM.

OPEN PUBLICATION LICENSE

One commonly used license is the Open Publication License, a cooperative effort of O'Reilly Publishing, New Riders Publishing, the Open Source Initiative, the OpenContent Project, VA Research, and others, written in 1999. The license was designed to be friendly to commercial publishers, such as O'Reilly and New Riders, who have published several books using the license—the full text of many of these books is available on the publisher's website.

The license is fairly short. It allows for commercial redistribution and modifications, provided that any modifications are identified and dated, that the original author and publisher are acknowledged, that the location of the original unmodified document be identified, and that the original authors' names not be used to endorse the new work without permission.

The license has two options that can be specified to prohibit the distribution of substantively modified versions without the explicit permission of the author and to prohibit any publication in book form for commercial purposes unless prior permission has been obtained from the copyright holder.

Note that an earlier, related license, the Open Content License, is often casually referred to as the "OPL." So if you see a reference to the OPL you will need to check to see which license it really indicates.

A copy of the Open Publication License can be found on the OpenContent website.[22]

GNU FREE DOCUMENTATION LICENSE (FDL)

The GNU Free Documentation License (FDL) is similar to the Open Publication License (with neither option specified), but it specifies everything in much greater detail. The FDL was written in early 2000. It is used by many open-source projects where the source code uses the GPL, such as the GNOME project. A number of books using the FDL have been published commercially.

The FDL distinguishes between the main technical content of a document and *secondary sections* that focus on the publisher or author, such as a preface or acknowledgments. These secondary sections can be declared invariant and required to be included in any derived works. Each author can also specify material that must be included on the front or back covers of any derived works.

People making modifications must add a history section to document their changes. A machine-readable copy of the document, in an accessible (that is, nonproprietary) format, must be made freely available.

The FDL does not include any warranty or liability disclaimers.

---

22. http://opencontent.org/openpub

A copy of the GNU FDL can be found on the Free Software Foundation website.[23]

PUBLIC DOCUMENTATION LICENSE (PDL)

The Sun Public Documentation License (PDL) is a revision of the Mozilla Public License modified to apply to documentation. It was first used in August 2002 as the license for OpenOffice documentation. It was designed to facilitate revisions to existing documents, requiring that all modifications be documented, but not going into the detail that the FDL requires. It also makes it possible to take pieces from one document and use them in another, provided that reasonable attribution is provided.

A copy of the PDL can be found on the OpenOffice website.[24]

FREEBSD DOCUMENTATION LICENSE

The FreeBSD Documentation License is just like the BSD license: It allows people to do anything they want with the licensed material as long as they retain the original copyright and disclaimers.

A copy of the FreeBSD Documentation License can be found on the FreeBSD website.[25]

CREATIVE COMMONS

The Creative Commons[26] is an organization "devoted to expanding the range of creative work available for others to build upon and share." It provides a set of licenses aimed primarily at artists, musicians, photographers, and writers that permits a variety of rights to consumers of the work, such as the right to create, distribute, and perform derivative works. These licenses can be used for documentation and, perhaps with some modifications made in conjunction with the Creative Commons, for software source code.

---

23. http://www.gnu.org/licenses/fdl.html

24. http://www.openoffice.org/licenses/PDL.html

25. http://www.freebsd.org/copyright/freebsd-doc-license.html

26. http://creativecommons.org

The Creative Commons in many ways exemplifies the principles and core values of the open-source community. Its website is a good place to visit to get a feel for how an even balance between the rights of the author and the rights of others can optimize opportunities for innovation.

Licenses

Open source is more than just a license and source code in a public place. The success of an open-source project is influenced mainly by how day-to-day matters are handled, not by the choice of license. Open source requires community, culture, shared vision, and a commitment to continuous design. That a project like Apache can succeed based on a minimal BSD-style license that does not even mention collaboration is proof that we need to look beyond the license. But the choice of a license can help set the tone for the project and define its legal boundaries. The license you choose also can determine how code from different contributors can be combined and which are the natural projects for you to collaborate with.

None of the advice in this chapter should be taken as legal advice. For the definitive meanings of the licenses described here or for help in drafting your own, please engage a lawyer.

CHAPTER 6

How To Do Open-Source Development

THERE IS NO ONE CORRECT WAY TO RUN AN OPEN-SOURCE PROJECT. Successful open-source projects can be quite different from each other. Some, such as Apache, are very democratic and volunteers are welcome to participate in all activities. Others, such as MySQL, where almost all of the developers work for one company, primarily do their development internally and then release the results; users and developers engage with each other to report bugs, request new features, and generally discuss the software, but development happens less visibly. There are even some projects that do not have a community at all, but consist of just a web page where new versions are made available for people to download, and perhaps an email address where comments can be sent.

The more a project encourages conversations and interactions among all of its community members, the more benefits it will get from using open-source. The key point about open source is that the development process must really be open: All the developers, both internal and external, need to have the same access to the source code and be able to fully participate in discussions and decisions about its design. If you currently have a geographically dispersed workgroup, then you are already probably aware of many of the issues involved. More traditional, collocated workgroups will probably need to change the way they currently work.

In this chapter we look at the major activities needed to do an open-source project and also discuss the process of creating a new release. As we do so, note the new jobs that need to be done. To have a successful open-source project requires that there be people to do those jobs, so you will need additional resources. We also discuss participating in an existing open-source project and using an open-source-like process, corporate source, within your company.

One other important point to keep in mind as you read on is that although most of the focus in this section is on developers, users are also a big part of the process. It is important to keep users involved in the process and not treat them as second-class citizens.

The Infrastructure Needed for an Open-Source Project

Every open-source project provides a public code archive to access the source code, documentation on both how to use and how to modify the code, mailing lists and newsgroups to discuss issues, a database to record bugs, and a website to provide access to the preceding facilities. These core features are the skeleton on which a healthy open-source project is built.

PUBLIC CODE ARCHIVE

A prime requirement for an open-source project is that the source code be publicly available.

- Any developer, whether inside or outside the company, should be able to get the latest version of the code anytime.

- A developer who is in charge of maintaining a module—the *module owner*—should be able to make changes directly to the source code.

- Contributions and bug fixes from developers who have not yet been granted write-access to the source code need to be integrated into the source code archive in a timely manner. This can be a major task and will most likely be done by the various module owners and other core developers.

- Builds of the source code must be done frequently (daily where possible) and made available for download by developers and users. Usually a less recent build that was fairly stable is also kept available for download. Users should always be able to download a working version of the code.

This is very different from the usual proprietary development model where the internal developers have their own private copy of the official source code that they periodically release to external developers. With everyone sharing the same source code archive, when any developer fixes a bug or makes a change, it is immediately available to all of the other developers; internal developers do not get special access. You do not want to discourage potential contributors by having them spend time tracking down a bug and fixing it, only to find that someone else has already done so.

Most open-source projects use CVS (Concurrent Versioning System) to maintain the repository of shared code. CVS provides a way for multiple developers to edit the source code without stepping on each other's changes. It also supports defining branches to create multiple versions of the code and makes it possible to roll back to an earlier version. CVS is itself an open-source project and is available for free.[1]

Whatever source control management (SCM) system your project uses, it is important that it be freely available to your project's developers. Someone working part-time on your project will not be willing to spend lots of money to purchase a proprietary SCM. Your current development team members may believe that whatever proprietary SCM your company uses is superior to CVS and that they will have to give up useful features if they are forced to switch. They need to understand that it is important that everyone uses the same SCM system and that the features they lose by using CVS will be made up in other ways by working with outside developers. It is hoped that the missing features will eventually be added either to CVS or to its replacement, Subversion. The Subversion project[2] is working to build a version control system that will be a compelling replacement for CVS in the open-source community.

Bonsai[3] is a tool used by the Mozilla project that lets developers perform queries on the contents of a CVS archive to determine recent changes and who was responsible for changing a particular line of code.

One job that must be assigned to a team member is to set up and maintain the CVS code server. A second job is to do the daily build and make sure it works—and if it doesn't, to find out why and to communicate the problem to the relevant developers. A third job, already mentioned, is to integrate bug fixes and contributions into the source code archive.

PROJECT DOCUMENTATION

In addition to the normal end-user documentation required for any software product, an open-source project needs to have good internal documentation for developers. You want to make it as easy as possible for new developers to learn their way around the source code. The easier it is to learn enough to get started, the more developers you'll attract. Conversely, if the internal documentation is poor or nonexistent, many potential developers will become frustrated and give up.

---

1. ftp://ftp.gnu.org/gnu/non-gnu/cvs or http://www.cvshome.org/downloads.html

2. http://subversion.tigris.org

3. http://mozilla.org/bonsai.html

Those developers who are working on the project as part of their normal day job will be prepared to devote whatever time is needed to come up to speed on how the code is organized and how it works. For them, poor documentation is just business as usual, but for people with only a few hours of free time in their off-hours who just want to fix an annoying bug or make a minor enhancement, the quality of the documentation can make the difference between success and failure. Initially new developers need to be able to locate the relevant locations in the source code and learn enough about how that code works to be able to modify it. If they are successful, then they are likely to do more work on the code. One web-based tool that can help developers search the source code is lxr, the Linux Cross-Reference tool.[4]

This means that all developers who contribute to the source code need to be encouraged to document their code. Someone also needs to write design documents and keep them up-to-date—especially needed is a high-level description of the software architecture. This could be an additional job for any technical writers that are available on your project. Mailing-list archives are also a good place for new (and old) developers to learn about various design decisions.

Another important document is a *project road map* that describes the current development plans for the overall project and the individual modules. The road map reflects what the core developers and module owners plan to work on based on discussions on the community mailing lists. The road map allows developers and users to get a sense of what changes they can expect and when they might happen. They can join in the official work then or, if their particular needs are for other changes, they know that they need to organize additional efforts. Many developers decide what they will work on by consulting the project road map, so it is vital that the road map be kept current. The road map, and the community discussions about what features are part of it, helps to focus your project and give it direction.

You will also want to create wish lists for the overall project and for each individual module. The wish lists are a good place for developers to look when they want to find something interesting to do that will help the project. The process of creating the wish list encourages users to speak up and participate in the design. Involving users as designers is essential if the project is to be really successful.

Your users will also need documentation. It is likely that some of them will be willing to help write it. The public user mailing list is an excellent source of information; organizing information in it into a list of frequently asked questions (FAQ) is a good first step.

---

4. http://lxr.linux.no

If you have professional technical writers working on your project, they will probably be the module owners for the documentation. Just as with code, others can send them suggestions and corrections, but they are the ones who decide what goes into the documentation. Of course, as with a code module, a volunteer who makes a number of good suggestions can earn the right to edit a document directly.

Be sure that the documentation you provide is in a format that people can easily read such as plain text or HTML. Don't require that your users and developers have special software to read the documentation—especially software they need to pay for! This rule also applies to the software needed to create the documentation. A number of open-source projects have discussed standardizing on DocBook/XML as the canonical format for open-source documentation.[5]

BUG DATABASE

Bugs happen. Being able to keep track of outstanding bugs is a must. The bug-tracking tool you choose should be as easy as possible for developers to use; otherwise they may not. Some developers prefer a bug tool that they can use via email so that bug reports are mailed to them and they can reply via email. Other developers prefer a web-based bug database.

Because users are a prime source of bug reports, it should to be easy for them to report bugs. Keep in mind that they have already suffered by discovering bugs—they may have lost their work and undoubtedly lost time—so don't make it painful for them to submit bug reports too. It makes sense to have a special, easy way for users to report bugs, different from the one developers use—it may be necessary for someone in the project to then check whether the bug has already been reported and, if not, to add it the bug database. Also, the more encouragement you can give to users to report bugs well, the more testers you will effectively have.

Another good practice is to have a developer who is responsible for reading the user mailing list and filing bug reports for problems reported there. It may make sense to have a separate mailing list just for bug reports.

The bug database may also be a good place to keep track of suggested enhancements. Any developer should be able to record an idea for a future improvement. Module owners should make sure that good ideas that come up in the mailing list are also recorded. Periodically, the suggestions recorded in the bug database should be used to update the wish lists for the overall project and for the individual modules.

---

5. http://www.oasis-open.org/docbook

An example of a bug-tracking system used by various open-source projects is Bugzilla.[6] It was originally created for the Mozilla project and the source code for it is freely available. The NetBeans open-source project is currently using Issuezilla, which is based on Bugzilla. Another open-source bug system being developed is Scarab.[7]

The work to maintain the bug database is another infrastructure job.

OPEN MAILING LISTS OR NEWSGROUPS

It is important that all the discussion about an open-source project be done in the open. All the users and developers should be using a public mailing list or newsgroup for their discussions. These discussions include announcements, bug reporting, problems and how to solve them, design issues, and proposals for future work. Your internal developers should also be participating there and not just using internal mailing lists. *Note:* For brevity's sake, in the following discussion, when we talk about using a public mailing list we also include using a public newsgroup or a web-based discussion forum.

Let Everyone Know What is Happening

It is vital that community members be involved in discussions with your internal developers. If it appears that your internal developers are doing their work in closed internal meetings and exchanges of private email, then outside developers will feel like they are being treated as second-class citizens and will not participate as much as they might. This is not to say that your internal developers must communicate only through public email lists or newsgroups, but when you have a meeting be sure to post notes from it to the list and consider inviting outside developers to attend the meeting, either in person or over the phone. Also, if you post the agenda beforehand, outside developers can express their viewpoints via email and these views can be considered at the meeting. Note that the more design work done via email, the easier it is to preserve it in a mailing list archive; often design decisions are never documented and this can create problems down the road when the assumptions underlying the design change or new people join the project and need to understand why certain decisions were made the way they were.

There are other reasons to let everyone know what is being considered. It is important to alert the community about any plans to make major changes to

6. http://www.mozilla.org/bugs

7. http://scarab.tigris.org

the code. The worst situation is when a module owner makes large changes to a module with no notification whatsoever. If other developers find out about the change because it breaks something they are working on or because when they go to do something with the module they find the code totally different, then they are not going to be happy. They are going to feel that they cannot depend on that module, because to them it has changed in an arbitrary manner. It is slightly better if the module owner announces that the code has been changed; the other developers may be just as bad off, but at least they know why sooner. The best thing to do is to announce in advance which changes are being considered, engage in open discussion with anyone concerned, and then announce what has been changed when the new code is checked in. Outside developers will feel they are part of the process because they really are part of it—plus the quality of the design will likely be improved because the discussions included more viewpoints.

On an Apache project mailing list in July 2000 there was a heated exchange of messages caused by private discussions. Two groups, one from Sun and the other from IBM, had each been discussing a particular major component primarily among themselves instead of using the public email list. When one group announced a new project to redo the component's architecture, the other—which had been developing that component—basically said "Hey, who are you to tell us what to do? That's our code and we'll take care of it ourselves, thank you very much." Lots of flames then flooded the mailing list. This case eventually had a satisfactory resolution, but the upset never needed to happen. It turns out that the group members who were originally developing the component had concluded in their private discussion that it should be redesigned, but that they didn't have the manpower internally to do so. Had they posted their discussion, they would have gotten lots of volunteers and retained their leadership position. Meanwhile, the other group of developers had privately discussed their problems with the current design, but didn't make them public until they announced the new project. Had they posted their comments earlier, everyone would have come out for a redesign, and they wouldn't have created a rift with the original development group.[8]

Posting Etiquette

In general, your internal developers have to be more careful about what they post than random, outside developers do. Even though they may think they are speaking as individuals, everyone else will take what they say as your company's

---

8. A short article on the exchange is available at http://www.xml.com/pub/a/2000/07/19/deviant/index.html and reproduced in Appendix D. The actual messages can be seen starting at http://marc.theaimsgroup.com/?l = xml-apache-general&m = 96942807201829&w = 2.

official policy. If an internal developer flames someone, it will not be seen as the action of an individual but rather as the action of "one of those arrogant guys" at your company. However, it is really important that your developers do participate, so you need to encourage them to do so. Some folks will never trust your company, but they may trust Ken, Yarda, and Stefan—employees of your company that the community comes to know as individuals.

As a rule, when sending a reply to a public mailing list or newsgroup remember that it will be read by everyone, taken out of context, and viewed suspiciously by folks trying to determine what your company is up to now. If you have a strong emotional feeling when writing the message, it might be best not to send it right away; instead, wait a day and see how it looks then. Often the first draft will let you get any angry feelings out of your system, and the second draft is the one that you should actually send.

One final point about messages: Don't be defensive. If someone attacks your company's actions, it is much better to wait a bit and see if, as often happens, another outsider will come to your company's defense. This will carry more weight than if the same message came from an employee of your company. Of course, if the original message points out an actual mistake that you have made, the sooner you admit that it is a mistake and explain how you plan to correct it, the better.

Types and Number of Mailing Lists/Newsgroups

Different mailing lists or newsgroups can be used for different purposes. A special moderated list for major announcements that receives only infrequent posts will be subscribed to by many users and developers. An unmoderated list with frequent postings on technical issues will have a smaller audience. In general, it is better to have too few mailing lists than to have too many.

Which would you prefer: to arrive at a party where the first room you see is comfortably filled with people talking animatedly, where the host greets you and starts introductions, and where groups move into nearby rooms when appropriate; or to arrive at a party where some rooms have only one or two people doing and saying nothing while the rest are empty? Following this analogy, you should strive to make your email lists like parties, each with a comfortable number of active conversations and an attentive host. To start this off, you should try to create one email list that is alive with activity, creating new lists only as needed. A host has an important job that must be done well because it helps set the tone for the community. Part of the host's job is to actively discourage flaming in order to make the list a safe place for people to post to.

A small project may need only a single mailing list for all project-related discussions. For a large, active project, each module might have several mailing lists. When the number of messages sent out each day grows too large, the people on the list might call for splitting it into several lists. Before you do so, make sure that it's not just a temporary increase in traffic. A single thread that lots of folks chime in on can easily double the message rate.

You will need a mailing list for users. Free software generally does not have a customer support hotline that users can call when they have a problem. They need a mailing list or newsgroup where they can post their questions. Developers or other users can then post replies to help them out.

In order to encourage people to answer other folks' questions, the Jini team had a policy of waiting 2 days before answering a general question. (Those that could be answered only by the core team, mostly "why was this done?" questions, were answered immediately.) This worked very well and has resulted in a mailing list where community members naturally answer most posted questions, with the core developers answering only the more difficult, technical ones.

It is important to keep an archive of each list. This is useful for new developers or new users so they can see if a particular issue has already been discussed. It's also useful as a group memory. Be sure to make searching the archives easy.

Mailing lists and archives serve another purpose: dispelling suspicions of an insider cabal. The health of any community is likely to become poisoned when its members believe that there is a group of people who are secretly making the important decisions. This suspicion can sap the morale of any organization, and it can happen even if it is well known and expected that decisions take place behind closed doors.

In an open-source project, the developers may feel that their efforts are being exploited when the project does not seem to embrace transparency. One of the best and easiest ways to avoid this potential problem is to have an archived mailing list (or lists) that has a clear influence on decision making.

Spam Concerns

With the continuing increase in the amount of unsolicited and unwanted email messages (spam) that flood the Internet, you want to do everything you can to keep spam from appearing on your project's mailing lists. If only a few spam messages make it through to your mailing lists, it's just a minor inconvenience—but if a large proportion of the messages are spam, then the mailing lists can become useless.

There are two types of spam to worry about in open-source projects: conventional spam which is typically advertising sent in bulk and spam email sent by project members but inappropriate for the list. An example of the second type of spam is a flame war on a topic unrelated to the project. Sometimes this can happen when politics or world events are mentioned.

Each project will have a slightly different definition of which messages are really spam. Is it okay for a company to post a product announcement that relates to the project? What about job offers? What about posting the same message to several of the project's mailing lists? What about continuing to argue after a decision has already been made? What about a humorous political cartoon?

Some open-source projects install spam filters to stop conventional spam from infecting their mailing lists. Others avoid conventional spam by restricting posts only to subscribers. Some allow anyone to post, but if the sender is not on an approved list then the message is first sent to a moderator. If the moderator confirms that it is a valid message, then it is forwarded on to the mailing list and the sender is added to the approved list. Sometimes messages can be delayed due to the need for moderation because it can take hours or even days before the moderator gets around to approving the message. Having several moderators located in different time zones around the globe can help.

For inappropriate messages, a moderator or other community leader can send a private note to the sender suggesting either that the email is not appropriate or that the email should be sent to individuals rather than to the whole list. For companies or individuals advertising related products or talking about possible jobs, a moderator or community leader should determine how appropriate the message is and either notify the sender if it's obviously out of line or bring it up with the community if it is a close call.

Whatever spam policy you decide on, be sure to make it clear to everyone. People need to have confidence that the mailing list software works well. It's generally better that a few spams make it through to the list than that legitimate messages be classified as spam and dropped. What constitutes spam depends on the culture of the community. A savvy community designer will post guidelines on the community website.

PROJECT WEBSITE

In addition to mailing lists, each project needs a website where potential users and developers can find out about the project and where news about the project can be posted. The website should be the portal to all aspects of the project. The site can have user guides, tutorials, archives of the mailing lists, and other documentation. And of course there should be a download page where folks can obtain the latest version of both the source code and ready-to-use binaries. There may also be pointers to web pages for commercial products associated with the project, although the main site should not have a strong commercial feel to it.

When people first hear of your project, the project's website is where they will go to find out about it. The website will help set their expectations about your project: What is the current project status? How can they download executables or source code? Does it seem professional? Are new developers welcomed? Is it a real community where they can fully participate, or is it more like a user group where their participation is limited? Is it an active effort or does it look dead? Why should they get involved? Is there help or tutorials available for beginners? Their experience of your project through the website will dictate whether they want to get involved as either users or developers, or whether they just leave.

For a small project, the website might be just a few pages. For a large project, the site might be quite large, with each module having its own set of pages. Maintaining the website and making sure the content on it is kept current is another infrastructure job that must have a person assigned to it. For large projects, an additional person is needed to be the editor-in-chief.

We say more about the project website in the section on creating a community of developers.

Software Life Cycle

We've looked at some of the infrastructure that supports an open-source project. Now let's look at some of the activities that need to happen as the project progresses.

PLANNING AND DECISION MAKING

All of the planning and decision making for an open-source project should take place either on the project's public mailing lists or at public community meetings. Small groups can, and should, get together in private to work up proposals and suggestions, but as soon as possible these need to be opened for community feedback.

Public discussion generally takes longer to make a decision than a proprietary development group does, but because the diversity of the viewpoints is greater for an open-source effort the resulting decision is likely to be of higher quality. This can translate into a shorter overall development cycle, because subsequent work will probably not need to be discarded because the *real* issues came up after, rather than during, the discussion period.

In an open-source project without explicit discussion cut-offs, the discussion can sometimes go on for a long time with diminishing benefit. In many of these cases, it is relatively clear what the sense of the decision is, but unless the discussion is cut off at the right time, the community will not seem crisp and well run. Therefore, it is crucial that someone be sensitive to when the discussion seems to be winding down. At that point, it is important to post a wrap-up message that summarizes the main issues and the consensus on what should be done. Part of the wrap-up is to list who has volunteered to actually do the work. Often the person who has initiated the discussion is the one to wrap things up, but some developers—especially those used to working in a hierarchical company—will expect someone else to make a decision and tell them what to do, which is not the way open-source works.

One of the most common reasons that a software project fails is because it does not meet the needs of its intended audience. This is much less likely to occur if the actual users of the project can join in the discussions where the project's functionality is being defined. For a really successful open-source project, it is probably the users that started this discussion in the first place. Only after the need has been clearly articulated and possible solutions have been debated can the developers work on a plan to implement a solution. If there are several proposed solutions, then the developers may choose to experiment by implementing trial versions of each, so that the users can try them all out to decide which is the best. Note that this process is called user-centered design or evolutionary design and is too seldom practiced by proprietary projects; the open-source process naturally encourages a user-centered approach.

Design decisions, and the rationale behind them, need to be recorded in the project's design documents. There should be a person assigned to keep them up to date. Scheduling decisions should be recorded in a project road map document. As already mentioned, the road map allows developers and users to get a sense of what changes they can expect and when they might happen. For a developer looking for a way to help, the road map can point them at work that needs to be done. It is very important that the road map be kept current; it is the definitive source of decision information on the project.

Scheduling takes on a very different flavor for an open-source project because many people are volunteers. Internal developers can be assigned to tasks based on your company's priorities, but outside developers choose what they will work on and set their own schedules. We say more later about how to do a release, but two points should be mentioned here. First, for a typical company-run project, the features that will go into the next release are defined, a schedule is made up, and the features are then coded. For an open-source project this process is reversed: new features are implemented, and, when there are a significant number of them, a release date is set. Second, setting a release date will motivate people who are working on almost finished modules to get them done in time for the next release. This process of setting a release date and then including in the release only those modules that are ready by that date is sometimes referred to as the "train model": any modules not ready must wait for the next train (that is, the next release).

Reliance on volunteers is another reason that it is important to assure that the project uses good modular design to enable decentralized development. In his book *Open Source Development with CVS*, Karl Fogel points out that "free projects optimize in favor of a distributed burden, lessening the vulnerability of the module to any one person's schedule (or lapse in judgment for that matter)" (p. 147).

In a hybrid open-source project directed by a company, the scheduling can have some aspects of company-run projects. Remember that in such a project, decisions are still made transparently, but the volunteers may agree to defining a feature set as the primary determiner of when a release will happen, as long as the company developers do that work. In this case, other features may still be added, and perhaps the release will be delayed for important or interesting additional features to be completed.

Deciding what internal developers focus on is a matter of private planning. However, if they are all working on matters peripheral to the main community activity, that can be bad—project leadership requires that they work to help achieve community goals. On the other hand, a company doesn't always need to demonstrate leadership. For example, your company might join an existing open-source project with the sole aim of adding a few features or porting it to another platform. But for an open-source project that your company initiates, ignoring the wishes of the community can be fatal: At best your company will be seen as irrelevant and the project will fork, and at worst the community will cease to participate and the project will be seen as a public failure that only your company cares about. In some cases, a company that starts an open-source project is best off ceding leadership to the community; cases where this makes sense include projects where the company is trying to make inroads in open-source-dominated markets or where the experts in the area are in the community and not in the company.

In the end, it's the people who write the code and who integrate the contributions who have the final say. The phrase "show me the code" often comes up in open-source project discussions.

INTEGRATING CONTRIBUTIONS

In a successful open-source effort, many developers contribute bug fixes and new features. Although everyone is allowed to read the source code archive, only a small group of developers are granted permission to directly modify it. In some projects, such as Linux or Mozilla, each module has one or more owners—the *module owners*—who are the only ones who can edit the source code for that module. Others wanting to make changes must submit their contributions to the official module owner, who may or may not accept them. Other projects, such as Apache, rely on a core group of developers—called *committers*—that jointly oversee the entire project; any one of them can modify code in any of the project's modules, although major changes are often reviewed and voted on by the entire core team. For simplicity, we refer to all the developers who can make changes to the official source code as module owners, but please keep in mind that some projects do not necessarily control access on a module-by-module basis. Also, for smaller projects, the original author may act as the project owner and be the only person with the right to make any changes.

When a developer who does not have write access to the source code submits a bug fix or modification, it is part of the job of the appropriate module owner to review the contribution and integrate it into the code base if it is both well written and in line with the project's goals. Accepting a contribution may involve some work, but it is fairly straightforward. Rejecting a contribution, however, requires some sensitivity.

Some proposed new features may introduce more complications then they are worth or they may be questionable in the first place. Module owners need to ensure the quality of the code they are responsible for and sometimes need to reject a contribution. For the health of the community, however, people making contributions should never be made to feel rejected. They have donated their time to make a contribution, and you want to encourage them to keep working on the project. Requesting that they make some changes to make their work better is one possible way to do this. Another is to reserve an official part of the CVS archive for nonstandard contributions; others can see them and incorporate them in their builds if they want to. Many open-source developers have gone on from receiving constructive rejections of their work to become productive project members. A healthy community helps to educate and develop its members.

Module owners must also be aware of the attitude of the community to their decisions. Module owners are allowed to make decisions only as long as they have the community's respect. Their authority is largely based on merit. If enough other developers disagree with the direction they are taking the project, they will either be replaced or the project will split into two factions—that is, the code will fork. It can become more difficult when a company sponsors an open-source project, because initially all the module owners are company employees. Module owners then have a manager to answer to in addition to the community. Moreover, that manager may or may not be responsive to community feedback. For this reason, it's important for a company starting an open-source project to educate the management chain and to put in place performance goals that reflect the success of the community and the open-source project.

How decisions get made varies among open-source projects

Roles associated with software development include architects, designers, implementors (sometimes called coders), quality assurance people (or testers), and release managers. Some of these roles have to do with managing or executing part of the development process (the implementors, release managers, and quality assurance people), whereas others are thought of as producing or creating important artifacts associated with the software (the architects and designers).

In the conventional view of software development, the requirements, specifications, architecture, and design are formal artifacts produced before implementation, although in even the most traditional development projects there is iterative refinement of them. In open-source projects, if there are similar artifacts, they may be either informal or reflected in the source code itself. Open source uses continuous (re)design, in which the design and even the architecture is fluid based on the use of the software and the desires of its developers. Any descriptions of the architecture and designs typically reside in discussion archives and other peripheral documents as well as in the source code itself. Requirements and specifications are likewise at best informal, captured in archives, source comments, and the source itself.

The majority of open-source projects have fewer than 20 developers working on them and rely on a single person, usually the originator of the code, to act as a "benevolent dictator" making the major decisions. For larger projects, decisions are often delegated to the senior developer in charge of each code module. Other open-source projects use a more democratic method. For example, each Apache Software Foundation project has a group of committers who vote on changes to the software and on who can become committers. Committers can be elected to be Foundation Members.

We say more on governance in the section "Who's in Charge?" later in this chapter when we discuss community issues.

Code reviews

A module owner should do at least an informal review of the code before accepting a contribution or bug fix. But who reviews the module owner's code? Actually, all of the code is continually being looked at by various developers. If there is code that is badly written, inefficient, confusing, or buggy, then someone is likely to complain and maybe even rewrite it. Some projects have a mailing list that is automatically sent a message whenever anyone makes a change to a file so that everyone subscribing to the list can review the changes as they happen. Code review can also take place in discussion about implementation issues on the project mailing lists. Some larger open-source projects, such as Mozilla, have a formal code review process that any new code must go through before it can be checked in.

An open-source project effectively has an ongoing, informal peer review of its code. This is what allows continuous evolution of the code. A proprietary project is much more likely to have important sections of code that only the original author has ever looked at.

DAILY BUILDS

A crucial requirement for an open-source project to be successful is that developers be able to make a small change to the latest source code, compile it, and see the outcome of the change. If they can't do this, they will be much less motivated to continue working on the project. This is why it is important to have working code that does something useful before asking developers to join a new open-source project. However, a problem can arise if someone has checked in code that includes fatal bugs or, even worse, causes the code not to build correctly; then other developers cannot test any of their work.

It is vital that there be someone who is responsible for making sure that the build is not broken. This buildmaster needs to identify the cause of any problems and fix the build as soon as possible, usually by reverting bad files to earlier, good versions. The buildmaster then needs to contact the developers who checked in the bad code and get them to fix it.

The Mozilla project has a special tool called tinderbox[9] that consists of a farm of machines whose sole purpose is to continually check out and build the source tree on various platforms and then display the status of the builds on a continually updated web page. This lets people know when it is safe to check in new changes.

To facilitate testing, it is important that the latest build (executable) be available for download by the testers. You want the smallest delay possible between when a developer checks in a fix for a bug and when the testers can download a new version containing that bug fix. The faster the feedback received the better. In the early days of Linux, Linus Torvalds on occasion made several releases of the Linux kernel in a single day. That's giving users and developers immediate gratification.

It is also very important to have the most recent stable build available for download. This is for your cutting-edge users who want the latest features that have been initially tested but have not yet gone through a full release cycle.

---

9. http://mozilla.org/tinderbox.html

TESTING

In a very real sense, everyone who uses an open-source application is part of the testing effort. The easier you make it for users to report a bug, the more likely they are to do so. However, the most significant difference between user-based testing in an open-source project and traditional alpha/beta testing for proprietary software is that, in addition to reporting a bug, some developers will isolate or track down the cause, and perhaps even submit a fix for the bug.

For some open-source projects, there is no formal testing; all the bugs are reported from actual use. For some other efforts, testers are recruited as part of the release cycle. In some sense, people are volunteering to help test code whenever they download the latest build or the last stable build. The cutting-edge users and developers are the first line of bug finders.

Looking at the quality of Linux, especially in comparison with other PC operating systems, we can see how successful this user testing can be. Another example is that the early users of Mozilla's 1.0 alpha and beta releases filed about 1000 bug reports per month.

Having users do the testing has extra benefits because they test not just that the new functionality has been correctly implemented but also that the functionality meets the users' actual needs. This is combining usability testing with QA.

It's important to thank your testers. Their efforts do not get the same visibility as the developers who contribute code or folks who write documentation. They should be acknowledged somewhere on the project's website and also in a README file that is part of the standard distribution.

For a larger project with more resources, doing some form of automatic regression testing can really help make sure old bugs do not recur. Jikes, for example, has a regression testing framework—which is itself an open-source project, called Jacks. Likewise, the Visualization Toolkit project uses extensive automated testing. If full-time QA people are available to do more formal testing, then so much the better.

RELEASES

Every time someone checks in a change to the source code, that is a new release. This is what open-source projects mean by continuous releases. For active developers this is great: They are guaranteed that they are working on the latest code. They won't waste time fixing a bug that someone else has already fixed. Other people can start using their contributions immediately—and report any bugs they find in those contributions.

But for some users, continuous releases are less desirable. Users want some stability in the programs they rely on. However, the amount of stability desired varies from one user to the next. Some want to be able to use the latest features, whereas others want something really solid and bug-free. It should be easy for a newcomer who wants to learn about your project to locate and download an executable that is known to work and has been well tested. This gives newcomers something to try out that will provide the best initial experience possible.

To satisfy these conflicting needs, many projects do a series of frequent, small incremental releases using code that has been mostly debugged, with infrequent major releases after the remaining bugs have been discovered and fixed. So the more adventurous users become the QA team to flush out the bugs in the minor releases.

When to do a major release is determined by the current state of the code: Have a number of serious bugs been fixed? Have significant new features been added? Has it been a long time since the last release? If the community decides the answer is yes, then the project enters a release cycle aimed at creating a stable version suitable for release.

The release process for an open-source project is very similar to that used for proprietary products. The main difference is that the open-source process is looser. For example, if the code for a new module is fairly stable and does useful things, then it may be included in a release even though the documentation for it is slim or nonexistent.

A release manager often is needed to coordinate the release process. This includes recruiting testers, coordinating the testing process, and even making sure that the testers are properly acknowledged afterward.

The release manager's job also includes helping to decide what goes into the release and what is not yet ready. This generally involves a code freeze, during which new functionality is not being added. Once it has been decided to do a new release, developers who are in the midst of writing new modules will be motivated to finish them quickly so that they can be included in the release. Motivating developers is good, but finishing the implementation of a module is not sufficient; it also must be debugged so that it is stable. Part of the release manager's job is to allow only stable code into the release. Even some bug fixes may not be included if the benefit of fixing the bug is outweighed by the possibility of new bugs that may be introduced by the fix. The release cycle is not the time to make big changes to the code.

In an open-source project (unlike many proprietary projects), ongoing development is likely to continue during the release process. Developers may want to continue to work on new and experimental modules that will not be included in the release. Projects that use a source control system such as CVS can start up a branch for the release activity while normal development continues on the main trunk. There are pros and cons to code freezing versus code branching. When code is branched for a release, developers can continue the work they're doing that's not related to the release; this maximizes ongoing work. But the cost is that any bug fixes made to the release version of the code must be merged into the main source branch, and changes made to the main branch while the release was being done can make such merges difficult. When code is frozen while a release is being done, developers who want to continue to work on new project code can be frustrated when they cannot check in their code and test it promptly. Such frustrations can sometimes lead developers to abandon the project.

When most of the known bugs have been fixed and the release is becoming stable, it is often a good idea to put out a beta release. More people are willing to try out a beta version because it has already undergone substantial testing. This second batch of testers will help catch the remaining bugs.

Finally, when the last major bugs have been fixed, the release is ready to be packaged for distribution and announced to the world. It is important that every release be given a unique release number so that everyone knows which is the newest version and so bugs can be reported against the correct version of the source code. Some projects, such as Linux, have adopted the convention of giving even version numbers to stable releases and odd numbers to untested ones. So in October 2002, the latest stable Linux kernel was version 2.4.19, the development version was 2.5.44, and the beta (prepatch) for the next stable kernel was version 2.4.20-pre11.

Companies such as Red Hat make their living packaging the major Linux releases and selling them to users who value stability, ease of installation, and product support. If your company plans on offering a branded product based on the open-source code, then it may follow a similar model.

SUPPORT

The various open-source licenses clearly state that open-source software comes with no support whatsoever. This is generally discussed as an opportunity for third parties to sell support, and indeed companies such as Red Hat make good money doing so.

But the support story is not so clear-cut. In fact, often the greatest source of support is from the other users and developers working on the project. These are the people who care about the software the most and know it the best. In a successful open-source project, the main mailing list is used by people to ask questions about problems they are having and quickly get answers. Some of the answers may not be the best, but generally with a little persistence people get the information to solve their problems. As long as people realize that they are asking for help, rather than demanding support, then the mailing list can be a major benefit for users of open-source software. But for those users who need someone to solve their problems for them, purchasing or contracting support from a third party is the way to go.

This is another way that user feedback can help improve the software. Developers get to see the problems real users are having and can modify the code accordingly. It's also just a small step from asking how to do something to suggesting something useful that the program could do.

ADDING A NEW MODULE OR SUBPROJECT

Contributing an entirely new module is one of the most exciting ways a developer can move an open-source project forward. This can add totally new capabilities to the software, often taking it in an unforeseen direction. But not every proposed new module will be a winner—some will be useful only to a small group of users, some will never work out, and some will just seem wacky— so it is important for the project to have a thorough but flexible approval process for new modules.

Many open-source projects have an experimental area where anyone can easily set up a new subproject to develop a new module. This provides a sandbox for developers to test new ideas and make them available to the community to try out. Generally the new module is not included in any of the project's official releases, but the developers working on the new module can create an experimental version that does include it and make it available for anyone who wants to download and play with it.

When the community decides that a new module provides important functionality, then it's time to move it out of the experimental area and make it an official part of the project. This can involve lots of effort, because the standards for an experimental module are quite different than for an official one. For an experimental module, all that matters is that it does something useful or neat, but making it "product quality" can require adding user documentation (possibly including online help), internationalization (I18N[10]), localization (L10N), accessibility (A11Y), usability testing, a build script to add it to the project build process, and a test suite; adopting the official project look and feel; and polishing whatever rough edges the module currently has.

---

10. This is a cute abbreviation style programmers and user interface designers have come to use for certain very long words. Here, "I18N" means that the abbreviated word starts with the letter "I," ends with the letter "N," and has 18 letters in between. The particular abbreviations shown here are widely used in the software engineering community, others are G11N (globalization) and D11N (documentation).

That's a lot of work, probably more than the original developer originally put into writing and debugging the module. Bringing the module up to the project's standards requires other developers to help out. That could involve employees from your company—UI team, graphics designers, technical writers, and QA folks—just as if it were a module you had developed.

There's a potential tension between wanting people to innovate by creating new modules and having high standards for the official product quality. You need to be careful not to make too high a barrier that prevents volunteer contributions from becoming part of the official release. One way to go about this is to let the community decide what the standards are for the open-source project, and then your company can choose to do additional work—such as writing more complete user documentation or more formal testing—to create your own branded version. Just be sure to contribute back as much as you can to the open-source effort.

Finally, it's important to periodically go through the list of subprojects and weed out those that are not being used and are no longer being worked on. Having too many abandoned subprojects makes it more difficult for people to find the live ones, and it may make the whole project seem dead. Approving subprojects and weeding out the dead ones are part of the community coordinator's job.

MAKING IT HAPPEN

As you can see, lots of work is needed for an open-source project to be successful. Here is a list of some of the jobs that you must commit resources to:

- Evangelist/community coordinator to encourage and coordinate developers, get publicity for the project, increase community involvement, host mailing lists, and in general just keep the project moving along. (We say more about these activities in the section on creating a community of developers.)

- Module owners to be responsible for the development of the code and to integrate contributions and bug fixes from other developers. They also need to participate on the project mailing lists.

- Infrastructure support for the CVS archive, mailing lists, bug database, and website.

- Website editor to keep the website alive with new content.

- People to document the system architecture and record reasons for design decisions.

- Buildmaster to oversee the build process and fix problems with broken builds.

- Release manager to coordinate release activities.

Going open-source is not a way to get something for nothing. It takes real work to make an open-source project successful. But putting in the required effort can yield a project that grows much more quickly than if you tried do to it all by yourself. For example, a year after Sun started the open-source Tomcat project it had 31 developers with commit access, only 9 of whom were Sun employees.

Building a Community

Okay. You've announced your project. You really want community involvement and participation, not just a user group. You've got a website, open mailing lists, a CVS archive, and a bug database. Your developers are standing by, eager to join in any discussions and ready to accept bug fixes and new features. What do you do next?

You want a healthy community involved with your project. This involvement takes many forms. First, you need users, people to actually use the software you are creating. John Ousterhout, the creator of TCL/TK, has said:

> *If an open source software package has a large enough number of users (where "large enough" seems to be around 5,000–10,000), you can be confident that it is functional, reliable, and fairly well documented. To see why this is true, consider the users. If they are non-expert users, there's no way that 5,000–10,000 of them will use a package unless it has these properties (furthermore, the developer would go crazy dealing with all of their questions and bug reports). On the other hand, if the users are expert and there are that many of them, then if there are problems they will simply fix them, which they can do since the package is open source.*

Having a large number of users makes things real and applies pressure on the developers. If you don't have users, you won't get developers. If you don't have users, then no one really cares about your project anyway and it will not be successful.

The distinction between a user and a developer will depend on your project. For Netscape's Mozilla browser, there's a big difference: Users run the browser; developers write the code that is the browser. For a project that is building a platform, for example, Java, there is less of a distinction: Users write Java programs; developers extend the classes in the official Java packages, most of which are themselves written as Java code. Someone writing a Java class library is somewhere in between.

In addition to just using software, which is of course the whole point of developing it, the users also help in many ways. First, they provide support to other users by discussing how to best use the software in their work, by helping to write product documentation, by answering questions posted to the various mailing lists, and by marketing the project to potential new users. Second, they can contribute any user-level customizations they make to the product, such as templates, macros, or preference settings. Third, they can help shape the future development of the product by suggesting improvements, identifying problem areas, and participating in design discussions. Finally, they help test the product by reporting the bugs they encounter; for most open-source projects, users act as the QA department. In all these ways the users become integral to the development of the software, unlike their role in a typical user group.

Some of your users will have sufficient technical skills to also work on the source code. They may contribute fixes for bugs that bother them. Others may get more involved by contributing code for a minor improvement or participating in design discussions on the mailing lists. Some may join in the ongoing work being done by the core developers, possibly earning the right to commit code to the CVS repository. A few may even become module owners.

There is a tendency in open-source projects to focus on the code, with the result that anyone who is not a developer is often treated as a second-class citizen. This is bad because the expertise and energy of users is a huge resource just waiting to be tapped. It's all too easy to become fixated on the source code, on the further development of the software itself; however, remember the whole point is to create something useful that lots of people will use. Writing a good tutorial can have a bigger payoff in attracting more new users then adding some spiffy new feature. Identifying a subset of your user community that has a common interest and creating a new mailing list for them to share ideas with each other can bring in lots of new members with a similar interest. For example, the OpenOffice project noticed that there were substantial numbers of community members who spoke languages other than English and so they decided to create separate mailing lists for German, French, Spanish, Italian, Dutch, and Portuguese native speakers. These native lists have been great for building community and have helped to attract new members. As of March 2004, there were native-language discussion forums in OpenOffice in over two dozen languages.

Keep in mind that your users and outside developers have diverse backgrounds. Some may be computer novices, whereas others may have more experience than your most senior people. Some will have worked on other open-source projects and have firm ideas about how they are run; for others your project will be their first involvement with open source, and they will have only hazy ideas of how to participate and will need to be educated in how open source really works.

As with all online communities, there is a natural progression from newbie, to regular member, to leader, to knowledgeable elder. The tone of the community you create will determine whether people's involvement will grow or not. If suggestions to the mailing lists are routinely flamed or if code contributions are harshly rejected, people will not want to participate. If the community encourages participation, even when the contribution is not very good, more people will be willing to participate and the level of everyone's participation will generally improve over time. Many open-source projects report that some of the current core developers started out by making somewhat clueless or half-baked contributions, but, by receiving encouragement and constructive feedback from other community members, they improved to the point of becoming key participants.

You can expect that as the community grows the number of people at any given level of participation will be roughly an order of magnitude less than the next lower one. For example, about a year after the Jini project was started over 40,000 people had downloaded the Jini source code, but only around 4000 had subscribed to the Jini-users mailing list. Of those, around 400 people were posting occasional messages, with most of the posts coming from a core group of around 40, of which 4 or so were considered elders.

Who's in charge?

As your project grows and develops, many decisions will need to be made. These will range from those affecting individual developers, such as whether a bug fix they have submitted is accepted or not, to ones affecting every developer and user, such as when to do a major release and what features will go into it. How these decisions are made and who makes them will either strengthen or undermine your project's sense of community.

If people feel that they are involved in the decision-making process and that their viewpoints are heard and respected, then the community will generally accept whatever decision is made. If people feel that a decision is being rammed down their throats, then they will object and, in the worst case, go elsewhere, possibly forking the source code and starting a competing project.

The exact decision-making process varies from one open-source project to the next, but in many it is based on the idea of a meritocracy: Those who have demonstrated their competency through their work on the project are the ones who make the decisions. In many cases, the project lead, often the originator of the code, has the final say. Likewise, module owners make decisions that affect their module. This works only as long as the "benevolent dictator" can maintain the respect of the developer community; otherwise, the community will call for a replacement.

Note that even in a meritocracy there will be lots of politics at play. First, there is the question of who judges whether someone has merit or not. There is no objective test that prospective contributors must pass. Instead, they must somehow prove themselves to the current core group. If their approach to the project is sufficiently different from the core group's then they may never be judged worthy. Second, having a good idea is not enough; it must be presented to the community in a clear manner that meshes with the current vision for the project. Even though a single module owner may make the final decision about whether to incorporate a new feature, being able to muster community support in favor of the feature can strongly influence the outcome. In both cases, there is a tension between the group's ability to maintain a narrow enough focus so as to be able to move forward and being open to innovation.

It should also be noted that a meritocracy based on the ability to write code has the direct effect of disenfranchising users—including users who are qualified developers, but who do not have the time or interest to contribute code to the project. Giving a say only to those who have contributed their time and effort has a certain appeal, especially if you are one of those people, but it has a negative result if the interests of those contributors are different from those of pure users. For example, a programmer's needs for a text editor are quite different from those of a person writing technical articles. So an open-source project developing a new text editor could easily put all its energy into adding features that make it easier to write computer programs rather than into features such as for the needs of footnotes or bibliographies. That's fine if the vision of the project is to create an editor for programmers, but if the original intent is to provide an open-source replacement for proprietary programs such as Microsoft Word then the project will be a failure. Success requires that all the users have a direct say in setting the priorities for the project. Letting everyone vote on which bugs are most important to fix is a small example of this. In any case, developers get the final vote by deciding what they will volunteer their time to work on.

For an open-source project where the majority, if not all, of the senior developers work for a single large company, this decision-making process can run into problems. Many open-source developers are suspicious of the motives of large companies, and they will suspect the senior developers of caring more about their company's needs than about the good of the open-source project. This makes decision making a problem until the outside developers get to know the senior developers as individuals and have reason to trust them. Even then, people will perceive the situation as potentially unfair.

To counter this, a more democratic process may be required. In some open-source projects, the senior developers vote on major decisions. For the Apache Software Foundation's projects, three positive votes and no negative votes are necessary for any decision. Moreover people voting no must give an explanation of why they are vetoing the proposal. A vote is also required to add a new member to the group of voting developers. The Apache HTTP Server Project guidelines and voting rules can be found on the Apache website.[11]

Another solution is to establish a neutral governing board that has final say and to which anyone can appeal a decision. The Jini, JXTA, and NetBeans projects have done this, establishing boards where Sun has only one-third of the total votes and the rest of the board consists of well-respected community members elected by the community. This has gone a long way toward gaining the trust of outside developers by showing that Sun cares about the success of the open-source project and is not trying to pull a fast one.

When choosing your company's representatives to such governing boards, you need to consider each board's purpose. For the Jini project, the board is primarily intended to provide technical oversight and so the initial Sun-appointed representatives included two of the core Jini architects. For the NetBeans project, the board is more of an appeals court and so the Sun representative has been someone knowledgeable about open source, but not directly involved with NetBeans day to day. Such a representative will be more likely to be unbiased if any major controversy happens; it also ensures that the Sun core NetBeans developers can freely advocate their positions without having to stay neutral. If your company is involved with other open-source projects, then the company employees working on those projects might be excellent potential board members for your project.

The Jini project has gone even further toward democracy by putting major decisions to a vote of the entire community. As mentioned earlier, Jini technology is a simple distributed computing model based on the Java programming language. Among other things, it was intended as a model for services—small bits of functionality—to discover each other dynamically and create a network of interoperating program parts. These services could be housed within devices—physically separate computing platforms as far as Jini is concerned. Because such a model is new, the definition of each service is likely to require a maturation period in which an initially immature service is defined and released, with perhaps numerous improvements subsequently being released. Service definitions are specified by Java interfaces (API).

A problem facing the Jini community was how to maintain the consistency and quality of Jini services, where all services must conform to the core Jini

---

11. http://httpd.apache.org/dev/guidelines.html

specifications (it's like TCP/IP) but where newly developed services need room to experiment and innovate. The community has developed a process that is fair, lightweight, and adaptable. It is lightweight because most people don't need to use it—they just write up specifications for their new Jini services and try to get people to use them. Only when they want something ratified or when they want to make a change to the core Jini services do they need to have the larger community vote.

To be fair means giving individuals and small companies a say equal to that of large companies. It also means recognizing that a large company may have many thousands of customers using its Jini-based products, and so it deserves a greater say than a lone individual. To balance these conflicting needs, members are divided into a general house and a commercial house. Both houses must approve any proposed standard. Acting as a sort of appeals court to oversee the process and further ensure fairness is a nine-member Technical Oversight Committee (TOC). The initial draft for this Jini Community Decision Process (JDP) is described in the Jini constitution.[12] The current, more detailed version 1.0 of the JDP was completed in December 2002.[13]

One final point is that none of the open-source licenses tries to describe how the community should be run—if a project forks, one branch could vote on everything, whereas the other could appoint an individual to make all the major decisions. If people do not like the governance structure you choose for your project, they may decide to set up a separate community with a decision-making process that they find more acceptable.

Likewise, the community has no direct say in changing the license—only the copyright owner of the code can do that. However community discussions on the project's mailing list in favor of changes to the licensing can be effective. The Mozilla project is an example; community feedback helped to shape the initial license and has also prompted the adoption of a dual-license structure. To give the community direct say, the copyright could be assigned to a foundation responsible to the community with the foundation's governing board elected by the members of the community. Then the community would have ultimate control over making changes to the license.

BUILDING TRUST

If you are just a private individual starting up a new open-source project, then you might be able to simply announce your project and then sit back and wait

---

12. http://www.jini.org/process/constitution.html

13. http://www.jini.org/jdp

for contributions to start rolling in. For a company, however, especially a large company, there's a suspicion that must be overcome before outside developers will feel comfortable contributing to the project. Basically, you have to earn their trust and prove that you do not have hidden motives. Further, there is a big difference between creating a successful users group and growing a successful open-source community.

If potential developers suspect that you will make money by selling the code that they contribute, then they are apt to be offended, and rightly so. And if they think that they might need to pay you in order to use a product that incorporates their contributions, then don't expect to receive many contributions.

You must clearly communicate what your business model is and that any money you make is for value that you are adding, such as higher-quality or additional proprietary features. If you really are profiting from the outside contributions made to the project, then even if you can explain how they also will benefit, it will be an uphill battle to recruit outside developers.

If developers must pay licensing or royalty fees, they will be less likely to contribute back to the project. If the license itself is too restrictive or seems to favor your company too much, outside participation will suffer. If publicity seems to slight contributions from external developers, then those developers will create negative press and leave.

The more you actually live a true open-source lifestyle, the easier it will be to earn the trust of your outside developers. Any incidents where your developers, or other people in your company, put a business-as-usual spin on things will make it harder for the project to succeed.

For example, Sun's reputation with the open-source community increased with the release of NetBeans under the Sun Public License and even more with the release of StarOffice under the LGPL and the support of Sun for the GNOME project. These overcame some of the bad feelings many developers had toward Sun because of the way Sun has retained control of Java. However, if any future problems arise between Sun and outside developers in the NetBeans or OpenOffice projects, the old suspicions may immediately resurface and need to be addressed.

It is vital that your company's developers participate in the project's mailing lists. This is how the community will come to know who they are and what sort of person each is. Remember that trust is built up between individuals. How your company's developers interact with community members will set the tone for the entire community. Because initially all of the module owners will be internal developers, how they accept and reject outside contributions will either create an atmosphere of real community or convince outsiders that it is an effort only by (or for the benefit of) your company.

You should have qualified outside developers receive check-in privileges as soon as possible. So keep an eye out for any outside developers who are contributing reasonable code; after they have made a few contributions, consider granting them CVS commit access. The sooner some module owners are outside developers, the better, so welcome anyone contributing what could be a new module. These are signals to everyone that it is a true open-source project. For example, a defining moment for the Tomcat project was the 3.1 Release, for which the release manager was from IBM and not from Sun. That let everyone know that Tomcat was no longer a Sun-only project.

Because many open-source developers are suspicious of large companies, it is important to recognize that it takes time to earn their trust and overcome any past mistakes.

Building trust also applies to people in other parts of your own company. When other groups in your company work with you through the open-source process, they will understand that your project is not business as usual and you will probably have a much easier time working with them. You should encourage developers outside your work group to contribute and when they do, consider granting them CVS commit access where appropriate. Note that the process of deciding who qualifies for CVS access should be the same regardless of whether a developer works for your company or outside of it.

GROWING A COMMUNITY OF USERS AND DEVELOPERS

You have a basic choice of sitting back and letting potential users and developers find you or going out and actively trying to recruit new participants. In either case, once people start to contribute to your project, you need to actively encourage them.

If you decide to go out and look for folks, then you need to know what types of people you are looking for. Who is your target audience? Or rather target audiences, because you need to grow both the number of active developers and the number of people using the resulting software.

To attract users, you need something that they can use. If all you have produced are some major pieces that will go into an actual product, then there may not be anything to use yet. This was a major problem with the Mozilla project when it first started. Without a working Mozilla browser, there were no users, and it was much harder to attract developers.

Once you have a working product, you increase your users just as with any other product: You make it better—easier to use with more features, better performance, fewer bugs, and better documentation. And you market it. Because the source code is publicly available, there should be a free version that users can easily download and install.

When you think in terms of starting with a small or minimal working useful piece of software, you encourage users and other developers to refine the requirements and specifications for it. In this way, open source can be very like the agile methodologies that produce many small releases guided by customer or user feedback.

A good user mailing list or newsgroup will also help grow the number of satisfied users, who will then help future novices. It is extremely important early on to help set a good tone on the mailing list. By encouraging group participation, you help to grow a real community. Out of this user community will come your future contributors, documentation writers, evangelists, and customers.

When the project is just starting, having a single communal mailing list is best. Resist the temptation to overdesign by creating many lists before any community has developed. As the volume grows on the mailing list, the community itself will decide when it is time to create additional lists.

In a traditional open-source project, people start out as users and become more involved because they value the product and wish to improve it. Again, your developers need to encourage people to participate in the design of new features and also in their implementation. For minor contributions, this can sometimes be frustrating to experienced developers who know that they could do it faster and better by themselves, but a few kind words now and then encouraging newcomers can really help.

Another source of contributors is other companies. If a company benefits from using an open-source product, then it may be willing to devote resources to that project. Actively seeking other companies to partner with may be a good strategy for growing the pool of contributors. Note that when a company gets involved, it may add many new developers who are focused on one or two modules. It is important that the module owner not be overwhelmed by their participation on the mailing lists and can promptly incorporate their contributed code and bug fixes. It isn't good if they have to wait weeks for their changes to get into the official CVS code archive. As soon as possible, some of their more experienced developers should be granted check-in privileges.

When working with teams from other companies, do not assume that things are going well just because no one is complaining. They might be unhappy but not know who to complain to or be unsure of what to expect because they are not familiar with open source. It is important that your community manager or some senior developer informally contact them to ask how they are doing and if they are encountering any problems.

One other source of developers is universities. Providing assistance—hardware, software, or funding—to a university research program can enlist the aid of large groups of students. For example, to promote use of the Eclipse open platform for tool integration, IBM announced the Eclipse Innovation Grant competition in November 2002 through which it would grant a total of $500,000 in awards to university faculty members and researchers to use the Eclipse open-source code base for teaching or research, or to actively promote the growth of Eclipse user communities. IBM also has an active Eclipse Fellowship Program to fund university-based research in the areas of programming languages, tools, and environments.

Many of these suggestions require your core developers to interact with and mentor people outside of your company. This can be done only by personal contact. By including community work in your open-source developers' performance review criteria, you encourage your developers to work with and mentor people in the larger community and thereby make the project more successful. If they receive the message it's important to work with outside developers, but they are evaluated only on how much code they've written, then it is likely that they will minimize their community participation. Without strong outside leadership to pick up the slack, the community will then stagnate and the project may become an effort done mostly by your company alone.

GIVE FOLKS A GOOD INITIAL EXPERIENCE

It is often difficult for a user to download and install a new piece of software. This can be due to a variety of reasons such as poorly written directions, the number of steps required for a successful install, or the difficulty of correctly configuring the software to the specific computer system. If your project is really compelling to potential users, then they will be highly motivated and willing to overcome whatever obstacles are in their way. For example, the first spreadsheet programs on the early personal computers created an urgency in many people, who needed the functionality of a spreadsheet so much that they were willing to ignore how difficult it was to use them. Of course, if your project is that exciting, then it may be that your business model should be based on commercial sales and not open source.

For most projects, however, the first obstacle people encounter may be enough to stop them from going any further. If they never hear about your project or can't find the project's website, then the project has essentially failed. If it's not clear how to download and install the software, folks will give up and look elsewhere. If they can't figure out how to use the program to do at least something simple or if it crashes on them right away, not only are they apt to drop it then and there, but they'll also let other people know what a loser the program is.

It is really important to make sure that people have a good initial experience when they locate, download, and try out your project's product. Making sure that the initial "out of the box" experience is a good one can be the difference between a successful project and one with no users. Make sure that it is easy for users to locate the correct version of the product to download. There should be a link on the project's home page that will take them directly to the correct download page. It should be crystal clear which download is the most recent stable release and which is the cutting-edge, buggy release that newcomers may not want. If there are known to be major problems with a release, then you should have a list of all of the major bugs or missing features posted somewhere that users can easily find—in fact, they should see the list before they try to download, so they can decide if the release is even worth their time to try out.

Any product installation process should be simple and straightforward. There should be a clearly written tutorial to get people started using the program. After they have had a taste of success with it, they will be more willing to put up with and overcome problems.

Trying to guarantee your users a good initial experience certainly makes sense as a goal for companies making commercial products, but why should an early version of an open-source project be so polished? It's certainly true that lots of open-source advocates are sophisticated computer users and expect early releases from open-source projects to be a bit rough. However, they only have so much time to devote to trying yours, and overcoming each obstacle eats into the time and energy they have available. Too many obstacles and they will give up and do something else. Remember, they don't need your program—they already make do without it and initially are just curious about it.

In some ways, this is a good situation, because it forces you early on to think about how people will actually install and use your program, instead of your waiting until the end of the development cycle to tackle it, if then. Dealing up front with user concerns always makes for a better final product.

Creating a good initial experience also goes for outside developers joining your project. What sort of reception do they get when they make their first bug reports, contribute their first bug fixes, or initially post to the mailing list? Are they welcomed or flamed? Does a more senior developer mentor them or reject their efforts? Even if their contributions are ultimately rejected, it is crucial that they feel that their efforts were appreciated and that they, as people, were not rejected.

An example of how to encourage outside contributors happened early on in the Jini project. One of the first code submissions had major problems. Rather than rejecting it, Ken Arnold (the module owner) basically rewrote it. Ken then talked privately with the original author about the need for the revisions and then announced to the world that the author had made this great contribution to the project—without mentioning that it had been rewritten. This broke the ice, and more outside developers started to contribute.

Other obstacles that developers face include how difficult it is to understand and work with the source code: Is it modular? Is there readable system-level documentation of the program's architecture and data structures? Is the build process straightforward or long and complex? Do they need special tools to compile or work on the code? These are all potential problems that can make developers decide not to devote their free time to working on your project.

Obstacles can hinder your project in other, more subtle ways. During the first few years of the Jini project, lots of energy was taken up addressing problems all newcomers seemed to face when they first tried to run an example Jini service. The problems stemmed from the underlying complexities of how the operating system handled multicasting (or not, in the case of Windows 2000), the network configuration, having the correct security policies set in the Java virtual machine, and other such issues that are outside of Jini's control but that are needed for Jini to function. Until the Jini project included tools to automatically detect these problems and then help users track down solutions to them, the beginner was faced with a major effort before achieving any success with the Jini technology. Some novices make use of the Jini FAQ and mailing list archives to solve their problems, whereas many more post their plight to the main mailing list. Going into its fifth year, the community continues to be incredibly supportive of new user problems, but it does take up the time of more senior members of the Jini community.

A COMMUNITY WEBSITE

People's first, and possibly only, exposure to your project is apt to be through your project's website. People working on your project will use the website as a place to meet, to post their work, and to find out about the current status of the project. The information presented on your website and how it is organized can help your project to be more successful. A good website helps create a sense of community.

At a minimum your website needs to have pages that do the following:

- Describe your project and its goals.

- Provide access for downloading the most recent releases, the latest experimental builds, and the current source code.

- Explain how to get involved.

- List recent news items concerning the project.

- Tell how to sign up for the project mailing lists and how to search the archive of previous messages.

- List the key developers working on the project and how to contact them.

Larger projects will also have web pages for:

- Tutorials and examples of how to use your product.

- User documentation.

- Developer documentation, including an up-to-date project road map.

- Accessing the files in the CVS archive.

- Reporting, searching, and editing bugs in the bug database.

- A list of FAQs about the project.

- Descriptions of each module.

- Pointers to web pages for commercial products associated with the project.

Many of these items will be created by your community members either directly (for example, someone writing an FAQ) or through community activities (for example, an online discussion of what milestones are in the project's road map). Other pages report on what community members are doing. Some projects allow participating developers to create additional web pages, possibly giving them personal directories to store files in where they can upload their own web pages or exchange files with other developers.

As you can see, the pages on the website must cover a large and diverse range of material. This material needs to be organized to meet the different needs of the various parts of the community. So there may be one section of the website dedicated to users and another more focused on developers' needs. The project's home page needs to clearly direct visitors to the web pages appropriate for their interests.

Moreover, the look and feel of the site will probably change as you move from the very public home page to more specialized, remote parts of the website. In a home, there is an intimacy gradient from the public parts of the house to the more private regions visited only by family and close friends. Similarly, a website's outer face should usually be more polished and standardized, while, further in, individual developers may use a variety of designs for the web pages that describe their subprojects.

As the project grows and changes, so too must the website. The community itself should be a major source of suggestions on how the website can be improved. Make sure it is easy for community members to suggest changes to the site and participate in its continual redesign. Some of this is easy to do by just posting on the web pages an email address for suggested changes. That is good mainly for minor corrections or adding pointers to web pages on other websites. For more substantial changes, it is usually better to have a website subproject that volunteers can join.

There is also a constant need to keep the website fresh. New content in the form of articles, status updates, news stories, and usage tips must be added regularly. Many people do not subscribe to the project mailing lists but rely on the project website to keep them up-to-date on things. This point came out quite dramatically when the OpenOffice project conducted a survey, advertised on all of the major OpenOffice community mailing lists and also on the website. When the results were analyzed it became clear that over half the people who responded did not read any of the mailing lists but instead relied solely on the website for news about OpenOffice.

The website is like a newspaper and, if the same old articles are there week after week, people stop visiting. One important project role is that of website editor. Just as a newspaper needs an editor, so does your website. The editor needs to solicit articles from developers, gather news related to the project, highlight work being done, profile key developers, and generally make sure that there is a good reason for anyone interested in your project to regularly visit your website.

A large project, such as OpenOffice, NetBeans, and Jini, will need its own independent website; it will also have the budget to pay for one. Smaller projects can join an existing website that hosts open-source projects, such as SourceForge,[14] Java.net,[15] or the Free Software Foundation's Savannah.[16] If a company has many small projects, it may make sense to gather them together on the same website. For example, Sun has a website for smaller Sun open-source projects called SunSource.net[17] and IBM has a similar site.[18] Appendix A contains URLs for other companies' websites.

---

14. http://sourceforge.net

15. http://www.java.net

16. http://savannah.gnu.org

17. http://sunsource.net

18. http://www-136.ibm.com/developerworks/opensource

MEETINGS

Mailing lists, websites, and other flavors of online communications are good, but to have a real community it is important for community members to actually meet each other in person. Being able to put a face with a name and to really interact with people—hearing their voices, seeing their facial expressions—is what is needed to create a true sense of community. Meeting in person also helps you to see people as individuals and to break down the barriers between companies.

Community meetings help the project to develop its own culture, which reinforces the community by helping to define a group identity and building stronger bonds between members. Each community will have its own flavor based on its shared values, its philosophy, the personalities of major members, and other unique properties. Attending a community meeting gives members a shared experience. It helps to create a larger context by exposing people to aspects of the project that they would otherwise not have seen.

Meetings are excellent places to do the following:

- Discuss and vote on major issues—sometimes it is much easier and quicker to reach consensus when meeting in person.

- Have individuals or subgroups present their work to the larger community.

- Conduct demonstrations of new products or subprojects.

- Connect developers and users.

- Start up a new subproject—people can more easily share their enthusiasm in person than through email.

- Acknowledge people who have contributed to the project.

- Perform informal market research and test out new ideas.

- Generate excitement for the project.

- Create a greater sense of community.

So it is very important that your project schedule regular community meetings. These can be full events in themselves or just a part of some larger event—the NetBeans community has scheduled meetings as part of the JavaOne conference and also at the O'Reilly Open Source Convention. Meetings can involve the entire community or just members of a subproject. If your project has working groups, committees, or a governing board that can be scheduled as part of a larger projectwide meeting, that will make it easier for individuals to justify traveling to participate in them.

Consider using formats other than the typical presentation and panel sessions. One idea is to have a *fishbowl discussion*. For a fishbowl, place five chairs in a circle in the middle of the room with the audience arranged around them. The session starts with four of the chairs occupied—usually with key project members—and one empty. The rule is that conversation can continue as long as at least one of the chairs is unoccupied—as soon as all five are occupied, the conversation must halt until someone gets up and leaves. The people initially in the four chairs start a discussion on some matter of importance to the community. Only the people sitting in the central chairs may speak. Someone in the audience who wants to say something must come up and sit in the empty chair, at which point one of the other people in the circle must leave (usually someone who has already spoken). The resulting discussion often has a more thoughtful tone than in other formats, partly because each person gets only a few chances to speak and so wants to make the most of each opportunity, and partly because the discussion is not dominated by back-and-forth discussions among a few people. At the Jini Community meetings, it has become something of a tradition to end the meeting with a fishbowl discussion about issues facing the community and the future of Jini technology.

Make sure to leave time for informal activities so people can meet up with folks with similar interests. Avoid the urge to schedule every minute. Encourage people to hang out together by having a reception with good food and drink. Have a group outing to some local landmark. Eat meals together. Make sure that your meeting space has places for people to sit together and talk. Sometimes the most valuable discussions happen outside the official sessions.

CORPORATE SOURCE ISSUES

Engaging a community can be more difficult in a corporate-source project than in an open-source project. This has to do with the nature of identity in the two arenas. People working for a company sometimes have a special corporate identity. By this we mean that employees adjust their behavior and attitudes to align themselves better with the corporate culture. For example, an employee might display more loyalty to the company while in the workplace than may be natural for that employee at home or at a ball game. But a commons-based project requires candor and a critical eye from participants in order to realize the benefits of the slowly dawning insights that commons-based approaches encourage. In an open-source setting, identity is a pseudonym because it may not be easy to find out someone's true identity behind the email address or people may not be inclined to look hard for that real identity. But in a company, it's easy to find out who is behind each email address and one's candid comments might figure into performance reviews and other employment decisions. This fear of exhibiting beliefs and behavior that would be good for a corporate source project but which might be considered contrary to the rah-rah culture of the company might inhibit employees and limit the effectiveness of the project.

Moreover, some developers are afraid of exposing their weaknesses—such as poor language skills—to an audience that could include managers who can fire them or withhold projects, raises, and promotions. When the context is a judgmental company project, some potential contributors might fear to expose a weakness that is otherwise not apparent. In an open-source project, in contrast, language skills do help a contributor, but there is generally tolerance for people who are not speaking their native language or who happen to be less skilled at writing than others in the project. Although the day-to-day dealings in open-source and corporate projects can be equally difficult and judgmental, corporate projects additionally brim with employment-related dangers. Whereas open-source projects thrive on candor, bottom-up action, and merit-based advancement, corporations may encourage strict team play, command-and-control, and hierarchy.

Sometimes experts are hesitant to expose their expertise because that might jeopardize their competitive advantage in the company. This hesitancy could boil down to a desire to get credit for contributions—in some cases people are more comfortable with disclosing information when there are audit trails that reveal who is accessing their disclosed information.

Project leaders and other managers advance by taking responsibility for a tough project and then delivering. But to some this can appear hard to do when control is relinquished to others, which is what happens when other people in the company, who do not report to the project leader or manager, are granted the right to check in or have write access to source code. And so project leaders and managers may not accept a corporate source project or may do so only reluctantly and therefore try to limit broad participation, at least unconsciously.

These are all impediments to building a strong community for a corporate source project. For corporate source to be truly effective, there needs to be a corporate culture that respects and celebrates speaking honestly.

THREE PRINCIPLES FOR COMMUNITY BUILDING

We end this section with three basic community design principles from Amy Jo Kim's book *Community Building on the Web* (pp. xv–xvi). We highly recommend this book, which describes the strategies needed to create a thriving online community.

First, design for growth and change. Don't overdesign your project up front. Start off small and focused. Grow in response to the needs of your community members. This echoes the development philosophy of open source: Start with a small but useful working version of the software and permit the community to continuously (re)design it. The poet, William Stafford, in speaking of writing, has provided a good definition of art:

[Art] is a reckless encounter with whatever comes along.

Building a community is an art.

Second, create and maintain feedback loops. You need to listen to your community in order to meet its needs. No one likes to be just a cog in someone else's machine. Doing this is harder than it sounds. Try to find someone to direct the evolution of the community part of your open-source project who is not heavily invested in the technology under development. Such an outsider is likely to care about the community more than the technology and therefore will be able to listen better.

Third, empower your community members over time. As your project "grows and matures, your members can and should play a progressively larger role in building and maintaining" the project. A common failure of the meritocracy is that the old guard hang on too long. Some elders develop a fear that only they know the true path for the software and that permitting someone else—anyone else—to have a definitive say will blow it. You should encourage your leaders to move on earlier rather than later. The following quotation is from an interview with a short-term participant in open source:

There's another [open-source] project whose technology I use and I want to develop further, but the "benevolent dictator" is simply a dictator ... the few developers who stick around are like that too ... who needs that?"[19]

Taken together, these three principles will help you to nurture and guide the excitement and energy of your users and developers to grow a successful project with an engaged community. The results will be much more than you could have done by yourself.

Ending an Open-Source Project

Open-source projects have a natural life cycle. They may start out slowly and then have a long period of growth when many new features are added and bugs fixed.

---

19. Quoted in Sonali Shah, Community-Based Innovation & Product Development: Findings from Open Source Software and Consumer Sporting Goods).

Eventually, they can mature and go into a maintenance phase when people still use the software, but no further major development is done. As your project matures and you achieve your main business goals for it, you may want to reallocate resources to other efforts. Also, a change in your company's situation might force a decrease in its level of involvement. It is natural for the founder of an open-source project to leave in order to move on to other interests. However, this does not necessarily mean just abandoning the project.

If your company decides to reduce or end its involvement in an open-source project, there are certain steps you need to take in order to assure a smooth transition and to avoid creating bad feelings toward your company. This is all very similar to how your company handles the end of life of its products in order not to antagonize its customers. Your company probably has a special process to approve ending a product. It should have a similar approval process for ending or decreasing participation in an open-source project that it has sponsored.

Right from the start of your project, you need to make it a practice to encourage community members to increase their participation. You should recruit active outside developers into the core team, giving them as much responsibility as they will take on. Each module owner should identify another developer who can take over as the new maintainer for the module if need be. For example, each module in Mozilla has an owner and one or more *peers* who can also approve code for check-in into the module; a peer is an obvious choice for replacing the current module owner. Involving outside developers in the running of your project early on is healthy for your project and creates a pool of people that you can turn the project over to should you need to.

As soon as the possibility that the company may need to decrease its level of involvement with the project arises, you need to plan out how to disengage. In your internal discussions, you may need to remind your managers and others that the company must not abruptly end its involvement—they need to understand that it will probably take several months to ramp down and turn the project over to the community.

It is important that you announce your company's intentions to your community as soon as possible. You want them to hear it from you, not through rumors or an article in the press. Remember that what you do here may hurt the company's reputation, making it harder to sponsor or participate in other open-source projects in the future.

If your company is currently paying for your project's website and it plans to stop doing so, then you need to work with your community to find a new home for it. Possibly one of your community members might be able to take over the hosting of it, or you may need to make use of one of the free open-source hosting services, such as SourceForge. You should help migrate over all of the website contents, CVS trees, bug databases, email archives, and other community documents. Be sure that the source code does not disappear when your company stops its support because your company may have a legal obligation to make sure the source code continues to be available for some specified time period. For example, the GPL requires the source code to be available for 3 years after the last release was distributed.

You need to decide the level of future involvement your company wishes to have with the project, if any. This includes whether you want to encourage your developers to continue working on it as part of their jobs or on their own time if they so choose. For example, will you permit your developers to take time to answer questions about the source code that only they may be able to answer?

How your company ends its involvement will leave a lasting impression. By doing things right, your company will be remembered for generously contributing its efforts to make the project a success. If your company just abandons the project, then it will be thought of as a company that doesn't care about open source and that is not a good partner.

Joining an Existing Open-Source Project

So far we have been discussing open-source projects that your company starts and provides the leadership for. If your work can build on an open-source project that already exists, then your needs are apt to be better met by joining that project and not by trying to start a new effort. You would definitely want to join an existing open-source project if your goal is just to port an open-source application to a new computer platform or to add a new feature to an existing open-source application or library.

Joining an already established open-source project is much easier than starting your own project because someone has already set up the infrastructure (website, CVS code archive, mailing lists, and bug database) and a community of developers is already working on it. Thus you can focus your efforts on adding the new functionality you need.

LICENSE ISSUES

Before joining an open-source project you need to check that its licenses are compatible with your business goals. For example, suppose that you are planning to combine the existing open-source code with proprietary code. If the project is using a GPL-style license then you will not be able to do so. However, if it is using any of the other common open-source licenses, including LGPL, then you will be okay.

BECOMING A GOOD COMMUNITY MEMBER

In theory, your involvement can be as limited as merely contributing a few bug fixes or small new features. Generally, your business goals will require you to do a bit more, and you will need to actively participate in the project and establish yourself as a valued community member.

Each open-source project has its own flavor, just as each Internet newsgroup or mailing list does. People are known to the community by their previous posts and contributions. It is very important that, before you start posting to the project mailing lists, you first lurk for a bit. Read over some of the mailing list archives to get a feel for how the project operates: Who is influential, what are the current major issues, and how are issues decided? You should also search the archives to see what has already been discussed about your particular areas of interest.

When you first post to the project to announce how you want to be involved, it is very important that you acknowledge the good work already done and explain how you plan to add value. You want to avoid appearing arrogant. You may also need to alleviate people's fears that your company is somehow trying to rip them off—sometimes just explaining why it is important to your company is enough to do that.

Keep in mind that you need to establish your reputation as an individual working on the open-source project. Other people working on the project don't care so much about your position at your company. What they care about is the quality of your posts and code contributions. The more they respect you, the easier it will be to work with them.

This might be a good place to mention some reasons why you should contribute any modifications you make back to the open-source project. First, it's the right thing to do. The community has made the code available to you, so you should return the favor by giving it any improvements that you make to the code. Second, it will help you build better relations with the community. If you are perceived as a good community member, then you are more apt to be listened to in discussions about the project's future. Finally, if you do not contribute your changes, then with each new release of the software you need to manually add your changes to the latest version of the source code—if the code has changed in ways that are incompatible with your modifications, you may need to do significant work to reincorporate your changes. When you give your changes back to the community, people who make additional changes will do whatever work is necessary to keep your code from breaking. By not contributing your changes, with each release you will need to do that work; you will be paying what is often called the stupidity tax.

THE OPEN-SOURCE DEVELOPMENT PROCESS

The key to open-source development is that it is an open process. This is especially to your benefit when joining an existing open-source project. By looking at the project's website, you should be able to learn everything you need to know about how the project is organized. In particular, you can read the project road map to get an understanding of what development is planned. You can identify the individuals responsible for the modules you will be working on. You can read the mailing list archives to get a sense of the project's history and character.

As you begin to work on the project, you need to make sure that you maintain this openness. Make sure that you use the project's public mailing lists and not a list internal to your company. Involve the community in any major design decisions that you need to make.

Being open in your intentions is quite important in your dealings with the project's module owners. These are the people who have the final say as to whether your proposed contributions are accepted into the official code base. That being the case, it is important that you post a message announcing your intentions what you want to do and how you plan to do it—before doing any major work. This will give the module owner and the other developers a chance to comment on your plans and evaluate how they fit in, or do not fit in, with the community's development plans. It is likely that you will need to make your work more general or extend the functionality to satisfy the rest of the project. It is also likely that the revised plan will be better overall. Note that if all you want to do is implement an API to your own proprietary code, that will not get much, if any, community support.

Some of the discussion may become a bit heated; many developers express themselves quite bluntly. Don't let the flames get to you. Remember that many of the people you are dealing with are volunteers and some may be quite inexperienced. Your replies should be aimed at the community and not at the "idiot" who just flamed you. Refer to the earlier section on "Posting Etiquette" for more on how to handle yourself when posting.

For more details of the day-to-day mechanics of an open-source project, please see the earlier section "How to Do Open-Source Development."

GETTING YOUR CONTRIBUTIONS ACCEPTED

To be effective when doing open-source development, it is very important to create realistic expectations on both sides. We have already talked about making sure that the community, and especially the module owners, have a clear expectation of what you want to contribute to the project. This will greatly increase the chances that your code will be accepted when you finish it. Another factor in your favor is that most people running an open-source project want their application to become popular and be used everywhere, so if your company is interested in modifying it a bit so it will be of interest to more people, you already have a leg up.

It is also important that you have realistic expectations about how the open-source project functions. For example, it may release a major stable version once a year, so if it has just finished a release cycle, then anything you contribute won't be officially released until the next year's major stable version. Likewise, if the project is in the middle of a release cycle, there may not be much community interest in discussing the wonderful new features that you are planning on—you may need to wait until the release is done before people have the energy to discuss major new features.

Another potential problem you face is that the particular module owner you are working with may be very slow in accepting your contributions. This may be because the module owner is busy with other matters or doesn't have much time to devote to the project. It may also be that your team of several developers is writing code much faster than the single module owner can digest it. If this is the case, you need to gain the trust of the module owner so that you can be allowed to check code in directly. It helps if you respect the coding style already used in the module when you write bug fixes, patches, or small changes.

A major role of the module owner is to guarantee the quality of the code base by screening contributed code. Some module owners are happy to share this screening function with developers who have shown that they are competent. Although module owners have the last word on what goes into their module, they are fine about letting delegated individuals check in the code when it is ready, as long as the general design had been discussed on the project's mailing list beforehand.

Sometimes, however a module owner refuses to delegate, and this can create a major problem. Some module owners insist on understanding every line of code in their modules, which is fine for small modules but may be impossible for a very large one. This is especially true for some original project owners who have never been willing to delegate responsibility to the various modules but instead insist on being a bottleneck that all major changes need to go through. If this turns out to be the case and the module/project owner is unwilling to change, you may need to muster community support for sharing responsibility. Otherwise, your only option is to fork the project. That is what happened with Emacs back in 1992: The XEmacs project came about when Lucid Inc., tried to contribute major changes to the display code and Richard Stallman refused to accept them.[20] A decade later, the two projects still remain separate.[21]

A successful example of a company joining an existing open-source project is IBM's work on the Linux operating system. In an interview on Slashdot, the IBM Linux Kernel hackers talked about getting their changes accepted into the Linux code base:

> QUESTION: *Is Linus accepting your changes well? How directly do you submit patches, and what are your experiences on the overall Linux kernel development style?*
>
> ANSWER: *Linus himself is wonderful about accepting patches on technical merit alone. He doesn't "grade" them differently if they come from ibm.com or mit.edu. We submit patches the exact same way that everyone else does: append the patch, mail to Linus and CC linux-kernel. If it's good, it gets in. If it sucks, you get flamed.*
>
> *However, the submission process can be more complicated than first appears. Often, you need to figure out who is maintaining a particular area of code, followed by talking to them to gauge if someone else is already working on the same thing. Once you submit your code to them and the appropriate list (isn't always lkml . . .), you may not get a response. This can be discouraging, but you have to find out why, or just simply resubmit, over and over and over. But, once you have a reputation, it does get easier to get quicker responses.*
>
> *Sometimes it's frustrating when you've put a lot of effort into something that doesn't get accepted, but there's normally a good reason for it. Even work that doesn't get accepted can influence other people's thinking and development in the future. On the flip side you can also just point out problems and other people fix them for you, so in general you win more than you lose;-)* [22]

Open Source within a Company

Everything mentioned so far about running an open-source project or joining an existing one also applies to corporate source, where all of the users and

---

20. http://www.jwz.org/doc/lemacs.html

21. http://www.xemacs.org/About/XEmacsVsGNUemacs.html

22. http://interviews.slashdot.org/interviews/02/06/18/1339201.shtml?tid=136

contributors are employees of your company. What changes when everything is done within a company is that the potential audience is much smaller, and depending on the company's culture, it may be more difficult to communicate and work with other participants.

In the normal world of open source, people working on a project come together because of their common interest in the project and generally do not have other connections between them. Sometimes volunteers might be in competing companies and that might influence their working relationship, but by and large everyone acts as individuals, albeit with their own personal technological biases.

Inside a company, however, there can be substantial barriers to cooperation and a tendency to use the official hierarchy of the company to force both how decisions are made and what developers will work on. This is very much at odds with the idea of creating a community-based project. When you are working within your company, there can be lots of pressure to do things the standard company way. In a company-sponsored open-source project, you can fight against this kind of pressure by pointing out the bad press that would ensue, but this tactic does not apply to internal projects.

This highlights the need to have strong executive sponsorship for corporate source projects. Without it, the time employees spend working on corporate source projects will often be questioned by their managers, and in hard times resources for the project will be the first to be cut. This is a typical problem—the work is good for the company as a whole but is not a priority for any specific department. It can take lots of nurturing to get a company's culture to embrace the cross-company cooperation needed for corporate source to be successful.

To justify a corporate source project, it helps to be able to point to successes within the company due to using the tools developed by the project. The crudest way to do this is just to measure how many times the tools have been downloaded. That gives some measure of interest in the project and can be useful for potential users—it highlights what others have found useful in the past. Another measure is to look at the number of people contributing to the project and the parts of the company they are in.

The normal wisdom is to try to minimize any barriers between an open-source project and a potential user. So we advise not requiring users to register in order to download. However, for their corporate source effort HP does require employees to register in order to download a tool. This, then, provides information on where in the company a tool is being used and enables HP to follow-up to see how it is being used. Part of the follow-up is an email message to the author or authors of the tool. This provides the authors with evidence of the use of their contributions, which can be used during performance reviews; it also provides an incentive for the authors to contribute more by improving the tool or contributing others. Thus, in this case, what would otherwise be a barrier is actually an enabler.

One of the major problems faced by efforts to encourage software reuse is making developers aware of existing code. Likewise, for corporate source, if customer engineers do not know that there's a great tool that a corporate source project has developed, they will never use it. It is vital to make sure that when good tools are developed that this be advertised across the company to all those employees who might benefit from it. This requires communication between parts of the company that traditionally do not interact much. It also calls for communication at the grassroots level rather than through the normal organizational channels. Messages from executive sponsors can help to make the corporate source projects more visible.

At HP Labs, the code repository was handed over to the corporate librarian, who organized it for easier search and retrieval. This constant attention to the contents of the repository for the purpose of making it easier to retrieve made a significant difference in the use and usefulness of the repository.

This is part of a common thread for the use of open source. The source code is produced by developers, who have, in general, the mindset of an engineer. Engineers are good at looking at a complex situation, understanding it, and then either repairing it or designing something that helps make it better. That is, they are good at puzzling things out. For many engineers working on an open-source project, once the code is done, everything is done. Perhaps this attitude comes from the belief that other people are like engineers and that therefore anyone should be able to figure out the rest. For example, engineers are sometimes poor writers because they believe that once the sentences are more or less on the page, the meaning can be puzzled out.

Therefore, we recommend that, for the documentation, the website, building the community, organizing meetings, and anything else that is not engineering the source code, you find people who are good at those things and who value them. The developers will appreciate it—perhaps without knowing why.

How to Do Open-Source Development

Doing open-source requires transparency and openness, and this extends to you, too. If art is a reckless encounter with whatever comes along, so is a successful open-source project. You need to give up some control and be willing to accept the direction the community takes the project because that is likely to be the direction where success lies.

CHAPTER 7

Going with Open Source

HOW AND WHY OPEN SOURCE WORKS was described in the previous chapters. In many cases, the idea of using open source originates with a project leader or mid-level manager in a company. This chapter and the two that follow address such leaders and managers more so than executives. Our aim is to help you decide whether open source is right for your project and describe steps you should take to proceed and missteps to avoid, if you so decide.[1]

Deciding to Do Open Source

After reading the first six chapters of this book, you are in a position to make an intelligent decision about whether open source is appropriate for your project. Here are some of the questions that you need to answer:

DO YOU BUY THE LIFESTYLE?

Are you willing to do your work in the open and collaborate with people outside your company? Will you use public mailing lists instead of internal ones? Are you willing to spend significant amounts of time discussing design and direction with outside community members? Is everyone working on your project willing to work this way? Are your managers (and their managers) willing to change how your project is run? Are you willing to give up total control and let the community make many of the decisions?

---

1. Because our primary experiences with starting open-source projects from within a company come from our efforts at Sun, most of the examples in this chapter are from there.

DOES YOUR BUSINESS MODEL SUPPORT IT?

What are your business goals? Are you trying to make a platform ubiquitous, gain developer mindshare, create a for-sale product, sell support or services, or something else? How does open source help you achieve these goals? How will your business model develop over time? Do you need to provide support for your product? If so, how will you support it?

CAN YOU LEGALLY OPEN SOURCE YOUR CODE?

Does your company own the rights to all of your source code? Does it include any third-party code? Does it use any third-party intellectual property (such as patents or trade secrets)?

IS YOUR PRODUCT OR PROJECT SOMETHING THAT AN OPEN-SOURCE COMMUNITY WILL CARE ABOUT?

Who is your target audience? Why will these people care about your project? What do they get out of it? What licenses are they currently using for related projects? Will your license be compatible with theirs? Will you be competing with an existing open-source project? Is there a working version of your code that people can use right now?

IS YOUR SOURCE CODE OPEN-SOURCE-FRIENDLY?

Large monolithic and poorly documented applications require lots of study before a developer can make even a small change. How easy is it for new people to learn their way around your code base? Is your code modular? Is there sufficient documentation? Are you willing to refactor the code? Are the main developers of the code willing to answer questions?

CAN YOU GET THE RESOURCES?

Doing open source requires some basic infrastructure. Can you provide the people to maintain the CVS archive, project mailing lists and archives, website, and bug database? Can you support a community coordinator, a website editor, and a buildmaster? Do you have a budget to design and host your project's website?

Do you have realistic and measurable goals?

How will you know whether your project is a success? How can you convince your managers and others at your company that you are achieving your goals? For an open-source project, success is more than just when you release and what features were implemented. Success includes the health of the community. What numbers are meaningful for your project goals (for example, market share, number of active outside developers, number of user contributions, or amount of email sent to mailing lists)?

What support do you need from your manager?

Is your management willing to allocate sufficient resources? Will they assess you on the success of the open-source effort? If the open-source community needs more time to make a decision or get a release out, is your management willing to slip schedules, or must you meet your company's internal schedules and deadlines at all costs? How about other managers at your company who run projects that depend on your project?

How to Prepare to Do Open Source at Your Company

If your answers to the previous questions support the use of open source for your project, then what? We now discuss some steps you can take to create a successful open-source project.

Resources at your company to help you

If your company is already participating in open source, then there are probably people in the company able to help you get started with your new open-source project—it might even be part of their job descriptions. Even if your project will be your company's first venture into the realm of open source, there are still apt to be internal company resources you can draw on to help make your project successful.

Possibly your company has established some sort of Open-Source Program Office to help launch and maintain company-sponsored open-source projects. This may include one or more people whose job is to monitor and advise groups in the company in their dealings with the open-source community. They can be very helpful in advising you on what license to use, negotiating with outside providers to host your project's website, training your team, and building the community, for example. They may have an internal company website on company procedures for open-source-related activities. There might also be an internal mailing list to discuss open-source issues.

Your company's legal department may have some people who know about open source, at least from a licensing perspective. We say more about legal issues later when we discuss getting source code ready to be made public and company policies for approving open-source projects.

You should definitely talk with the folks in any other projects within your company that use or develop open source. They are the ones who are in the best position to help you understand what you are getting yourself into.

EDUCATE YOURSELF AND YOUR TEAM ABOUT OPEN SOURCE

The best way to prepare to do open source is to participate in an existing open-source project. You or someone from your team should find an open-source project of interest and join it. Download the project's code and play with it. Follow the mailing lists. Perhaps fix a bug or contribute a small modification. Other members of your team should also participate in open-source projects that interest them.

Doing this for a few weeks will give you and your teammates a good idea of what an open-source project really feels like. You will also gain an appreciation for what it's like to be an outsider. Were you treated courteously in your interactions with the project's module owners and core developers? Were your suggestions and contributions dealt with promptly? Did you feel accepted and encouraged? This should give you plenty to think about when you are running your own open-source project.

Another way to learn about the open-source culture firsthand is to join discussions on websites such as Slashdot.[2] Read the postings to see the range of people who make up the open-source community—from clueless newbies to experienced professionals. Post your own comments on topics you personally care about. Please avoid flaming. If you post with an email address from your company, you might check whether your comments are treated specially. Don't feel that you always need to defend your company—that's best done by people who don't work for your company.

Not all developers are suited for the open way that open-source projects must be run. Getting a taste from participating in someone else's project may aid in identifying whether you, or someone on your team, is not well-suited for open source.

---

2. http://slashdot.org

EDUCATE YOUR MANAGER ABOUT OPEN SOURCE

Developing open-source software is quite different from creating proprietary software. You will need the support of your manager to succeed. Your manager, and probably his or her manager, will also need to understand how open source works along with its advantages and disadvantages.

You need to make sure that your manager does not believe any of the various myths and misconceptions about open source (see "Common Open-Source Myths, Misconceptions, and Questions" in Chapter 3).

Does your manager understand how an open-source development process will change how you do your work? Is it clear how the business model for the project is supported by open source? Most important, does your manager agree that the benefits gained by creating an open-source community around your project is worth more than your company keeping total control?

It is vital to your project that your manager understands the basics of open source, especially after approving your use of it. If your manager has unrealistic expectations, you need to correct them immediately; they are certain to create major problems for you down the road. For example, some managers believe that open source will allow them to cut back on the number of company-employed developers working on the project because community volunteers will take up the programming load. When after a year you ask for more head count, they will feel deceived and you will probably be lucky to keep the resources you already have.

DEVELOP YOUR BUSINESS MODEL

If you haven't already developed the business model for your project, now is the time to do so. Your business model should make it clear what your business goals are and how they fit with the company's goals. It should explain how using an open-source development model helps you achieve your goals. For more information, refer to "Business Reasons for Choosing to Open Source Your Code" in Chapter 4.

DESIGN APPROPRIATE REVIEW CRITERIA

You and your manager will need to establish proper criteria to measure the success of your project. You need to include both the traditional metrics on the code itself and ways to measure the success of the community working on your project. Based on your business model, you need to decide which numbers are meaningful—for example, release dates, feature sets, market share, number of active outside developers, number of user contributions, or amount of email sent to mailing lists.

You and your manager also need to meet with your human resources representative to design appropriate performance review criteria that measure developers on both their contributions designing and writing code and on their contributions to making the open-source community a success by responding to messages on project mailing lists, incorporating contributions and bug fixes from outside developers, and performing other community-related activities.

CHOOSING A LICENSE

When you choose a license for your project, it is best to use one of the well-known, existing licenses rather than trying to create a new one. Even a short, clearly written new license is an additional hurdle that limits outside participation—and most new licenses tend to be neither short nor clear. Legal departments in universities and in other, noncommercial organizations are reluctant even to read a new license for their clientele, so if you want to address the university user and developer communities, writing your own license will probably backfire. For a fuller discussion of the various licenses, refer to Chapter 5; for the full text of each license discussed see Appendix B.

Here are some questions that will help you select an open-source license:

- Does your project currently use any open-source code? If so, then you need to use the same license that the open-source code uses or another license that is compatible with it.

- Will your project need to work with any other existing open-source groups or code? If so, then you need to use a license that is compatible with theirs. For example, working with GNOME or Linux groups will be easier if your project uses the GNU General Public License (GPL) or Lesser General Public License (LGPL), but working with an Apache-related project will be easier if your project uses a Berkeley Software Distribution (BSD)-style license.

- Whom do you see as your potential contributors: companies or individuals? If the answer is companies, then don't use the GPL because many companies are still reluctant to use that style of license; instead consider using the Mozilla Public License (MPL) or BSD so that proprietary products are possible. If the answer is individuals, then GPL may be a good choice. If you want to minimize barriers as much as possible, consider a BSD-style license.

- Does your code define a platform or infrastructure? If so, then a gated-community license or GPL will be better suited to your needs—something similar to the Sun Community Source License (SCSL) if the technology needs a strong central organization to move it forward or GPL if the technology is more mature.

- Are you primarily trying to establish a standard? If so, then you may not need to develop any source code and don't need a license. Instead, you need to establish a standards group. If the standard already exists and you want to promote it, then using a license similar to the Sun Industry Standards Source License (SISSL) may be appropriate.

- Will your company or others want to include your source code in commercial products? Both the MPL and any BSD-style licenses support creating proprietary larger works, LGPL can also be considered.

- Is compatibility critical? If so, then a variation on either the SISSL or the SCSL may be appropriate. Alternatively, the license could not try to control the technology at all but, rather, you could require that any products pass a set of compatibility tests before they can use the trademarked name or logo.

- Are you worried that predators will try to embrace and extend the technology? If so, then using the GPL or SISSL would force them to reveal any extensions they might make. Using something such as the SCSL would not allow them to release an incompatible product, but that may also reduce community involvement.

- Are you or others at your company unwilling to give up control of the technology? SCSL was designed in part to allow Sun to keep enough control of Java to prevent incompatible versions. The effect of the license has been balanced by changes to the Java Community Process (JCP) that now give other companies an equal say in decisions about changes to Java. Be aware that the refusal to let the community take charge may limit your effort. Wanting to keep control is often a sign that you should not consider using open source at all.

- Do you plan to sell software developed by your project? Many companies do sell software developed under an open-source license. For example, Red Hat charges for its version of Linux. Other companies use an open-source code base, create their own proprietary products on top, and charge for those products. Whatever you choose as a business model, remember that with open-source licenses, your base code will be free for anyone to view.

- If you are willing to let anyone use the technology for free, but want to charge for the use of a name or logo, then you can use any license for the technology and have a separate logo license for anyone who is willing to pay to use the logo.

- Is there any IP that you do not want to make publicly available? It is possible to make your source code freely available using open source, but require people to license your patents before they can distribute any software based on the source code. If you want to limit the technology to be used only by the project, then you need to use a license that is explicit about IP such as MPL, SISSL, or SCSL.

- Are there two disjoint communities that you need to work with? If so, then you may need to use a dual license so that each community uses the license best suited to it. However, this will complicate your life, so if at all possible try to use a single license.

You also need to decide on what a developer must agree to in order to contribute source code to your project. Refer to the section "Supplementing the License—Contributor Agreements" in Chapter 5 for more details.

If you are thinking of joining an existing open-source project, then a license has already been selected by the project. You need to consider whether you can achieve your business goals under that license. If you are planning to combine the open-source code with proprietary code, then GPL will not work, but any of the other licenses, including LGPL, will be okay.

GETTING YOUR SOURCE CODE READY TO RELEASE

If you are starting a new open-source project, then you need to have working code in order to attract people to your project. Your code probably was not developed from scratch with the intent of making it available to the public, so you will need to get it ready before you can release it. There are two major aspects of the code to consider: design and legal ownership.

Design Issues

One aspect of proprietary code development is that most of the code is seen only by the developer who originally wrote it. It is not apparent to anyone else if the code has gotten ugly, if a rough prototype intended to be thrown away has instead become the production code, or if changes and patches have been force fit over an antiquated design in order to add new functionality. The prospect of opening up the source code to the scrutiny of outside developers can be quite unsettling.

Before the source code is released, it is important to do a thorough design review of it to avoid embarrassment. We would all like the code to be perfect and polished, but that is never the case and not something that any open-source developer expects. But do check to make sure that the code is not truly awful; if chunks of it are truly awful, they may need to be worked on. Sometimes all that is needed is a comment explaining matters, for example, saying that something is a quick hack to provide functionality needed to test another module or that it handles only the basic case and needs to have special cases added later. If outside developers understand why a design or implementation decision was made, they will not make unreasonable criticisms of the code. However, they will be justifiably harsh if the code is really bad and there are no extenuating circumstances.

Think of the source code as a work in progress, an approximation of what you want that is going to grow and change over time. Some parts will be exquisite jewels, whereas others will be lumps of coal. What is most important is that it is possible for an outside developer to make small changes to the code (for bug fixes or minor improvements) without breaking everything.

Part of the design review, then, is to make sure that the code is open-source-friendly. It is critical that the source code builds or is usable in a working application that people can use right now. If the code is still in development and cannot be used to do anything interesting yet, then it may need more work before it is ready for release. Also, if the code is not already modular, you may need to make it so. Large monolithic applications that require the developer to know all of the code in order to modify a small part are not suited to open-source development.

Another part of the design review is to examine the project documentation. If you do not already have a good architectural overview, clear instructions for installation, and a documented build process, then you need to write those documents. Your user community will also need a good user's manual.

Legal Issues

Before you can release any source code, you need to do *due diligence* on the code to make sure there are no legal problems. You must first be sure that your company legally has the right to release the source code. This means that you must check all of the code to see whether any of it was developed by a third party or whether it makes use of any third-party intellectual property (for example, patents or trade secrets). If any third-party work is found, you need to check the terms of the license that your company has to use it to see whether you can distribute it.

For example, the Sun StarOffice office suite product contains third-party code for printing and spell checking that Sun cannot legally make available, so those modules could not be included when Sun created the OpenOffice open-source project based on StarOffice. Hence, OpenOffice started out with no printing or spell-checking code. The project has since written new code for printing and has incorporated a new spell checker developed by another open-source project.

The StarOffice example illustrates the need to check the source code itself rather than assuming that when your company acquires another company that all the source code in any of its products automatically is fully owned by your company. Code can be third party because it was third party to the company that your company acquired. The only safe way to identify all third-party code is to actually go and examine all the source code.

Searching your code for third-party IP can take a lot of time. Some of the searching can be done with automated tools (for example, using grep on all of the files for the word *copyright*), but much must be done by hand. It is often very useful to bring fresh eyes to this task, so not just the engineers who have been working on the code should conduct the search. Don't forget budget concerns when you request engineers from other projects within your company to review your source code.

It is also important to identify any of your company's IP in the source code that you might not want to make generally available, for example, code for which patents have not yet been filed. Which IP should be shared and which should not is a business decision.

The source code may contain information about internal aspects of your company that you may want to remove, such as your future plans relating to other products or the names of former developers. There are many reasons why developers involved in creating proprietary software may not want their names associated with it when the code is open sourced; for example, they may not be proud of the code they wrote or they may not want to be bothered with questions about it. This means that you may also need to clean out CVS logs or entries in your current bug database.

Finally, it is necessary to scrub the code of any nasty comments or inappropriate language. It can be embarrassing to your company if people find disparaging comments about other companies or individuals. If your code base is not too large, this is tedious but not too time consuming; if you have several million lines of code to scrub, as in StarOffice, this can be a major undertaking.

One other legal issue concerns what to call the open-source application if it needs a different name than your company's branded product. You should have your company's trademark department check on any names you plan on using. It often does not make sense to trademark an open-source product name.

CREATE A RATIONAL DEVELOPMENT PLAN

If your business model involves building a branded product (whether proprietary or not) on top of your open-source project, then you need to be very clear on how the development of the two efforts will be tied together. You need to decide how you will merge changes developed in one effort into the other. Will you periodically take a snapshot of the open-source project and incorporate that into the branded product? Or will you do your sampling only after a major release of the open-source project? Will you incorporate the entire open-source code base or only selected parts of it? What is your process?

Because the open-source project involves volunteer developers from outside of your company, you will not be able to dictate its release cycle; the community will decide on the schedule for doing a release and what features will be in it. If your derived, branded product has a fixed release date, what will you do if the open-source release is delayed? Can you slip your schedule for the branded product?

One good process is to base the branded version on a stable release of the open-source project. Changes made to the branded product then flow back into the open-source code base. This process guarantees that both code bases are as similar as possible and minimizes problems of version skew. It also forces the schedule for the branded product to be tightly coupled with the open-source project release cycle. Figure 7.1 shows this, graphically. In the figure, the lower line is the ongoing open-source development effort and the upper line is the branded development effort. The numbers label the following events:

1. Incorporation of changes from the open-source version into the branded product code base.

2. Start of the open-source release process; the solid line is work on the next stable release; the dotted line is ongoing development (new or experimental) aimed at some future release.

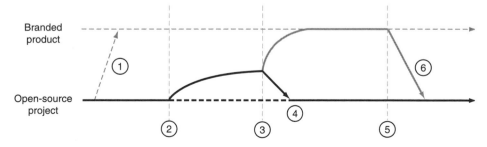

FIGURE 7.1 Branded product built on stable open-source project release.

3. End of the open-source release cycle—a stable version is now available— and start of the branded release process, based on the stable open-source version.

4. Merger of the open-source stable version with the main open-source development branch.

5. End of the branded product release cycle—a stable version of the branded product is now available.

6. Merger of the stable branded product code back into open-source code base. *Note:* Some changes might have been merged back earlier (between points 4 and 6).

A major assumption in this process is that there will be no major differences between the open-source version and the corresponding parts of the branded product. The branded version may include additional functionality, but those parts in common with the open-source version will be a strict subset of the official open-source release. The only exceptions will be temporary improvements in the branded version, such as bug fixes or updated documentation, that will be migrated back to the open-source code base.

An alternative, less desirable development process is to maintain two separate code bases and have the developers of the branded product decide both when to merge in code from the open-source project and when to submit changes back to it. This certainly gives you the most flexibility, but also the most management complexity because the two code bases will evolve independently. Graphically this process is shown in Figure 7.2. The lower line in the figure is the ongoing open-source development effort and the upper line is the branded development effort. The numbers label the following events and processes:

1. Incorporation of changes from the open-source version into the branded product code base.

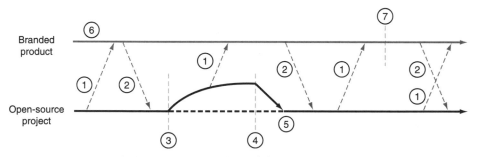

FIGURE 7.2 Branded product independent of the open-source project release cycle.

2. Incorporation of changes from the branded product into the open-source code base.

3. Start of the open-source release process; the solid line is work on the next stable release; the dotted line is ongoing development (new or experimental) aimed at some future release.

4. End of the open-source release cycle—a stable open-source version is now available.

5. Merger of the open-source stable version with the main open-source development branch.

6. Ongoing branded release process.

7. End of branded product release cycle—a stable version of the branded product is now available.

Notice that the development of the open-source version and the branded product happen in parallel; there is no relationship between the release cycles of the two efforts. Code is taken from one effort and incorporated into the other whenever some developer thinks it is appropriate.

The assumption here is that the two versions can have different features. They are now two separate products, sharing only a family resemblance. Over time, their differences will most likely increase unless there is some strong pressure to bring the two versions together.

This style of development makes sense when the branded product includes proprietary features. Sometimes, as with early versions of GhostScript, these features will eventually be contributed to the open-source version. For other projects, such as sendmail, the open-source version is used to increase the quality by incorporating the feedback from many people using sendmail in real situations. In both these cases, the main developers must work extensively with the open-source community.

A third (undesirable) development process that we warn you against is to use the development of the branded product to drive things forward. This is shown in Figure 7.3. Again the lower line in the figure is the ongoing open-source development effort and the upper line is the branded development effort. The numbers label the following events and processes:

1. Ongoing branded release process.

2. End of branded product release cycle—a stable version of the branded product is now available.

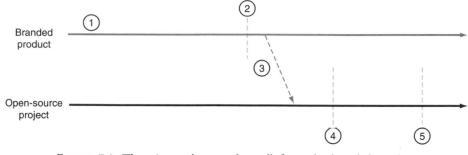

FIGURE 7.3 Throwing code over the wall from the branded product to the open-source project.

3. Incorporation of changes from the branded product into the open-source code base.

4. Start of the open-source release process.

5. End of the open-source release cycle—a stable open-source version is now available.

Here the development of the branded version takes place internally, and when it is done the new code is "thrown over the wall" to the open-source project. Note that improvements to the open-source project are never incorporated back into the branded product. Companies using this model probably have all their internal developers working only on the branded version, leaving the open-source effort solely to outside volunteers. This process treats the open-source project as a second-class effort, and as a result the open-source project will probably fail or at best become more like a user group. This development process is what we expect for proprietary software development. This is also the process that managers in your company may be most comfortable with and the one that they may try to force your project to use. However, using it will mean that you will not get any of the benefits from open source and that you will enjoy the negative publicity from a failing open-source project.

BUDGETING RESOURCES FOR YOUR PROJECT: PEOPLE AND WEBSITE

Chapter 6 describes a number of tasks that you need to do in order to have a successful project. You need to assign people to the following jobs:

- Evangelist/community manager/community coordinator
- Website editor

- Scribe to document the system architecture and record reasons for design decisions

- Module owners

- Developers or system administrators to support the CVS archive, mailing lists, bug database, and website

- Buildmaster

- Release manager

For a new project, all of these will initially need to be done by your company's employees. As your project grows, outside developers may volunteer to take on some of the tasks. If you are joining an existing open-source project, then you may need to handle only the module owners' tasks for the code you contribute.

Your project's website provides the place for your community of developers to live. For more information on what the website needs to do, refer to "A Community Website" in Chapter 6. If you are starting a new open-source project, then you may also need to create a new website. If you join an existing project, there is probably an existing website that you will be able to build on.

CHOOSING THE COMMUNITY MANAGER

The community manager (or evangelist or community coordinator) is the company's voice to the community. This person is the Linus Torvalds of your project. Your project will be associated with this person at least as much as your project is associated with your company. The community manager has to be able to speak on a variety of technical, political, social, and community levels. Therefore, this person must be chosen carefully and must have a rare combination of skills. The following is a list of some of the most important ones:

- Must be able to speak both to experts and to novices with natural style and grace.

- Must be able to speak about vision, strategy, engineering, source code, architecture, design, release management, and testing.

- Must understand what a community is like and how to build and sustain one, and must be able to speak clearly about these issues—or else must have a trusted partner who does.

- Must be fair and be able to act without bias when operating on behalf of the community, especially when the aims of the community don't match the aims of the company.

- Should be a known person in the outside computing world (this is often not possible, but the community manager will become well-known outside the company if all goes well).

Natural community managers share some things you can recognize: project leaders want them on their teams, marketing people ask them to make presentations, and email from them is clear, crisp, and definitive.

Finding this person will not be easy. You may hesitate to assign anyone with these capabilities and qualities to a project role that might not seem to be the most profitable use of such talents. This shows exactly how seriously you should take the decision to go with open source—it must be worth assigning one of your most talented developers to what some would call a babysitting role.

CREATING A WEBSITE

If you even suspect that you might want to create a website for your project, immediately acquire the rights to the appropriate domain name. Do it now.

Your website will need to provide the following services:

- A webserver that supports downloads

- A CVS server for the source code

- A mailing list server with a searchable archive

- A newsgroup feed of the mailing lists

- A bug-tracking system

- Disk space for developers and projects

If you are doing internal open source where everyone involved is a company employee, then you want a website inside your company's firewall. For a gated-community or a true open-source project where people outside your company will participate, then for security reasons you probably want to host your website outside of your company's firewall. You have three choices:

- Pay a company that does web hosting for open-source projects to run your website.

- Use one of the free open-source-project hosting sites.
- Do it yourself, possibly as part of your company's website.

Which one you pick will depend on your budget and project needs.

Before your website can go live you need to have your company's legal and trademark folks take a look at it to check that there are not any legal or trademark problems. You should reserve time with them so they can look over your web pages well in advance of when you make the website accessible to the public.

Contract with a Company that Does Web Hosting of Open-Source Projects

Companies such as CollabNet[3] provide many of the services your open-source project will need. They also charge a significant fee per year to do so.[4] In addition to providing the computers and software to host your website, the services also include a person to check that the community is functioning properly and perhaps another person to be the website editor. If your project has any special needs, you can contract for additional features. For a large project, having CollabNet host the website may make sense. Sun uses CollabNet to host a number of its sponsored open-source projects such as NetBeans and OpenOffice. Note that it can easily take 3–4 weeks to finalize a contract for your project, so don't leave creating your website until the last minute.

For its Collaborative Development Program (CDP), Hewlett-Packard's printing and imaging division contracted with CollabNet to provide web hosting. CDP is a gated community where HP's worldwide employees can collaborate on software development projects along with HP's business partners and customers.

Sun has a special website called SunSource.net[5] for smaller Sun-sponsored open-source projects. This website is also hosted by CollabNet. Because the web infrastructure is shared by a number of projects, the cost is much less than setting up and running many separate project websites. However, because the infrastructure is shared it is harder to add special features for a specific project.

One benefit of using a company such as CollabNet is that its staff includes people with lots of experience with numerous open-source projects. They can

---

3. http://www.collab.net

4. In fall 2003, for a significant community the fee could be several hundred thousand dollars a year.

5. http://sunsource.net

help train your team in how to do open source and how to interact with the open-source community. Another benefit is that they know what tools an open-source project needs and they provide them as part of their basic offering. Be aware, however, that they may not be able to provide support for additional features or to customize your project's pages. Be sure to check out several open-source projects that they host to determine whether they provide the features that you want for your project.

Use a Free Open-Source-Project Hosting Site

Because many open-source projects are composed largely of developers working in their free time with no sponsoring organization, websites have sprung up, such as VA Software Corporation's SourceForge[6] or the Free Software Foundation's Savannah,[7] that provide free hosting of open-source projects. This is great for developers and projects with no budgets, but it means you are limited to whatever basic features the hosting organization provides, which may include banner ads on your web pages. For a small project with limited resources, SourceForge or Savannah may be the only possible alternative.

For a small project that may not be very visible, having it live on a website that lots of open-source developers regularly visit can only improve your chances of potential volunteers stumbling across your project. Be sure to include a complete description of your project when you register it so that anyone searching through the current projects can find yours.

In summer 2004, there were over 83,000 projects hosted on SourceForge and over 2000 on Savannah.

Do It Yourself

Many of the large well-known open-source projects, such as Apache and Mozilla, are self-hosted. Project volunteers maintain and support all the infrastructure for the website, CVS tree, bug database, and mailing lists.

Versions of all the tools needed to host an open-source project are themselves available as open source. So if you choose to, you can do it yourself and set up your own website. You will need either to have use of a company-owned web server outside your corporate firewall or to contract with a company that does web hosting. You then do all the work to set up web pages, mailing lists, CVS trees, and your bug database. The website for Jini.org was at one point run on a workstation owned by the Jini group and collocated at Best.com.

---

6. http://sourceforge.net

7. http://savannah.gnu.org

The IBM subsidiary that originally developed the code that became the Eclipse project originally hosted the Eclipse website alongside the subsidiary's public website.

It is also possible to buy versions of the software used by the open-source-project hosting websites mentioned: VA Software sells SourceForge and CollabNet sells its successor to SourceCast—called CollabNet Enterprise Edition—to companies to set up for their external open-source projects or for internal open-source or gated communities. An open-source version of SourceForge called Gforge[8] is also available.

If you host your project's website on one of your company's web servers, then there are several potential problems you need to watch out for. First, and most important: make sure your open-source project is distinct from the corporate website. In order to create a real community, you need to give your project's web pages a look and feel that is different from those of your company's web pages. Ideally, your project will have its own domain name and not use a URL that includes your company's domain name. Check that your company's policy is flexible enough to let your project have its own flavor.

Next, you need to check your company's policy on the types of materials that can be posted on a company-sponsored website. The needs of an open-source project are quite different from those of a corporate website. Posting third-party content is often avoided on a corporate website, but it is the lifeblood of a successful open-source project. Make sure that keeping an archive of messages sent by community members, which might include comments critical of your company or one of your competitors, is all right. Check that contributions from the community can be made available as downloadable files. How involved will your company's legal people be in approving what goes on your website (such as, liability issues, use of trademarks, and compliance with export regulations)? Will you be more restricted by being hosted on one of your company's web servers than if you had contracted with an external web-hosting company?

Third, find out whether you can directly edit your website or whether someone in your company's IT department must do this. Having your IT department maintain your web server is a major plus, but if the result is that minor changes take weeks to enact that won't work very well.

Some projects combine the do-it-yourself approach with the use of one of the free open-source-hosting websites. For example, JBoss, an open-source Java application server project, has its own website[9] with project information and

---

8. http://gforge.org

9. http://www.jboss.org

discussion forums, but relies on SourceForge[10] to provide its CVS tree, bug database, file downloading, and task management.

MAKING USE OF AN EXISTING WEBSITE

If you are joining an existing open-source project, then you will probably be able to use the project's website and not have to create a new site of your own. If you are joining in on the work of ongoing modules, then all of the mailing lists, CVS archives, and bug databases should already exist; you just need to subscribe to the mailing lists and start contributing.

If you are developing new modules, then you will probably need a new mailing list for each module. If it is a large project, then it very likely that there is an easy (possibly automated) way to create a new subproject, complete with archived mailing lists and a directory in the CVS tree. Some open-source efforts, such as Apache, require that you either be a member of the Apache Software Foundation (ASF) or have a member's sponsorship in order to start a new subproject.

Adding a new subproject to an existing website generally will not put a strain on the site's resources. If you expect your project will be a significant burden due to the size of the code base or the traffic on the discussion lists, then you might want to consider donating server machines or making a monetary contribution. Talk to the website maintainers and find out what they need to make the website better. It's always good to volunteer resources, but don't assume they will be accepted (for example, a Linux-based website will probably not be interested in a Solaris-based web server). Having your company listed as a supporter of the website is also a plus.

YOUR WEBSITE NEEDS AN EDITOR-IN-CHIEF

Your project may be making great progress as developers work on the source code, but, if no one is reporting the improvements on your website and general mailing lists, then to the outside world your project will look dead. A stale website will turn people away, so you need to have someone assigned to keep the website home page up-to-date with the latest project news. You want your website to attract both users and potential developers. The larger your project, the more important it is to have a person whose job it is to let everyone know what's happening. Editing the website may be part of the community coordinator's job.

---

10. http://sourceforge.net/projects/jboss

CROSS-LINKING WITH YOUR COMPANY'S WEB PAGES

You should have pointers to your project's web pages from appropriate places on your company's main website. For example, on IBM's website,[11] the IBM WebSphere Studio Workbench product web pages have pointers to the Eclipse website,[12] and on Sun's website[13] the Sun Java Studio product web pages have links to the NetBeans website.[14] The editor of your website should coordinate with the people managing your company's website so that it has up-to-date news of your project. Often, when your project is first announced there will be lots of stories and links on several of your company's web pages, but months later nothing will have changed. Stale references make it seem as if your project has not progressed.

You also should make sure that any link from your open-source website back to a commercial website is appropriate. Having a banner ad for Sun on the NetBeans website would be in very bad taste, as would giving Sun preferential treatment with links to Sun products. However, having a page of links to companies offering commercial NetBeans plug-in modules, including ones from Sun, would be okay.

Getting Approval from Your Company

Before you can announce your open-source project to the world, you have one last hurdle to clear: getting official approval from your company. Working with open source is similar to introducing a new product or making use of another company's proprietary code. In both cases, your company is making a legal agreement that can limit future choices and create future obligations. This is all part of normal business and so your company should have an established procedure for approving the use of open source in company activities. Just as most companies require approval before a new product is introduced or an old product is retired, there should be an official approval process to create a new open-source project or end participation in an existing one.

A small company might do this casually, whereas a larger company will probably have a formal approval process. If you've done all of the steps mentioned so far in this chapter, then you should have answers to the questions that will be

---

11. http://www.ibm.com

12. http://www.eclipse.org

13. http://www.sun.com

14. http://www.netbeans.org

asked during the approval process, and you should have no trouble getting your project approved.

Most companies will have different approval procedures depending on whether a project is intended to create a new open-source project to release source code developed internally (outbound open source) or whether code from an existing open-source project will be used in-house or incorporated into one of the company's products (inbound open source). There may be still a third process to approve joining an existing open-source project, where you plan to both contribute company-developed source code and make use of externally developed code.

Your company should also have an approval process for employees who are working on an open-source project as individuals on their own time. Although this is primarily to protect that individual and the open-source project they are participating in, it can also benefit your company by signalling its support for open source.

Finally, there needs to be an approval process for stopping work on an open-source project or decreasing the company resources allocated to it. Just as every company needs to control how it ends the life of a product, similar end-of-life (EOL) considerations apply to stopping work on an open-source project.

Different issues and concerns are important for each of these situations; we discuss each in turn. Note that each company will have its own process, so you need to contact your company's legal department for details of your company's policy.

WHO SHOULD BE APPROVING OPEN-SOURCE ACTIVITIES?

Because of the possibly serious implications and requirements associated with both inbound and outbound open source, it is important that any approval body consist of executives at the same level as those who approve new products. The approval board should include senior executives from development, marketing, product planning, and legal. The reviewing team may include the head of your business unit.

It is vital that the approval of a company-sponsored open-source project come from a level higher than that of the manager who will be running the project, and it should come from a level above all of the groups that will be affected by the project.

If you are creating a new approval process for your company, be sure to announce it to everyone who might be involved. Especially when it comes to downloading source code from the Internet, many engineers may not realize that they are potentially exposing the company to harm.

GETTING APPROVAL TO RELEASE SOURCE CODE DEVELOPED BY YOUR COMPANY

Creating a new open-source project is almost like releasing a new product—it consumes company resources, its quality reflects on your company, and it implies a certain commitment. If you start a new project and it fails, this will probably generate bad publicity for and bad will toward your company. The approval process needs to weed out the badly conceived projects and make sure that proposed projects have not neglected anything important.

There are two parts to a basic approval process for creating a new open-source project: a business analysis to explain your business strategy and make the case for doing open source and due diligence to guarantee that the source code does not include any embarrassing comments or third-party encumbrances. Only after both steps have been successfully completed can the project be started. In fact, no announcement of your company's intent to release the code should be made until both steps have been completed.

Requirements for the Business Analysis

The business analysis should require you to examine two main areas: the suitability of the source code for public distribution and the strategic significance for your company of releasing the code.

Steps for determining suitability include the following:

- Identifying the source code.

- Determining what stage of development the code is in—is it mature code?

- Confirming that the source code is free of viruses.

- Confirming that there is adequate documentation.

- Confirming that the source code is sufficiently modular and buildable that outside developers will be able to use it.

- Identifying the engineers who will participate on the due-diligence team.

- Identifying the employees who will interact with the community created by the new open-source project and confirming that they all understand how to interact.

Steps for determining strategic significance include the following:

- Listing the business goals for making the source code public.

- Identifying the audience/community that will use the code.

- Identifying the factors critical to the success of the effort, including the resources needed.

- Specifying which licensing model your project will use.

- Identifying what the financial impact on your company will be.

- Specifying a schedule for the project, including the target date to announce the release of the source code.

This information should be reviewed by your approval board, and if they decide that there are suitable business reasons for using open source, then you need to start the due diligence process.

Requirements for Due Diligence

Due diligence includes a review of the source code and documentation by your company's legal and technical staff to determine whether any third-party technology or proprietary information has been incorporated into the source code you are planning to release. This is done by examining the source code thoroughly to determine the origin of each part. Any code not developed by your company must be checked to determine whether it is under a license that allows you to include it in a public release, and, if not, the code must be replaced or relicensed.

The due diligence effort also includes the following:

- Confirming that appropriate copyright, trademark, and patent filings have been made.

- Determining whether there are any export restrictions.

- Removing any inappropriate, derogatory, or offensive statements or references in the source code.

Upon successful completion of the due diligence process, the approval board that reviewed the business analysis should either approve the project itself or pass a recommendation to an appropriate senior executive for final approval. Once the project has been approved, you may announce the project and release the source code.

GETTING APPROVAL TO USE SOURCE CODE DEVELOPED OUTSIDE YOUR COMPANY

If you are planning on downloading source code that has been released under an open-source license, then before you can incorporate that code into a company product or use it internally you will first need to get company approval. This is to ensure that your business unit, any affected functional groups (for example, support), and your upper management are making informed decisions when they acknowledge and accept the risks and obligations dictated by the license that the downloaded code uses.

These risks include the following:

- No warranties, which means that if the source code infringes the intellectual property rights of a third party, your company could be required to stop shipping products containing the downloaded code and could be forced to pay monetary damages.

- No support, so, if needed, your company must resolve performance, customer support and maintenance, internationalization, and localization issues. (Of course, providing support for an open-source product can be an excellent business opportunity.)

- Limits on what your company can do with a product based on the open-source code, which means that your company may not be able to release a larger work under a desired license.

- Additional requirements on your company, such as that all source code in any derived work must be made publicly available.

- Indiscriminate dissemination of the downloaded source code within your company, which could permit it to be unknowingly used in some other, inappropriate company product.

The approval process needs to review the business case for using the downloaded code, including how these risks will be minimized or handled. Issues that must be addressed fall into three main categories: business analysis, strategic analysis, and legal review.

Business Analysis

First you must do the following:

- Identify and describe the technology you wish to use.

- Explain the strategic significance of the technology: What gap does it fill? What is its benefit to your company? What alternatives are there?

- Identify which of your company's products will use the technology and how they will use it: Will it be embedded in the product or just bundled with it? If embedded, will the downloaded code be used as is or will it be modified?

- Describe how your company will distribute the technology (for example, in source or binary): Will the technology's functionality be segregated from your company's proprietary code?

- State whether there will be any license fees or royalties for the company products that will include the technology.

- Explain how the technology will be maintained and supported.

- Describe the proposed licensing model for any of your company products developed using the downloaded source code.

- Estimate the difficulty and the time required to remove or replace the downloaded technology if that should become necessary.

Strategic Analysis

Next, someone from your company's corporate strategy and planning department must do the following:

- Ensure that your company's strategic rationale and business purposes for downloading the technology are consistent with your company's long-term technical and business objectives.

- Check with your company's support division that the appropriate support and engineering resources are available to support the downloaded source code once it has been embedded in one of your company's products.

Legal Review

And, finally, your legal department needs to do the following:

- Identify licensing requirements, such as needing to publish the modified source code.

- Identify any legal risks associated with using the downloaded technology.

- Identify any steps or measures to minimize the risks or to comply with the licensing requirements.

Once you have the information required by these steps, the approval board can review matters. Only after approval is granted can the downloaded source code be incorporated into a company product. Once it has, your group will be responsible for making sure that your company complies with any requirements imposed by the download license.

Several groups in a company might want to use a specific downloaded technology—especially one used only internally and not in any company products, such as Emacs, Apache, or Tomcat. For these cases, it might make sense to create a fast-track approval process that can be used to quickly approve requests to use downloaded software that has already been fully reviewed. The only thing that needs to be checked is that the software will be used the same way.

It may also be possible to automatically approve software downloaded for an employee's individual use, such as a calendar manager, address book, news reader, or web browser. The key point here is that the employee is not modifying or redistributing the software. But even in these cases it is important to check that the license used by the software does not preclude its commercial use, the use of the software as part of an individual's job.

GETTING APPROVAL TO PARTICIPATE IN AN EXISTING OPEN-SOURCE PROJECT

If you are planning on having your company's employees participate in an existing open-source project, then before they can do any work with it you need to get the proper approval. This approval process will probably be similar to that for participating in a joint effort with another company or an industry consortium. In some cases, all that may be required is that the direct managers give their approval to the participating engineers. For example, a small, focused effort by one of your engineers to help an open-source project adapt its code to run well with one of your company's products should not require a heavyweight approval process.

If code previously developed by your company will be contributed to the project or if the code developed by the project will be incorporated into one of your company's products, then one, or both, of the previous policies may apply and require an additional approval process.

The steps that should be followed before any of your company engineers may participate involve the details of the open-source project such as the following:

- Describe the overall open-source project.

- Determine the primary reasons that your company should participate.

- Determine the precise goals and objectives for your company personnel working on the project.

- Determine which open-source license the project uses.

- Determine how IP is handled. Does the project allow contributors to retain copyright on contributed code?

- Identify other companies participating in the project.

There are also steps involving risks to your company's intellectual property rights, as follows:

- Identify the procedures you will put in place to prevent any of the open-source code developed by your company personnel from subsequently getting mixed with your company's proprietary code.

- Determine the likelihood that your company personnel developing open-source code will later be asked to develop similar functionality in your company's proprietary code.

- Determine whether any existing company patents fall within the scope of the project.

- Outline the steps you will take while working on the project to identify possible future patents.

- Determine whether participation in the project will increase the risk that company personnel could disclose trade secrets.

Once this information has been obtained and your management grants approval, then you can start to participate in the open-source effort.

GETTING APPROVAL AS AN INDIVIDUAL

Many software engineers choose to spend part of their personal time contributing to open-source projects. By doing so, they learn new technologies, get feedback on their coding abilities, and otherwise grow and develop. This is a benefit to the company they work for because it makes them more valuable as employees. However, it can create a problem if their open-source work conflicts in some way with the company's business.

A company may have legitimate concerns about work employees do in their spare time. If the open-source work is similar to an employee's job then there is the danger that the employee will disclose proprietary information concerning technical ideas or business plans. This could make it impossible to file patents on work the company has done. Likewise, the employee might inappropriately take ideas or code from the open-source project and use it in a company product, thereby tainting it.

Even when an employee's open-source work and normal work assignment are in different areas, the company might have a product that competes with that of the open-source project. That can create a conflict of interest for the employee.

Many companies require their employees to sign an agreement when they are hired that specifies that the company owns anything that the employees invent. Students who are receiving support from their university may be in a similar situation. If the employees or students contribute to an open-source project, then their employer may claim ownership of their work. There have been several stories reported at places such as Slashdot in which this has indeed happened and people had to stop their participation in the open-source project and have their code removed from it. This is bad for the project, is very bad for the individual, and gives the company a bad name. No one benefits from a situation like this.

All these potential problems can be avoided by having a simple process for employees to get approval to participate in an open-source project. The process should ensure that the employees understand company policy regarding intellectual property and conflicts of interest. General guidelines should be established and communicated to the employees. These typically include that any open-source work should be done on the employees' own time, should not be done while at work or using company equipment, and should not be similar to what their normal job duties are. A form amending the original employee agreement should be signed by an appropriate-level company executive and the employees should receive a copy. The form should state that the company gives up any claim to the work done by the employees as part of the open-source project and that the employees have the right to assign their copyrights to the open-source project.

The need for approval arises largely because of the agreement many companies have new employees sign. One suggestion from Slashdot is that when starting a new job the new employee should rewrite any offending clauses to restrict the scope of that agreement. The following is an excerpt from that posting:

A lot of people think they have no negotiating ability. You do. When you're thinking of signing on with some company, and they send you a boiler-plate contract to sign, don't just sign it and send it back. Read it carefully. Alter it as you see fit, striking out sections, adding sections, and initialing each change. Then sign it, make a copy for yourself, and send it back.

Where it says:

```
company owns the rights to all work produced during the term of employment
```

Just strike it out, and change it to:

```
company owns the rights to code written during working hours and in direct
furtherance of any tasks assigned by the company
```

See how much nicer that reads? Now, when you do this, there are two possibilities: either the company will ignore it and hire you, or they will object to your alteration of the contract.[15]

Many Slashdot posters have described how they did this when they started a new job and that their employers had no problem with making any reasonable changes.

GETTING APPROVAL TO STOP OR LESSEN PARTICIPATION IN A SPONSORED OPEN-SOURCE PROJECT

There will come a time when you need to reduce the number of people and resources devoted to an open-source project that your company has been sponsoring. Because it is an open-source project, this is a much more public announcement than reducing the number of employees working on some internal proprietary product. If handled badly, it can hurt your company's reputation in other open-source projects you sponsor or participate in—developers will question your company's commitment to open source. You can also expect news stories reporting your company's change in focus.

Naturally, how damaging such a reduction in support can be depends on the size and prominence of the project. If it is something as large as IBM's support for Eclipse, then reducing commitment will probably be written about in the mainstream press, whereas if it's a small company with a small project, there might be hardly any notice taken outside that project's community. The community surrounding even a trivial project, however, can be vocal and influential beyond the apparent importance of the project itself, and it is sometimes hard to know for sure who is watching the project. So be wary of how you try to reduce your company's commitment.

Because of the potential for damage to your company's reputation, it is important to have an approval process in place to review any decreases in your participation in publicly visible open-source projects. The last thing your CEO wants is for the press to announce that your company is making major changes in strategy all because some low-level manager has laid off or transferred the employees most visible to one of your open-source projects. We've seen this happen—a company laid off the employee providing the technological leadership for one of their open-source projects—along with the subsequent damage control the company needed to recover from it.

---

15. http://slashdot.org/article.pl?sid=02/03/21/0139244

If you want to minimize the negative impact of reducing your commitment to an open-source project that your company sponsors, the questions that must be answered include the following:

- Is this a decrease in effort, or are you ending your participation in the project?

- How will it be announced?

- What will the public perception of the reduction be?

- How will the community of the open-source project react?

- How will this affect other open-source projects your company is participating in?

If you are ending your sponsorship of the project, there must be a plan and schedule for disengaging. You will need to answer the following additional questions:

- Who from the community will take over the project?

- Where will the project's website be hosted? How will any transition take place?

- What obligations do you need to fulfill (for example, continuing to post the source code)?

- Is it okay for your developers to continue to participate on their own time if they wish to?

Making sure all of these questions have satisfactory answers before taking any public actions should minimize any possible harm to your company and keep the respect of the open-source world.

WHAT ABOUT SMALL PROJECTS OR END-OF-LIFE PRODUCTS?

For a small project, all of this may seem like overkill. However, the same steps must be followed whether you are releasing 500 lines of code or 500,000. Of course, it is much easier to do due diligence on 500 lines of source code so it can be released.

To be successful, open source requires fostering a community around the code, and that takes work. At a minimum, someone who understands the code must filter suggested changes and help developers work with it. It also requires an archived mailing list or newsgroup and at least a handful of web pages, including one that lets people download the source code and executable versions.

Most open-source projects are fairly small, consisting of fewer than 20 developers and several hundred users. So, the effort required is only the discussion and coding needed to move the project along. As long as the user community is happy with the rate of progress, the project is alive and healthy. For a mature project there may not be many, if any, changes being made to the code—the community will stay healthy from active discussions on how to best use the software.

Because a small project will have a limited budget (and an EOL project may have no budget), it will probably not be able to afford to have a dedicated website. If your company already has a website for small company-sponsored open-source projects, then you can host your project there. For example, a number of smaller Sun open-source projects are hosted at SunSource.net.[16] If your company does not have such a website then you will need to use a free website provider, such as SourceForge.[17]

For EOLed code that is no longer being supported, but that you don't want to die, the amount of effort needed to make it open source may seem to be orders of magnitude more than the work you expect your group will put into the code in the future. Remember that open source is not magic: It takes a lot of work to create a community and make an open-source project successful. You will still need to determine an appropriate license for the software. To give a community a chance to grow, you should expect that you will need to commit one or two engineers for at least a year to engage with the community and to continue working on the code.

For a product that you are about to stop supporting, you may just want to provide the source code to current customers so they can continue to use it. That is, you want to keep your customers happy even though you are discontinuing the product, but you are not interested in creating a community. In such a case, it may be sufficient to make the source code and supporting material, such as build scripts and internal documentation, available for download on your regular corporate website. You should also make sure that there is an email list or forum set up so that your customers can help each other—plan for some of your engineers to participate on that list.

---

16. http://sunsource.net

17. http://sourceforge.net

Problems You Can Expect to Encounter

Once you have approval for your project and have begun open-source development, there are a number of problems that you are likely to encounter. We end this chapter by discussing some of the more common ones along with ways to handle them. These difficulties crop up in virtually every open-source project just because of how people act when they try to collaborate. These are the problems that you'll see even when you do everything right. There is a whole other class of problems that results from mistakes being made in how an open-source project is run, which we cover in Chapter 9.

GETTING ENGAGEMENT

The first problem you may face when you start up your open-source project is that no one seems to care about it—no potential users download your application to try it out; perhaps no one even visits your project's website. If so, you need to publicize your project, telling people how and why it helps them. See the section on "Marketing Your Project" in Chapter 8 for suggestions on ways to do this.

Another problem you may encounter is that once you start getting users, only a few bug reports or contributions are submitted. People are downloading your application and, you hope, using it, but they are not providing the feedback or improvements you had hoped for. It may be because it just takes time for a community to develop, but it also may be that you are discouraging outside participation. Some things that you can do to increase participation are described in the section "Focus on Your Users and Contributors" in Chapter 8.

A third problem you may see is that many user questions posted to your project's mailing lists go unanswered. If outside individuals are posting only questions to your mailing lists and your team is answering all of them, you will quickly become overwhelmed trying to answer everybody. When you start up the open-source project, tell your developers to use the rule of delaying answering a posted question for a day or two. This will encourage your users to answer them. If a question has not been not answered after a day or two, then one of your developers should answer it. Typically, the community manager is the one to answer such questions, but make sure those you assign are capable of answering the more difficult questions asked by your intermediate and advanced community members—these members, knowing their questions will be answered by one of the experts you've assigned, will have a reason to stay on the list, and they will be just the ones to provide answers to the easier queries. Check the attitude expressed in the messages your team posts: Is it arrogant? Does your team embarrass people when they are wrong? You need to make the mailing list a safe place for people to participate.

It is very important to build up a community of givers rather than takers. Open source is very much a gift economy. The more personally connected your team members are with other individuals in the community and the more they are perceived as giving to and caring about the community, the greater will be the community involvement and participation in the project. Conversely, if your developers act as if they are just doing their jobs, then do not expect much in the way of outside volunteers or for a community to develop—at best you will have a user group.

PLAYS WELL WITH OTHERS

Software developers often have strong opinions and are not shy about expressing them. Some might even be accused of lacking in social skills. When they interact, sparks can fly and lots of unproductive flaming can result. In every open-source project, there will often be major differences of opinion on what is the best architecture or technical solution to any given problem. Too many battles can split a community, causing some developers to leave to start a competing project. To avoid this fate for your project, it is important that your developers learn to help arbitrate any flame wars that occur. Even when they disagree with some community member, they need to keep the conversation civil and focus the community on its common goals. Make sure people feel they are being heard and that their viewpoint is seen as a positive contribution to the project even if it is not the direction chosen. Figure out a way to explicitly recognize and reward those of your team who douse flames well.

A related problem is that some discussions never seem to resolve: Various viewpoints get expressed, but no solution is agreed on. In some projects, the project founder or a module owner plays the role of final decision maker. In other projects, there is no one individual in charge. For those other projects, each issue needs to have a person assigned to bring it to conclusion—often this is the person who brought up the issue or the one who will undertake implementing whatever solution is chosen. It might also be a person with good project management skills, who can listen to what developers are saying. This person needs to follow-up on each issue raised during the discussion, get a sense of how the community feels about each, and summarize matters when the discussion winds down or when nothing new is being said. The summary should indicate what was decided and who will do any associated work to implement it.

The decision about an issue can also falter because only a few people participate in the discussion. It might be necessary to solicit the opinions of specific community members who are knowledgeable on the particular issue. Lack of discussion may also indicate that the community does not consider the issue to be important, and so the appropriate decision might be to do nothing for now.

Sometimes there will be lots of noise on the project's mailing lists, often by people who think they know more than they actually do or who have an extreme viewpoint—noise in the form of extended discussion on how to approach a particular problem or a new idea about what to add or a direction to go. There will always be some noise like this on the lists, but too much can drive valued community members away. However, it's important to consider whether some discussion really is noise or whether it is important information that differs from the prejudices of the main project developers—sometimes it is hard to tell the difference. Often the best solution is to suggest that those in favor of the new idea should create a new subproject and implement a prototype. This at least moves the discussion to another list and your community might be pleasantly surprised when they get to see the idea put into practice. As for those few folks who continue to send flames, you may need to send them a private message asking them what's going on and to please tone it down—sometimes they don't realize that they are acting inappropriately.

Managing community expectations is another common problem. No matter how much you do, you can count on people requesting additional features—in fact you want them to. Some of these requests will be for things that everyone agrees would be great, whereas others may be more questionable or not fit with the project's main direction. In any case, your company has only so many employees who can work on your project, so there will always be more than you can do. It is very important that you establish a community of peers where it is taken for granted that anyone can and does contribute to the project. In such a community, the person who proposes a new feature is a logical choice for who should implement it. Although some open-source projects adopt the attitude that anyone who proposes a change or feature must "show me the code," you shouldn't fall prey to it. Sometimes a gifted designer or someone who understands the user community very well is not a gifted coder, and you should encourage outside developers to work with such people. What you do not want is a community where everyone expects that all significant work will be done only by your company. When there is a feature that you do not wish to have your employees work on, you want the community's energies directed at implementing the feature itself, not at trying to convince you to do so.

DEALING WITH YOUR OWN COMPANY

Sometimes it's not just the community outside your company that insists on telling you what to do. Sometimes other groups inside your own company demand that you add features for them that you either do not have the resources to do or that clash with the publicly stated road map of your project. The more you can encourage other parts of your company to actively participate through the open-source process, the better. Once other groups learn that they can submit bug fixes and new features directly, they will understand that they can control their own schedules and not be dependent on your group. This is the same form of risk reduction that a company enjoys when it has a source-code escrow agreement with a supplier or it uses an open-source solution and the original supplier or support company is unresponsive or goes out of business: The source code can be fixed and improved without the intercession of the original development group. In this way, open source can reduce risks for other parts of your company.

If your current managers have problems resolving disputes among your developers, then making your project open source can make things worse. As already mentioned, the open-source method of making decisions via public discussion on project mailing lists often does not reach a clear consensus. If your own developers do not agree with the direction the project is taking, they can air their objections in the public discussion and use the ensuing uncertainty to block others from taking action. It is important that your developers be able to express themselves freely on the project mailing lists, but you do not want them using those discussions to further their private agendas. This can sometimes be a tough call, and it requires that your project managers be willing to step in when necessary and make decisions about what your company's developers should be working on. An example of this problem that we've seen occur is when a developer who does not want to implement what a user-interface designer has proposed uses disagreements with the proposal on the mailing lists as a reason to do whatever that developer prefers. In a traditional proprietary project, the developer would not have a choice, but would need to implement what the UI expert thought best.

Another common problem occurs when there is a change in management in your company and your new management doesn't understand open source. If this happens, you need to immediately start to educate them about open source and make it clear how your use of open source helps your company. If your old manager can help explain why open source makes sense, so much the better. A failure on your part to sell your new management on the value of open source can have disastrous consequences, both when resource decisions need to be made and when you and your project come up for review.

CONTRIBUTING TO OTHER PROJECTS

The last problem we consider here is you as an individual having trouble getting your contributions accepted when you are participating in an open-source project that is run by someone else. You've fixed a major bug or written some nifty new feature, but you cannot get the open-source project to accept it. It can be very frustrating when you are trying to help, but are being ignored.

There are several reasons why this may be the case. The first is that the community might not know you. If this is your first contribution, then people will be wondering who you are and why should they pay any attention to what you say. It is very important that you build up your reputation with the community by helping to fix small bugs and participating in discussions. Contributions that show people that you are competent and that affirm that you share in the project's goals will give you standing in the community. Only then will people be willing to listen to you when you make suggestions that go beyond the current project road map. You and the rest of your team may be the authorities within your company, but unless you are also world famous, you will need to establish a track record through your participation in the open-source project. It's not just a question of your competency, but also one of trust. This is especially important because companies are often viewed suspiciously and many will assume your company is trying somehow through you to rip off the work done by the open-source community. You need to demonstrate that you, as an individual, are someone the community can trust.

Another reason your contribution may not be accepted is that your proposed solution is not seen by the community as adding any value. This may be because you are concerned about a different set of issues—for example, you may be extending the software to work in a complex enterprise setting, whereas the project's focus is on an individual using a single machine; or you may be interested in making the software more usable by novices, whereas the community is mostly expert power users. It's up to you to convince the community members—or at least the relevant module owner—that what you are proposing has value. In any such discussion, you should listen carefully to any objections raised by the community. It is very likely that you will need to modify your proposed solution to take the community's concerns into account. You should start this dialog as soon as you know that you need to fix some bug or add some feature, well before you write any code. If you wait until after you have all the code written and then surprise the community with it, you will probably be the one surprised.

You may find that the project or module owner isn't responding to your email messages. Remember that a lot of open-source developers are volunteers, so they may be busy with their real jobs or other work, they might be on vacation, or they may be temporarily burned out on open source. By looking at the traffic on the project's mailing lists and in the mail archives, you should be able to determine whether the project owner is ignoring just you or is simply not currently active at all. Also, as previously mentioned, if no one knows who you are, then on a busy mailing list your comments will be easy to overlook, especially if they are on a topic far from the project's current focus.

For more discussion see the section "Getting Your Contributions Accepted" in Chapter 6.

Going with Open Source

Going with open source is not a simple task, nor is it inexpensive. Your company should have a clear, long-term vision of the business goals of such a project. Because the commitment is expensive and lengthy, the primary business goals that make sense are strategic ones. If you find yourself thinking of using open source as a tactic, you should think very hard because when the time for the tactic is over, you might have to pay a price out of balance with the tactical gain you realized.

We have provided here a good general idea of the questions to ask and considerations to take into account when deciding whether to go with open source and preparing to execute the decision. If you've read this book and absorbed the philosophy, principles, and practices of open source, you should be able to work your way through any other questions or issues that come up that we haven't covered.

CHAPTER 8

How To Build Momentum

THE PREVIOUS CHAPTERS OF THIS BOOK HAVE DESCRIBED all the elements that go into creating and running an open-source project. In this chapter, we discuss some things you can do to increase your project's chances for success. This builds on the material in the section "Building a Community" in Chapter 5, which covers the basic things to do. The next chapter focuses on what *not* to do based on lessons learned from the failures and mistakes we've observed in various open-source projects.

The ideas in this chapter apply to any open-source project; however, we want to emphasize that a company engaging in an open-source project has many additional resources that can be used to further the project in ways that are not available to individual volunteers. In addition to developers, a company also employs technical writers, user-interface experts, graphic artists, website designers, technology evangelists, marketing people, project managers, and people with other skills, all of whom can help with different aspects of the project. Once they understand the open-source process, these folks can make major contributions to help the project become a success. All the activities that your company does to support a proprietary product—marketing, advertising, support, and training— are also needed for an open-source project.

As you read over this chapter, remember what your business goals are and focus on how to achieve them. Creating a successful open-source project is only part of your strategy. As the project grows and develops, it will take on a life of its own. You need to balance the needs of the open-source community against your business goals. For the most part, they should be aligned toward a common purpose, and developers from both inside and outside of your company will work together to achieve them. Where they are orthogonal, you should let the community proceed on its own. If they are opposed, you need to be very upfront about communicating your plans and reach some agreement that does not alienate or frustrate your community.

For example, one of the business goals of the NetBeans project was for Sun to sell proprietary modules that added functionality to the basic NetBeans IDE. Developing similar modules as open source in NetBeans would undermine this goal because the functionality would then be available for free. However, outside developers have every right to expect that any useful modules they create can become part of NetBeans. So the decision was made that any module could be developed for NetBeans. It also was decided that when a NetBeans module duplicated the functionality of one of Sun's proprietary modules the Sun version would be open sourced. In this way, the functionality level of NetBeans would continually go up, which would be good for the health of the project. Sun could make this decision because the Sun engineers were confident that they would always be able to develop new proprietary modules that Sun could sell, so they did not need to hold tightly to their existing ones.

Marketing Your Project

As with any product, marketing plays a key role in the success of your project. For you to be successful, people need to hear about your project, understand what it does, and see how it can help them. Getting the message out about your project is one job marketing can help with.

WHAT IS YOUR PROJECT'S STORY?

Before your project is ever announced to the world, you need to come up with a compelling story that describes what your project is aiming at—something to get people excited about it. This is the message that will attract people to your project both as users and potential developers. If the story is not appealing, then people will not be interested in participating and won't get involved.

For most open-source projects, this story is focused on the technology being developed. For example, the Apache HTTP Server Project exists to build the best web server. The following are statements of the story for Apache.

> *The Apache Project is a collaborative software development effort aimed at creating a robust, commercial-grade, featureful, and freely-available source code implementation of an HTTP (Web) server.*[1]

---

1. http://httpd.apache.org/ABOUT_APACHE.html

The goal of this project is to provide a secure, efficient and extensible server which provides HTTP services in sync with the current HTTP standards.[2]

Other projects have a more user-centered focus, as seen in the following comment about GNOME.

The GNOME project was born as an effort to create an entirely free desktop environment for free systems. From the start, the main objective of GNOME has been to provide a user friendly suite of applications and an easy-to-use desktop.[3]

You need to determine what sort of people you are hoping to attract to your project. If you want to mainly target end-users, then you need to talk about what they can do with the software you are developing, which of their problems your software solves. If you want to focus on developers who will contribute code to your project, then emphasizing the technological aspects may work, but remember that most people working on open-source projects do so because they need to use the resulting software—your developers will also be users.

Creating a good story is hard work. The story needs to express the shared purpose behind your project. It will attract people who share this vision and are willing to work to make it real. Moreover, the story should infuse all aspects of the project so that it provides guidance whenever a strategic decision must be made. In literary theory, such a story is called a *topos* and can be defined as follows:

a conventionalized expression or passage in text which comes to be used as a resource for the composition of additional texts.[4]

Topos literally means "place" or "location" in Greek, and a topos is a place from which similar stories can be woven. An example from literature is the story of the Garden of Eden. Anyone in a Western Judeo-Christian culture when asked to tell a story about the Garden of Eden will probably come up with a story consistent with the vision of creation the Garden of Eden presents. An example of a technology-related topos is Moore's Law, which is regularly used as the basis of stories about the future of computing.

For an example of the power of a good story, consider the one developed for the Jini project. As described earlier, Jini technology is a thin layer built on top

---

2. http://httpd.apache.org

3. http://www.gnome.org/intro/findout.html

4. *The New Princeton Encyclopedia of Poetry and Poetics*, p. 1294.

of Java that allows applications to be written as remote services that can be dynamically deployed and located over a network. The obvious story is that Jini is another middleware framework for distributed applications. But this story has a technology focus that would have severely limited the spread of the Jini message— indeed the term *middleware* causes even developers to yawn. Instead, the Jini marketing team built a story around what Jini technology would mean to users; that story generated lots of excitement in developers, the press, and the marketplace.

The Jini topos speaks of a world of "intelligent services" that "simply connect" to form "spontaneous networks" and describes a set of home, office, and automobile scenarios derived from this topos. The concepts "simply connect" and "spontaneous networks" address how people relate to the technology. The Jini topos was highly effective and created a thriving community and associated technology—as hoped—along with thriving E-Speak, UPnP, and SOAP communities and associated technologies.

This type of story is especially important for any project with ubiquity as a goal. For Jini, success did not rest in extensive development of the core Jini protocols but rather in nurturing communities to create a wide range of Jini-based services. The story needed to inspire companies to want their products—be they printers, cameras, or whatever—to "simply connect" by using Jini technology.

Contrast this with the Apache topos (described earlier) which speaks of web servers and technology for making them effective. Whereas Jini projects tend to fan out, creating new services for people to use, the Apache Software Foundation's projects tend to focus on adding web server functionality and adopting related technologies such as Java Server Pages, servlets, and XML.

Topoi and storytelling, however, might not go over well with your highly technical developers. Although the developers at Sun in the Jini group were involved in the story-making, they quickly came to believe that the story was misguided, because it talked exclusively about a world of small devices when in fact Jini was also capable in middleware and other high-end applications, such as distributed and scientific computing. They became upset that Sun was actually not working diligently in the device space and so to them the story was a lie.

The idea of a topos, however, is that a topos enables people to make their own stories about their own areas of interest. In fact, most middleware application writers had little trouble understanding that "simply connect" and "spontaneous networks" were either literally or metaphorically true for them, although they worried that less sophisticated people might not be able to understand the connection.

If you decide to build a topos, make sure your developers understand what it's for and buy into the topos you create.

At its best, the topos as a story-making story attracts and provides room for experimentation and variation beyond what the initiators envisioned.

THE NAME MATTERS

What you call your open-source project is important. You need to choose a name that will attract developers. In effect, you are creating a brand identity just like any commercial product. You want to create an identity that matches your target audience and that is consistent with your story. Most important, you don't want a name that is too slick or connected with a commercial product.

This can be complicated if part of your business plan is to develop a commercial product based on the open-source version. You need to recognize the different naming requirements for each version.

For example, when Sun was deciding how to name its various Java IDE products, it used the more formal "Forte for Java" name for the Sun-branded versions and the more developer-friendly "NetBeans" name for the open-source version. Keeping the NetBeans name was important for historical reasons, but as a name it does not really describe the project—a Java IDE and more generally a portable tools platform—so another name might have been better.

GETTING THE MESSAGE OUT

Once you have a good story about your project, you need to tell it to people. This is a traditional role for marketing. When you have a major piece of news, such as when you first announce your project, your company's marketing machine can see to it that the world hears about it. For very important announcements, this can include major stories in the press. For instance, the initial stories about Sun's Jini technology appeared in the *New York Times, Business Week,* and *Wired.* When top Sun executives such as Scott McNealy and Bill Joy gave talks or met with the press, they made sure to talk about what was new with Jini, JXTA, NetBeans, OpenOffice, and the other open-source projects Sun was working on. Major stories were also featured on Sun's website, along with links to stories elsewhere on the Web.

In addition to the big-splash type of announcement, you should also maintain ongoing low-key press coverage. This is essential because there is often a long time between the initial announcement and the final release. You don't want people to think that your project is dead, so be sure to publicize ongoing activities such as community meetings, working group meetings, and significant milestones. These can be as short as a single sentence in a column of industry news in a magazine. Such stories should also be featured on the home page of your project's website. Note that some PR folks are interested only in handling major stories and will balk at the smaller scale needed for ongoing coverage. If they won't do it, then you need to find someone else who will.

If your project involves infrastructure or something that can be used as part of another application or website, try to find ways to take advantage of the pride some people find in using open-source code or in the technology of your project. Create a logo, a graphic, or a sound that can easily be cut and pasted onto the splash screen of other applications or onto the website of some proud user of your stuff. The logo can link to your website, drawing traffic.

GOING BEYOND STANDARD MARKETING

The conventional marketing channels—major newspapers and magazines, trade press, and trade shows—are important, but an open-source project has other ways to reach potential users and developers, including newsgroups, mailing lists, webzines, and weblogs. Use all of these channels to market your project. You should encourage your developers and users to post to whatever online forums are appropriate.

It is important to use a different writing style for material sent over these alternative channels. This is a matter of *voice*. Richard Rhodes, author of *The Making of the Atomic Bomb*, wrote:

> *Every work of writing, no matter how modest, no matter how seemingly "objective," no matter how "true," is composed in one or more fictional voices. "Someone" "tells" every story, even the copy on the back of cereal boxes, even a legal contract, even a street sign. We may not pause to puzzle out who "someone" is—the author may not even have thought about her choice of voice in advance—but we register "someone"'s presence and assess his statements accordingly.*[5]

Almost every reader is aware of the voice behind any writing, and so if you want to build a community, you need to make that community feel like a group of people, people with distinct and human voices. Company writing typically tries to appear as neutral as possible, as much like an encyclopedia as possible, so there is little possibility of a reader hearing a voice behind the writing, a voice expressing an opinion. The company in many cases wants the reader to believe that what

---

5. Richard Rhodes, *How to Write: Advice and Reflections*, p. 36.

is written is objectively true. Marketing writing often puts a cheerleading sort of voice behind the words.

Anything that has a slick marketing feel or inauthentic voice will be rejected and probably will give people a negative view of your project. Avoid hype. What *does* work is honest talk from developer to developer or user to user. As such, it is the opposite of the typical anonymous marketing message broadcast to a target audience. Instead, it is a message from a real person attempting to engage in an ongoing conversation with other individuals. Each message helps establish the reputation of the writer. Your employees need to become known and respected members of the community in order to best communicate about your project. A big test of their honesty is their being able to admit errors or mistakes and to acknowledge the successes of other projects.

One last point is that it is very important to give credit to the folks who did the work. If a number of outside developers contributed to your open-source project, be sure to acknowledge their efforts. You may even want to feature their efforts because it shows that the project goes beyond your company.

Focus on Your Users and Contributors

One of the most crucial factors in your project's success is releasing a useful product—one that works and solves a real problem. This is exactly the same problem faced by any company releasing a commercial software application. Open source works best with at least several thousand users, so your product must first attract that many. Then the open-source process will encourage those users to provide feedback that will make your project more in tune with the needs of potential users. Remember that one of the main points of doing open source is continuous design, which requires that you pay attention to the continuous feedback you're getting from the community.

If you have such a large code base that you plan on releasing it in several installments in order to give you time to scrub it, then make sure that the first release can build a complete and useful product. Try to release the parts that are most valuable to users and developers first. As you release subsequent pieces, additional news stories about your project will be generated.

TARGET YOUR POTENTIAL AUDIENCE

As with any product, you need to identify what sort of person will benefit from using your product. You need to make sure your message reaches those people. This is where you can make use of standard marketing and advertising.

You also should target other companies that will benefit either from using your product directly or using it to add value to their customers. For example, any company doing Java development can use NetBeans to increase the productivity of its programmers. Other companies create commercial products that run on top of NetBeans. In both cases, companies have an incentive to assign their own developers to work on NetBeans to add features they need, and indeed a number of companies have already done so. For any open-source project, companies provide a good source of potential developers.

MAKE USERS SUCCESSFUL

Installing and learning to use a piece of new software is always a major hurdle for people. As discussed in "Give Folks a Good Initial Experience" in Chapter 6, it is important that you make things as easy as possible. Every person who can't install your application or who is unable to get it to run will be sure to mention those problems to other potential users. You want the message sent by word of mouth to be that people should try your product, not that it should be avoided.

Good documentation, tutorials, and training will also help your users to succeed. The ideas behind open source encourage users to help each other, so provide ways for them to do so via your project's website: Create user mailing lists and discussion forums. Compile FAQs. Do everything you can to encourage the formation of an active user community. There may even be more than one, so you may need to foster several developing communities. They might be separated by what they do with the product (for example, Java vs. C programmers) or by other factors (for example, French vs. German speakers). For large projects, work with a publisher to get a book written about how to best use your software.

Most active communities have an email-based communications flavor to them. One reason that urban settings seem energized is that there are constant noise and interruptions—actual evidence of energy. A community that thrives on email is one that interrupts people with frequent email. Some community members— often the most active ones—are eager for such interruptions. A community with no such interruptions, with only a website (even with wikis and weblogs) will seem placid and low energy by comparison. When people need to go see whether something is happening, they tend to go see a little less frequently as time goes on. For energetic email-based communities, there needs to be a way for people to get respite and opt to come around to see what's happening or receive relatively infrequent email digests.

Do releases as frequently as makes sense. Small frequent releases give people a greater sense of progress than infrequent large ones.

Let your users help make your project more successful. You need to listen to their needs when designing future versions of your product. In fact, your users should be part of your project's design team.

ENCOURAGE OUTSIDE DEVELOPERS

When you first open your source code to the outside world, the initial reaction of outside developers is usually very positive. You can expect comments such as "Wow! You really meant it! There's a lot here!" After a few weeks, the warts will start to show as developers realize how much work will be required to add the features they want, to improve performance, or to do whatever they care about. You need to expect this change in attitude and react appropriately: Acknowledge the problems and don't be defensive.

Any developer beginning to work on your project needs help to come up to speed. New developers at your company can often just walk across the hall to ask one of the original developers. Outside developers do not have that option. You need to provide them with a systems overview, internal documentation, and email access to the original developer team.

Make sure your developers welcome outside comments and do not respond with flames. Your team needs to encourage outside contributors. Some have lots of expertise and need to be treated as peers. Others may lack experience and need mentoring. The tone you set when you respond to the first suggestions, bug reports, bug fixes, and outside contributions will determine what role people outside your team will play in your project. It is much easier to start off right than to try to recover later.

HELP OUTSIDE EFFORTS MEET PROJECT QUALITY STANDARDS

Every open-source project establishes a level of quality that new modules and features need to reach in order to become part of the official release. For some projects, this may mean just that the new code adds more features than bugs. However, other projects may require documentation of the new features; support for internationalization, localization, and accessibility; user-interface (UI) consistency with the project's look and feel; usability testing; adherence to coding style guidelines; or any of various other common requirements for product-quality software. For volunteers who have developed some cool new functionality and want to contribute it to your project, meeting this full list of requirements can easily involve much more work than they spent writing and debugging the code in the first place.

This creates a potential problem: You want your project releases to be of high quality, but you do not want to treat outside contributions as second-class code that doesn't make it into the official release. This situation arises in part because a company-sponsored project usually includes technical writers, graphic artists, UI specialists, and others who work with your company's engineers. One possible solution is to have these people also share their skills with outside developers.

The NetBeans project did this—graphic design for icons was available on request, the Sun UI team was available to provide advice on the user interface for a contributed module, and the Sun documentation team generally took responsibility for documenting everything in the NetBeans standard distribution. Other assistance was also available to include the new module in the automatic project build scripts.

This doesn't guarantee that all contributed code will be brought up to product quality. It is common for open-source projects to have an experimental modules section containing new code in various stages of readiness for adventurous users to play with. Those modules that the community finds promising are candidates for your team along with the rest of the community to improve further.

MAKE SURE ADEQUATE RESOURCES ARE ALLOCATED

An open-source project requires more resources than a conventional proprietary one. If you skimp on providing for the additional needs, it will slow down, or even cripple, your project. The rate-limiting factor for your project should be the enthusiasm and effort of your community, not the person maintaining the project's website who is too busy to update it or your internal developers who are so overworked they have no time to integrate outside contributions and bug fixes. Starting up an open-source project implies a commitment to engage with your community and to support it.

Moreover, feedback you receive from your community provides important information you should use to set priorities. If all your employees are fully assigned to tasks in order to meet your company's goals, then you will be unable to benefit from what you learn from your community. You need to be able to reassign developers to work on what will make your project most successful, where success is defined in large part by your users. If your schedule and plans are inflexible, you will miss one of the major benefits of open source—design help from your community. You also run the risk of alienating members of your community when they see that you do not listen to their ideas, suggestions, and requests.

Of course, you do have limited resources, so you need to identify when your lack of resources is the bottleneck and see if the community can provide the additional manpower. For example, what if one of your developers who is in charge of a module has so much work to do that it prevents a prompt reply to bug fixes or modifications submitted by outside developers? In such a case, one or more other developers need to be allowed to also check in changes to that module. This may be an outside developer who has submitted changes to the module. As soon as possible, you should grant qualified outside developers check-in privileges.

However, that same overworked module owner must make time to participate in any community discussions relating to that module. If that is not possible, then another person who can engage with the community needs to take over ownership of the module. It is okay to delegate work on the module to others, but leadership regarding the module's development requires active participation.

Good project management can make a difference. A good project manager makes sure that when the project is being hurt by a lack of adequate resources either more resources from within your company are allocated or the community is solicited to provide the additional help.

GOVERNANCE MAY NEED TO CHANGE AS YOUR COMMUNITY GROWS

What works for making decisions when you first launch your project will probably change as your community develops. Initially only your developers will understand the source code and what is needed to change it; the community is mostly in the role of users commenting on how well the product meets their needs. That makes it easy for your developers to be the ones who make all the major decisions, especially because they are the ones doing the bulk of the work. As time goes by and outside contributors become more involved with the project, they will naturally want more of a say in how the project moves forward. This will include what features go into it, what bugs should be fixed first, and when and how releases are done.

At this point you have a choice: You can try to keep total control, minimizing community involvement, or you can encourage the community to take on a larger role. In the latter case, the open-source project will blossom beyond just your company, even though it will still be the largest contributor.

Governance is how things are decided and by whom. Every community and every open-source project has some sort of governance because decisions must be made all the time. Governance does not necessarily imply some sort of hierarchy, voting procedures, or strict process. People who join open-source projects expect some sort of meritocracy in which good work (merit) is rewarded with more rights and responsibilities. Most open-source projects have good meritocracies, but not all do.

In a company-sponsored open-source project, people who would otherwise be thought of as good-natured dictators might not always be seen as working toward the best interests of the project and community but might be seen as serving some corporate goals. In these cases, it's a good idea to think about alternatives to pure meritocracy for governance.

The community will typically ignore early discussions on governance—they will be happy letting you run things. Most developers and users simply want to do their work; they don't want to have to think about process and governance. But at some point, people in your community will start to demand a say and may even complain about how evil your company is to try to run everything. At that point, little you do will be seen as good and many messages posted will contain suspicions about your motives. It's like a rebellion, and you just need to expect it and ride it out.

For most company-sponsored open-source projects, some kind of exception-based governance with an appeals body is the best lightweight mechanism to put in place. Sometimes you need to put something related to governance in the contract with the web-hosting company. For example, if an appeals body needs to be able to direct the hosting company to give check-in privileges to someone, that will need to go into the contract between your company and the hosting company—otherwise, your company will retain that power.

When your community starts to request a greater say in how the project is run, it is likely that most of the email will come from just a few people. Do not think that they are just a few malcontents and that everyone else is basically happy with the status quo. If you do, you will miss your chance to involve your community more in your project—and you may not get another chance. It is better to think of the few vocal folks as early adopters, who represent the leading edge of your community's thoughts on governance. Work with them to get more community participation. If you don't engage with them, then they will almost certainly cut back their efforts; even worse, you will give the rest of your community the impression that you do not want to work with them—that they are somehow second-class citizens, that they should stay in their place and let you call the shots for the project. Changing this impression later will be difficult. It is better to not give it in the first place. Working with your community, you have a chance to make the project a true community effort.

Even after you have made it over this hurdle and your community is actively involved in making important decisions about the project, you should expect this process to continue and governance to adapt as your project continues to develop. In large part, this will be caused by your project's growing in size, both in terms of the number of people involved and the number of active subprojects. For example, as the original Apache project added more and more subprojects, it needed to create a Project Management Committee to oversee each project. Further growth led to the creation of the nonprofit Apache Software Foundation with an elected governing board. As your project grows in size, your project's organization will also need to change.

PROVIDE FOR THE DIFFERING NEEDS OF YOUR COMMUNITY MEMBERS

Everyone in your community is unique. Their reasons for participating, the length of their involvement, how much they contribute, and how much they know all vary from person to person. In her book *Community Building on the Web*, Amy Jo Kim describes a five-stage membership life cycle that runs from visitor to novice to regular to leader to elder. Most people will not progress through all five stages—in fact you should expect the number of visitors to be several orders of magnitude larger than all the other stages combined. To attract and retain people, you need to understand their differing needs and how to encourage people to become more involved.

Guide Your Visitors

A visitor is someone who simply wants to see what your community is about. Like a tourist, a visitor wants to easily find the interesting places and painlessly get an idea of what's up with the project.

Are visitors to your project's website able to easily find answers to their questions or do they become lost as they try to locate information? A good website has a section devoted to newcomers. This Visitors Center should contain the following:

- A project mission statement and road map.

- Answers to frequently asked questions.

- Instructions on how to download the current release.

- Tutorials and getting-started documents.

- Press releases and articles about the project.

- A site map and a way to search the website.

- Policies and guidelines for participating in the project.

Most of the larger open-source projects make it easy for visitors to find this type of information. Two good examples are Mozilla[6] and GNOME.[7]

You may want to have a separate area for each different category of visitors. This might be as minimal as having additional sections in your FAQs, or you might have multiple web pages with specialized documents for each group. For example the OpenOffice project[8] has localized versions of much of its website for speakers of different languages (for example, Czech, French, German, and Japanese), whereas the GNOME project provides separate web pages for users and for application developers.

Another question you must address is how much visitors can participate. Can they browse mail archives, subscribe to mailing lists, post to mailing lists, add comments to discussion forums, or edit wiki pages? Generally, you want to maximize how much information visitors can see on your website and minimize barriers to entry. However, you also need to worry about possible disruptions of conversations; furthermore your community members may not want to discuss controversial topics in public.

Although many visitors will be new to your project and may need help navigating your website, others will be quite knowledgeable about your project—they may visit your project's website frequently to see what's new. Do not assume that all the people who care about your project get their news via the mailing lists; feature news about your project on the home page and update it frequently.

The definition of *visitor* is someone without a community identity, so any participation visitors do is done anonymously. It is not necessary to encourage your visitors to join. However, you should make clear what the benefits and requirements of membership are. The main reason people join an online community is to do something that requires membership. For an open-source project, that something is typically being able to ask questions in order to get help in using the project's code and participating in the discussion of the project's future.

Welcome Your Novices

Novices are people who have taken the step to join your project. They may have registered on your project's website or maybe just subscribed to one of your project's mailing lists. They are interested in your project, but need to learn the

---

6. http://www.mozilla.org

7. http://www.gnome.org

8. http://www.openoffice.org

ropes about how your community functions. They need to learn what they can do as members and how to behave.

When they join, you need to welcome them into your community. A simple way to do this is by sending a welcoming email message. This note should be from a real person, even if it is sent automatically from the mailing list server. Have either the project's founder or your community manager write this welcoming message. It should confirm the novice's membership and explain how the community works. You shouldn't overload new members with information but rather provide links to what they are likely to need to know as they get started working on your project.

On your website, you should help novices learn who's who in your community. Include a page listing the major contributors, community leaders, and module owners. If you can include pictures of folks, all the better. Introduce novices to your regulars and leaders at community meetings.

Depending on your project, you may want to have a special mailing list, discussion forum, or even a subproject for newcomers to get their initial questions answered. This can keep the same basic questions from constantly being posted to your main mailing lists. It lets novices help each other, which sets a good tone for later. This is another reason to have good FAQ lists and to regularly link to them in the major mailing lists.

Be sure to encourage a friendly attitude that is tolerant of inappropriate postings by novices on project mailing lists. Gently let the offenders know how your project does things, without personally attacking them. Redirect inappropriate messages to the correct mailing list. Discourage flaming. This attitude encourages novices to participate and is good for your community of regulars too.

Reward Your Regulars

Regulars are the lifeblood of your project; they are the folks who do the work to make your project a success. They answer questions on the mailing lists, report bugs and bug fixes, contribute code and new ideas, tell others about your project, and do all the other work necessary for your project to move forward. Do everything you can to encourage your regulars to participate and to retain their interest in your project.

Because many open-source projects are meritocracies, be sure to recognize people doing good work. Be sure to add them to the project's list of contributors. Reward them by granting them CVS commit privileges. Invite them to be part of the core group. Encourage them to take responsibility for part of the design or a module of code.

A good way to show appreciation for the work your regulars do is to have a spotlight feature on your website's home page or in your project's newsletter that highlights individuals and their work. You can also encourage them to give a presentation at a community meeting. Not only does it reward them directly, but it also can educate your community about new functionality and encourage other regulars and novices by giving them an example of what your community values.

Another way to show that you value your regulars is to use resources from your company to further refine one of their contributions to help bring it up to project-quality standards, as described earlier. Even having one of your graphic artists create a cool logo for a subproject may be appreciated. Just be sure they feel you are working with them and not trying to take over from them.

The ultimate way to retain your best regulars is to hire them! It is always hard to find top talent and especially to know how they will function in your company's culture. With open source, you have a way to try out people and determine whether they fit in with your current team. Even if they do not live near any of your company's offices you already know that they can work productively from wherever they do live (that is, remotely). For example, Sun Labs is supporting a small open-source project called Electric, a computer-aided design system for electrical circuits. When one volunteer really distinguished himself by his contributions, Sun hired him—even though he lives in Moscow and the Sun Labs team is in California.

Empower Your Leaders

Your leaders are the people who keep your community running. Some will be outside volunteers and some will be your employees—a successful project will have a healthy mix of both. Some will have formal leadership roles, such as module owner, but many roles will be more informal. For an open-source project, leadership is all about having a vision and working with others to make it happen; it's not about being in charge, making decisions, or giving orders.

The leaders in your community will naturally take on many different roles:

- Welcoming newcomers to the project and answering their questions.

- Answering technical and procedural questions on your project mailing lists.

- Guiding discussions to help them reach a conclusion.

- Selecting high-quality content to highlight on your website or in your newsletter.

- Coordinating activities such as releases, community meetings, or trade-show demos.

- Providing quality checks on contributed code.

- Policing community discussions to keep them civil, and redirecting messages to the correct mailing list.

- Resolving conflicts and helping the community to make decisions.

- Solving complex technical problems.

- Creating compelling visions and directions for the project.

You need to watch your regulars to see which are starting to assume any of these roles and encourage them to do so. Try to recruit outside volunteers to oversee visible project-related activities such as module owner, release manager, or newsletter editor. Establish as soon as possible that community members do important things.

Be sure to provide support for new leaders. It may be as simple as your community manager trading some tips via email on guiding discussions or assigning an experienced module owner to mentor a new one. You may want to give all new module owners training on the various tools your project uses. But recognize that volunteers have limited time, so don't push them to act like full-time employees.

When you have project-related discussions and meetings inside your company, try to invite outside volunteer leaders to participate. Be sure to keep them informed on any decisions you make. All of your project's leaders need to be kept in the loop. You do not want to create an us-versus-them attitude.

You can reward your leaders and make them more visible by giving them a special place to express their ideas and opinions. This could be a column in the community newsletter or a series of articles on your website—you could encourage them to write weblogs featured on the project's website. If a leader is not interested in writing, then post an interview instead.

Honor Your Elders

Elders are respected long-time regulars and leaders who are your community's mentors, teachers, and advisors. They provide role models for newcomers and regulars on how to behave properly. They may have stepped down from more active roles such as a leader or contributor, but your community can still benefit from their sharing their knowledge.

Some projects take no notice of when major contributors move on; at most they may add their names to a list of emeritus contributors and also remove them from the list of active developers. The Apache Software Foundation's projects have a rule that committers who have been inactive for 6 months or more may lose their status as committers. Although people can regain their committer status by just requesting it on the project's developer mailing list, the fact that they lost it indicates a certain indifference toward formerly valued community members.

Try to identify potential elders and encourage them to continue to participate in some way. They may not have time to write code, but perhaps they would like to follow various design discussions—they certainly have the knowledge to do so, including knowledge of your project's history and why previous decisions were made the way they were. If any of your senior developers move on to another project in your company, see whether you can get their new managers to approve their continuing, though perhaps minimal, involvement on your project mailing lists.

One way to show that you value your elders is to have a special mailing list for them where the community can ask their opinions on important matters that come up. You can also try to solicit their advice on the regular project mailing lists. Include them in activities at your community meetings and interview them on your website or in your newsletter.

COMMUNICATION CREATES COMMUNITY

Everyone involved with your project—users, designers, developers, and evangelists—should know what is happening with it. Everyone needs to know what's new and be able to participate in discussions about various project issues, plans, and designs. As is mentioned in the section "Let Everyone Know What Is Happening" in Chapter 6, it is crucial that your internal developers use public mailing lists for their discussions so that the entire community can participate.

Your project should start off with as few mailing lists as possible in order to focus things (see the section "Types and Number of Mailing List/Newsgroups" in Chapter 6). This might be one moderated list for infrequent project announcements, one unmoderated list for all user-related questions and comments (including design suggestions), and one unmoderated list for all general developer-related messages (mostly implementation issues).

Your team needs to set a friendly tone on these lists to encourage others to participate (see the section "Posting Etiquette" in Chapter 6). You should encourage people from outside of your company to respond to questions from other users/developers. We recommend the Jini team's policy of waiting 2 days before answering a general user question. Questions that can be answered by only the core team should be answered immediately. This should result in a mailing list where users naturally answer most of the posted questions, and the core developers answer only the more difficult, technical ones.

Mailing lists are great for discussions, but not everyone has the time to follow them. To keep people informed on current issues, you should start a project newsletter. This newsletter should be published on a regular schedule, ranging from weekly to monthly depending on how active your project is. The contents of the newsletter should be featured on your project's website. An example newsletter topic might be a "contributor spotlight" that focuses on some individual who is doing interesting work on the project. The NetBeans project publishes both a brief weekly newsletter, consisting mostly of links to interesting discussions on its mailing lists, and a monthly newsletter with full articles covering such things as project-related news, feature stories on developers and projects, and pointers to press articles about NetBeans.

Community Meetings

To create a real community for your project requires that people get to know one another. Some of this can happen over mailing lists, but far better are face-to-face meetings. Have a community meeting as soon as possible and at regular intervals afterward. For smaller projects, you might need to hold your community meeting as part of some larger event, for example as a birds-of-a-feather (BoF) session at conferences such as JavaOne or LinuxWorld. Try to hold meetings in different locations so more of your community can attend.

A community meeting is a great way to raise the overall level of excitement about your project. Avoid dull status-reporting sessions. Plan for more interactive formats to take advantage of people being together. Users and developers usually have lots of questions they would like to ask the core developers, so be sure they get a chance. Introduce major contributors so people can associate faces with names. Your developers should also become known as individuals. Reserve time for people to schedule BoFs during the meeting. Include time for people to informally chat and network.

Don't be constrained by regular meeting formats. The Jini project has held several open celebrations that they call Jini Fest! where they show off cool aspects of Jini technology and provide an occasion for Jini developers to socialize and network. These have been more free-form events held during the annual JavaOne conference where groups are invited to show off their work with Jini—both companies using Jini and various Jini Community projects are invited. Each group hosts a table in a big room. Add food and drink, plus several hundred Jini enthusiasts, and you have an exciting event. They even filmed part of the event as part of a webcast about Jini technology featured at JavaOne.

Community meetings are also a great place to hold working group meetings. Getting the major players into a room can speed up decision-making on open issues. (Be sure to report back via email to the full community on any decisions made at the meeting.)

Other meeting options include phone conferences and online chat sessions. You might also consider using a webcast to present status updates or other information to your worldwide community. The Jini project has done several webcasts. Although webcasts are not as interactive as a meeting, they are good at helping your community to get to know the people presenting material. Putting a human face on your main developers and contributors helps to build community. An open-source project has by definition a distributed work group, and you need to explore ways to facilitate communications among the members.

Events

Sometimes you can create a strong sense of community and attract others to your project by sponsoring events, such as a reception at a larger conference. In many cases, conference organizers are receptive to the idea of a special event or sponsorship at their conference to add texture at low cost to them. Conference organizers often contract with a hotel or conference center to lease a fixed set of the facilities for the entire duration of the conference, and therefore these facilities might be available at low or no cost to you.

A good example is IBM and Eclipse. At the ACM Conference on Object-Oriented Programming, Systems, Languages, and Applications (OOPSLA) in both 2002 and 2003, IBM sponsored Eclipse receptions. In 2003, the reception featured a few short speeches but lots of food and demonstrations. There were no other conference events that evening, so attendance was high. The event was held in one of the main conference halls, which cost IBM nothing, and the entire affair cost less than $20,000 for the food and drinks. It was at this conference and reception that Erich Gamma and Kent Beck's book on contributing to Eclipse went public.

NEW FORMS OF COMMUNICATION: WIKIS AND WEBLOGS

The tools available for online communication continue to evolve. As they do, new opportunities arise for people in open-source projects to interact and collaborate with each other. Two particularly promising new technologies are the wiki and the weblog.

The WikiWikiWeb

A wiki is a website that allows people to edit web pages collaboratively. A wiki makes it easy for anyone to view, edit, and create web pages using just a web browser. A very simple markup scheme allows basic text formatting. In the original wiki, a link to another wiki page was automatically created by writing several words with their first letters capitalized and with no spaces between them, for example, OpenSource or CollaborativeDevelopment. If there was not already a page with that name, a new one was created.

A wiki is a great way for a community to create a group document. As members browse the existing pages, any time they see mistakes or want to make additions all they need to do is press the *Edit this page* button displayed at the bottom of the page. This loads the current text of the page into a form in which it can be edited. The *Save page* button in the form saves a new version of the page, which is immediately made available for all to see.

The first wiki website[9] was established by Ward Cunningham in 1995. Ward originally called it the WikiWikiWeb from the word *wiki wiki*, which means "quick" in the Hawaiian language. For another example, check out the Wikipedia,[10] where, in only 3 years, the online community has created an open-content encyclopedia of almost 300,000 entries (as of July 2004). Open-source projects have recently begun to use wikis. The Apache Software Foundation has a wiki[11] used by its various projects, and the GNOME project has set up a wiki[12] to provide support.

Writing in wiki pages consists of either unsigned, deliberately anonymous text that is intended to be community material which others are encouraged to update and improve (for example, a page on the Apache wiki describing how to do log rotation for the James mail/news server) or a series of signed comments where people hold a form of conversation as they try to reach an understanding of the issues involved (for example, a page discussing which Java IDE to use, also on the Apache wiki). Anyone can both reorganize the conversational threads to clarify the material, possibly moving them to new pages, and revise the community material based on the comments made. Over time more and more community-owned text is created expressing the community consensus and the concluded discussions may be removed. Many wikis provide simple version-control mechanisms so that no text is lost, and archiving important versions of a wiki page can make looking at history easy.

Most wikis have a special *RecentChanges* page that displays an automatically generated index of all the wiki pages that have been changed recently.

---

9. http://c2.com/cgi/wiki

10. http://www.wikipedia.org

11. http://wiki.apache.org/general

12. http://gnomesupport.org/wiki

Many people check the *RecentChanges* page frequently to see what is new on the wiki.

Many people's immediate reaction when they first hear about wiki is that it cannot possibly work. People worry that someone will come along and delete what is there or write random garbage all over pages. This indeed can, and does occasionally, happen, but as soon as the wiki's community members notice the problem, one of them erases the graffiti and restores the page's original contents from the previous archived version. After continually having their "work" removed, the offending individuals usually quickly give up and go elsewhere.

A more common problem is that no community consensus emerges, possibly because the community is split into opposing viewpoints on some issue. Then it is important that the community try to express each of the viewpoints rather than resolving the issue to a single "correct" one. This requires a real sense of community and a respect for the beliefs of other community members. The Wikipedia calls this writing with a *neutral point of view* and has a good description of how to do this.[13]

Another reason that discussions sometimes do not resolve is that the community is exploring a new area and just doesn't know enough yet. In this case, the discussions remain visible as a reminder that the issue is still open. As individuals and hence the community learn more, people may eventually add to the discussion and reorganize it.

The wide-open nature of the wiki and most people's unfamiliarity with wikis can present a barrier. People can be afraid of what will happen to what they write or unsure what type of contributions are acceptable. The tone set by the community will either encourage new folks to join in or discourage them from doing so. Once people contribute and begin to edit wiki pages, they gain a feeling of empowerment and often develop a vested interest in overseeing the wiki as a whole.

A wiki is a community effort and each develops its own culture. In general, the sense of working together to build a better understanding seems to encourage people to be more polite than many other Internet activities do—perhaps because on a wiki any flames, spam, and trivia can be easily deleted, while the constructive comments typically expand and grow.

Coming to a common place, sharing a vocabulary, and working together over time on common goals all help to make the people using a wiki into an actual community.

For more information on wikis, see the book *The Wiki Way: Collaboration and Sharing on the Internet* by Bo Leuf and Ward Cunningham.

---

13. http://en.wikipedia.org/wiki/Neutral_point_of_view

Weblogs or Blogs

A weblog (also known by its contraction, "blog") is an online journal with entries on whatever topic or topics interest the author, usually including links to online articles, news, or other blogs. Blogs enable people without much web experience to create, format, and post diarylike entries with ease. Blogs are a great way for an individual to have a place to express opinions.

We have discussed mostly communities built up by collaboration, but the blog focuses on the individual. Helping to create a strong individual identity also helps to build community—community is about getting to know the individual members in the community better over time, something that blogs help to do. They also help to bridge the gaps among multiple communities that the blogger is a member of. Many people who write blogs include a list of links to other blogs that they read. This *blogroll* helps to define the blogging community that a person identifies with.

A good way for an open-source project to make use of blogs is to have a news page that displays the latest blog entries from selected community members or a project group blog. Most blogs provide an RSS (*Rich Site Summary* or *Really Simple Syndication*) feed that other web pages can subscribe to. Using this RSS feed, a project can feature on its home page headlines for the most recent relevant blog entries.

Having key people in your project write a blog (called "blogging") is another channel for getting important information to your community; it is also a good way to reach people outside of your community who are interested in your project. Anyone can subscribe to the RSS feeds from your blogs and thus get timely updated news concerning your project.

A good book on how to write a blog is *The Weblog Handbook: Practical Advice on Creating and Maintaining Your Blog* by Rebecca Blood.

Community Outreach

Your project does not exist in a vacuum. Strengthen your connections with other open-source projects. Do this to be a good citizen and because it will benefit your project. If your software engineers establish good reputations with the open-source community it will benefit your company.

Being active in the larger world of open source will help you with your open-source project. Your project infrastructure undoubtedly will use many open-source tools such as CVS, Bugzilla, and Perl, so you may want to become involved in the debates about their future development. Seeing how other projects are run will give you ideas about what your project should or should not do.

Market your project to other open-source efforts. These provide a natural audience for the software you develop and are a source of potential contributors. For example, if you create an application that runs on Linux, then you should work with groups creating Linux distributions so that your application will be included—OpenOffice is part of the Linux distributions from RedHat, SuSE, and Mandrake.

ESTABLISHING CREDIBILITY WITH THE OPEN-SOURCE CROWD

Beyond the day-to-day activities of your project, there are some other things you can do to establish better credibility with the larger open-source community. The bigger and more visible your project is, the more important it is for people working on other open-source projects to see you as being part of this larger open-source community.

First, it will help if you are using a license that has been blessed by the more well-known spokespeople for open source, such as Richard Stallman, Tim O'Reilly, Bruce Perens, and Eric Raymond. If your project uses an OSI-certified open-source license such as BSD, Mozilla, or the GNU GPL, then these spokespeople will be able to go on record as saying your project is true open source and a Good Thing. If your project is using a proprietary or shared source license, they and the press will be sure to point out that your project is not open source. This issue arose with Sun's Jini project, which uses the Sun Community Source License (SCSL)—even though Sun was quite clear in stating that it was creating a gated community and not trying to do true open source, the press and some open-source pundits kept saying, "Yes, but it's not open source." This deflected attention from the Jini technology and slowed down the growth of the project around it.

Second, you should establish strong, positive connections with other open-source projects. If your project uses tools or modules developed by other open-source projects or your project produces tools or modules that other open-source projects could benefit from, then not only should you be involved with these other projects, but you should try to entwine their projects and yours as much as possible. An ideal situation is for your project to be part of the planning process—for future features and the timing of releases—for those other projects. The OpenOffice project started with the intent to integrate its office productivity suite with the GNOME desktop, so it became involved in the GNOME community, contributing code and bug fixes back to the GNOME project. As the collaboration deepened, technologies and components from each project became part of the other, so that OpenOffice can be said to be deeply embedded into GNOME. The more your project is seen as not only supporting but deeply integrated with other open-source efforts, the more your project—and thus your company—will be considered a good member of the larger open-source community.

You should also establish dialogs with open-source developers not involved with your project. Have your internal developers both read and post to places such as Slashdot.[14] Encourage them to start individual weblogs. The more individuals from your company that people see participating in open-source forums—especially when their email addresses include your company's domain name—the harder it will be for them to see your company as a large faceless corporation. It is fine for your company's developers to express whatever views they have, but they should strive for some restraint and avoid too much flaming. As mentioned in the section on "Email Etiquette"(Chapter 6), they need to remember that even though they are posting as individuals, people will read their notes as being your company's official policy. When your company's actions are attacked, they should wait a bit to first give outside people a chance to defend your company—statements from people not employed by your company are more effective than statements from employees. Of course, if the criticism is valid, your developers should immediately acknowledge it and fix things.

Harvesting Innovation

If you're trying to do innovation based on your open-source project, then you need to do more than just successfully run the project—you need to harvest what we have called triggers. Harvesting from your community doesn't involve any sort of thievery or unethical behavior—it means simply finding out what your community members are doing; what problems they're having; what books, trends, and technologies they are engaged in; what conferences they attend; and how they are using your open-source software.

Your community manager can lead the way by being sociable and getting to know the active members of the community. Your developers can also get to know community members. Without being intrusive, you can easily come to find out what kinds of uses your community members are making of your open-source software. Are there problems that seem beyond the scope of the open-source project itself? Are there related problems that could be addressed with other products or add-ons? Are people using your technology clustering in application areas you didn't anticipate? Are they talking about a new technology or reading a new book? Are they working on some particular other open-source projects? Are they upgrading their hardware in a pattern?

---

14. http://slashdot.org

When you hold your community meetings, try to arrange for community members to talk about how they are using the project's technology. Use these opportunities to learn about the people who have come to your technology on their own. And learn about what they are doing with it.

Get your developers together periodically to share what's been learned and brainstorm new opportunities. Have a variety of people in your company look at the community. When you think you have something, it might turn out that some community members your community manager is friendly with are willing to discuss your ideas.

The key is just to keep your eyes open—don't pry and don't do official-looking surveys. Simply be aware of what your community is up to, who is in it, and what they share voluntarily about what they are doing and the problems they're having.

Welcome the Unexpected

One of the strengths of open source is that contributors always surprise you. When someone submits a new module that takes things in a new direction, be willing to devote some resources to making it a bigger success. If some people start using your product in ways you didn't expect, check it out and see whether there's a whole new market waiting for you. Most of all, listen to what your community tells you it wants and needs. You have made an investment of company resources in order to use open source, so be sure to get the greatest possible return on that investment by harvesting the innovation that your community creates.

CHAPTER 9

What To Avoid—Known Problems and Failures

AS YOU WORK TO MOVE YOUR PROJECT FORWARD, it is inevitable that you will make some mistakes. How you respond to them can be critical to your project's success. If you are honest with your community about what was done and take steps to correct matters, then your project can move forward with strengthened mutual respect between you and your community. If you refuse to admit that there is a problem or ignore the wishes of your community members, then they will have less trust in you and your intentions. This is especially critical for large companies, because outside developers often start off with a low level of trust concerning the company's motives. Any act that reinforces their fears hurts your project's chances of success. When your actions demonstrate your respect for your community members' opinions, you earn their trust and improve the chances of your project recovering from any future problems.

In this section, we look at some problems that can cause open-source projects to stumble. We hope that by being aware of them you can avoid them in your project.

Not Understanding Open Source

The first problems can arise when people making decisions about whether to use open source for a project do not understand how open source works. A typical failure is for decision makers to not believe the philosophical tenets of open source (see "Philosophical Tenets of Open Source" in Chapter 3) or to believe one or more of the myths about open source (see "Common Open-Source Myths, Misconceptions, and Questions" in Chapter 3). As a result, they decide not to use open source because they imagine there are insurmountable problems, or, even worse, they choose open source but have unrealistic expectations. The first case causes the company to miss a possible opportunity, whereas the second can doom the project to failure.

One common fear decision makers have is that by choosing to make a project open source the core developers will be swamped by having to answer thousands of email messages from outside user developers. (Fear of developers being swamped by questions and requests is one reason that managers isolate engineers working on proprietary projects from customers.) Indeed, the core team will need to spend some of its time engaging with the community and answering questions; however, the bulk of the questions that arise on project mailing lists should end up being answered by other community members—the community naturally provides the necessary resources.

Another common misconception is that open sourcing one product means that everything connected with it, including totally separate programs, must also be open sourced. In the past, Microsoft and others who were opposed to open source have tried to play on this fear in statements and articles where they have called open source both "un-American" and "a cancer."[1] The reality is that even under a strong open-source license such as the GPL only the actual source code of the application is affected. Other open-source licenses, such as the LGPL, Mozilla, and BSD, make it easy to combine proprietary and open-source code. There are real issues about what IP an open-source project will share, but they are not as horrific or all-devouring as people uninformed on the details of open source might fear. Note that because open-source licenses have yet to be thoroughly tested in court, lawyers are prone to be overly cautious when they first read an open-source license.

Many people believe that the point of doing open source is to get hundreds of outside developers to work for them for free. When this doesn't happen—and it almost certainly won't—they declare the project a failure. Moreover, managers who believe that open source is just a way to cut costs may not allocate sufficient resources to the project—starving it to death.

A related misconception is that you will get hundreds of developers contributing lots of random low-quality code that you will somehow need to deal with. This just doesn't happen. If you are lucky, you might get a number of

---

1. Microsoft CEO Steve Ballmer called Linux a "cancer" because of its use of GPL, in an interview in the *Chicago Sun Times* on June 1, 2001. Microsoft's operating systems chief Jim Allchin said the following in a statement originally reported by *Bloomberg News* on February 14, 2001: "I'm an American; I believe in the American way . . . I worry if the government encourages open source, and I don't think we've done enough education of policymakers to understand the threat." One of the many online discussions of both these remarks can be found at http://www.computerweekly.com/articles/article.asp?liArticleID = 123866&liFlavourID = 1&sp = 1. Since these statements, Microsoft has launched a number of shared-source programs, and at this time sponsors two small open-source projects on SourceForge (http://sourceforge.net/projects/wtl and http://sourceforge.net/projects/wix).

outside developers experimenting with your source code trying to fix bugs or make improvements, but you will never hear from most of them. Like most people, developers do not want to appear foolish in a public forum. If they think that their potential contributions are not so great, they will most likely never show them to anyone. In fact, your problem is more apt to be the opposite: trying to convince potential contributors to submit code that they feel is less than perfect.

A common mistake is believing that a company can open source a project to get good PR while playing the same old proprietary game. The outside world will quickly see this for the sham it is, and no one will join the project. Doing an open-source project for the wrong reasons will probably get you a lot of bad press coverage and alienate outside developers.

A different type of problem is starting to occur as more people learn about open source: People sometimes believe that any open-source project they create must work exactly the same way as an existing open-source project. Projects such as Apache, Mozilla, and Linux are being held up as exemplars of the only way to run an open-source project. Although it is important to learn from successful open-source projects, we are still just beginning to understand the landscape of open source. To succeed requires adopting an open-source attitude and innovating new ways to do things.

Another mistake is not understanding that starting an open-source project is like launching a new product. They have similar life-cycle issues, the most important being that neither can be ended abruptly without upsetting your customers, which includes the community in the case of an open-source project. Open-source projects, like products, require an end-of-life plan. For more details, please refer to the section on "Ending an Open-Source Project" in Chapter 6.

Don't Needlessly Duplicate an Existing Effort

In pure voluntary open source, there generally will be only one open-source project in a given area. Innovation and invention are still possible, but the open-source philosophy is, as much as possible, to resist diversity and instead to press forward with a single solution with maximum effort. The few instances where there are two open-source projects trying to produce similar results are due to political issues: GNOME happened because of unhappiness with the license used by KDE, XEmacs came about because of a disagreement over how to add display support to Emacs, and Linux started up while AT&T was battling legally with Berkeley over BSD.

There are only so many open-source developers interested in a given area, and it is hard enough to create one community of them, let alone two. So if there is already an open-source project with goals similar to yours, then you should endeavor to join that project. If there is some very good reason why you cannot join with them—and it had better be an extremely compelling reason, such as they are using GPL and your business aim is to produce a proprietary version—then you should rethink whether you should be doing open source at all.

Sometimes diversity is what's needed. If you decide to start a project building something with the same basic intent as an existing open-source project, you need to understand that you will get fewer volunteers and that the differences must be clear and distinct. Over time, you might convince people that your differences are worthwhile and thereby attract more developers and users; and over the very long run you might be in a position to merge back with the original open-source project once the relative importance and attractiveness of the different design and implementation decisions become clear through use.

The story of XEmacs is illustrative here because it is perhaps the first instance of a commercial company working on free or open source as part of a business strategy, and it was also probably the first and most visible fork of an open code base.

In 1991, a company named Lucid, Inc.,[2] was working on a product called Energize, which was an integrated development environment (IDE) for C and C++ on Unix. The design of this development environment involved very tight integration among the various tools: compilers, linkers, debuggers, graphers, and editors. The IDE needed a powerful editor to tie the whole thing together, and the Lucid designers chose Emacs. Moreover, the IDE was graphics based: It assumed a window system such as X rather than the character-oriented terminals of the day.

The then-current version of GNU Emacs from the Free Software Foundation was Emacs 18, which was a terminal-based editor relying on simple character placement for its visual display rather than on a graphics-based environment, which is standard today. At the time, there was another version of GNU Emacs called Epoch that had been developed at NCSA; this was a set of patches to Emacs 18 that gave it much better GUI support.

Also at that time, the next major release of Emacs, Emacs 19, was expected to integrate features from Epoch, but was long overdue. The Epoch maintainers themselves saw Epoch as an interim measure, awaiting the release of Emacs 19.

The developers at Lucid didn't want to tie themselves to the soon-to-be-obsolete Emacs 18 or to Epoch because those code bases were considered obsolete

---

2. Richard Gabriel was the founder of Lucid, originally and primarily a company that provided Common Lisp systems for all the hardware manufacturers when artificial intelligence was all the rage. Ron Goldman was an employee of Lucid for several years.

even by their maintainers. The Lucid developers wanted to use Emacs 19; the idea was that Energize would operate with the off-the-shelf version of Emacs 19, which most people would already have installed on their system anyway. In that way, Energize would make use, to some extent, of tools developers already had and were already using.

But because Emacs 19 wasn't done yet, Lucid decided to provide funding and resources to help get Emacs 19 finished. Many of the Lucid developers were fans of the Free Software Foundation and contributed to free software projects, so all their work on Emacs 19 was released under GPL, and they assigned copyright on all their work back to the Free Software Foundation. Lucid had no proprietary interest in Emacs per se—it was simply a tool that would enhance the value of their proprietary product, and they hoped there would be good PR associated with releasing the GUI-based Emacs when Emacs 19 had been delayed so long. Among the other work Lucid did for Emacs was to produce a user manual, which would be required for the proprietary product.

Unfortunately, the relationship with the Free Software Foundation broke down, primarily for two reasons:

- There was a dispute over the design of a hypertextlike addition to Emacs.

- There was a dispute about how display and redisplay could best be done on window systems such as X.

Moreover, the Free Software Foundation was not in a position to work as quickly as Lucid needed, so Lucid bundled its work into what became Lucid Emacs and released it as a GPLed open-source editor.

After Lucid went out of business in 1994 (for unrelated reasons), Lucid Emacs became XEmacs. To this day, XEmacs is about as popular as FSF Emacs because it still provides features and a design that many people find superior to the FSF's version.

As of fall 2003, the XEmacs project was looking at merging back into FSF Emacs, but there were still too many irreconcilable differences in the way the two projects viewed technical, programming, design, and organizational matters to make a merge possible. Although some commentators consider XEmacs to have been a divisive fork, others consider the competition between the two groups as positive for the rapid advancement of Emacs over the last decade.

If you decide to start a competing project it is very important that you establish good relations with the developers of the existing project. The last thing you want is to have them bad-mouthing your project on forums such as Slashdot. Also, you probably share many common goals with them and there are apt to be many subprojects you can work on together, such as establishing common file formats.

There will sometimes be cases where creating a competing open-source effort cannot be avoided. For example, when Sun released their StarOffice code as OpenOffice it overlapped with two existing open-source projects: Gnumerics and AbiWord. StarOffice was an existing proprietary office suite built to compete with Microsoft office. The lead developer for Gnumerics had been engaged in conversations with Sun about this overlap before OpenOffice was announced, and, as a result, he viewed the OpenOffice project in a good light and was receptive to working with Sun. However, no one on the AbiWord project was consulted before or after the OpenOffice announcement; worse, one of the AbiWord developers tried to start a discussion on one of the OpenOffice mailing lists about developing a common XML file format, but never received any replies from the StarOffice engineers. The result was that the AbiWord developers became suspicious of Sun's motives and did not work with Sun, and both efforts are the worse because of this.

One final point about creating a competing open-source project: Do not expect any people working on existing projects to switch to your project. Your outside contributors will come from people who have not yet gotten involved with either project, and you will be in direct competition with the other project for potential new developers. In the OpenOffice example, none of the Gnumerics or AbiWord developers switched over to work on OpenOffice.

Licensing Issues

The license you choose can create problems if it is unfamiliar to your target audience or inappropriate for your project.

It is a bad idea to create a new license for your project. There is a set of existing, mature open-source licenses that open-source developers are familiar with, and it is unlikely that your concerns are not addressed by one of them. If people are unfamiliar with a license they tend to be suspicious of it and shy away from the project. When Sun first introduced the Sun Community Source License (SCSL), no one quite knew what to make of it; it was also hard to understand. Using a new license requires taking on a large community education effort—time that might be better spent working on your project.

The Mozilla project has decided that it wants to be able to engage more with a number of projects that use the GPL. As a result, it is in the messy process of contacting all the people who have ever contributed code to Mozilla to get their permission to multiply license the code under MPL, GPL, and LGPL. This highlights two problems: how letting contributors hold the copyright for their contribution prevents changing licensing terms and how the choice of license can limit who will work on the code.

Beware of trying to change either the license or the contributor agreement after your project is underway. Sometimes doing this is no problem; for example, OpenOffice changed from requiring contributors to assign copyright of their submissions to Sun to requiring contributors to sign a joint copyright agreement (JCA), which gave contributors more rights and was accepted by the community almost without comment. However, when the NetBeans project, which had not previously required copyright assignment, announced it was adopting the same joint copyright requirement for contributors, several community members complained that Sun was acting unfairly, because it took away the right of exclusive ownership. Had NetBeans started with a JCA, it is likely that the issue would never have arisen. Part of the problem with almost any change you make is that it will act as a lightning rod, opening the door to larger-scale criticism if your community has major unresolved issues with the way you are leading the project.

In general, when a company sponsoring an open-source project decides to make a major change to the license, the code, the architecture, the community, or anything else visible and important, the outside community will tend to view such decisions with suspicion. It will wonder whether there is some hidden, sinister reason for the change that is not decipherable and hence represents a trap. Therefore, make changes with care and involve the community as early as possible in discussions about important changes.

Design Issues

Earlier we have mentioned that low-code quality can be an issue. Similarly, a poor or otherwise deficient system design can lead to less success than could be hoped for. In large part, successful open-source projects have been either copies of good designs (Linux, for example) or have been designed by extraordinary designers. In some cases, their work had already been proven in the form of a series of excellent designs, and in others they were new talents in the making.

A company should think carefully about how good a design it is thinking of offering as an open-source project. In most cases, a company should offer software designed by proven designers or else do a careful design review before releasing the code, followed by revisions if needed.

An interesting but complex example of this is NetBeans versus Eclipse—this illustrates the design quality issue and also the first-mover myth. NetBeans started as a student project (originally called Xelfi) in the Czech Republic in 1996. The goal was to write a Delphi-like Java IDE in Java. A company was formed around this project, called NetBeans. Sun acquired the company in 1999 and soon thereafter open sourced the code. Eclipse was designed and initially implemented by OTI, a Canadian company that had previously been acquired by IBM. OTI had extensive experience developing programming environments. Eclipse was released as open source several years after NetBeans.

The two designs differ dramatically in maturity and quality. Part of this has to do with the experience levels of the two design groups, but some has to do with when the designs were done and the different knowledge levels—1996 versus 2000 and students versus older professionals. The later Eclipse design has a sophisticated but easy-to-handle plug-in architecture with XML manifests, which reflected the growing use of XML that was apparent to OTI but hidden in the future for the NetBeans student team.

At this point (spring 2004), Eclipse is regarded as superior and has more mind- and market share, but NetBeans has a considerable following and is making design and architecture changes. Nevertheless, any company would be wise to be sure of the quality and maturity of a design before releasing it.

Code Issues

One of the first hurdles an open-source project faces is whether the code is complete and builds a working application. The classic complaint about Mozilla in its early days was that the source code Netscape released was incomplete and could not make a working web browser. The Mozilla team was committed to the work, so the project continued. Once a working browser began to emerge, more casual contributors have also been able to participate.

This is also a common problem for small projects that are started because someone has a cool idea: A group of people may exchange messages about the idea and suggest ways to improve it, but somehow no one ever gets around to writing any code! Remember that open source only works to incrementally improve what's there—if you have only design ideas, then that's what the community will improve. Someone needs to write the code for a minimal but working version before the community will contribute any code.

A second hurdle is making sure that the user succeeds when trying out your application for the first time. This was a noticeable problem with Jini, not because of a problem with the Jini code but rather because of a problem configuring Windows systems to properly support multicasting. The lesson here is that even though your code is fine, problems with other software may cause your project to suffer. You need to go to some lengths to anticipate initial usage patterns and skill levels of the users when code is released to the community. In the Jini case, it was expected that mostly Solaris users would try out Jini and that any Windows users would be able to figure out how to configure multicast properly. This expectation proved to be false on both counts.

Another stumbling block occurs when outside developers have trouble navigating the source code. This could be because the code is too difficult to understand (in which case it should be rewritten), there is inadequate system documentation, or the code base is too large. Developers who want to work on the OpenOffice project have a steep learning curve due to the tremendous amount of code involved. This is a particularly common problem as a project moves from being proprietary to open source because of the vastly different levels of developer involvement—even an incredibly well-documented proprietary project still assumes a full-time commitment from a new developer.

Marc Fleury and Juha Lindfors wrote in "Enabling Component Architectures with JMX" about how modularity increased open-source productivity in the JBoss project:

> *Modularity in open source is not just a good idea. Modularity is the only way a project can mature. Successful open source projects are usually measured by the number of people that participate in the development. It is common for very successful teams to have a tightly knit core team of developers working on core functionality, but the key to growing the codebase is to enable lots of developers to work on modules around the core.*
>
> *JBoss 1.0 was near completion when the core developers came to a simple conclusion: it was too hard for the casual developer to come in and contribute over the course of a week. One would have to spend at least a week to understand the code before making any contribution. The situation was typical of second generation open source projects: lots of people wanted to participate but very few could actually do so.*
>
> *For the third iteration, JBoss embraced JMX. Within a week, an alternate SOAP-based invocation layer was submitted to the JBoss group. Modularity is needed for open source development and management. JMX is a natural way to enforce modularity in a design. The increased productivity and the ease of component integration to the server has made JBoss and JMX a success.[3]*

A related problem cropped up in the JXTA project. The JXTA source code was deliberately released early so that the community could help design it. This led to some developers being confused about which aspects of JXTA were not yet defined and which had just not been documented yet. Once adequate

---

3. Java Management Extensions (JMX) technology provides the tools for building distributed, web-based, modular, dynamic solutions for managing and monitoring devices, applications, and service-driven networks. Quote taken from: http://www.onjava.com/pub/a/onjava/2001/02/01/jmx.html

documentation was written that made this clear, the discussion was able to move forward smoothly.

A different type of problem can happen when a project has a slow release cycle. One way that the outside world judges how well a project is doing is by how long it has been since the last release. If a project goes too long without a release, people will start to consider the project dead or a failure. For example, many people thought that the Mozilla project was in trouble after its first year because no working browser had been released. The frequent releases starting in mid-2001, leading up to version 1.0 in June 2002 and continuing since, have dispelled this feeling and now people outside of the Mozilla project have good evidence that it is alive and making progress.

If your project has not released anything for a long time, you should consider putting less into your next release and trying to do smaller, more frequent releases. You should also make sure that your project website is updated regularly—a stale website is another indication of a dying or dead project.

Another potential problem relates to subprojects. As we discussed in the earlier section "Don't Needlessly Duplicate an Existing Effort," there is usually only one open-source project in a given area. This also applies within an open-source project: Once someone contributes a new module to your project, it will be difficult for a similar module to compete. Stated another way, the first code to show up usually wins.[4] For example, as part of the Apache XML Project, the Xerces XML parser appeared first making it difficult for another XML parser, the Crimson subproject, to be adopted. In fact, the best parts of Crimson have been merged into the Xerces code base and work on the Crimson subproject has been halted.

A problem comes from believing that developing the code is all that is required. If all of your attention is on developing the code, you are likely to lose track of your main business goals. For example, if ubiquity is a goal, then marketing the technology to potential partners should have a high priority—internal development resources should be focused on helping partners succeed. If you can get a large company such as IBM or HP to adopt the technology, you can be sure they will contribute their own developers to help work on the code. Unfortunately, the natural tendency is to try to do everything yourself, and so larger opportunities are often neglected.

Another way this problem can hurt your project is if the developers, both internal and external, are the only ones to decide on the project's future direction.

---

4. This is in contrast to the case in the commercial world, where the first to market is rarely the winner ("Creativity" in Chapter 2). Unlike in the commercial world, the open-source community tends to perform relentless and continuous design and redesign, thereby quickly turning a possibly flawed first attempt into a polished winner.

The whole idea of open source as a meritocracy focused on coding tends to disenfranchise anyone who does not contribute code, which means that users, UI designers, marketing people, and the like are often not able to fully participate. This results in software that is designed by developers for developers, and this is why much open-source software is not appropriate for the general public. If you are seeking "world domination," then this can be a major problem that you need to overcome.

One way to make the focus go beyond the code is to actively make roles for nondevelopers such as UI designers and documentation writers. For example, NetBeans has a communitywide mailing list dedicated to the design and discussion of UI issues. There is also a NetBeans project focusing on UI development and issues, plus a process through which other developers can get UI design assistance from the members of the UI project. When the NetBeans project first started, there was a hesitancy to add nondeveloper roles like this because that wasn't something that the high-profile open-source projects such as Apache or Linux did. You may encounter similar resistance.

It should be noted that the UI community traditionally has worked in a test-first design atmosphere in which usability testing takes place before committing anything to code, so there could be a basic mismatch of working styles between your UI folks and the open-source developers. This has been known to hurt open-source projects in general, so you should make sure that the UI folks you include in your open-source project are educated in continuous (re)design and buy into the approach.

Trying to Control Too Much

One of the surest ways to cripple an open-source project is for the original developers to refuse to give up control. At best this turns potential outside developers into a user group, and at worst it kills the project. There are many ways that the original developers can try to keep control.

A common mistake is that the internal development group believes that it does not need to change how it works. Very often the internal developers continue to use a private company mailing list to carry on discussions about project issues. Although not every email message needs to be sent to the public project mailing list, if essential design discussions are carried out in private, then one of the main benefits of open source—feedback from users and outside developers—is lost. A further problem is that when the internal developers do post to the rest of the community, they are announcing what they have decided rather than starting a community discussion. For a successful open-source project, the internal development team needs to shift its email discussions to the project's public mailing lists.

The other major way that internal developers keep control of the development process is by keeping a private code archive, often one that relies on a proprietary code versioning tool instead of CVS. Some projects do not even have a public code archive, just tar[5] files with the source code for the most recent release. This sends a clear message to potential outside developers that they are second-class citizens who can look at the code but never touch it meaningfully—in fact they cannot even see the most recent changes but need to wait until the public copy is updated. A real open-source project has one public code archive that all developers use, although not everyone will have full write-access to it.

Another problem arises when developers want their design or code to be perfect before letting anyone else see it. A major shift in attitude is needed to go from a proprietary development environment where, in many cases, no one ever looks at your code, to an open-source world where everyone may see what you've done, warts and all. Whether it's a single developer or the entire internal development team, waiting too long before releasing a design or code is a mistake that hurts the overall project. It is important that everyone thinks in terms of a work in progress, developed in the open to maximize possible feedback from others. Remind folks that nothing is final; it is always subject to modification as the project's needs change.

A more general problem is common to both proprietary and open-source projects: developers and managers try to make a master plan and then carry it out. Planning is good, but, carried to the extreme of not adapting to change, it can hurt your project. For example, some open-source projects try to figure out all the appropriate mailing lists and set them up so they will be ready when the project is first announced. Unfortunately, the needs of a project that has just started up are often quite different from those of one that has been running for a while. A better approach is to start with one or two main mailing lists and to create more lists only when the number of daily messages grows too large. Engineering in general often tries to do the "right thing" in one step rather than taking a number of smaller steps in whatever direction currently seems best. A decision maker who believes strongly in master planning will probably not buy into the fundamental philosophical tenets of open source (see "Philosophical Tenets of Open Source" in Chapter 3).

---

5. "Tar" stands for tape archive. Originally the tar program was used to store files in archives on magnetic tape, but the modern generalization of it can create a single file that holds both files and directories, which is convenient for emailing, uploading, and downloading source code files for an entire system or large program. Such files are called "tar files" or, more properly, "tar archives"; a colorful variant is "tarball."

A very bad problem occurs when the internal developers do not have respect for the outside developers. If any member of the core team thinks of the outside developers as bozos who should be ignored, then you can be sure that the community will pick up on that attitude and react negatively. You should remember that there are more smart people outside your company than inside it, and one major reason for making your project open source is to be able to engage with such people as much as possible. In an email discussion about a project where the core developers were not engaging with the community, Alan Cox, one of the primary Linux kernel developers, put it like this: "Give feedback and you get more than repaid. Ignore people and you lose them forever."[6]

This problem can often be seen when core developers refuse to engage with outside developers in design discussions on the project's mailing lists—often the core developers don't even read the public mailing lists. Refusing to listen to community concerns hurts the project because it both kills a sense of community and results in developing the wrong product. Keep in mind that approximately half of all software projects fail, not for technical reasons but because they produce a result that does not match the needs of the target audience. Feedback from the community in an open-source project increases the probability that what is produced is what is wanted. Make sure you listen to what your community members say; they are probably right.

If your community encounters difficulties in working with your developers because of any of these problems, then you should not expect much in the way of outside contributions. Any external developers interested in your project will probably work well outside the core area that your internal developers have laid claim to. Contributions of new plug-ins or new modules are possibilities; major improvements to existing modules are not.

Even if you have been doing everything correctly, the community will mostly leave improvements to the core to you until there are visible or a significant number of outside developers working on core modules. That's why it is very important to publicize any outside developer activities or contributions to the core area, to break down the view that your company handles everything related to it. This will take time, so be sure that the metrics you use to measure the success of your project reflect this.

This is not a problem just for company-sponsored projects; traditional open-source projects also encounter it. For example, in April 2003 a fork of the XFree86 project was started because of the feeling that the core team was controlling development too tightly and not listening to the rest of the community. Problems identified by the community included limited development resources

---

6. http://www.xfree86.org/pipermail/forum/2003-April/000983.html

(fewer contributors than for much smaller open-source projects), slow release schedules, lack of cooperation with other projects such as KDE and GNOME, and an opaque development process (core team using a private mailing list and no information available on the XFree86 home page on how to become an XFree86 developer). Part of the problem came from the way the project was initially structured in order to satisfy requirements of a contract with X.org. The rest came from not changing the decision-making process as the project grew. More details can be found in an online interview with a former XFree86 core team member.[7]

The day-to-day operation of a project offers many opportunities to make mistakes by people trying to retain control. Creating a real community requires that the community participate in making decisions. There is no real community when the only developers who can check in code to the CVS archive work for your company, where every important module is owned by a developer employed by your company, or where the governance board consists solely of your company's employees. So grant outside developers the right to check in code as soon as possible, put an outside developer in charge of a module as soon as possible, and have outside developers on your governance board.

You can alienate outside developers if your company's employees are automatically given check-in privileges while outside developers have to earn them by making good contributions. This is a common mistake for open-source projects with a core team from a single company. It is important that all developers be treated according to the same standards regardless of which company they work for. Sometimes new developers at your company may have made contributions that the outside community doesn't see because they have handed over their code to the module owner in private, so be sure to make the activity of new folks visible to all.

Another mistake some open-source projects make is for the module owners to be too slow to accept outside contributions and check them in to the official code archive—or even worse, to refuse to accept them. This might be because the module owner is too busy to deal with any contributions from the community. It might also be because the module owner is being too controlling over what goes into the module. Part of the module owner's job is to maintain the quality of the code, but another, equally important job is to be responsive to the directions set by the community.

If another company is contributing so much code that the module owner becomes a bottleneck, then it is important that one or more of the outside contributors be granted the right to also check in code. The alternatives might be

---

7. http://lwn.net/Articles/27673

that few will make additional contributions or, more likely, that the outside developers will fork the project, as happened when the XEmacs developers started a second open-source project to develop Emacs faster and in a different direction than the original Emacs effort.

In summary, one of the worst things you can do to your open-source project is to try to control it too much. Although other mistakes you could make will slow down or limit your project, your keeping too much control will minimize outside contributions and make it likely that someone will fork the project. Rather than trying to control everything, you should provide positive leadership. If you set goals that the community agrees on, then everyone will be working together to advance the project. If you don't engage the community, you will lose it because everyone will stop trying to work with you and go elsewhere. One final point is that not all engineers and managers are cut out for open source: If they refuse to give up control, then they may do more harm than good for your project.

Many of these problems stem from not thoroughly buying into the philosophy and practices of open source. If the development team and management will not buy into loosening control and valuing active community participation, you should abandon pushing for using an open-source methodology in your company.

Marketing Issues

A big mistake many company-initiated open-source projects make is not actively marketing themselves and the applications they are creating. No marketing means fewer users and fewer contributors. For a low-key effort this may be fine, but if you really want your project to take off, people need to hear about it.

When they hear about it is also important. Some companies make a big announcement well before the project is underway and the code is available. This can drum up quite a bit of interest in the project, but if there's nothing for potential outside contributors to do, it can be a wasted opportunity. For example, in mid-July 2000, Sun announced that the StarOffice source code would be made available, and created a project website at Openoffice.org. This generated lots of interest and many people flocked to the Openoffice.org mailing lists. Unfortunately, there was no documentation about the soon-to-be released code, and only a few, junior StarOffice developers participated on the mailing lists. As a result, potential community members ended up spinning their wheels speculating about how StarOffice worked until the code was finally released in mid-October and more senior members of the StarOffice development team joined the mailing lists. If you were having a party at your house, you would not think of making your guests wait outside for hours before letting them in, and, if they did have to wait outside you would go out and welcome them, not leave them to fend for themselves.

Big announcements that get major press coverage are great for your project—when they have real content and are not simply hype. Many marketing and PR people are trained to sell benefits (and never mention possible drawbacks) as part of making announcements, but to technical people expecting to hear about a down-to-earth open-source project, such selling can sound like hype. Many marketing and PR people do not consider it worthwhile to make announcements in which they cannot sell benefits, and so you end up having relatively infrequent, large announcements with long gaps between them. During these gaps, people might conclude that your project is dead because they haven't heard any recent news about it. This happened to the Jini project in the several-year interval between when the technology was first announced and when products based on Jini began to appear in the marketplace. Any new technology will have a similar interim period. Following a huge initial announcement with a very long and noticeable silence will invite people to think the project has failed. You should make sure that the many small but significant events associated with your project are properly communicated to the public. Frequent short mentions of your progress lets people know that your project is alive and well. An ideal way to communicate current news of your project is to post it on your project's website.

Letting your project website become stale is a surefire way to make people think that your project is dead. Many people interested in your project never subscribe to the project's mailing lists—they periodically surf to your project's website to see what's happening. If the project's home page hasn't changed, they may conclude that no major work has been done and are less likely to check again. Make sure that someone is assigned to update your website on a regular basis.

One of the worst marketing mistakes a company can make is failing to give proper credit for the work done by outside developers. For example, back in December 1999 at a large trade show, Sun announced the release of a Linux version of the Java 2 Platform, Standard Edition (J2SE) that had been done in collaboration with Borland Software Corporation (at the time of this incident, it was named the Inprise Corporation; it was originally named Borland International Inc.). The press release failed to mention that much of the work that lay behind this version of J2SE had been done by the Linux Blackdown Porting Team, a group of open-source programmers devoted to Java. The open-source community was stung by the omission and started to lose trust in Sun. It turned out that this major error happened because the marketing person writing the press release was unaware of the work done by the Blackdown project. Sun immediately released another announcement giving proper credit to the Blackdown team, and the Sun engineers in charge of the Linux port personally apologized to the Blackdown group. Promptly admitting the mistake and correcting it was crucial to Sun's regaining trust with the open-source community.

The Blackdown incident highlights another mistake: Sun failed to publicize participation by Sun engineers in the Blackdown work and other open-source projects. If people inside of Sun had known about this, then the press-release mistake would never have happened. Moreover, many in the open-source community are unaware of Sun's many contributions to open-source projects, which causes Sun to not receive the credit it has earned. According to the Orbiten Free Software Survey[8] done in May 2000, Sun was in fact ranked as the second largest contributor of code to open-source projects. Your company needs to let others know about its contributions to open-source projects to get the credit it deserves—but without overemphasizing or hyping its participation.

Tension between an Open-Source Project and the Rest of Your Company

It's not enough that everyone working on your open-source project interact appropriately with the outside world, you also have to deal with the rest of your company. If others inside your company do not understand why you are using open source and the implications of that for their work, then your project can run into major trouble. Open-source projects need different resources than proprietary ones and have different constraints on how they operate. If this is not understood by those outside your project, then they likely will work against you in the normal internal politics that go on inside every company.

One mistake your open-source project can make is to fail to market itself within your company. Moreover, your message needs to have a different emphasis from the one used for people outside of your company. You need to communicate how the goals of your project help further your company's business goals. If you fail to do this, then your project may be seen as irrelevant and other, proprietary efforts will be given precedence. This marketing must be an ongoing activity, especially when there are changes in upper management.

You must educate people at your company about what metrics will be used to measure the success of your project. These are likely to be quite different

---

8. Formerly located at http://orbiten.org/ofss/01.html, the text of the survey can still be found at http://amsterdam.nettime.org/Lists-Archives/nettime-bold-0005/msg00106.html

from the more familiar metrics used for proprietary projects. Anyone opposed to your project, for whatever reason, will have a much harder time proving it a failure if everyone understands the appropriate metrics for measuring it.

The results of a lack of internal marketing and poor metrics can be devastating to your project if your company hits hard times and needs to look for people to lay off. This happened at Sun in 2001 when the size of the Jini development team was reduced. Particularly hard hit were those folks working on community issues, including the main community manager (who was also one of the original developers of Jini) and the person working on updating the Jini.org website. These were very visible cuts, and the community began to conclude that they signalled that Sun was pulling back from Jini technology. It took several messages from Sun executives to reassure the community that Jini was still important to the company.

A common management mistake we have seen is to have people trying to serve two masters. Developers helping to grow the community while writing code to meet internal deadlines for proprietary work will feel pressure from the company to make the proprietary work higher priority. It is necessary to separate developers into those focused on the open-source activities of the project and those doing work on proprietary projects. Otherwise, local pressure from managers and coworkers will ensure that the proprietary aspects are given priority. A failure to include community-related metrics in the performance reviews of those involved with open-source activities is a common mistake, with the direct result that those community activities tend to be neglected.

The worst type of mistake that projects make is to try to cheat or put something over on their communities. This could be as minor as sneaking code into the code base or as major as blocking a competing company from checking in code it needs. Any actions that treat the open-source project as if it were a proprietary effort owned by your company destroys the community's trust in your company—both for your project and also for any other open-source projects that your company is involved in. People who think that they can get good PR for an open-source project while playing the same old proprietary game are sadly mistaken. If someone tries to avoid, ignore, or otherwise fool your project's community, you need to point out that your company has made a public commitment to your open-source community and any monkey business will get your company bad publicity. Any activity that does not show respect to the community and the approved community processes should be avoided, even when apparently done with good intentions.

Tension between the proprietary side of your company and your open-source project is apt to arise over your project's schedule. Groups doing proprietary efforts within your company expect you to have control over when your project does a release and what features are included in it. If their products depend on yours, this may cause them to make unrealistic plans. You need to educate them so that they understand that your community has a major say in the release process.

Community Issues

So far we have discussed some of the worst mistakes that can hurt the growth of your project's community. These include mistakes such as continuing to work in a proprietary style without engaging the community, trying to plan out the entire community ahead of time rather than letting it develop more organically, starting up the project website and mailing lists before you are ready to participate, and acting as if you owned the entire project.

Another set of mistakes stems from a belief that the community will arise by itself. That will never happen. For example, it is common to believe that the community doesn't need face-to-face meetings—that email communication alone will create the needed connections between people. This just isn't the case. Meeting in person allows folks to put faces with names and to see each other as people; it helps to break down the barriers between your company's employees and outside contributors. A related mistake is believing that all that is needed to have a community meeting is to announce it a few months in advance, and then it will just happen. This also doesn't work. As for any meeting, it is important to plan out what topics will be discussed and to post an agenda well in advance. It is also necessary to talk up the meeting in community discussions. People need to be motivated to want to attend, especially for the first few meetings when the community is just getting established. Creating a vibrant community can occur only if you and your team nurture it by encouraging contributors, holding community meetings, and supporting community activities.

Another problem occurs when your company's developers send harsh or acrimonious messages—*flames*—to a project mailing list. Flaming rarely improves matters, and the community will consider the flame to have come from your company. Make sure you and your teammates follow good posting etiquette and avoid attacking outside developers. Even if you know that the person you want to flame is comfortable with that sort of exchange, remember that public messages are seen by all the community members, many of whom do not appreciate flames. You should think of the entire mailing list as being the audience for any emails you send—don't focus on a specific individual. Because the mailing lists are the major way people in your community communicate, it is crucial that everyone feels safe posting to them. Flaming and harsh criticism in messages discourage many people from participating.

A similar problem is that any opinions or comments posted by an employee of your company will often be taken as official company policy. You need to be sure to indicate which postings are just your personal thoughts and which are really company policy.

Not telling the rest of the community what you are planning is another all too common problem. For a project that you are leading, this behavior will generally discourage community involvement; for a project that you are only a participant in, it will make it harder for you to get your contributions accepted. In both cases, you also lose out by not getting feedback early on when it can do the most good—so your eventual result will not be as good as it could have been. You may be acting with the best of intentions, but others in the community will not know that and are likely to assume otherwise. The article reproduced in Appendix D gives an example of what can happen when a company's developers do not communicate their plans to the community in advance.

Another set of problems center on how easy it is for community members to create new subprojects for modules they are working on. On Jini.org, any registered community member can create a new subproject; however, old subprojects that die are not cleaned up. As a result, it is very confusing to Jini developers who want to join an existing subproject because they are confronted with a list of over 100 subprojects, many of which are defunct. For any open-source project, someone in the community needs to be responsible for pruning inactive subprojects. On the other hand, diversity is good—it's how innovation and creativity come about. So it's good when many subprojects get started, even if many of them die out. And when a subproject is dead, it should be moved to an inactive list rather than to the dumpster in case someone later wishes to pick it up.

Evangelize active projects so potential participants know about them. Both the Jini and the JXTA project home web pages have a section spotlighting one or two community projects.

The opposite problem occurs when it is too hard for someone to start up a new project. Both NetBeans and JXTA have an approval process for creating a new project. A public discussion is required before a new project can be approved. This works to avoid duplication and to inform the rest of the community about the new project, but in a way this may prevent some types of projects from being started. People are generally conservative, and, when a project sounds like it is outside what is normal or usual, people tend to discount or discredit it. So, if you ask people what they think about a project that is innovative in some way, they may tend to disparage it. In contrast, if you simply let the project proceed, then once people try out a working version of it perhaps they will understand its value. That is, a deliberate approval process can screen out innovative projects because of a kind of fear. Many technical people, particularly software people, try to create tidy logical structures and ontologies and then place things into them. When an area is not thoroughly known, it isn't possible to make such tidy structures, but that doesn't inhibit the impulse. Some new projects won't fit into one of these imagined tidy structures and might be criticized because of it. Hence, a better approach might be to allow anyone to create a new project and then have a community coordinator monitor the project's health; should it die, the community coordinator can then move it to a list of inactive projects.

A final community-related problem concerns one-size-fits-all project infrastructure tools. Make sure that the company providing the infrastructure for your project (website, CVS tree, mailing lists, and bug database) does not treat your project as a generic open-source project. Every open-source project will naturally do things slightly differently, and, where this is significant, you don't want your project constrained by your infrastructure provider. For example, the NetBeans project had decided to use a model where any developer trusted to commit changes to one module was trusted to commit changes to every module. This model encourages community members to trust each other, and relies on social rather than technological means to enforce rules for code changes. The original open-source infrastructure provided by CollabNet, the NetBeans infrastructure provider, had supported this model. CollabNet later decided to upgrade their infrastructure, and the new design (SourceCast) assumed as universal the practice some open-source projects adopted of limiting developers' CVS access to just those modules that they have been explicitly granted access to. The NetBeans project discovered this only after the upgrade, and it caused some ruffled feathers in the community when developers' privileges disappeared without warning. CollabNet agreed to change their software to be more policy neutral. This example illustrates two things: technological concerns should not dominate design; and there is not one true way to do open source.

Lack of Resources

The underlying cause of a number of the mistakes we have been discussing is a lack of resources, most notably people to work on some necessary aspect of your project. These people can be employees of your company who are assigned to work on your project, or they can be volunteers, including employees of other companies.

Many projects do not have anyone assigned to be a community manager or coordinator. That can compound any resource problems because the community coordinator is the person who recruits volunteers from the community to help out. For a smaller project, this can be done by the project owner, whereas for bigger projects, it might be part of the product manager's job. For large projects, it can become a full-time job.

The most common reason a project's website becomes stale is that no one has time to update it. Outside contributions can get ignored when module owners are too busy. Someone needs to write the internal documentation needed to orient potential contributors. Make sure that you don't let critical tasks remain undone: Assign an employee of your company or find an outside volunteer.

One of the primary reasons to do an open-source project is to benefit from feedback from outside your company. If you do not have the resources to take advantage of this community feedback, then you are missing out on a major opportunity. Many company-sponsored open-source projects suffer from this problem by having inflexible plans made without consulting their communities. In addition to not acting on the good ideas suggested by your community members, you alienate them by ignoring what they are trying to tell you. They will stop wasting their time trying to interact with you and devote their energy elsewhere.

A related problem is using the wrong resources. An open-source project is a development effort that exploits continuous design but with further opportunities for marketing-related and other strategic efforts. Nevertheless, the heart of the activity is development with development goals and practices. Things can go wrong if an organization other than engineering or development is the home for open-source projects and open-source oversight. For example, sometimes a company will determine that it needs to build a community of developers for some strategic purpose such as executing on a "developer capture" program designed to lure more developers into the company's camp. Because this is a marketing activity, it might seem natural to locate oversight in a marketing group, so that, for example, measurements of progress and of the nature of the developers captured can be made. However, a marketing group is unlikely to know enough about software development to oversee the community, nor is it likely to have a reason to care about ongoing software development once the developers have been "captured."

Recovering from Mistakes

Everyone makes mistakes. It's what you do after a mistake that really matters. Here's what you need to do:

- Admit that a mistake was made.
- Take steps to set things right.

Honestly discussing with the community what happened and how to make sure it does not happen again is the only way to proceed if you want to have a successful open-source project. Doing the right thing will give your community a reason to trust you more in the future. Being defensive, refusing to admit there is a problem, and refusing to fix things are just further mistakes that will alienate potential users and contributors and erode their trust in you.

CHAPTER 10

Closing Thoughts

OPEN SOURCE IS A WAY OF BUILDING CLOSER RELATIONSHIPS with your customers and better relationships with your developers. An open-source project breaks down organizational boundaries both within your company and between your company and the outside world. Open source results in software that better meets the needs of its users, both in terms of better fit and higher reliability.

In an article taking a broad look at open source, Brian Behlendorf wrote:

> *What the open-source community has proven is that individuals—and, by extension, companies—can work together on a much more discrete, iterative level. People are starting to understand that having interaction between developers on a daily basis during development is far more valuable than waiting through the typical product-revision cycles. It may seem chaotic at times; for programmers, balancing the requirements of their employers with that of the other participants may be a constant challenge. But it can work.[1]*

Barn raising is an excellent metaphor for many (but not all) aspects of open source. Traditionally, and even today, barn raising is how most Amish barns are built. When a couple gets married or when a disaster destroys a barn, the entire community gets together on a particular day or over a weekend to raise a new barn. The foundation is poured and other components are made beforehand, but all the heavy lifting is scheduled to be done with the full crew on the special day or weekend. All the able-bodied men pitch in. The older, experienced men direct the activities, and the boys act as gofers. The women and girls prepare and serve food and drink, and they also provide first aid. It's an activity that unifies the entire community, and it is done without any thought that it is something special—it is the most ordinary thing in the world.

---

1. http://news.cnet.com/news/0-1276-210-6659302-1.html

Barn raising requires thinking in a gift-economy way. Each person working on the raising—whether by wielding a hammer or by baking a pie—knows without thinking that the gift being given is part of a cycle of gifts that includes, in the case of the Amish, the gifts given to them by God.

Barn raising captures the fact that collaboration on a grand scale is common and ancient. But for open source barn raising is just a metaphor: It doesn't capture cleanly the idea of continuous design, nor does it address well the ways that commercial and business advantages can be had by using open source cleverly.

Competition and collaboration contribute to innovation and creativity in two distinct ways. Competition works through diversity and selection; collaboration works through refinement and improving.

In a competitive atmosphere, each organization or entity tries to gain an advantage by producing things that are different from the others in ways thought to have advantage. The process producing diversity may not be random, but with enough variety, it is likely that there will be artifacts with better designs or better conformance to actual requirements. Then it's a matter of selecting the best designs from this variety. Sometimes a pure market situation is not ideal for the selection because an artifact that is just a little better than adequate in many dimensions will be selected more often than one that is excellent in just a few.

In a collaborative situation, a competently designed artifact can be perfected through the application of many individual acts of improvement. In such a situation, people with talents spanning a variety of areas will apply their expertise to the artifact, and perhaps it will become as good as it can be based on where it started. This approach depends on the starting point being relatively good in a number of dimensions. Writers' workshops and remodeling efforts work this way.

Open source provides opportunities for both types of innovation and creativity. The competitive type derives from interactions and conversations with the communities surrounding the source code, which can provide triggers leading to innovations. The collaborative type happens when a piece of software undergoes a long and continuous process of redesign based on a set of slowly dawning insights. This method of design depends on the belief that master planning is difficult when it is possible at all—not that the act of master planning is impossible, but that the results of master planning are frequently less than desirable and that revisions and other kinds of maintenance are required to repair the implementation and design flaws.

Resistance to continuous (re)design comes, we believe, from a hidden belief that bugs and other flaws are a matter of right versus wrong or even good versus evil—that a bug in a design represents something wrong with the designer and that the presence of the bug is the result of the machinations of evil. The better, more productive attitude is that errors happen because the makers are human, that there are shades of gray when it comes to errors, and that the noble thing to do in the face of bugs is to fix them rather than judge the maker.

The story of Levittown on Long Island is our favorite example of how people acting in their own interests can effect a positive redesign of a community that has suffered from extreme master planning.

The first Levittown—once called *Island Trees*—was a postwar innovation in low-cost housing in which a potato patch on Long Island was turned into the first mass-produced housing tract. After the foundations were laid, specialized crews descended on each lot, one after another, so fast that 18 houses were completed in the 8 AM to noon shift—we could say they used an especially brutal and efficient master plan. Many lamented the approach. Peter Bacon Hales, art historian from the University of Illinois at Chicago, wrote of the criticism:

> *The accusations against Levittown from the first focused on its relentless homogeneity, the cramped quarters of its interiors, and the raw, unfinished quality of its landscape.*[2]

Architects, artists, and even some computer scientists have used Levittown as an example of how modernism—the belief in reductionism and the ultimate value of the machine—can lead to what some call the deathlike morphology of late-20th- and early-21st-century life, the unimaginably dulling effect of sameness and inhumanity on ordinary lives.

Postwar Americans needed affordable housing near their jobs to raise the first wave of baby-boomers, not unaffordable aesthetics. The houses were snapped up while trucks hauling tools and pulling trailers carrying bulldozers drove away toward their next project. The architects, designers, builders, and developers did not care to learn from their projects, and the United States experienced an unending string of housing projects since then that imposed a planned living experience on people bent more on living than on planning.

Levittown relied on wood framing, but many other projects cast their designs literally in concrete. The Pruitt-Igoe apartments in St. Louis won architectural awards in the mid-1950s for low-cost housing design. But the two complexes were simply steel and concrete high-rise warrens in the mold of the Swiss architect Le Corbusier, who said,

> *a house is a machine to live in*[3]

2. http://www.uic.edu/~pbhales/Levittown

3. Quoted in Peter Hall, *Cities of Tomorrow*, p. 205.

And also:

> *the design of cities is too important to be left to the citizens*[4]

Seventeen years after being completed, the Pruitt-Igoe complex was demolished, creating a vacant lot still mostly vacant, signaling the beginning of the postmodern era.

So in 1951, the designers of Levittown watched as families poured in to begin life in the carefully planned and constructed warrens relentlessly devised according to modernist principles of machine love.

Nature and the Levittown community did not care about the master plan: The bulldozed landscape began to sprout trees and shrubs, and over a period of years, as economic realities changed, the community developed a sense of innovation and its inhabitants a control of their own destinies. Not being trained as architects or builders did not faze them. They thought locally and acted locally. The community, through small acts of repair, transformed a homogenized and orderly Levittown into a place deserving the name Island Trees. Through customization, additions, remodels, landscaping, disorder, the community, acting as a multitude or aggregation of individuals regarded as not individually important—as a mob—made Levittown over.

Peter Bacon Hales wrote the following about the transformation of Levittown:

> *The raw, new quality of the landscape, too, didn't seem so awful to new renters and (a little later) owners, who knew that the trees and grass would quickly grow, and who understood the Levitt salesman's pitch promising opportunities to personalize the interior and exterior of your Levittown house. Life [magazine] ran a contest, seeking the best-decorated Levittown house, and the winner was a rather startling red-themed Mandarin-Revival Sino-Asian extravaganza. Over time, Levittown houses changed character, as their occupants rose in status and in economic wealth, and as families expanded and community standards of innovation and growth trickled from the home-improvement seminars at the Community Center and later the High School, out into the Saturday projects and summer vacation plans of Levittown residents. Today's heterogeneous Levittown is a testimony to the resilience of the community...*[5]

Levittown is not much different from many towns: The people who live there have inherited its earlier form from people who are gone and whose cares and requirements are perhaps passé. The specifications, needs, and criteria for the evolving town are being invented communitywide on-the-fly—and why should it

---

4. Quoted in Peter Hall, *Cities of Tomorrow*, p. 207.

5. http://www.uic.edu/~pbhales/Levittown

be any different for software, which, unlike towns, doesn't have the benefit of a long and visible history?

In open source, many of the activities are progressive and uncertain; they are formulated as needed and in response to local needs—of the module owners or of committers or others associated with small pieces of the software and sometimes of the users who, through their complaints and suggestions, are hoping to engage in participatory usability.

In an open-source project, community building and software building are intertwined because the changing needs of the software translate into a new set of players or players at different levels of maturity and expertise. As the software becomes more mature and valuable, it needs to become more stable and the changes need to be smaller and better planned. As people come to rely on the software, its caretakers need to listen more equitably, which sometimes can require being more formal or more process oriented. A cavalier governance that is perfect for the start-up phase of a project might not work later on.

Companies are now starting to use open source for more of their work: Some companies are adopting open-source software as part of their products, often the commodity parts, whereas others are sponsoring open-source projects to create markets, to make a ubiquity play, to attract developers, and for a variety of other business reasons. A company sponsoring an open-source project is not exactly like an all-volunteer effort, and you need to take special care running one. But the benefits can be significant if you do it right: transparency, continuous (re)design, innovation in the product, innovation by learning from your community, distributed development, better reuse, developer capture, PR, reduced support costs, and on and on.

When you start your first company-sponsored open-source project, you should realize that you will learn and continuously redesign your processes and practices for running them. When first starting out, it is a good idea to model your project on one of the established open-source projects, such as Apache or Linux. Once you have gotten the proper feel for things, you will be able to evolve how your project is run so as to better meet your specific needs. Just as your project will change as it matures, there is also an arc of maturity for all of your company's sponsored open-source projects. With the first project, Jini, Sun was just learning to let go of control. With Tomcat, NetBeans, and OpenOffice, the basic skills of running an open-source project began to spread within Sun. Only then did it became possible to do more experimental projects such as JXTA. It takes a while for trust in the open-source approach to spread within an organization. But once it does, the scope of possible projects that can be open sourced increases, as does the company's ability to innovate in how those projects are run.

Open source is an evolving methodology with its own arc of maturity. As existing open-source projects face new problems, they need to innovate in how they operate. The Apache Software Foundation is grappling with how to resolve conflicts over competing approaches. The Linux project is trying to increase compatibility among Linux distributions and prevent the fracturing that plagued Unix in the 1980s and 1990s. Open-source projects are experimenting with various governance methods, new licenses, and different ways to work together.

We believe that as the focus of programming shifts from stand-alone applications to interacting web services we will see a new way of developing software arise that we call *mob software*. Mob software takes the self-organizing and open-ended aspects of open source and goes much, much further with them. Imagine all people, not just programmers, being able to modify the software they use. With millions of contributors sharing a multitude of improvements, mob software will transform how we create and think about software.[6]

In this book, we've recounted what we've learned over the past 15 years about open source, collaboration, creativity, innovation, and software development as it relates to commons-based collaboration. We believe that open source can mature and expand to even more interesting projects and that the practice can be applied to more areas of design and building. The ideas of open source are old; they merely fell a little out of grace for the last few hundred years as people came to rely more on capitalistic solutions. Now they are coming back as we find that writing software gets easier only when there is a sophisticated base of software to support the new work and that it's unlikely that for-profit organizations can provide all of it at an affordable cost.

And even though this book is aimed at companies and the managers and project leaders in them, we also intend this book to be for people who are looking at expanding their skills as developers and software engineers. For you, the message of this book is that you can learn about the real process of creating software from open source and that you can see a variety of real code by the great and not-so-great designers and implementors by looking at open-source code. Unlike proprietary software efforts, open-source projects produce an open software literature that can be studied and even savored. And as time goes on, knowledge of both open-source software systems and how to do open-source development will become a more important skill to have.

~

Open source is not a new idea—we've seen it throughout history in the form of commons-based building. As Paul Freiberger and Michael Swaine recount in,

---

6. *Mob Software: The Erotic Life of Code* available at http://www.dreamsongs.com/Essays.html

Fire in the Valley: The Making of the Personal Computer, we can see it even in unexpected places:

> *In the late 1960s, just outside Seattle, a group of teenagers met after school each day and biked to a local company. As it closed for the day and its employees began heading home, the boys were just getting started. They thought of themselves as the firm's unofficial night shift, and in fact they routinely worked until long after dark, pounding on the keys of the company's DEC computer and gorging on carry-out pizza and soft drinks. The two leaders of the group [Paul Allen and Bill Gates] were considered a little odd by their class-mates. They were "computer nuts," completely absorbed in the technology. All the boys worked for free ... Computer Center Corporation, which they called "C Cubed," let them come in to find errors in the DEC computer's programming. ... [A]s long as C Cubed could show that DEC's program had bugs (errors that caused the programs to malfunction or "crash"), the firm didn't have to pay DEC for using the computer.*

Open source is not for everyone, but if you have the right attitude then it can be a major success factor for your project. You must be willing to give up control and share decision making with your community. Working together you can create something much better than you could by working alone. Good luck!

APPENDIX A

Resources

Further Reading

Blood, Rebecca. (2002). *The Weblog Handbook: Practical Advice on Creating and Maintaining Your Blog.* Cambridge, MA: Perseus Publishing.

Boston Consulting Group Hacker Survey. (2002). Available at: http://www.osdn.com/bcg/index.html

Brooks, Frederick P. (1995). *The Mythical Man-Month: Essays on Software Engineering.* Reading, MA: Addison-Wesley.

Chesbrough, Henry. (2003). *Open Innovation: The New Imperative for Creating and Profiting from Technology.* Cambridge, MA: Harvard Business School Press.

DeMarco, Tom, and Timothy Lister. (1999). *Peopleware: Productive Projects and Teams,* 2nd ed. New York: Dorset House.

DiBona, Chris, Sam Ockman, and Mark Stone (eds.). (1999). *Open Sources: Voices from the Open Source Revolution.* Sebastopol, CA: O'Reilly & Associates, Available at: http://www.oreilly.com/catalog/opensources/book/toc.html

Dinkelacker, Jamie, Pankaj K. Garg, Rob Miller, and Dean Nelson. (2001). *Progressive Open Source.* Palo Alto: HP Laboratories. Available at: http://www.hpl.hp.com/techreports/2001/HPL-2001-233.html

FLOSS—Free/Libre Open Source Software: Survey and Study, Berlecon Research. (2002). Available at: http://www.infonomics.nl/FLOSS/report

Fogel, Karl. (1999). *Open Source Development with CVS.* Scottsdale, AZ: CoriolisOpen Press.

Gabriel, Richard P. (1990). *Lisp: Good News, Bad News, How to Win Big.* Available at: http://dreamsongs.com/WorseIsBetter.html

Gabriel, Richard P., and Ron Goldman. (2000). *Mob Software: The Erotic Life of Code.* Available at http://www.dreamsongs.com/Essays.html

Hugo, Richard. (1992). *The Triggering Town: Lectures and Essays on Poetry and Writing.* New York: W. W. Norton.

Kim, Amy Jo. (2000). *Community Building on the Web.* Berkeley, CA: Peachpit Press.

Leuf, Bo, and Ward Cunningham. (2001). *The Wiki Way: Collaboration and Sharing on the Internet.* Boston: Addison-Wesley.

Moody, Glyn. (2001). *Rebel Code: Inside Linux and the Open Source Revolution.* Cambridge, MA: Perseus Publishing.

Raymond, Eric. (1999). *The Cathedral & the Bazaar.* Sebastopol, CA: O'Reilly & Associates. Original paper available at: http://www.catb.org/~esr/writings/cathedral-bazaar/

Tellis, Gerard J., and Peter N. Golder. (2002). *Will & Vision: How Latecomers Grow to Dominate Markets.* New York: McGraw-Hill.

Websites of Interest

Agile Manifesto: http://agilemanifesto.org/principles.html
Apache Software Foundation: http://www.apache.org
Apple Darwin: http://developer.apple.com/darwin
Cisco-centric Open Source Community: http://cosi-nms.sourceforge.net
CollabNet: http://www.collab.net
Creative Commons: http://creativecommons.org
Eclipse: http://www.eclipse.org
Fink: http://fink.sourceforge.net
Free Software Foundation: http://www.gnu.org
Free Software Foundation's Savannah: http://savannah.gnu.org
GForge: http://gforge.org
HP open-source projects: http://opensource.hp.com
IBM open-source projects: http://www-136.ibm.com/developerworks/opensource
Intel open-source projects: http://www.intel.com/cd/ids/developer/asmo-na/eng/52779.htm
Java Community Process: http://www.jcp.org
Mozilla: http://mozilla.org
Novell open-source projects: http://forge.novell.com
Open Source Initiative: http://www.opensource.org
Oracle open-source projects: http://oss.oracle.com
SGI open-source projects: http://oss.sgi.com
Slashdot: http://slashdot.org
SourceForge: http://sourceforge.net
Sun open-source projects: http://www.sunsource.net
Symbian: http://www.symbian.com/developer/opensource_index.html

Visualization ToolKit (VTK): http://vtk.org

Tools

Bonsai (to query about changes to a CVS archive): http://mozilla.org/bonsai.html
Bugzilla bug-tracking tool: http://www.mozilla.org/bugs
CVS: ftp://ftp.gnu.org/gnu/non-gnu/cvs and http://www.cvshome.org/downloads.html
Linux Cross-Reference tool, lxr: http://lxr.linux.no
Tinderbox (to show build status of source tree): http://mozilla.org/tinderbox.html

Licenses

Apache: http://www.apache.org/licenses/LICENSE-2.0
Artistic License: http://www.perl.com/pub/a/language/misc/Artistic.html
BSD: http://www.opensource.org/licenses/bsd-license.html
CPL: http://www.ibm.com/developerworks/oss/CPLv1.0.htm
Creative Commons licenses: http://creativecommons.org/license
FDL: http://www.gnu.org/licenses/fdl.html
FreeBSD Documentation License: http://www.freebsd.org/copyright/freebsd.doc-license.html
GPL: http://www.gnu.org/copyleft/gpl.html
LGPL: http://www.gnu.org/copyleft/lesser.html
Microsoft Shared Source: http://www.microsoft.com/recources/sharedsource/default.asp
MPL: http://www.mozilla.org/MPL/MPL-1.1.html
Open Publication License: http://opencontent.org/openpub
PDL: http://www.openoffice.org/licenses/PDL.html
SCSL (Jini version): http://www.sun.com/jini/licensing/licenses.html
SISSL: http://www.openoffice.org/licenses/sissl_license.html
SPL: http://www.netbeans.org/about/legal/spl.html

APPENDIX B

Licenses

In this appendix are the full texts for all the open-source licenses mentioned in this book. Included with each is a pointer to where the license may be found online.

Apache Software License

Artistic License

Berkeley Software Distribution (BSD)

FreeBSD Documentation License

GNU Free Documentation License (FDL)

GNU General Public License (GPL)

GNU Lesser General Public License (LGPL)

IBM Common Public License (CPL)

Microsoft Shared Source License for CLI, C# and JScript

Microsoft Shared Source License for Windows CE .NET

MIT or X License

Mozilla Public License (MPL)

Open Publication License

Sun Community Source License (SCSL)

Sun Industry Standards Source License (SISSL)

Sun Public Documentation License (PDL)

Apache Software License

taken from: http://www.apache.org/licenses/LICENSE-2.0

Apache License
Version 2.0, January 2004
http://www.apache.org/licenses/

TERMS AND CONDITIONS FOR USE, REPRODUCTION, AND DISTRIBUTION

1. **Definitions**.

"License" shall mean the terms and conditions for use, reproduction, and distribution as defined by Sections 1 through 9 of this document.

"Licensor" shall mean the copyright owner or entity authorized by the copyright owner that is granting the License.

"Legal Entity" shall mean the union of the acting entity and all other entities that control, are controlled by, or are under common control with that entity. For the purposes of this definition, "control" means (i) the power, direct or indirect, to cause the direction or management of such entity, whether by contract or otherwise, or (ii) ownership of fifty percent (50%) or more of the outstanding shares, or (iii) beneficial ownership of such entity.

"You" (or "Your") shall mean an individual or Legal Entity exercising permissions granted by this License.

"Source" form shall mean the preferred form for making modifications, including but not limited to software source code, documentation source, and configuration files.

"Object" form shall mean any form resulting from mechanical transformation or translation of a Source form, including but not limited to compiled object code, generated documentation, and conversions to other media types.

"Work" shall mean the work of authorship, whether in Source or Object form, made available under the License, as indicated by a copyright notice that is included in or attached to the work (an example is provided in the Appendix below).

"Derivative Works" shall mean any work, whether in Source or Object form, that is based on (or derived from) the Work and for which the editorial revisions, annotations, elaborations, or other modifications represent, as a whole, an original work of authorship. For the purposes of this License, Derivative Works shall not include works that remain separable from, or merely link (or bind by name) to the interfaces of, the Work and Derivative Works thereof.

"Contribution" shall mean any work of authorship, including the original version of the Work and any modifications or additions to that Work or Derivative Works thereof, that is intentionally submitted to Licensor for inclusion in the Work by the copyright owner or by an individual or Legal Entity authorized to submit on behalf of the copyright owner. For the purposes of this definition, "submitted" means any form of electronic, verbal, or written communication sent to the Licensor or its representatives, including but not limited to communication on electronic mailing lists, source code control systems, and issue tracking systems that are managed by, or on behalf of, the Licensor for the purpose of discussing and improving the Work, but excluding communication that is conspicuously marked or otherwise designated in writing by the copyright owner as "Not a Contribution."

"Contributor" shall mean Licensor and any individual or Legal Entity on behalf of whom a Contribution has been received by Licensor and subsequently incorporated within the Work.

2. Grant of Copyright License. Subject to the terms and conditions of this License, each Contributor hereby grants to You a perpetual, worldwide, non-exclusive, no-charge, royalty-free, irrevocable copyright license to reproduce, prepare Derivative Works of, publicly display, publicly perform, sublicense, and distribute the Work and such Derivative Works in Source or Object form.

3. Grant of Patent License. Subject to the terms and conditions of this License, each Contributor hereby grants to You a perpetual, worldwide, non-exclusive, no-charge, royalty-free, irrevocable (except as stated in this section) patent license to make, have made, use, offer to sell, sell, import, and otherwise transfer the Work, where such license applies only to those patent claims licensable by such Contributor that are necessarily infringed by their Contribution(s) alone or by combination of their Contribution(s) with the Work to which such Contribution(s) was submitted. If You institute patent litigation against any entity (including a cross-claim or counterclaim in a lawsuit) alleging that the Work or a Contribution incorporated within the Work constitutes direct or contributory patent infringement, then any patent licenses granted to You under this License for that Work shall terminate as of the date such litigation is filed.

4. Redistribution. You may reproduce and distribute copies of the Work or Derivative Works thereof in any medium, with or without modifications, and in Source or Object form, provided that You meet the following conditions:

a. You must give any other recipients of the Work or Derivative Works a copy of this License; and

b. You must cause any modified files to carry prominent notices stating that You changed the files; and

c. You must retain, in the Source form of any Derivative Works that You distribute, all copyright, patent, trademark, and attribution notices from the Source form of the Work, excluding those notices that do not pertain to any part of the Derivative Works; and

d. If the Work includes a "NOTICE" text file as part of its distribution, then any Derivative Works that You distribute must include a readable copy of the attribution notices contained within such NOTICE file, excluding those notices that do not pertain to any part of the Derivative Works, in at least one of the following places: within a NOTICE text file distributed as part of the Derivative Works; within the Source form or documentation, if provided along with the Derivative Works; or, within a display generated by the Derivative Works, if and wherever such third-party notices normally appear. The contents of the NOTICE file are for informational purposes only and do not modify the License. You may add Your own attribution notices within Derivative Works that You distribute, alongside or as an addendum to the NOTICE text from the Work, provided that such additional attribution notices cannot be construed as modifying the License.

You may add Your own copyright statement to Your modifications and may provide additional or different license terms and conditions for use, reproduction, or distribution of Your modifications, or for any such Derivative Works as a whole, provided Your use, reproduction, and distribution of the Work otherwise complies with the conditions stated in this License.

5. **Submission of Contributions.** Unless You explicitly state otherwise, any Contribution intentionally submitted for inclusion in the Work by You to the Licensor shall be under the terms and conditions of this License, without any additional terms or conditions. Notwithstanding the above, nothing herein shall supersede or modify the terms of any separate license agreement you may have executed with Licensor regarding such Contributions.

6. **Trademarks.** This License does not grant permission to use the trade names, trademarks, service marks, or product names of the Licensor, except as required for reasonable and customary use in describing the origin of the Work and reproducing the content of the NOTICE file.

7. **Disclaimer of Warranty.** Unless required by applicable law or agreed to in writing, Licensor provides the Work (and each Contributor provides its Contributions) on an "AS IS" BASIS, WITHOUT WARRANTIES OR CONDITIONS OF ANY KIND, either express or implied, including, without limitation, any warranties or conditions of TITLE, NON-INFRINGEMENT, MERCHANTABILITY, or FITNESS FOR A PARTICULAR PURPOSE. You are solely responsible for determining the appropriateness of using or redistributing the Work and assume any risks associated with Your exercise of permissions under this License.

8. **Limitation of Liability.** In no event and under no legal theory, whether in tort (including negligence), contract, or otherwise, unless required by applicable law (such as deliberate and grossly negligent acts) or agreed to in writing, shall any Contributor be liable to You for damages, including any direct, indirect, special, incidental, or consequential damages of any character arising as a result of this License or out of the use or inability to use the Work (including but not limited to damages for loss of goodwill, work stoppage, computer failure or malfunction, or any and all other commercial damages or losses), even if such Contributor has been advised of the possibility of such damages.

9. **Accepting Warranty or Additional Liability.** While redistributing the Work or Derivative Works thereof, You may choose to offer, and charge a fee for, acceptance of support, warranty, indemnity, or other liability obligations and/or rights consistent with this License. However, in accepting such obligations, You may act only on Your own behalf and on Your sole responsibility, not on behalf of any other Contributor, and only if You agree to indemnify, defend, and hold each Contributor harmless for any liability incurred by, or claims asserted against, such Contributor by reason of your accepting any such warranty or additional liability.

END OF TERMS AND CONDITIONS

APPENDIX: How to apply the Apache License to your work

To apply the Apache License to your work, attach the following boilerplate notice, with the fields enclosed by brackets "[]" replaced with your own identifying information. (Don't include the brackets!) The text should be enclosed in the appropriate comment syntax for the file format. We also recommend that a file or class name and description of purpose be included on the same "printed page" as the copyright notice for easier identification within third-party archives.

```
Copyright [yyyy] [name of copyright owner]

Licensed under the Apache License, Version 2.0 (the "License");
you may not use this file except in compliance with the License.
You may obtain a copy of the License at

       http://www.apache.org/licenses/LICENSE-2.0

Unless required by applicable law or agreed to in writing, software
distributed under the License is distributed on an "AS IS" BASIS,
WITHOUT WARRANTIES OR CONDITIONS OF ANY KIND, either express or implied.
See the License for the specific language governing permissions and
limitations under the License.
```

Artistic License

taken from: http://www.perl.com/pub/a/language/misc/Artistic.html

The Artistic License
August 15, 1997

Preamble

The intent of this document is to state the conditions under which a Package may be copied, such that the Copyright Holder maintains some semblance of artistic control over the development of the package, while giving the users of the package the right to use and distribute the Package in a more-or-less customary fashion, plus the right to make reasonable modifications.

Definitions

"Package" refers to the collection of files distributed by the Copyright Holder, and derivatives of that collection of files created through textual modification.

"Standard Version" refers to such a Package if it has not been modified, or has been modified in accordance with the wishes of the Copyright Holder as specified below.

"Copyright Holder" is whoever is named in the copyright or copyrights for the package.

"You" is you, if you're thinking about copying or distributing this Package.

"Reasonable copying fee" is whatever you can justify on the basis of media cost, duplication charges, time of people involved, and so on. (You will not be required to justify it to the Copyright Holder, but only to the computing community at large as a market that must bear the fee.)

"Freely Available" means that no fee is charged for the item itself, though there may be fees involved in handling the item. It also means that recipients of the item may redistribute it under the same conditions they received it.

1. You may make and give away verbatim copies of the source form of the Standard Version of this Package without restriction, provided that you duplicate all of the original copyright notices and associated disclaimers.

2. You may apply bug fixes, portability fixes and other modifications derived from the Public Domain or from the Copyright Holder. A Package modified in such a way shall still be considered the Standard Version.

3. You may otherwise modify your copy of this Package in any way, provided that you insert a prominent notice in each changed file stating how and when you changed that file, and provided that you do at least ONE of the following:

   a. place your modifications in the Public Domain or otherwise make them Freely Available, such as by posting said modifications to Usenet or an equivalent medium, or placing the modifications on a major archive site such as uunet.uu.net, or by allowing the Copyright Holder to include your modifications in the Standard Version of the Package.

    b. use the modified Package only within your corporation or organization.

    c. rename any non-standard executables so the names do not conflict with standard executables, which must also be provided, and provide a separate manual page for each non-standard executable that clearly documents how it differs from the Standard Version.

    d. make other distribution arrangements with the Copyright Holder.

4. You may distribute the programs of this Package in object code or executable form, provided that you do at least ONE of the following:

    a. distribute a Standard Version of the executables and library files, together with instructions (in the manual page or equivalent) on where to get the Standard Version.

    b. accompany the distribution with the machine-readable source of the Package with your modifications.

    c. give non-standard executables non-standard names, and clearly document the differences in manual pages (or equivalent), together with instructions on where to get the Standard Version.

    d. make other distribution arrangements with the Copyright Holder.

5. You may charge a reasonable copying fee for any distribution of this Package. You may charge any fee you choose for support of this Package. You may not charge a fee for this Package itself. However, you may distribute this Package in aggregate with other (possibly commercial) programs as part of a larger (possibly commercial) software distribution provided that you do not advertise this Package as a product of your own.

    You may embed this Package's interpreter within an executable of yours (by linking); this shall be construed as a mere form of aggregation, provided that the complete Standard Version of the interpreter is so embedded.

6. The scripts and library files supplied as input to or produced as output from the programs of this Package do not automatically fall under the copyright of this Package, but belong to whomever generated them, and may be sold commercially, and may be aggregated with this Package. If such scripts or library files are aggregated with this Package via the so-called "undump" or "unexec" methods of producing a binary executable image, then distribution of such an image shall neither be construed as a distribution of this Package nor shall it fall under the restrictions of Paragraphs 3 and 4, provided that you do not represent such an executable image as a Standard Version of this Package.

7. C subroutines (or comparably compiled subroutines in other languages) supplied by you and linked into this Package in order to emulate subroutines and variables of the language defined by this Package shall not be considered part of this Package, but are the equivalent of input as in Paragraph 6, provided these subroutines do not change the language in any way that would cause it to fail the regression tests for the language.

8. Aggregation of this Package with a commercial distribution is always permitted provided that the use of this Package is embedded; that is, when no overt attempt is made to make this Package's interfaces visible to the end user of the commercial distribution. Such use shall not be construed as a distribution of this Package.

9. The name of the Copyright Holder may not be used to endorse or promote products derived from this software without specific prior written permission.

10. THIS PACKAGE IS PROVIDED "AS IS" AND WITHOUT ANY EXPRESS OR IMPLIED WARRANTIES, INCLUDING, WITHOUT LIMITATION, THE IMPLIED WARRANTIES OF MERCHANTIBILITY AND FITNESS FOR A PARTICULAR PURPOSE.

The End

Berkeley Software Distribution (BSD)

taken from: http://www.opensource.org/licenses/bsd-license.html

Copyright (c) 1998, The Regents of the University of California. All rights reserved.

Redistribution and use in source and binary forms, with or without modification, are permitted provided that the following conditions are met:

1. Redistributions of source code must retain the above copyright notice, this list of conditions and the following disclaimer.

2. Redistributions in binary form must reproduce the above copyright notice, this list of conditions and the following disclaimer in the documentation and/or other materials provided with the distribution.

3. Neither name of the University nor the names of its contributors may be used to endorse or promote products derived from this software without specific prior written permission.

FreeBSD Documentation License

taken from: http://www.freebsd.org/copyright/freebsd.doc.license.html

FreeBSD Documentation License

Copyright © 1995, 1996, 1997, 1998, 1999 by The FreeBSD Documentation Project

Redistribution and use in source (SGML DocBook) and 'compiled' forms (SGML, HTML, PDF, PostScript, RTF and so forth) with or without modification, are permitted provided that the following conditions are met:

1. Redistributions of source code (SGML DocBook) must retain the above copyright notice, this list of conditions and the following disclaimer as the first lines of this file unmodified.

2. Redistributions in compiled form (transformed to other DTDs, converted to PDF, PostScript, RTF and other formats) must reproduce the above copyright notice, this list of conditions and the following disclaimer in the documentation and/or other materials provided with the distribution.

Important: THIS DOCUMENTATION IS PROVIDED BY THE FREEBSD DOCUMENTA-TION PROJECT "AS IS" AND ANY EXPRESS OR IMPLIED WARRANTIES, INCLUDING, BUT NOT LIMITED TO, THE IMPLIED WARRANTIES OF MERCHANTABILITY AND FITNESS FOR A PARTICULAR PURPOSE ARE DISCLAIMED. IN NO EVENT SHALL THE FREEBSD DOCUMENTATION PROJECT BE LIABLE FOR ANY DIRECT, INDIRECT, INCIDENTAL, SPECIAL, EXEMPLARY, OR CONSEQUENTIAL DAMAGES (INCLUDING, BUT NOT LIMITED TO, PROCUREMENT OF SUBSTITUTE GOODS OR SERVICES; LOSS OF USE, DATA, OR PROFITS; OR BUSINESS INTERRUPTION) HOWEVER CAUSED AND ON ANY THEORY OF LIABILITY, WHETHER IN CONTRACT, STRICT LIABILITY, OR TORT (INCLUDING NEGLIGENCE OR OTHERWISE) ARISING IN ANY WAY OUT OF THE USE OF THIS DOCUMENTATION, EVEN IF ADVISED OF THE POSSIBILITY OF SUCH DAMAGE.

GNU Free Documentation License (FDL)

taken from: http://www.gnu.org/licenses/fdl.html

GNU Free Documentation License

Version 1.1, March 2000

0. PREAMBLE

The purpose of this License is to make a manual, textbook, or other written document "free" in the sense of freedom: to assure everyone the effective freedom to copy and redistribute it, with or without modifying it, either commercially or noncommercially. Secondarily, this License preserves for the author and publisher a way to get credit for their work, while not being considered responsible for modifications made by others.

This License is a kind of "copyleft", which means that derivative works of the document must themselves be free in the same sense. It complements the GNU General Public License, which is a copyleft license designed for free software.

We have designed this License in order to use it for manuals for free software, because free software needs free documentation: a free program should come with manuals providing the same freedoms that the software does. But this License is not limited to software manuals; it can be used for any textual work, regardless of subject matter or whether it is published as a printed book. We recommend this License principally for works whose purpose is instruction or reference.

1. APPLICABILITY AND DEFINITIONS

This License applies to any manual or other work that contains a notice placed by the copyright holder saying it can be distributed under the terms of this License. The "Document," below, refers to any such manual or work. Any member of the public is a licensee, and is addressed as "you."

A "Modified Version" of the Document means any work containing the Document or a portion of it, either copied verbatim, or with modifications and/or translated into another language.

A "Secondary Section" is a named appendix or a front-matter section of the Document that deals exclusively with the relationship of the publishers or authors of the Document to the Document's overall subject (or to related matters) and contains nothing that could fall directly within that overall subject. (For example, if the Document is in part a textbook of mathematics, a Secondary Section may not explain any mathematics.) The relationship could be a matter of historical connection with the subject or with related matters, or of legal, commercial, philosophical, ethical or political position regarding them.

The "Invariant Sections" are certain Secondary Sections whose titles are designated, as being those of Invariant Sections, in the notice that says that the Document is released under this License.

The "Cover Texts" are certain short passages of text that are listed, as Front-Cover Texts or Back-Cover Texts, in the notice that says that the Document is released under this License.

A "Transparent" copy of the Document means a machine-readable copy, represented in a format whose specification is available to the general public, whose contents can be viewed and edited directly and straightforwardly with generic text editors or (for images composed of pixels) generic paint programs or (for drawings) some widely available drawing editor, and that is suitable for input to text formatters or for automatic translation to a variety of formats suitable for input to text formatters. A copy made in an otherwise Transparent file format whose markup has been designed to thwart or discourage subsequent modification by readers is not Transparent. A copy that is not "Transparent" is called "Opaque".

Examples of suitable formats for Transparent copies include plain ASCII without markup, Texinfo input format, LaTeX input format, SGML or XML using a publicly available DTD, and standard-conforming simple HTML designed for human modification. Opaque formats include PostScript, PDF, proprietary formats that can be read and edited only by proprietary word processors, SGML or XML for which the DTD and/or processing tools are not generally available, and the machine-generated HTML produced by some word processors for output purposes only.

The "Title Page" means, for a printed book, the title page itself, plus such following pages as are needed to hold, legibly, the material this License requires to appear in the title page. For works in formats which do not have any title page as such, "Title Page" means the text near the most prominent appearance of the work's title, preceding the beginning of the body of the text.

2. VERBATIM COPYING

You may copy and distribute the Document in any medium, either commercially or noncommercially, provided that this License, the copyright notices, and the license notice saying this License applies to the Document are reproduced in all copies, and that you add no other conditions whatsoever to those of this License. You may not use technical measures to obstruct or control the reading or further copying of the copies you make or distribute. However, you may accept compensation in exchange for copies. If you distribute a large enough number of copies you must also follow the conditions in section 3.

You may also lend copies, under the same conditions stated above, and you may publicly display copies.

3. COPYING IN QUANTITY

If you publish printed copies of the Document numbering more than 100, and the Document's license notice requires Cover Texts, you must enclose the copies in covers that carry, clearly and legibly, all these Cover Texts: Front-Cover Texts on the front cover, and Back-Cover Texts on the back cover. Both covers must also clearly and legibly identify you as the publisher of these copies. The front cover must present the full title with all words of the title equally prominent and visible. You may add other material on the covers in addition. Copying with changes limited to the covers, as long as they preserve the title of the Document and satisfy these conditions, can be treated as verbatim copying in other respects.

If the required texts for either cover are too voluminous to fit legibly, you should put the first ones listed (as many as fit reasonably) on the actual cover, and continue the rest onto adjacent pages.

If you publish or distribute Opaque copies of the Document numbering more than 100, you must either include a machine-readable Transparent copy along with each Opaque copy, or state in or with each Opaque copy a publicly-accessible computer-network location containing a complete Transparent copy of the Document, free of added material, which the general network-using public has access to download anonymously at no charge using public-standard network protocols. If you use the latter option, you must take reasonably prudent steps, when you begin distribution of Opaque copies in quantity, to ensure that this Transparent copy will remain thus accessible at the stated location until at least one year after the last time you distribute an Opaque copy (directly or through your agents or retailers) of that edition to the public.

It is requested, but not required, that you contact the authors of the Document well before redistributing any large number of copies, to give them a chance to provide you with an updated version of the Document.

4. MODIFICATIONS

You may copy and distribute a Modified Version of the Document under the conditions of sections 2 and 3 above, provided that you release the Modified Version under precisely this License, with the Modified Version filling the role of the Document, thus licensing distribution and modification of the Modified Version to whoever possesses a copy of it. In addition, you must do these things in the Modified Version:

A. Use in the Title Page (and on the covers, if any) a title distinct from that of the Document, and from those of previous versions (which should, if there were any, be listed in the History section of the Document). You may use the same title as a previous version if the original publisher of that version gives permission.

B. List on the Title Page, as authors, one or more persons or entities responsible for authorship of the modifications in the Modified Version, together with at least five of the principal authors of the Document (all of its principal authors, if it has less than five).

C. State on the Title page the name of the publisher of the Modified Version, as the publisher.

D. Preserve all the copyright notices of the Document.

E. Add an appropriate copyright notice for your modifications adjacent to the other copyright notices.

F. Include, immediately after the copyright notices, a license notice giving the public permission to use the Modified Version under the terms of this License, in the form shown in the Addendum below.

G. Preserve in that license notice the full lists of Invariant Sections and required Cover Texts given in the Document's license notice.

H. Include an unaltered copy of this License.

I. Preserve the section entitled "History", and its title, and add to it an item stating at least the title, year, new authors, and publisher of the Modified Version as given on the Title Page. If there is no section entitled "History" in the Document, create one stating the title, year, authors, and publisher of the Document as given on its Title Page, then add an item describing the Modified Version as stated in the previous sentence.

J. Preserve the network location, if any, given in the Document for public access to a Transparent copy of the Document, and likewise the network locations given in the Document for previous versions it was based on. These may be placed in the "History" section. You may omit a network location for a work that was published at least four years before the Document itself, or if the original publisher of the version it refers to gives permission.

K. In any section entitled "Acknowledgements" or "Dedications", preserve the section's title, and preserve in the section all the substance and tone of each of the contributor acknowledgements and/or dedications given therein.

L. Preserve all the Invariant Sections of the Document, unaltered in their text and in their titles. Section numbers or the equivalent are not considered part of the section titles.

M. Delete any section entitled "Endorsements". Such a section may not be included in the Modified Version.

N. Do not retitle any existing section as "Endorsements" or to conflict in title with any Invariant Section.

If the Modified Version includes new front-matter sections or appendices that qualify as Secondary Sections and contain no material copied from the Document, you may at your option designate some or all of these sections as invariant. To do this, add their titles to the list of Invariant Sections in the Modified Version's license notice. These titles must be distinct from any other section titles.

You may add a section entitled "Endorsements", provided it contains nothing but endorsements of your Modified Version by various parties—for example, statements of peer review or that the text has been approved by an organization as the authoritative definition of a standard.

You may add a passage of up to five words as a Front-Cover Text, and a passage of up to 25 words as a Back-Cover Text, to the end of the list of Cover Texts in the Modified Version. Only one passage of Front-Cover Text and one of Back-Cover Text may be added by (or through arrangements made by) any one entity. If the Document already includes a cover text for the same cover, previously added by you or by arrangement made by the same entity you are acting on behalf of, you may not add another; but you may replace the old one, on explicit permission from the previous publisher that added the old one.

The author(s) and publisher(s) of the Document do not by this License give permission to use their names for publicity for or to assert or imply endorsement of any Modified Version.

5. COMBINING DOCUMENTS

You may combine the Document with other documents released under this License, under the terms defined in section 4 above for modified versions, provided that you include in the combination all of the Invariant Sections of all of the original documents, unmodified, and list them all as Invariant Sections of your combined work in its license notice.

The combined work need only contain one copy of this License, and multiple identical Invariant Sections may be replaced with a single copy. If there are multiple Invariant Sections with the same name but different contents, make the title of each such section unique by adding at the end of it, in parentheses, the name of the original author or publisher of that section if known, or else a unique number. Make the same adjustment to the section titles in the list of Invariant Sections in the license notice of the combined work.

In the combination, you must combine any sections entitled "History" in the various original documents, forming one section entitled "History"; likewise combine any sections entitled "Acknowledgements", and any sections entitled "Dedications". You must delete all sections entitled "Endorsements."

6. COLLECTIONS OF DOCUMENTS

You may make a collection consisting of the Document and other documents released under this License, and replace the individual copies of this License in the various documents with a single copy that is included in the collection, provided that you follow the rules of this License for verbatim copying of each of the documents in all other respects.

You may extract a single document from such a collection, and distribute it individually under this License, provided you insert a copy of this License into the extracted document, and follow this License in all other respects regarding verbatim copying of that document.

7. AGGREGATION WITH INDEPENDENT WORKS

A compilation of the Document or its derivatives with other separate and independent documents or works, in or on a volume of a storage or distribution medium, does not as a whole count as a Modified Version of the Document, provided no compilation copyright is claimed for the compilation. Such a compilation is called an "aggregate", and this License does not apply to the other self-contained works thus compiled with the Document, on account of their being thus compiled, if they are not themselves derivative works of the Document.

If the Cover Text requirement of section 3 is applicable to these copies of the Document, then if the Document is less than one quarter of the entire aggregate, the Document's Cover Texts may be placed on covers that surround only the Document within the aggregate. Otherwise they must appear on covers around the whole aggregate.

8. TRANSLATION

Translation is considered a kind of modification, so you may distribute translations of the Document under the terms of section 4. Replacing Invariant Sections with translations requires special permission from their copyright holders, but you may include translations of some or all Invariant Sections in addition to the original versions of these Invariant Sections. You may include a translation of this License provided that you also include the original English version of this License. In case of a disagreement between the translation and the original English version of this License, the original English version will prevail.

9. TERMINATION

You may not copy, modify, sublicense, or distribute the Document except as expressly provided for under this License. Any other attempt to copy, modify, sublicense or distribute the Document is void, and will automatically terminate your rights under this License. However, parties who have received copies, or rights, from you under this License will not have their licenses terminated so long as such parties remain in full compliance.

10. FUTURE REVISIONS OF THIS LICENSE

The Free Software Foundation may publish new, revised versions of the GNU Free Documentation License from time to time. Such new versions will be similar in spirit to the present version, but may differ in detail to address new problems or concerns. See http://www.gnu.org/copyleft/.

Each version of the License is given a distinguishing version number. If the Document specifies that a particular numbered version of this License "or any later version" applies to it, you have the option of following the terms and conditions either of that specified version or of any later version that has been published (not as a draft) by the Free Software Foundation. If the Document does not specify a version number of this License, you may choose any version ever published (not as a draft) by the Free Software Foundation.

How to Use this License for your Documents

To use this License in a document you have written, include a copy of the License in the document and put the following copyright and license notices just after the title page:

```
Copyright (c) YEAR  YOUR NAME.
Permission is granted to copy, distribute and/or modify this document
under the terms of the GNU Free Documentation License, Version 1.1
or any later version published by the Free Software Foundation;
with the Invariant Sections being LIST THEIR TITLES, with the
Front-Cover Texts being LIST, and with the Back-Cover Texts being LIST.
A copy of the license is included in the section entitled "GNU
Free Documentation License".
```

If you have no Invariant Sections, write "with no Invariant Sections" instead of saying which ones are invariant. If you have no Front-Cover Texts, write "no Front-Cover Texts" instead of "Front-Cover Texts being LIST"; likewise for Back-Cover Texts.

If your document contains nontrivial examples of program code, we recommend releasing these examples in parallel under your choice of free software license, such as the GNU General Public License, to permit their use in free software.

GNU General Public License (GPL)

taken from: http://www.gnu.org/copyleft/gpl.html

GNU GENERAL PUBLIC LICENSE

Version 2, June 1991

```
Copyright (C) 1989, 1991 Free Software Foundation, Inc.
59 Temple Place-Suite 330, Boston, MA 02111-1307, USA
```

```
Everyone is permitted to copy and distribute verbatim copies of this license document, but
changing it is not allowed.
```

Preamble

The licenses for most software are designed to take away your freedom to share and change it. By contrast, the GNU General Public License is intended to guarantee your freedom to share and change free software—to make sure the software is free for all its users. This General Public License applies to most of the Free Software Foundation's software and to any other program whose authors commit to using it. (Some other Free Software Foundation software is covered by the GNU Library General Public License instead.) You can apply it to your programs, too.

When we speak of free software, we are referring to freedom, not price. Our General Public Licenses are designed to make sure that you have the freedom to distribute copies of free software (and charge for this service if you wish), that you receive source code or can get it if you want it, that you can change the software or use pieces of it in new free programs; and that you know you can do these things.

To protect your rights, we need to make restrictions that forbid anyone to deny you these rights or to ask you to surrender the rights. These restrictions translate to certain responsibilities for you if you distribute copies of the software, or if you modify it.

For example, if you distribute copies of such a program, whether gratis or for a fee, you must give the recipients all the rights that you have. You must make sure that they, too, receive or can get the source code. And you must show them these terms so they know their rights.

We protect your rights with two steps: (1) copyright the software, and (2) offer you this license which gives you legal permission to copy, distribute and/or modify the software.

Also, for each author's protection and ours, we want to make certain that everyone understands that there is no warranty for this free software. If the software is modified by someone else and passed on, we want its recipients to know that what they have is not the original, so that any problems introduced by others will not reflect on the original authors' reputations.

Finally, any free program is threatened constantly by software patents. We wish to avoid the danger that redistributors of a free program will individually obtain patent licenses, in effect making the program proprietary. To prevent this, we have made it clear that any patent must be licensed for everyone's free use or not licensed at all.

The precise terms and conditions for copying, distribution and modification follow.

TERMS AND CONDITIONS FOR COPYING, DISTRIBUTION AND MODIFICATION

0. This License applies to any program or other work which contains a notice placed by the copyright holder saying it may be distributed under the terms of this General Public License. The "Program," below, refers to any such program or work, and a "work based on the Program" means either the Program or any derivative work under copyright law: that is to say, a work containing the Program or a portion of it, either verbatim or with modifications and/or translated into another language. (Hereinafter, translation is included without limitation in the term "modification.") Each licensee is addressed as "you."

Activities other than copying, distribution and modification are not covered by this License; they are outside its scope. The act of running the Program is not restricted, and the output from the Program is covered only if its contents constitute a work based on the Program (independent of having been made by running the Program). Whether that is true depends on what the Program does.

1. You may copy and distribute verbatim copies of the Program's source code as you receive it, in any medium, provided that you conspicuously and appropriately publish on each copy an appropriate copyright notice and disclaimer of warranty; keep intact all the notices that refer to this License and to the absence of any warranty; and give any other recipients of the Program a copy of this License along with the Program.

You may charge a fee for the physical act of transferring a copy, and you may at your option offer warranty protection in exchange for a fee.

2. You may modify your copy or copies of the Program or any portion of it, thus forming a work based on the Program, and copy and distribute such modifications or work under the terms of Section 1 above, provided that you also meet all of these conditions:

    a) You must cause the modified files to carry prominent notices stating that you changed the files and the date of any change.

    b) You must cause any work that you distribute or publish, that in whole or in part contains or is derived from the Program or any part thereof, to be licensed as a whole at no charge to all third parties under the terms of this License.

    c) If the modified program normally reads commands interactively when run, you must cause it, when started running for such interactive use in the most ordinary way, to print or display an announcement including an appropriate copyright notice and a notice that there is no warranty (or else, saying that you provide a warranty) and that users may redistribute the program under these conditions, and telling the user how to view a copy of this License. (Exception: if the Program itself is interactive but does not normally print such an announcement, your work based on the Program is not required to print an announcement.)

These requirements apply to the modified work as a whole. If identifiable sections of that work are not derived from the Program, and can be reasonably considered independent and separate works in themselves, then this License, and its terms, do not apply to those sections when you distribute them as separate works. But when you distribute the same sections as part of a whole which is a work based on the Program, the distribution of the whole must be on the terms of this License, whose permissions for other licensees extend to the entire whole, and thus to each and every part regardless of who wrote it.

Thus, it is not the intent of this section to claim rights or contest your rights to work written entirely by you; rather, the intent is to exercise the right to control the distribution of derivative or collective works based on the Program.

In addition, mere aggregation of another work not based on the Program with the Program (or with a work based on the Program) on a volume of a storage or distribution medium does not bring the other work under the scope of this License.

3. You may copy and distribute the Program (or a work based on it, under Section 2) in object code or executable form under the terms of Sections 1 and 2 above provided that you also do one of the following:

a) Accompany it with the complete corresponding machine-readable source code, which must be distributed under the terms of Sections 1 and 2 above on a medium customarily used for software interchange; or,

b) Accompany it with a written offer, valid for at least three years, to give any third party, for a charge no more than your cost of physically performing source distribution, a complete machine-readable copy of the corresponding source code, to be distributed under the terms of Sections 1 and 2 above on a medium customarily used for software interchange; or,

c) Accompany it with the information you received as to the offer to distribute corresponding source code. (This alternative is allowed only for noncommercial distribution and only if you received the program in object code or executable form with such an offer, in accord with Subsection b above.)

The source code for a work means the preferred form of the work for making modifications to it. For an executable work, complete source code means all the source code for all modules it contains, plus any associated interface definition files, plus the scripts used to control compilation and installation of the executable. However, as a special exception, the source code distributed need not include anything that is normally distributed (in either source or binary form) with the major components (compiler, kernel, and so on) of the operating system on which the executable runs, unless that component itself accompanies the executable.

If distribution of executable or object code is made by offering access to copy from a designated place, then offering equivalent access to copy the source code from the same place counts as distribution of the source code, even though third parties are not compelled to copy the source along with the object code.

4. You may not copy, modify, sublicense, or distribute the Program except as expressly provided under this License. Any attempt otherwise to copy, modify, sublicense or distribute the Program is void, and will automatically terminate your rights under this License. However, parties who have received copies, or rights, from you under this License will not have their licenses terminated so long as such parties remain in full compliance.

5. You are not required to accept this License, since you have not signed it. However, nothing else grants you permission to modify or distribute the Program or its derivative works. These actions are prohibited by law if you do not accept this License. Therefore, by modifying or distributing the Program (or any work based on the Program), you indicate your acceptance of this License to do so, and all its terms and conditions for copying, distributing or modifying the Program or works based on it.

6. Each time you redistribute the Program (or any work based on the Program), the recipient automatically receives a license from the original licensor to copy, distribute or modify the Program subject to these terms and conditions. You may not impose any further restrictions on the recipients' exercise of the rights granted herein. You are not responsible for enforcing compliance by third parties to this License.

7. If, as a consequence of a court judgment or allegation of patent infringement or for any other reason (not limited to patent issues), conditions are imposed on you (whether by court order, agreement or otherwise) that contradict the conditions of this License, they do not excuse you from the conditions of this License. If you cannot distribute so as to satisfy simultaneously your obligations under this License and any other pertinent obligations, then as a consequence you may not distribute the Program at all. For example, if a patent license would not permit royalty-free redistribution of the Program by all those who receive copies directly or indirectly through you, then the only way you could satisfy both it and this License would be to refrain entirely from distribution of the Program.

If any portion of this section is held invalid or unenforceable under any particular circumstance, the balance of the section is intended to apply and the section as a whole is intended to apply in other circumstances.

It is not the purpose of this section to induce you to infringe any patents or other property right claims or to contest validity of any such claims; this section has the sole purpose of protecting the integrity of the free software distribution system, which is implemented by public license practices. Many people have made generous contributions to the wide range of software distributed through that system in reliance on consistent application of that system; it is up to the author/donor to decide if he or she is willing to distribute software through any other system and a licensee cannot impose that choice.

This section is intended to make thoroughly clear what is believed to be a consequence of the rest of this License.

8. If the distribution and/or use of the Program is restricted in certain countries either by patents or by copyrighted interfaces, the original copyright holder who places the Program under this License may add an explicit geographical distribution limitation excluding those countries, so that distribution is permitted only in or among countries not thus excluded. In such case, this License incorporates the limitation as if written in the body of this License.

9. The Free Software Foundation may publish revised and/or new versions of the General Public License from time to time. Such new versions will be similar in spirit to the present version, but may differ in detail to address new problems or concerns.

Each version is given a distinguishing version number. If the Program specifies a version number of this License which applies to it and "any later version," you have the option of following the terms and conditions either of that version or of any later version published by the Free Software Foundation. If the Program does not specify a version number of this License, you may choose any version ever published by the Free Software Foundation.

10. If you wish to incorporate parts of the Program into other free programs whose distribution conditions are different, write to the author to ask for permission. For software which is copyrighted by the Free Software Foundation, write to the Free Software Foundation; we sometimes make exceptions for this. Our decision will be guided by the two goals of preserving the free status of all derivatives of our free software and of promoting the sharing and reuse of software generally.

NO WARRANTY

11. BECAUSE THE PROGRAM IS LICENSED FREE OF CHARGE, THERE IS NO WARRANTY FOR THE PROGRAM, TO THE EXTENT PERMITTED BY APPLICABLE LAW. EXCEPT WHEN OTHERWISE STATED IN WRITING THE COPYRIGHT HOLDERS AND/OR OTHER PARTIES PROVIDE THE PROGRAM "AS IS" WITHOUT WARRANTY OF ANY KIND, EITHER EXPRESSED OR IMPLIED, INCLUDING, BUT NOT LIMITED TO, THE IMPLIED WARRANTIES OF MERCHANTABILITY AND FITNESS FOR A PARTICULAR PURPOSE. THE ENTIRE RISK AS TO THE QUALITY AND PERFORMANCE OF THE PROGRAM IS WITH YOU. SHOULD THE PROGRAM PROVE DEFECTIVE, YOU ASSUME THE COST OF ALL NECESSARY SERVICING, REPAIR OR CORRECTION.

12. IN NO EVENT UNLESS REQUIRED BY APPLICABLE LAW OR AGREED TO IN WRITING WILL ANY COPYRIGHT HOLDER, OR ANY OTHER PARTY WHO MAY MODIFY AND/OR REDISTRIBUTE THE PROGRAM AS PERMITTED ABOVE, BE LIABLE TO YOU FOR DAMAGES, INCLUDING ANY GENERAL, SPECIAL, INCIDENTAL OR CONSEQUENTIAL DAMAGES ARISING OUT OF THE USE OR INABILITY TO USE THE PROGRAM (INCLUDING BUT NOT LIMITED TO LOSS OF DATA OR DATA BEING RENDERED INACCURATE OR LOSSES SUSTAINED BY YOU OR THIRD PARTIES OR A FAILURE OF THE PROGRAM TO OPERATE WITH ANY OTHER PROGRAMS), EVEN IF SUCH HOLDER OR OTHER PARTY HAS BEEN ADVISED OF THE POSSIBILITY OF SUCH DAMAGES.

END OF TERMS AND CONDITIONS

How to Apply These Terms to Your New Programs

If you develop a new program, and you want it to be of the greatest possible use to the public, the best way to achieve this is to make it free software which everyone can redistribute and change under these terms.

To do so, attach the following notices to the program. It is safest to attach them to the start of each source file to most effectively convey the exclusion of warranty; and each file should have at least the "copyright" line and a pointer to where the full notice is found.

```
one line to give the program's name and an idea of what it does.
Copyright (C) yyyy  name of author

This program is free software; you can redistribute it and/or modify it under the terms of
the GNU General Public License as published by the Free Software Foundation; either
version 2 of the License, or (at your option) any later version.

This program is distributed in the hope that it will be useful, but WITHOUT ANY WARRANTY;
without even the implied warranty of MERCHANTABILITY or FITNESS FOR A PARTICULAR PURPOSE.
See the GNU General Public License for more details.

You should have received a copy of the GNU General Public License
along with this program; if not, write to the Free Software Foundation, Inc.,
59 Temple Place—Suite 330, Boston, MA 02111-1307, USA.
```

Also add information on how to contact you by electronic and paper mail.

If the program is interactive, make it output a short notice like this when it starts in an interactive mode:

```
Gnomovision version 69, Copyright (C) yyyy name of author
Gnomovision comes with ABSOLUTELY NO WARRANTY; for details
type 'show w'. This is free software, and you are welcome
to redistribute it under certain conditions; type 'show c' for details.
```

The hypothetical commands 'show w' and 'show c' should show the appropriate parts of the General Public License. Of course, the commands you use may be called something other than 'show w' and 'show c'; they could even be mouse-clicks or menu items—whatever suits your program.

You should also get your employer (if you work as a programmer) or your school, if any, to sign a "copyright disclaimer" for the program, if necessary. Here is a sample; alter the names:

```
Yoyodyne, Inc., hereby disclaims all copyright
interest in the program 'Gnomovision'
(which makes passes at compilers) written
by James Hacker.

signature of Ty Coon, 1 April 1989
Ty Coon, President of Vice
```

This General Public License does not permit incorporating your program into proprietary programs. If your program is a subroutine library, you may consider it more useful to permit linking proprietary applications with the library. If this is what you want to do, use the GNU Library General Public License instead of this License.

GNU Lesser General Public License (LGPL)

taken from: http://www.gnu.org/copyleft/lesser.html

GNU LESSER GENERAL PUBLIC LICENSE

Version 2.1, February 1999

```
Copyright (C) 1991, 1999 Free Software Foundation, Inc.
59 Temple Place, Suite 330, Boston, MA 02111-1307 USA
Everyone is permitted to copy and distribute verbatim copies
of this license document, but changing it is not allowed.
```

Preamble

The licenses for most software are designed to take away your freedom to share and change it. By contrast, the GNU General Public Licenses are intended to guarantee your freedom to share and change free software—to make sure the software is free for all its users.

This license, the Lesser General Public License, applies to some specially designated software packages—typically libraries—of the Free Software Foundation and other authors who decide to use it. You can use it too, but we suggest you first think carefully about whether this license or the ordinary General Public License is the better strategy to use in any particular case, based on the explanations below.

When we speak of free software, we are referring to freedom of use, not price. Our General Public Licenses are designed to make sure that you have the freedom to distribute copies of free software (and charge for this service if you wish); that you receive source code or can get it if you want it; that you can change the software and use pieces of it in new free programs; and that you are informed that you can do these things.

To protect your rights, we need to make restrictions that forbid distributors to deny you these rights or to ask you to surrender these rights. These restrictions translate to certain responsibilities for you if you distribute copies of the library or if you modify it.

For example, if you distribute copies of the library, whether gratis or for a fee, you must give the recipients all the rights that we gave you. You must make sure that they, too, receive or can get the source code. If you link other code with the library, you must provide complete object files to the recipients, so that they can relink them with the library after making changes to the library and recompiling it. And you must show them these terms so they know their rights.

We protect your rights with a two-step method: (1) we copyright the library, and (2) we offer you this license, which gives you legal permission to copy, distribute and/or modify the library.

To protect each distributor, we want to make it very clear that there is no warranty for the free library. Also, if the library is modified by someone else and passed on, the recipients should know that what they have is not the original version, so that the original author's reputation will not be affected by problems that might be introduced by others.

Finally, software patents pose a constant threat to the existence of any free program. We wish to make sure that a company cannot effectively restrict the users of a free program by obtaining a restrictive license from a patent holder. Therefore, we insist that any patent license obtained for a version of the library must be consistent with the full freedom of use specified in this license.

Most GNU software, including some libraries, is covered by the ordinary GNU General Public License. This license, the GNU Lesser General Public License, applies to certain designated libraries, and is quite different from the ordinary General Public License. We use this license for certain libraries in order to permit linking those libraries into non-free programs.

When a program is linked with a library, whether statically or using a shared library, the combination of the two is legally speaking a combined work, a derivative of the original library. The ordinary General Public License therefore permits such linking only if the entire combination fits its criteria of freedom. The Lesser General Public License permits more lax criteria for linking other code with the library.

We call this license the "Lesser" General Public License because it does Less to protect the user's freedom than the ordinary General Public License. It also provides other free software developers Less of an advantage over competing non-free programs. These disadvantages are the reason we use the ordinary General Public License for many libraries. However, the Lesser license provides advantages in certain special circumstances.

For example, on rare occasions, there may be a special need to encourage the widest possible use of a certain library, so that it becomes a de-facto standard. To achieve this, non-free programs must be allowed to use the library. A more frequent case is that a free library does the same job as widely used non-free libraries. In this case, there is little to gain by limiting the free library to free software only, so we use the Lesser General Public License.

In other cases, permission to use a particular library in non-free programs enables a greater number of people to use a large body of free software. For example, permission to use the GNU C Library in non-free programs enables many more people to use the whole GNU operating system, as well as its variant, the GNU/Linux operating system.

Although the Lesser General Public License is Less protective of the users' freedom, it does ensure that the user of a program that is linked with the Library has the freedom and the wherewithal to run that program using a modified version of the Library.

The precise terms and conditions for copying, distribution and modification follow. Pay close attention to the difference between a "work based on the library" and a "work that uses the library." The former contains code derived from the library, whereas the latter must be combined with the library in order to run.

TERMS AND CONDITIONS FOR COPYING, DISTRIBUTION AND MODIFICATION

0.   This License Agreement applies to any software library or other program which contains a notice placed by the copyright holder or other authorized party saying it may be distributed under the terms of this Lesser General Public License (also called "this License"). Each licensee is addressed as "you."

A "library" means a collection of software functions and/or data prepared so as to be conveniently linked with application programs (which use some of those functions and data) to form executables.

The "Library," below, refers to any such software library or work which has been distributed under these terms. A "work based on the Library" means either the Library or any derivative work under copyright law: that is to say, a work containing the Library or a portion of it, either verbatim or with modifications and/or translated straightforwardly into another language. (Hereinafter, translation is included without limitation in the term "modification.")

"Source code" for a work means the preferred form of the work for making modifications to it. For a library, complete source code means all the source code for all modules it contains, plus any associated interface definition files, plus the scripts used to control compilation and installation of the library.

Activities other than copying, distribution and modification are not covered by this License; they are outside its scope. The act of running a program using the Library is not restricted, and output from such a program is covered only if its contents constitute a work based on the Library (independent of the use of the Library in a tool for writing it). Whether that is true depends on what the Library does and what the program that uses the Library does.

1. You may copy and distribute verbatim copies of the Library's complete source code as you receive it, in any medium, provided that you conspicuously and appropriately publish on each copy an appropriate copyright notice and disclaimer of warranty; keep intact all the notices that refer to this License and to the absence of any warranty; and distribute a copy of this License along with the Library.

You may charge a fee for the physical act of transferring a copy, and you may at your option offer warranty protection in exchange for a fee.

2. You may modify your copy or copies of the Library or any portion of it, thus forming a work based on the Library, and copy and distribute such modifications or work under the terms of Section 1 above, provided that you also meet all of these conditions:

a) The modified work must itself be a software library.

b) You must cause the files modified to carry prominent notices stating that you changed the files and the date of any change.

c) You must cause the whole of the work to be licensed at no charge to all third parties under the terms of this License.

d) If a facility in the modified Library refers to a function or a table of data to be supplied by an application program that uses the facility, other than as an argument passed when the facility is invoked, then you must make a good faith effort to ensure that, in the event an application does not supply such function or table, the facility still operates, and performs whatever part of its purpose remains meaningful.

(For example, a function in a library to compute square roots has a purpose that is entirely well-defined independent of the application. Therefore, Subsection 2d requires that any application-supplied function or table used by this function must be optional: if the application does not supply it, the square root function must still compute square roots.)

These requirements apply to the modified work as a whole. If identifiable sections of that work are not derived from the Library, and can be reasonably considered independent and separate works in themselves, then this License, and its terms, do not apply to those sections when you distribute them as separate works. But when you distribute the same sections as part of a whole which is a work based on the Library, the distribution of the whole must be on the terms of this License, whose permissions for other licensees extend to the entire whole, and thus to each and every part regardless of who wrote it.

Thus, it is not the intent of this section to claim rights or contest your rights to work written entirely by you; rather, the intent is to exercise the right to control the distribution of derivative or collective works based on the Library.

In addition, mere aggregation of another work not based on the Library with the Library (or with a work based on the Library) on a volume of a storage or distribution medium does not bring the other work under the scope of this License.

3.   You may opt to apply the terms of the ordinary GNU General Public License instead of this License to a given copy of the Library. To do this, you must alter all the notices that refer to this License, so that they refer to the ordinary GNU General Public License, version 2, instead of to this License. (If a newer version than version 2 of the ordinary GNU General Public License has appeared, then you can specify that version instead if you wish.) Do not make any other change in these notices.

Once this change is made in a given copy, it is irreversible for that copy, so the ordinary GNU General Public License applies to all subsequent copies and derivative works made from that copy.

This option is useful when you wish to copy part of the code of the Library into a program that is not a library.

4.   You may copy and distribute the Library (or a portion or derivative of it, under Section 2) in object code or executable form under the terms of Sections 1 and 2 above provided that you accompany it with the complete corresponding machine-readable source code, which must be distributed under the terms of Sections 1 and 2 above on a medium customarily used for software interchange.

If distribution of object code is made by offering access to copy from a designated place, then offering equivalent access to copy the source code from the same place satisfies the requirement to distribute the source code, even though third parties are not compelled to copy the source along with the object code.

5.   A program that contains no derivative of any portion of the Library, but is designed to work with the Library by being compiled or linked with it, is called a "work that uses the Library." Such a work, in isolation, is not a derivative work of the Library, and therefore falls outside the scope of this License.

However, linking a "work that uses the Library" with the Library creates an executable that is a derivative of the Library (because it contains portions of the Library), rather than a "work that uses the library." The executable is therefore covered by this License. Section 6 states terms for distribution of such executables.

When a "work that uses the Library" uses material from a header file that is part of the Library, the object code for the work may be a derivative work of the Library even though the source code is not. Whether this is true is especially significant if the work can be linked without the Library, or if the work is itself a library. The threshold for this to be true is not precisely defined by law.

If such an object file uses only numerical parameters, data structure layouts and accessors, and small macros and small inline functions (ten lines or less in length), then the use of the object file is unrestricted, regardless of whether it is legally a derivative work. (Executables containing this object code plus portions of the Library will still fall under Section 6.)

Otherwise, if the work is a derivative of the Library, you may distribute the object code for the work under the terms of Section 6. Any executables containing that work also fall under Section 6, whether or not they are linked directly with the Library itself.

6.   As an exception to the Sections above, you may also combine or link a "work that uses the Library" with the Library to produce a work containing portions of the Library, and distribute that work under terms of your choice, provided that the terms permit modification of the work for the customer's own use and reverse engineering for debugging such modifications.

You must give prominent notice with each copy of the work that the Library is used in it and that the Library and its use are covered by this License. You must supply a copy of this License. If the work during execution displays copyright notices, you must include the copyright notice for the Library among them, as well as a reference directing the user to the copy of this License. Also, you must do one of these things:

a) Accompany the work with the complete corresponding machine-readable source code for the Library including whatever changes were used in the work (which must be distributed under Sections 1 and 2 above); and, if the work is an executable linked with the Library, with the complete machine-readable "work that uses the Library," as object code and/or source code, so that the user can modify the Library and then relink to produce a modified executable containing the modified Library. (It is understood that the user who changes the contents of definitions files in the Library will not necessarily be able to recompile the application to use the modified definitions.)

b) Use a suitable shared library mechanism for linking with the Library. A suitable mechanism is one that (1) uses at run time a copy of the library already present on the user's computer system, rather than copying library functions into the executable, and (2) will operate properly with a modified version of the library, if the user installs one, as long as the modified version is interface-compatible with the version that the work was made with.

c) Accompany the work with a written offer, valid for at least three years, to give the same user the materials specified in Subsection 6a, above, for a charge no more than the cost of performing this distribution.

d) If distribution of the work is made by offering access to copy from a designated place, offer equivalent access to copy the above specified materials from the same place.

e) Verify that the user has already received a copy of these materials or that you have already sent this user a copy.

For an executable, the required form of the "work that uses the Library" must include any data and utility programs needed for reproducing the executable from it. However, as a special exception, the materials to be distributed need not include anything that is normally distributed (in either source or binary form) with the major components (compiler, kernel, and so on) of the operating system on which the executable runs, unless that component itself accompanies the executable.

It may happen that this requirement contradicts the license restrictions of other proprietary libraries that do not normally accompany the operating system. Such a contradiction means you cannot use both them and the Library together in an executable that you distribute.

7.   You may place library facilities that are a work based on the Library side-by-side in a single library together with other library facilities not covered by this License, and distribute such a combined library, provided that the separate distribution of the work based on the Library and of the other library facilities is otherwise permitted, and provided that you do these two things:

a) Accompany the combined library with a copy of the same work based on the Library, uncombined with any other library facilities. This must be distributed under the terms of the Sections above.

b) Give prominent notice with the combined library of the fact that part of it is a work based on the Library, and explaining where to find the accompanying uncombined form of the same work.

8.   You may not copy, modify, sublicense, link with, or distribute the Library except as expressly provided under this License. Any attempt otherwise to copy, modify, sublicense, link with, or distribute the Library is void, and will automatically terminate your rights under this License. However, parties who have received copies, or rights, from you under this License will not have their licenses terminated so long as such parties remain in full compliance.

9.   You are not required to accept this License, since you have not signed it. However, nothing else grants you permission to modify or distribute the Library or its derivative works. These actions are prohibited by law if you do not accept this License. Therefore, by modifying or distributing the Library (or any work based on the Library), you indicate your acceptance of this License to do so, and all its terms and conditions for copying, distributing or modifying the Library or works based on it.

10.   Each time you redistribute the Library (or any work based on the Library), the recipient automatically receives a license from the original licensor to copy, distribute, link with or modify the Library subject to these terms and conditions. You may not impose any further restrictions on the recipients' exercise of the rights granted herein. You are not responsible for enforcing compliance by third parties with this License.

11.   If, as a consequence of a court judgment or allegation of patent infringement or for any other reason (not limited to patent issues), conditions are imposed on you (whether by court order, agreement or otherwise) that contradict the conditions of this License, they do not excuse you from the conditions of this License. If you cannot distribute so as to satisfy simultaneously your obligations under this License and any other pertinent obligations, then as a consequence you may not distribute the Library at all. For example, if a patent license would not permit royalty-free redistribution of the Library by all those who receive copies directly or indirectly through you, then the only way you could satisfy both it and this License would be to refrain entirely from distribution of the Library.

If any portion of this section is held invalid or unenforceable under any particular circumstance, the balance of the section is intended to apply, and the section as a whole is intended to apply in other circumstances.

It is not the purpose of this section to induce you to infringe any patents or other property right claims or to contest validity of any such claims; this section has the sole purpose of protecting the integrity of the free software distribution system which is implemented by public license practices. Many people have made generous contributions to the wide range of software distributed through that system in reliance on consistent application of that system; it is up to the author/donor to decide if he or she is willing to distribute software through any other system and a licensee cannot impose that choice.

This section is intended to make thoroughly clear what is believed to be a consequence of the rest of this License.

12.   If the distribution and/or use of the Library is restricted in certain countries either by patents or by copyrighted interfaces, the original copyright holder who places the Library under this License may add an explicit geographical distribution limitation excluding those countries, so that distribution is permitted only in or among countries not thus excluded. In such case, this License incorporates the limitation as if written in the body of this License.

13.   The Free Software Foundation may publish revised and/or new versions of the Lesser General Public License from time to time. Such new versions will be similar in spirit to the present version, but may differ in detail to address new problems or concerns.

Each version is given a distinguishing version number. If the Library specifies a version number of this License which applies to it and "any later version," you have the option of following the terms and conditions either of that version or of any later version published by the Free Software Foundation. If the Library does not specify a license version number, you may choose any version ever published by the Free Software Foundation.

14.   If you wish to incorporate parts of the Library into other free programs whose distribution conditions are incompatible with these, write to the author to ask for permission. For software which is copyrighted by the Free Software Foundation, write to the Free Software Foundation; we sometimes make exceptions for this. Our decision will be guided by the two goals of preserving the free status of all derivatives of our free software and of promoting the sharing and reuse of software generally.

NO WARRANTY

15.   BECAUSE THE LIBRARY IS LICENSED FREE OF CHARGE, THERE IS NO WARRANTY FOR THE LIBRARY, TO THE EXTENT PERMITTED BY APPLICABLE LAW. EXCEPT WHEN OTHERWISE STATED IN WRITING THE COPYRIGHT HOLDERS AND/OR OTHER PARTIES PROVIDE THE LIBRARY "AS IS" WITHOUT WARRANTY OF ANY KIND, EITHER EXPRESSED OR IMPLIED, INCLUDING, BUT NOT LIMITED TO, THE IMPLIED WARRANTIES OF MERCHANTABILITY AND FITNESS FOR A PARTICULAR PURPOSE. THE ENTIRE RISK AS TO THE QUALITY AND PERFORMANCE OF THE LIBRARY IS WITH YOU. SHOULD THE LIBRARY PROVE DEFECTIVE, YOU ASSUME THE COST OF ALL NECESSARY SERVICING, REPAIR OR CORRECTION.

16.   IN NO EVENT UNLESS REQUIRED BY APPLICABLE LAW OR AGREED TO IN WRITING WILL ANY COPYRIGHT HOLDER, OR ANY OTHER PARTY WHO MAY MODIFY AND/OR REDISTRIBUTE THE LIBRARY AS PERMITTED ABOVE, BE LIABLE TO YOU FOR DAMAGES, INCLUDING ANY GENERAL, SPECIAL, INCIDENTAL OR

CONSEQUENTIAL DAMAGES ARISING OUT OF THE USE OR INABILITY TO USE THE LIBRARY (INCLUDING BUT NOT LIMITED TO LOSS OF DATA OR DATA BEING RENDERED INACCURATE OR LOSSES SUSTAINED BY YOU OR THIRD PARTIES OR A FAILURE OF THE LIBRARY TO OPERATE WITH ANY OTHER SOFTWARE), EVEN IF SUCH HOLDER OR OTHER PARTY HAS BEEN ADVISED OF THE POSSIBILITY OF SUCH DAMAGES.

END OF TERMS AND CONDITIONS

How to Apply These Terms to Your New Libraries.

If you develop a new library, and you want it to be of the greatest possible use to the public, we recommend making it free software that everyone can redistribute and change. You can do so by permitting redistribution under these terms (or, alternatively, under the terms of the ordinary General Public License).

To apply these terms, attach the following notices to the library. It is safest to attach them to the start of each source file to most effectively convey the exclusion of warranty; and each file should have at least the "copyright" line and a pointer to where the full notice is found.

```
one line to give the library's name and an idea of what it does.
Copyright (C) year  name of author

This library is free software; you can redistribute it and/or
modify it under the terms of the GNU Lesser General Public
License as published by the Free Software Foundation; either
version 2 of the License, or (at your option) any later version.

This library is distributed in the hope that it will be useful,
but WITHOUT ANY WARRANTY; without even the implied warranty of
MERCHANTABILITY or FITNESS FOR A PARTICULAR PURPOSE. See the GNU
Lesser General Public License for more details.

You should have received a copy of the GNU Lesser General Public License
along with this library; if not, write to the Free Software Foundation,
Inc., 59 Temple Place, Suite 330, Boston, MA 02111-1307 USA
```

Also add information on how to contact you by electronic and paper mail.

You should also get your employer (if you work as a programmer) or your school, if any, to sign a "copyright disclaimer" for the library, if necessary. Here is a sample; alter the names:

```
Yoyodyne, Inc., hereby disclaims all copyright interest in
the library 'Frob' (a library for tweaking knobs) written
by James Random Hacker.

signature of Ty Coon, 1 April 1990
Ty Coon, President of Vice
```

That's all there is to it!

IBM Common Public License (CPL)

taken from: http://www.ibm.com/developerworks/oss/CPLv1.0.htm

Common Public License – V 1.0

THE ACCOMPANYING PROGRAM IS PROVIDED UNDER THE TERMS OF THIS COMMON PUBLIC LICENSE ("AGREEMENT"). ANY USE, REPRODUCTION OR DISTRIBUTION OF THE PROGRAM CONSTITUTES RECIPIENT'S ACCEPTANCE OF THIS AGREEMENT.

1. DEFINITIONS

"Contribution" means:
- a) in the case of the initial Contributor, the initial code and documentation distributed under this Agreement, and
- b) in the case of each subsequent Contributor:
  - i) changes to the Program, and
  - ii) additions to the Program;
    where such changes and/or additions to the Program originate from and are distributed by that particular Contributor. A Contribution 'originates' from a Contributor if it was added to the Program by such Contributor itself or anyone acting on such Contributor's behalf. Contributions do not include additions to the Program which: (i) are separate modules of software distributed in conjunction with the Program under their own license agreement, and (ii) are not derivative works of the Program.

"Contributor" means any person or entity that distributes the Program.

"Licensed Patents" mean patent claims licensable by a Contributor which are necessarily infringed by the use or sale of its Contribution alone or when combined with the Program.

"Program" means the Contributions distributed in accordance with this Agreement.

"Recipient" means anyone who receives the Program under this Agreement, including all Contributors.

2. GRANT OF RIGHTS

- a) Subject to the terms of this Agreement, each Contributor hereby grants Recipient a non-exclusive, worldwide, royalty-free copyright license to reproduce, prepare derivative works of, publicly display, publicly perform, distribute and sublicense the Contribution of such Contributor, if any, and such derivative works, in source code and object code form.

- b) Subject to the terms of this Agreement, each Contributor hereby grants Recipient a non-exclusive, worldwide, royalty-free patent license under Licensed Patents to make, use, sell, offer to sell, import and otherwise transfer the Contribution of such Contributor, if any, in source code and object code form. This patent license shall apply to the combination of the Contribution and the Program if, at the time the Contribution is added by the Contributor, such addition of the Contribution causes such combination to be covered by the Licensed Patents. The patent license shall not apply to any other combinations which include the Contribution. No hardware per se is licensed hereunder.

c) Recipient understands that although each Contributor grants the licenses to its Contributions set forth herein, no assurances are provided by any Contributor that the Program does not infringe the patent or other intellectual property rights of any other entity. Each Contributor disclaims any liability to Recipient for claims brought by any other entity based on infringement of intellectual property rights or otherwise. As a condition to exercising the rights and licenses granted hereunder, each Recipient hereby assumes sole responsibility to secure any other intellectual property rights needed, if any. For example, if a third party patent license is required to allow Recipient to distribute the Program, it is Recipient's responsibility to acquire that license before distributing the Program.

d) Each Contributor represents that to its knowledge it has sufficient copyright rights in its Contribution, if any, to grant the copyright license set forth in this Agreement.

3. REQUIREMENTS

A Contributor may choose to distribute the Program in object code form under its own license agreement, provided that:

a. it complies with the terms and conditions of this Agreement; and

b. its license agreement:

    i) effectively disclaims on behalf of all Contributors all warranties and conditions, express and implied, including warranties or conditions of title and non-infringement, and implied warranties or conditions of merchantability and fitness for a particular purpose;

    ii) effectively excludes on behalf of all Contributors all liability for damages, including direct, indirect, special, incidental and consequential damages, such as lost profits;

    iii) states that any provisions which differ from this Agreement are offered by that Contributor alone and not by any other party; and

    iv) states that source code for the Program is available from such Contributor, and informs licensees how to obtain it in a reasonable manner on or through a medium customarily used for software exchange.

When the Program is made available in source code form:

a) it must be made available under this Agreement; and

b) a copy of this Agreement must be included with each copy of the Program.

Contributors may not remove or alter any copyright notices contained within the Program.

Each Contributor must identify itself as the originator of its Contribution, if any, in a manner that reasonably allows subsequent Recipients to identify the originator of the Contribution.

4. COMMERCIAL DISTRIBUTION

Commercial distributors of software may accept certain responsibilities with respect to end users, business partners and the like. While this license is intended to facilitate the commercial use of the Program, the Contributor who includes the Program in a commercial product offering should do so in a manner which does not create potential liability for other Contributors. Therefore, if a Contributor includes the Program in a commercial product offering, such Contributor ("Commercial Contributor") hereby agrees to defend and indemnify every other Contributor ("Indemnified Contributor") against any losses, damages and costs (collectively "Losses") arising from claims, lawsuits and other legal actions brought by a third party against the Indemnified Contributor to the extent caused by the acts or omissions of such Commercial Contributor in connection with its distribution of the Program in a commercial product offering. The obligations in this section do not apply to any claims or Losses relating to any actual or alleged intellectual property infringement. In order to qualify, an Indemnified Contributor must: a) promptly notify the Commercial Contributor in writing of such claim, and b) allow the Commercial Contributor to control, and cooperate with the Commercial Contributor in, the defense and any related settlement negotiations. The Indemnified Contributor may participate in any such claim at its own expense.

For example, a Contributor might include the Program in a commercial product offering, Product X. That Contributor is then a Commercial Contributor. If that Commercial Contributor then makes performance claims, or offers warranties related to Product X, those performance claims and warranties are such Commercial Contributor's responsibility alone. Under this section, the Commercial Contributor would have to defend claims against the other Contributors related to those performance claims and warranties, and if a court requires any other Contributor to pay any damages as a result, the Commercial Contributor must pay those damages.

5. NO WARRANTY

EXCEPT AS EXPRESSLY SET FORTH IN THIS AGREEMENT, THE PROGRAM IS PROVIDED ON AN "AS IS" BASIS, WITHOUT WARRANTIES OR CONDITIONS OF ANY KIND, EITHER EXPRESS OR IMPLIED INCLUDING, WITHOUT LIMITATION, ANY WARRANTIES OR CONDITIONS OF TITLE, NON-INFRINGEMENT, MERCHANT-ABILITY OR FITNESS FOR A PARTICULAR PURPOSE. Each Recipient is solely responsible for determining the appropriateness of using and distributing the Program and assumes all risks associated with its exercise of rights under this Agreement, including but not limited to the risks and costs of program errors, compliance with applicable laws, damage to or loss of data, programs or equipment, and unavailability or interruption of operations.

6. DISCLAIMER OF LIABILITY

EXCEPT AS EXPRESSLY SET FORTH IN THIS AGREEMENT, NEITHER RECIPIENT NOR ANY CONTRIBUTORS SHALL HAVE ANY LIABILITY FOR ANY DIRECT, INDIRECT, INCIDENTAL, SPECIAL, EXEMPLARY, OR CONSEQUENTIAL DAMAGES (INCLUDING WITHOUT LIMITATION LOST PROFITS), HOWEVER CAUSED AND ON ANY THEORY OF LIABILITY, WHETHER IN CONTRACT, STRICT LIABILITY, OR TORT (INCLUDING NEGLIGENCE OR OTHERWISE) ARISING IN ANY WAY OUT OF THE USE OR DISTRIBUTION OF THE PROGRAM OR THE EXERCISE OF ANY RIGHTS GRANTED HEREUNDER, EVEN IF ADVISED OF THE POSSIBILITY OF SUCH DAMAGES.

7. GENERAL

If any provision of this Agreement is invalid or unenforceable under applicable law, it shall not affect the validity or enforceability of the remainder of the terms of this Agreement, and without further action by the parties hereto, such provision shall be reformed to the minimum extent necessary to make such provision valid and enforceable.

If Recipient institutes patent litigation against a Contributor with respect to a patent applicable to software (including a cross-claim or counterclaim in a lawsuit), then any patent licenses granted by that Contributor to such Recipient under this Agreement shall terminate as of the date such litigation is filed. In addition, if Recipient institutes patent litigation against any entity (including a cross-claim or counterclaim in a lawsuit) alleging that the Program itself (excluding combinations of the Program with other software or hardware) infringes such Recipient's patent(s), then such Recipient's rights granted under Section 2(b) shall terminate as of the date such litigation is filed.

All Recipient's rights under this Agreement shall terminate if it fails to comply with any of the material terms or conditions of this Agreement and does not cure such failure in a reasonable period of time after becoming aware of such noncompliance. If all Recipient's rights under this Agreement terminate, Recipient agrees to cease use and distribution of the Program as soon as reasonably practicable. However, Recipient's obligations under this Agreement and any licenses granted by Recipient relating to the Program shall continue and survive.

Everyone is permitted to copy and distribute copies of this Agreement, but in order to avoid inconsistency the Agreement is copyrighted and may only be modified in the following manner. The Agreement Steward reserves the right to publish new versions (including revisions) of this Agreement from time to time. No one other than the Agreement Steward has the right to modify this Agreement. IBM is the initial Agreement Steward. IBM may assign the responsibility to serve as the Agreement Steward to a suitable separate entity. Each new version of the Agreement will be given a distinguishing version number. The Program (including Contributions) may always be distributed subject to the version of the Agreement under which it was received. In addition, after a new version of the Agreement is published, Contributor may elect to distribute the Program (including its Contributions) under the new version. Except as expressly stated in Sections 2(a) and 2(b) above, Recipient receives no rights or licenses to the intellectual property of any Contributor under this Agreement, whether expressly, by implication, estoppel or otherwise. All rights in the Program not expressly granted under this Agreement are reserved.

This Agreement is governed by the laws of the State of New York and the intellectual property laws of the United States of America. No party to this Agreement will bring a legal action under this Agreement more than one year after the cause of action arose. Each party waives its rights to a jury trial in any resulting litigation.

Microsoft Shared Source License for CLI, C# and JScript

taken from: http://msdn.microsoft.com/MSDN-FILES/027/002/097/ShSource CLILicense.htm

Microsoft Shared Source CLI, C# and JScript License
March 27, 2002

This License governs use of the accompanying Software, and your use of the Software constitutes acceptance of this license.

You may use this Software for any non-commercial purpose, subject to the restrictions in this license. Some purposes which can be non-commercial are teaching, academic research, and personal experimentation. You may also distribute this Software with books or other teaching materials, or publish the Software on websites, that are intended to teach the use of the Software.

You may not use or distribute this Software or any derivative works in any form for commercial purposes. Examples of commercial purposes would be running business operations, licensing, leasing, or selling the Software, or distributing the Software for use with commercial products.

You may modify this Software and distribute the modified Software for non-commercial purposes, however, you may not grant rights to the Software or derivative works that are broader than those provided by this License. For example, you may not distribute modifications of the Software under terms that would permit commercial use, or under terms that purport to require the Software or derivative works to be sublicensed to others.

You may use any information in intangible form that you remember after accessing the Software. However, this right does not grant you a license to any of Microsoft's copyrights or patents for anything you might create using such information.

In return, we simply require that you agree:

1. Not to remove any copyright or other notices from the Software.

2. That if you distribute the Software in source or object form, you will include a verbatim copy of this license.

3. That if you distribute derivative works of the Software in source code form you do so only under a license that includes all of the provisions of this License, and if you distribute derivative works of the Software solely in object form you do so only under a license that compiles with this License.

4. That if you have modified the Software or created derivative works, and distribute such modifications or derivative works, you will cause the modified files to carry prominent notices so that recipients know that they are not receiving the original Software. Such notices must state: (i) that you have changed the Software; and (ii) the date of any changes.

5. THAT THE SOFTWARE COMES "AS IS", WITH NO WARRANTIES. THIS MEANS NO EXPRESS, IMPLIED OR STATUTORY WARRANTY, INCLUDING WITHOUT LIMITATION, WARRANTIES OF MERCHANTABILITY OR FITNESS FOR A PARTICULAR PURPOSE OR ANY WARRANTY OF TITLE OR NON-INFRINGEMENT.

ALSO, YOU MUST PASS THIS DISCLAIMER ON WHENEVER YOU DISTRIBUTE THE SOFTWARE OR DERIVATIVE WORKS.

6. THAT MICROSOFT WILL NOT BE LIABLE FOR ANY DAMAGES RELATED TO THE SOFTWARE OR THIS LICENSE, INCLUDING DIRECT, INDIRECT, SPECIAL, CON-SEQUENTIAL OR INCIDENTAL DAMAGES, TO THE MAXIMUM EXTENT THE LAW PERMITS, NO MATTER WHAT LEGAL THEORY IT IS BASED ON. ALSO, YOU MUST PASS THIS LIMITATION OF LIABILITY ON WHENEVER YOU DISTRIBUTE THE SOFTWARE OR DERIVATIVE WORKS.

7. That if you sue anyone over patents that you think may apply to the Software or anyone's use of the Software, your license to the Software ends automatically.

8. That your rights under the License end automatically if you breach it in any way.

9. Microsoft reserves all rights not expressly granted to you in this license.

Microsoft Shared Source License for Windows CE.Net

taken from: http://msdn.microsoft.com/embedded/usewinemb/ce/sharedsrccode/eula/default.aspx

Microsoft Windows CE 5.0 Shared Source License Agreement ("License")
June 28, 2004

Microsoft gives you a license to use the accompanying Software on the following terms:

You may:

1. Correct errors in Your hardware and software operating on the Windows CE platform.

2. Create derivative works of the Software to debug, improve and optimize Windows CE.

3. Use the Software as a reference to develop Enhancements. "Enhancements" means technologies that enhance or extend the functionality or features of the Windows CE operating system and do not include any of the Software or any derivative work of the Software.

4. Provide system integration and technical support services to Your customers to assist them in their development, testing, or use of hardware and software, as applicable, based on the Windows CE platform.

5. Compile the Software and any derivative works of the Software that You create under the terms of this License and then publicly perform and display that compiled code in operation in Your device in public demonstrations at tradeshows, lectures and similar events.

6. Distribute derivative works of the Software only in object code form as part of Your Windows CE-based embedded product provided that You have signed a standard, royalty-bearing agreement of distribution of Windows CE.

7. Microsoft reserves all rights not expressly granted.

You may not:

1. Use the Software or information derived from the Software for any project related to, or to make any Enhancements or derivative works of the Software for use with, a non-Microsoft operating system or related to a device or piece of hardware based on a non-Microsoft operating system.

2. Use the Software for patent-mining purposes, such as (i) determining if any features, functions or processes provided by the Software are covered by any patents or patent applications or (ii) using the Software as a reference or using specific knowledge of the Software to modify existing patents or patent applications or creating any continuation, continuation in part, or extension of existing patents or patent applications.

In return, we simply require that you agree:

1. Not to remove any copyright notices from the Software.

2. Identify all derivative works of the Software, and Yourself as the author of such derivative works.

3. Not to provide end-user support for your derivative works.

4. Not to combine or distribute the Software (or any derivative works) with other software that is licensed pursuant to terms that seek to require that the Software (or any intellectual property in it) be licensed to or otherwise shared with others.

5. That if you distribute the Software in source code form, then you do so only under this License (i.e. you must include a complete copy of this License with your distribution), and if you distribute the Software solely in object form you only do so under a license that compiles with this License.

6. That if you distribute any derivative works of the Software, you will defend, indemnify and hold Microsoft harmless from any claims, losses or damages arising from any actions brought by a third party against Microsoft to the extent caused by Your acts or omissions in connection with such distribution.

7. **That the Software comes "as is", with no warranties. None whatsoever. This means no express, implied or statutory warranty, including without limitation, warranties of merchantability or fitness for a particular purpose or any warranty of non-infringement. Also, you must pass this disclaimer on whenever you distribute this Software.**

8. **That neither Microsoft, its affiliates, nor its suppliers are liable for any damages, including those types of damages known as indirect, special, consequential, or incidental related to the Software or this License, to the maximum extent the law permits, no matter what legal theory its based on. Also, you must pass this limitation of liability on whenever you distribute the Software.**

9. That if you sue anyone over patents that you think may apply to this Software for a person's use of this Software, your license to this Software ends automatically.

10. Not to assert patents owned or licensable by You that claim (i) any inventions in any Enhancements or derivative works You develop using the Software or (ii) any inventions You derive from the Software (collectively, Your patents) against Microsoft, Microsoft affiliates, and Microsoft Licensees (as defined below), excluding OEM/ODM Licensees (as defined below), for infringement of Your Patents on account of the making, use, sale, offer for sale, importation or other disposition or promotion of any version or portion of Windows CE, portion thereof, or a redistributed portion thereof, then You and Your affiliates agree to offer licenses to such OEM/ODM Licensees under commercially reasonable and non-discriminatory terms and pricing.

11. If You assign any of Your Patents or rights to enforce any of Your Patents, You will require that the assignee(s) agree to be bound by this Section. Any such assignment by You not in accordance with this Section will be null and void.

12. "Microsoft Licensee" means any third party that is directly or indirectly licensed by Microsoft to exercise any legal rights with respect to Windows CE or a portion thereof or a redistributed portion thereof, including authorized distributors or Windows CE, users of Windows CE and end users of any redistributed portions of Windows CE. OEM/ODM Licensee means an original equipment/device manufacturer directly or indirectly licensed by Microsoft to use binaries incorporated in that OEM/ODMs embedded system(s).

13.   That the patent rights Microsoft is licensing only apply to the Software, not to any derivatives you make.

14.   That your rights under this License end automatically if you breach this License in any way.

If you would like to suggest changes, modifications or improvements to the Softwarem e-mail us at cesrc@microsoft.com.

MIT or X License

taken from: http://www.xfree86.org/current/LICENSE2.html

(*Note that the original MIT version did not include the final two paragraphs.*)

X Copyright

Copyright ©1987 X Consortium

Permission is hereby granted, free of charge, to any person obtaining a copy of this software and associated documentation files (the "Software"), to deal in the Software without restriction, including without limitation the rights to use, copy, modify, merge, publish, distribute, sublicense, and/or sell copies of the Software, and to permit persons to whom the Software is furnished to do so, subject to the following conditions:

The above copyright notice and this permission notice shall be included in all copies or substantial portions of the Software.

THE SOFTWARE IS PROVIDED "AS IS," WITHOUT WARRANTY OF ANY KIND, EXPRESS OR IMPLIED, INCLUDING BUT NOT LIMITED TO THE WARRANTIES OF MERCHANTABILITY, FITNESS FOR A PARTICULAR PURPOSE AND NONINFRINGE-MENT. IN NO EVENT SHALL THE X CONSORTIUM BE LIABLE FOR ANY CLAIM, DAMAGES OR OTHER LIABILITY, WHETHER IN AN ACTION OF CONTRACT, TORT OR OTHERWISE, ARISING FROM, OUT OF OR IN CONNECTION WITH THE SOFTWARE OR THE USE OR OTHER DEALINGS IN THE SOFTWARE.

Except as contained in this notice, the name of the X Consortium shall not be used in advertising or otherwise to promote the sale, use or other dealings in this Software without prior written authorization from the X Consortium.

X Window System is a trademark of X Consortium, Inc.

Mozilla Public License (MPL)

taken from: http://www.mozilla.org/MPL/MPL-1.1.html

MOZILLA PUBLIC LICENSE
Version 1.1

1. **Definitions**

    1.0.1. "Commercial Use" means distribution or otherwise making the Covered Code available to a third party.

    1.1. "Contributor" means each entity that creates or contributes to the creation of Modifications.

    1.2. "Contributor Version" means the combination of the Original Code, prior Modifications used by a Contributor, and the Modifications made by that particular Contributor.

    1.3. "Covered Code" means the Original Code or Modifications or the combination of the Original Code and Modifications, in each case including portions thereof.

    1.4. "Electronic Distribution Mechanism" means a mechanism generally accepted in the software development community for the electronic transfer of data.

    1.5. "Executable" means Covered Code in any form other than Source Code.

    1.6. "Initial Developer" means the individual or entity identified as the Initial Developer in the Source Code notice required by **Exhibit A**.

    1.7. "Larger Work" means a work which combines Covered Code or portions thereof with code not governed by the terms of this License.

    1.8. "License" means this document.

    1.8.1. "Licensable" means having the right to grant, to the maximum extent possible, whether at the time of the initial grant or subsequently acquired, any and all of the rights conveyed herein.

    1.9. "Modifications" means any addition to or deletion from the substance or structure of either the Original Code or any previous Modifications. When Covered Code is released as a series of files, a Modification is:

    > A. Any addition to or deletion from the contents of a file containing Original Code or previous Modifications.

    > B. Any new file that contains any part of the Original Code or previous Modifications.

    1.10. "Original Code" means Source Code of computer software code which is described in the Source Code notice required by **Exhibit A** as Original Code, and which, at the time of its release under this License is not already Covered Code governed by this License.

    1.10.1. "Patent Claims" means any patent claim(s), now owned or hereafter acquired, including without limitation, method, process, and apparatus claims, in any patent Licensable by grantor.

1.11. "Source Code" means the preferred form of the Covered Code for making modifications to it, including all modules it contains, plus any associated interface definition files, scripts used to control compilation and installation of an Executable, or source code differential comparisons against either the Original Code or another well known, available Covered Code of the Contributor's choice. The Source Code can be in a compressed or archival form, provided the appropriate decompression or de- archiving software is widely available for no charge.

1.12. "You" (or "Your") means an individual or a legal entity exercising rights under, and complying with all of the terms of, this License or a future version of this License issued under Section 6.1. For legal entities, "You" includes any entity which controls, is controlled by, or is under common control with You. For purposes of this definition, "control" means (a) the power, direct or indirect, to cause the direction or management of such entity, whether by contract or otherwise, or (b) ownership of more than fifty percent (50%) of the outstanding shares or beneficial ownership of such entity.

2. Source Code License.

2.1. The Initial Developer Grant.
The Initial Developer hereby grants You a world-wide, royalty-free, non-exclusive license, subject to third party intellectual property claims:

(a) under intellectual property rights (other than patent or trademark) Licensable by Initial Developer to use, reproduce, modify, display, perform, sublicense and distribute the Original Code (or portions thereof) with or without Modifications, and/or as part of a Larger Work; and

(b) under Patent Claims infringed by the making, using or selling of Original Code, to make, have made, use, practice, sell, and offer for sale, and/or otherwise dispose of the Original Code (or portions thereof).

(c) the licenses granted in this Section 2.1(a) and (b) are effective on the date Initial Developer first distributes Original Code under the terms of this License.

(d) Notwithstanding Section 2.1(b) above, no patent license is granted: 1) for code that You delete from the Original Code; 2) separate from the Original Code; or 3) for infringements caused by: (i) the modification of the Original Code or (ii) the combination of the Original Code with other software or devices.

2.2. Contributor Grant.
Subject to third party intellectual property claims, each Contributor hereby grants You a world-wide, royalty-free, non-exclusive license

(a) under intellectual property rights (other than patent or trademark) Licensable by Contributor, to use, reproduce, modify, display, perform, sublicense and distribute the Modifications created by such Contributor (or portions thereof) either on an unmodified basis, with other Modifications, as Covered Code and/or as part of a Larger Work; and

(b) under Patent Claims infringed by the making, using, or selling of Modifications made by that Contributor either alone and/or in combination with its Contributor Version (or portions of such combination), to make, use, sell, offer for sale, have made, and/or otherwise dispose of: 1) Modifications made by that Contributor (or portions thereof); and 2) the combination of Modifications made by that Contributor with its Contributor Version (or portions of such combination).

(c) the licenses granted in Sections 2.2(a) and 2.2(b) are effective on the date Contributor first makes Commercial Use of the Covered Code.

(d) Notwithstanding Section 2.2(b) above, no patent license is granted: 1) for any code that Contributor has deleted from the Contributor Version; 2) separate from the Contributor Version; 3) for infringements caused by: (i) third party modifications of Contributor Version or (ii) the combination of Modifications made by that Contributor with other software (except as part of the Contributor Version) or other devices; or 4) under Patent Claims infringed by Covered Code in the absence of Modifications made by that Contributor.

3. **Distribution Obligations.**

    3.1. Application of License.
    The Modifications which You create or to which You contribute are governed by the terms of this License, including without limitation Section 2.2. The Source Code version of Covered Code may be distributed only under the terms of this License or a future version of this License released under Section 6.1, and You must include a copy of this License with every copy of the Source Code You distribute. You may not offer or impose any terms on any Source Code version that alters or restricts the applicable version of this License or the recipients' rights hereunder. However, You may include an additional document offering the additional rights described in Section 3.5.

    3.2. Availability of Source Code.
    Any Modification which You create or to which You contribute must be made available in Source Code form under the terms of this License either on the same media as an Executable version or via an accepted Electronic Distribution Mechanism to anyone to whom you made an Executable version available; and if made available via Electronic Distribution Mechanism, must remain available for at least twelve (12) months after the date it initially became available, or at least six (6) months after a subsequent version of that particular Modification has been made available to such recipients. You are responsible for ensuring that the Source Code version remains available even if the Electronic Distribution Mechanism is maintained by a third party.

    3.3. Description of Modifications.
    You must cause all Covered Code to which You contribute to contain a file documenting the changes You made to create that Covered Code and the date of any change. You must include a prominent statement that the Modification is derived, directly or indirectly, from Original Code provided by the Initial Developer and including the name of the Initial Developer in (a) the Source Code, and (b) in any notice in an Executable version or related documentation in which You describe the origin or ownership of the Covered Code.

    3.4. Intellectual Property Matters.
    (a) Third Party Claims.
    If Contributor has knowledge that a license under a third party's intellectual property rights is required to exercise the rights granted by such Contributor under Sections 2.1 or

2.2, Contributor must include a text file with the Source Code distribution titled "LEGAL" which describes the claim and the party making the claim in sufficient detail that a recipient will know whom to contact. If Contributor obtains such knowledge after the Modification is made available as described in Section 3.2, Contributor shall promptly modify the LEGAL file in all copies Contributor makes available thereafter and shall take other steps (such as notifying appropriate mailing lists or newsgroups) reasonably calculated to inform those who received the Covered Code that new knowledge has been obtained.

(b) Contributor APIs.

If Contributor's Modifications include an application programming interface and Contributor has knowledge of patent licenses which are reasonably necessary to implement that API, Contributor must also include this information in the LEGAL file.

(c) Representations.

Contributor represents that, except as disclosed pursuant to Section 3.4(a) above, Contributor believes that Contributor's Modifications are Contributor's original creation(s) and/or Contributor has sufficient rights to grant the rights conveyed by this License.

3.5. Required Notices.

You must duplicate the notice in **Exhibit A** in each file of the Source Code. If it is not possible to put such notice in a particular Source Code file due to its structure, then You must include such notice in a location (such as a relevant directory) where a user would be likely to look for such a notice. If You created one or more Modification(s) You may add your name as a Contributor to the notice described in **Exhibit A**. You must also duplicate this License in any documentation for the Source Code where You describe recipients' rights or ownership rights relating to Covered Code. You may choose to offer, and to charge a fee for, warranty, support, indemnity or liability obligations to one or more recipients of Covered Code. However, You may do so only on Your own behalf, and not on behalf of the Initial Developer or any Contributor. You must make it absolutely clear than any such warranty, support, indemnity or liability obligation is offered by You alone, and You hereby agree to indemnify the Initial Developer and every Contributor for any liability incurred by the Initial Developer or such Contributor as a result of warranty, support, indemnity or liability terms You offer.

3.6. Distribution of Executable Versions.

You may distribute Covered Code in Executable form only if the requirements of Section 3.1–3.5 have been met for that Covered Code, and if You include a notice stating that the Source Code version of the Covered Code is available under the terms of this License, including a description of how and where You have fulfilled the obligations of Section 3.2. The notice must be conspicuously included in any notice in an Executable version, related documentation or collateral in which You describe recipients' rights relating to the Covered Code. You may distribute the Executable version of Covered Code or ownership rights under a license of Your choice, which may contain terms different from this License, provided that You are in compliance with the terms of this License and that the license for the Executable version does not attempt to limit or alter the recipient's rights in the Source Code version from the rights set forth in this License. If You distribute the Executable version under a different license You must make it absolutely clear that any terms which differ from this License are offered by You alone, not by the Initial Developer or any Contributor. You hereby agree to indemnify the

Initial Developer and every Contributor for any liability incurred by the Initial Developer or such Contributor as a result of any such terms You offer.

3.7. Larger Works.
You may create a Larger Work by combining Covered Code with other code not governed by the terms of this License and distribute the Larger Work as a single product. In such a case, You must make sure the requirements of this License are fulfilled for the Covered Code.

4. Inability to Comply Due to Statute or Regulation.

If it is impossible for You to comply with any of the terms of this License with respect to some or all of the Covered Code due to statute, judicial order, or regulation then You must: (a) comply with the terms of this License to the maximum extent possible; and (b) describe the limitations and the code they affect. Such description must be included in the LEGAL file described in Section 3.4 and must be included with all distributions of the Source Code. Except to the extent prohibited by statute or regulation, such description must be sufficiently detailed for a recipient of ordinary skill to be able to understand it.

5. Application of this License.

This License applies to code to which the Initial Developer has attached the notice in **Exhibit A** and to related Covered Code.

6. Versions of the License.

6.1. New Versions.
Netscape Communications Corporation ("Netscape") may publish revised and/or new versions of the License from time to time. Each version will be given a distinguishing version number.

6.2. Effect of New Versions.
Once Covered Code has been published under a particular version of the License, You may always continue to use it under the terms of that version. You may also choose to use such Covered Code under the terms of any subsequent version of the License published by Netscape. No one other than Netscape has the right to modify the terms applicable to Covered Code created under this License.

6.3. Derivative Works.
If You create or use a modified version of this License (which you may only do in order to apply it to code which is not already Covered Code governed by this License), You must: (a) rename Your license so that the phrases "Mozilla," "MOZILLAPL," "MOZPL," "Netscape," "MPL," "NPL" or any confusingly similar phrase do not appear in your license (except to note that your license differs from this License) and (b) otherwise make it clear that Your version of the license contains terms which differ from the Mozilla Public License and Netscape Public License. (Filling in the name of the Initial Developer, Original Code or Contributor in the notice described in **Exhibit A** shall not of themselves be deemed to be modifications of this License.)

7. DISCLAIMER OF WARRANTY.

COVERED CODE IS PROVIDED UNDER THIS LICENSE ON AN "AS IS" BASIS, WITHOUT WARRANTY OF ANY KIND, EITHER EXPRESSED OR IMPLIED,

INCLUDING, WITHOUT LIMITATION, WARRANTIES THAT THE COVERED CODE IS FREE OF DEFECTS, MERCHANTABLE, FIT FOR A PARTICULAR PURPOSE OR NON-INFRINGING. THE ENTIRE RISK AS TO THE QUALITY AND PERFORMANCE OF THE COVERED CODE IS WITH YOU. SHOULD ANY COVERED CODE PROVE DEFECTIVE IN ANY RESPECT, YOU (NOT THE INITIAL DEVELOPER OR ANY OTHER CONTRIBUTOR) ASSUME THE COST OF ANY NECESSARY SERVICING, REPAIR OR CORRECTION. THIS DISCLAIMER OF WARRANTY CONSTITUTES AN ESSENTIAL PART OF THIS LICENSE. NO USE OF ANY COVERED CODE IS AUTHORIZED HEREUNDER EXCEPT UNDER THIS DISCLAIMER.

8. TERMINATION.

8.1. This License and the rights granted hereunder will terminate automatically if You fail to comply with terms herein and fail to cure such breach within 30 days of becoming aware of the breach. All sublicenses to the Covered Code which are properly granted shall survive any termination of this License. Provisions which, by their nature, must remain in effect beyond the termination of this License shall survive.

8.2. If You initiate litigation by asserting a patent infringement claim (excluding declaratory judgment actions) against Initial Developer or a Contributor (the Initial Developer or Contributor against whom You file such action is referred to as "Participant") alleging that:

(a) such Participant's Contributor Version directly or indirectly infringes any patent, then any and all rights granted by such Participant to You under Sections 2.1 and/or 2.2 of this License shall, upon 60 days notice from Participant terminate prospectively, unless if within 60 days after receipt of notice You either: (i) agree in writing to pay Participant a mutually agreeable reasonable royalty for Your past and future use of Modifications made by such Participant, or (ii) withdraw Your litigation claim with respect to the Contributor Version against such Participant. If within 60 days of notice, a reasonable royalty and payment arrangement are not mutually agreed upon in writing by the parties or the litigation claim is not withdrawn, the rights granted by Participant to You under Sections 2.1 and/or 2.2 automatically terminate at the expiration of the 60 day notice period specified above.

(b) any software, hardware, or device, other than such Participant's Contributor Version, directly or indirectly infringes any patent, then any rights granted to You by such Participant under Sections 2.1(b) and 2.2(b) are revoked effective as of the date You first made, used, sold, distributed, or had made, Modifications made by that Participant.

8.3. If You assert a patent infringement claim against Participant alleging that such Participant's Contributor Version directly or indirectly infringes any patent where such claim is resolved (such as by license or settlement) prior to the initiation of patent infringement litigation, then the reasonable value of the licenses granted by such Participant under Sections 2.1 or 2.2 shall be taken into account in determining the amount or value of any payment or license.

8.4. In the event of termination under Sections 8.1 or 8.2 above, all end user license agreements (excluding distributors and resellers) which have been validly granted by You or any distributor hereunder prior to termination shall survive termination.

9.   LIMITATION OF LIABILITY.

UNDER NO CIRCUMSTANCES AND UNDER NO LEGAL THEORY, WHETHER TORT (INCLUDING NEGLIGENCE), CONTRACT, OR OTHERWISE, SHALL YOU, THE INITIAL DEVELOPER, ANY OTHER CONTRIBUTOR, OR ANY DISTRIBUTOR OF COVERED CODE, OR ANY SUPPLIER OF ANY OF SUCH PARTIES, BE LIABLE TO ANY PERSON FOR ANY INDIRECT, SPECIAL, INCIDENTAL, OR CONSE-QUENTIAL DAMAGES OF ANY CHARACTER INCLUDING, WITHOUT LIMITA-TION, DAMAGES FOR LOSS OF GOODWILL, WORK STOPPAGE, COMPUTER FAILURE OR MALFUNCTION, OR ANY AND ALL OTHER COMMERCIAL DAMAGES OR LOSSES, EVEN IF SUCH PARTY SHALL HAVE BEEN INFORMED OF THE POSSIBILITY OF SUCH DAMAGES. THIS LIMITATION OF LIABILITY SHALL NOT APPLY TO LIABILITY FOR DEATH OR PERSONAL INJURY RESULTING FROM SUCH PARTY'S NEGLIGENCE TO THE EXTENT APPLICABLE LAW PROHIBITS SUCH LIMITATION. SOME JURISDICTIONS DO NOT ALLOW THE EXCLUSION OR LIMITATION OF INCIDENTAL OR CONSEQUEN-TIAL DAMAGES, SO THIS EXCLUSION AND LIMITATION MAY NOT APPLY TO YOU.

10.   U.S. GOVERNMENT END USERS.

The Covered Code is a "commercial item," as that term is defined in 48 C.F.R. 2.101 (Oct. 1995), consisting of "commercial computer software" and "commercial computer software documentation," as such terms are used in 48 C.F.R. 12.212 (Sept. 1995). Consistent with 48 C.F.R. 12.212 and 48 C.F.R. 227.7202-1 through 227.7202-4 (June 1995), all U.S. Government End Users acquire Covered Code with only those rights set forth herein.

11.   MISCELLANEOUS.

This License represents the complete agreement concerning subject matter hereof. If any provision of this License is held to be unenforceable, such provision shall be reformed only to the extent necessary to make it enforceable. This License shall be governed by California law provisions (except to the extent applicable law, if any, provides otherwise), excluding its conflict-of-law provisions. With respect to disputes in which at least one party is a citizen of, or an entity chartered or registered to do business in the United States of America, any litigation relating to this License shall be subject to the jurisdiction of the Federal Courts of the Northern District of California, with venue lying in Santa Clara County, California, with the losing party responsible for costs, including without limitation, court costs and reasonable attorneys' fees and expenses. The application of the United Nations Convention on Contracts for the International Sale of Goods is expressly excluded. Any law or regulation which provides that the language of a contract shall be construed against the drafter shall not apply to this License.

12.   RESPONSIBILITY FOR CLAIMS.

As between Initial Developer and the Contributors, each party is responsible for claims and damages arising, directly or indirectly, out of its utilization of rights under this License and You agree to work with Initial Developer and Contributors to distribute such responsibility on an equitable basis. Nothing herein is intended or shall be deemed to constitute any admission of liability.

13. MULTIPLE-LICENSED CODE.

Initial Developer may designate portions of the Covered Code as "Multiple- Licensed". "Multiple-Licensed" means that the Initial Developer permits you to utilize portions of the Covered Code under Your choice of the MPL or the alternative licenses, if any, specified by the Initial Developer in the file described in **Exhibit A.**

Exhibit A—Mozilla Public License Notice.

"The contents of this file are subject to the Mozilla Public License Version 1.1 (the "License"); you may not use this file except in compliance with the License. You may obtain a copy of the License at http://www.mozilla.org/MPL/

Software distributed under the License is distributed on an "AS IS" basis, WITHOUT WARRANTY OF ANY KIND, either express or implied. See the License for the specific language governing rights and limitations under the License.

The Original Code is _____.

The Initial Developer of the Original Code is _____. Portions created by _____ are Copyright (C) _____. All Rights Reserved.

Contributor(s): _____.

Alternatively, the contents of this file may be used under the terms of the _____ license (the "[___] License"), in which case the provisions of [___] License are applicable instead of those above. If you wish to allow use of your version of this file only under the terms of the [___] License and not to allow others to use your version of this file under the MPL, indicate your decision by deleting the provisions above and replace them with the notice and other provisions required by the [___] License. If you do not delete the provisions above, a recipient may use your version of this file under either the MPL or the [___] License."

[NOTE: The text of this Exhibit A may differ slightly from the text of the notices in the Source Code files of the Original Code. You should use the text of this Exhibit A rather than the text found in the Original Code Source Code for Your Modifications.]

Open Publication License

taken from: http://opencontent.org/openpub

Open Publication License
Draft v1.0, 8 June 1999

I. REQUIREMENTS ON BOTH UNMODIFIED AND MODIFIED VERSIONS

The Open Publication works may be reproduced and distributed in whole or in part, in any medium physical or electronic, provided that the terms of this license are adhered to, and that this license or an incorporation of it by reference (with any options elected by the author(s) and/or publisher) is displayed in the reproduction.

Proper form for an incorporation by reference is as follows:

> Copyright (c) <year> by <author's name or designee>. This material may be distributed only subject to the terms and conditions set forth in the Open Publication License, vX.Y or later (the latest version is presently available at http://www.opencontent.org/openpub/).

The reference must be immediately followed with any options elected by the author(s) and/or publisher of the document (see section VI).

Commercial redistribution of Open Publication-licensed material is permitted.

Any publication in standard (paper) book form shall require the citation of the original publisher and author. The publisher and author's names shall appear on all outer surfaces of the book. On all outer surfaces of the book the original publisher's name shall be as large as the title of the work and cited as possessive with respect to the title.

II. COPYRIGHT

The copyright to each Open Publication is owned by its author(s) or designee.

III. SCOPE OF LICENSE

The following license terms apply to all Open Publication works, unless otherwise explicitly stated in the document.

Mere aggregation of Open Publication works or a portion of an Open Publication work with other works or programs on the same media shall not cause this license to apply to those other works. The aggregate work shall contain a notice specifying the inclusion of the Open Publication material and appropriate copyright notice.

SEVERABILITY. If any part of this license is found to be unenforceable in any jurisdiction, the remaining portions of the license remain in force.

NO WARRANTY. Open Publication works are licensed and provided "as is" without warranty of any kind, express or implied, including, but not limited to, the implied warranties of merchantability and fitness for a particular purpose or a warranty of non-infringement.

334 Appendix B *Licenses*

IV. REQUIREMENTS ON MODIFIED WORKS

All modified versions of documents covered by this license, including translations, anthologies, compilations and partial documents, must meet the following requirements:

1. The modified version must be labeled as such.

2. The person making the modifications must be identified and the modifications dated.

3. Acknowledgement of the original author and publisher if applicable must be retained according to normal academic citation practices.

4. The location of the original unmodified document must be identified.

5. The original author's (or authors') name(s) may not be used to assert or imply endorsement of the resulting document without the original author's (or authors') permission.

V. GOOD-PRACTICE RECOMMENDATIONS

In addition to the requirements of this license, it is requested from and strongly recommended of redistributors that:

1. If you are distributing Open Publication works on hardcopy or CD-ROM, you provide email notification to the authors of your intent to redistribute at least thirty days before your manuscript or media freeze, to give the authors time to provide updated documents. This notification should describe modifications, if any, made to the document.

2. All substantive modifications (including deletions) be either clearly marked up in the document or else described in an attachment to the document.

3. Finally, while it is not mandatory under this license, it is considered good form to offer a free copy of any hardcopy and CD-ROM expression of an Open Publication-licensed work to its author(s).

VI. LICENSE OPTIONS

The author(s) and/or publisher of an Open Publication-licensed document may elect certain options by appending language to the reference to or copy of the license. These options are considered part of the license instance and must be included with the license (or its incorporation by reference) in derived works.

A. To prohibit distribution of substantively modified versions without the explicit permission of the author(s). "Substantive modification" is defined as a change to the semantic content of the document, and excludes mere changes in format or typographical corrections.

To accomplish this, add the phrase "Distribution of substantively modified versions of this document is prohibited without the explicit permission of the copyright holder." to the license reference or copy.

B. To prohibit any publication of this work or derivative works in whole or in part in standard (paper) book form for commercial purposes is prohibited unless prior permission is obtained from the copyright holder.

To accomplish this, add the phrase "Distribution of the work or derivative of the work in any standard (paper) book form is prohibited unless prior permission is obtained from the copyright holder." to the license reference or copy.

Sun Community Source License (SCSL)

taken from: http://www.sun.com/jini/licensing/licenses.html

Sun Community Source License
Version 3.0

Jini Technology Specific Attachment v 1.0
(SCSL3/Jini TSA 1.0)

Contents

I. Definitions
II. Purposes
III. Research Use Rights
IV. Restrictions & Community Responsibilities
V. Governance

Attachment A-1: Community Member Certificate Attachment
Attachment A-2: Student Acknowledgment
Attachment B: (Additional Terms/Responsibilities)
Commercial Use Supplement to Sun Community Source Code License
Technology Specific Attachment to the Sun Community Source License

I. DEFINITIONS

"Community Code" means Reference Code, Contributed Code, and any combination thereof.

"Community Member" means You, Original Contributor and any other party that has entered into and has in effect a version of this License (or who is similarly authorized and obligated by Sun) for the Technology with Original Contributor.

"Contributed Code" means Error Corrections, Shared Modifications and any other code other than Reference Code made available to all Community Members in accordance with this License.

"Contributed Code Specifications" means the functional, interface and operational specifications and documentation for Contributed Code.

"Contributor" means any Community Member who makes available Contributed Code.

"Covered Code" means any and all code (including Modifications) implementing all or any portion of the Technology Specifications.

"Error Correction(s)" mean Modifications which correct any failure of Community Code to conform to any aspect of the Technology Specifications.

"Interfaces" means classes or other programming code or specifications designed for use with the Technology comprising a means or link for invoking functionality, operations or protocols and which are additional to or extend the interfaces designated in the Technology Specifications.

"Modifications" means any (i) change or addition to Covered Code, or (ii) new source or object code implementing any portion of the Technology Specifications, but (iii) excluding any incorporated Reference Code.

"Original Contributor" means Sun Microsystems, Inc., its affiliates, successors and assigns.

"Reference Code" means source code for the Technology designated by Original Contributor at the Technology Site from time to time.

"Research Use" means research, evaluation, development, educational or personal and individual use, excluding use or distribution for direct or indirect commercial (including strategic) gain or advantage.

"Shared Modifications" means those Modifications which Community Members elect to share with other Community Members pursuant to Section III.B.

"Technology Specifications" means the functional, interface and operational specifications and documentation for the Technology designated by Original Contributor at the Technology Site from time to time.

"Technology" means the technology described in and contemplated by the Technology Specifications and which You have received pursuant to this License.

"Technology Site" means the website designated by Original Contributor for accessing Community Code and Technology Specifications.

"You" means the individual executing this license or the legal entity or entities represented by the individual executing this license. "Your" is the possessive of "You."

II. PURPOSES

Original Contributor is licensing the Reference Code and Technology Specifications and is permitting implementation of Technology under and subject to this Sun Community Source License (the "License") to promote research, education, innovation and product development using the Technology.

COMMERCIAL USE AND DISTRIBUTION OF TECHNOLOGY IS PERMITTED ONLY UNDER OPTIONAL SUPPLEMENTS TO THIS LICENSE.

III. RESEARCH USE RIGHTS

A. From Original Contributor. Subject to and conditioned upon Your full compliance with the terms and conditions of this License, including Sections IV (Restrictions and Community Responsibilities) and V.E.7 (International Use), Original Contributor:

1. grants to You a non-exclusive, worldwide and royalty-free license to the extent of Original Contributor's copyrights and trade secret rights in and covering the Reference Code and Technology Specifications to do the following for Your Research Use only:

    a) reproduce, prepare derivative works of, display and perform the Reference Code, in whole or in part, alone or as part of Covered Code;

    b) reproduce, prepare derivative works of and display the Technology Specifications;

c) distribute source or object code copies of Reference Code, in whole or in part, alone or as part Covered Code, to other Community Members or to students; and

d) distribute object code copies of Reference Code, in whole or in part, alone or as part of object code copies of Covered Code, to third parties.

2. will not, during the term of Your License, bring against You any claim alleging that Your using, making, having made, importing or distributing Community Code for Your Research Use, insofar as permitted under Section III.A.1 of this License, necessarily infringes any patent now owned or hereafter acquired by Original Contributor whose claims cover subject matter contained in or embodied by the Reference Code or which would necessarily be infringed by the use or distribution of any and all implementations of the Technology Specifications.

3. grants to You a non-exclusive, worldwide and royalty-free license, to the extent of its intellectual property rights therein, to use (a) Original Contributor's class, interface and package names only insofar as necessary to accurately reference or invoke Your Modifications for Research Use, and (b) any associated software tools, documents and information provided by Original Contributor at the Technology Site for use in exercising the above license rights.

B. Contributed Code. Subject to and conditioned upon compliance with the terms and conditions of this License, including Sections IV (Restrictions and Community Responsibilities) and V.F.7 (International Use), each Community Member:

1. grants to each Community Member a non-exclusive, worldwide and royalty-free license to the extent of such Community Member's copyrights and trade secret rights in and covering its Contributed Code, to reproduce, modify, display and distribute Contributed Code, in whole or in part, in source code and object code form, to the same extent as permitted under such Community Member's License with Original Contributor (including all supplements thereto).

2. will not, during the term of the Community Member's License, bring against any Community Member any claim alleging that using, making, having made, importing or distributing Contributed Code as permitted under this License (including any supplements) infringes any patents or patent applications now owned or hereafter acquired by such Community Member which patents or patent applications are infringed by using, making, having made, selling, offering for sale, importing or otherwise transferring the Contributed Code ("Community Member Patents"). This covenant shall apply to the combination of the Contributed Code with other Covered Code if, at the time the Contributed Code is posted, such addition of the Contributed Code causes such combination to be covered by the Community Member Patents. The covenant shall not apply to any other combinations which include the Contributed Code or to the use or distribution of modified Contributed Code where the modifications made by the Community Member add to the functions performed by the Contributed Code in question and where, in the absence of such modifications, there would be no infringement of a Community Member Patent.

3. grants to Original Contributor, in addition to the rights set forth in Sections III.B.1 and III.B.2, the right to sublicense all such rights in Contributed Code, in whole or in part, as part of Reference Code or other technologies based in whole or in part on Reference Code or Technology and to copy, distribute, modify and prepare derivative works of

Contributed Code Specifications, in whole or in part, in connection with the exercise of such rights.

C. Subcontracting. You may provide Covered Code to a contractor for the sole purpose of providing development services exclusively to You consistent with Your rights under this License. Such Contractor must be a Community Member or have executed an agreement with You that is consistent with Your rights and obligations under this License. Such subcontractor must assign exclusive rights in all work product to You. You agree that such work product is to be treated as Covered Code.

D. No Implied Licenses. Neither party is granted any right or license other than the licenses and covenants expressly set out herein. Other than the licenses and covenants expressly set out herein, Original Contributor retains all right, title and interest in Reference Code and Technology Specifications and You retain all right, title and interest in Your Modifications and associated specifications. Except as expressly permitted herein, You must not otherwise use any package, class or interface naming conventions that appear to originate from Original Contributor.

IV.   RESTRICTIONS AND COMMUNITY RESPONSIBILITIES

As a condition to Your license and other rights and immunities, You must comply with the restrictions and responsibilities set forth below, as modified or supplemented, if at all, in Attachment B, Additional Research Use Terms and Conditions.

A. Source Code Availability. You must provide source code and any specifications for Your Error Corrections to Original Contributor as soon as practicable. You may provide other Contributed Code to Original Contributor at any time, in Your discretion. Original Contributor may, in its discretion, post Your Contributed Code and Contributed Code Specifications on the Technology Site. You may post Your Contributed Code and/or Contributed Code Specifications on another website of Your choice; provided, source code of Community Code and Technology Specifications must be provided to Community Members only and only following certification of Community Member status as required under Section IV.D.

B. Notices. You must reproduce without alteration copyright and other proprietary notices in any Covered Code that You distribute. The statement, "Use and Distribution is subject to the Sun Community Source License available at http://sun.com/software/communitysource" must appear prominently in Your Modifications and, in all cases, in the same file as all Your copyright and other proprietary notices.

C. Modifications. You must include a diff file with Your Contributed Code that identifies and details the changes or additions You made, the version of Reference Code or Contributed Code You used and the date of such changes or additions. In addition, You must provide any Contributed Code Specifications for Your Contributed Code. Your Modifications are Covered Code and You expressly agree that use and distribution, in whole or in part, of Your Modifications shall only be done in accordance with and subject to this License.

D. Distribution Requirements. You may distribute object code of Covered Code to third parties for Research Use only pursuant to a license of Your choice which is consistent with this License. You may distribute source code of Covered Code and the Technology Specifications for Research Use only to (i) Community Members from whom You have first obtained a certification of status in the form set forth in Attachment A-1, and (ii) students from whom You have first obtained an executed acknowledgment in the form set forth in Attachment A-2. You must keep a copy of each such certificate and acknowledgment You obtain and provide a copy to Original Contributor, if requested.

E. Extensions.

1. You may create and add Interfaces but, unless expressly permitted at the Technology Site, You must not incorporate any Reference Code in Your Interfaces. If You choose to disclose or permit disclosure of Your Interfaces to even a single third party for the purposes of enabling such third party to independently develop and distribute (directly or indirectly) technology which invokes such Interfaces, You must then make the Interfaces open by (a) promptly following completion thereof, publishing to the industry, on a non-confidential basis and free of all copyright restrictions, a reasonably detailed, current and accurate specification for the Interfaces, and (b) as soon as reasonably possible, but in no event more than thirty (30) days following publication of Your specification, making available on reasonable terms and without discrimination, a reasonably complete and practicable test suite and methodology adequate to create and test implementations of the Interfaces by a reasonably skilled technologist.

2. You shall not assert any intellectual property rights You may have covering Your Interfaces which would necessarily be infringed by the creation, use or distribution of all reasonable independent implementations of Your specification of such Interfaces by a Community Member or Original Contributor. Nothing herein is intended to prevent You from enforcing any of Your intellectual property rights covering Your specific implementation of Your Interfaces or functionality using such Interfaces other than as specifically set forth in this Section IV.E.2.

V. GOVERNANCE.

A. License Versions.

Only Original Contributor may promulgate new versions of this License. Once You have accepted Reference Code, Technology Specifications, Contributed Code and/or Contributed Code Specifications under a version of this License, You may continue to use such version of Reference Code, Technology Specifications, Contributed Code and/or Contributed Code Specifications under that version of the License. New code and specifications which You may subsequently choose to accept will be subject to any new License in effect at the time of Your acceptance of such code and specifications.

B. Disclaimer of Warranties.

1. COVERED CODE, ALL TECHNOLOGY SPECIFICATIONS AND CONTRIBUTED CODE SPECIFICATIONS ARE PROVIDED "AS IS," WITHOUT WARRANTIES OF ANY KIND, EITHER EXPRESS OR IMPLIED INCLUDING, WITHOUT LIMITA-TION, WARRANTIES THAT ANY SUCH COVERED CODE, TECHNOLOGY SPECIFICATIONS AND CONTRIBUTED CODE SPECIFICATIONS ARE FREE OF DEFECTS, MERCHANTABLE, FIT FOR A PARTICULAR PURPOSE OR NON-INFRINGING OF THIRD PARTY RIGHTS. YOU AGREE THAT YOU BEAR THE ENTIRE RISK IN CONNECTION WITH YOUR USE AND DISTRIBUTION OF ANY AND ALL COVERED CODE, TECHNOLOGY SPECIFICATIONS AND

CONTRIBUTED CODE SPECIFICATIONS UNDER THIS LICENSE. NO USE OF ANY COVERED CODE, TECHNOLOGY SPECIFICATIONS OR CONTRIBUTED CODE SPECIFICATIONS IS AUTHORIZED EXCEPT SUBJECT TO AND IN CONSIDERATION FOR THIS DISCLAIMER.

2. You understand that, although each Community Member grants the licenses set forth in the License and any supplements hereto, no assurances are provided by any Community Member that Covered Code or any specifications do not infringe the intellectual property rights of any third party.

3. You acknowledge that Reference Code and Technology Specifications are neither designed nor intended for use in the design, construction, operation or maintenance of any nuclear facility.

C. Limitation of Liability.

1. Infringement. Each Community Member disclaims any liability to all other Community Members for claims brought by any third party based on infringement of intellectual property rights. Original Contributor represents that, to its knowledge, it has sufficient copyrights to allow You to use and distribute the Reference Code as herein permitted (including as permitted in any Supplement hereto) and You represent that, to Your knowledge, You have sufficient copyrights to allow each Community Member and Original Contributor to use and distribute Your Shared Modifications and Error Corrections as herein permitted (including as permitted in any supplements to the License). You agree to notify Original Contributor should You become aware of any potential or actual infringement of the Technology or any of Original Contributor's intellectual property rights in the Technology, Reference Code or Technology Specifications.

2. Suspension. If any portion of, or functionality implemented by, the Reference Code, Technology or Technology Specifications becomes the subject of a claim or threatened claim of infringement ("Affected Materials"), Original Contributor may, in its unrestricted discretion, suspend Your rights to use and distribute the Affected Materials under this License. Such suspension of rights will be effective immediately upon Original Contributor's posting of notice of suspension on the Technology Site. Original Contributor has no obligation to lift the suspension of rights relative to the Affected Materials until a final, non-appealable determination is made by a court or governmental agency of competent jurisdiction that Original Contributor is legally able, without the payment of a fee or royalty, to reinstate Your rights to the Affected Materials to the full extent contemplated hereunder. Upon such determination, Original Contributor will lift the suspension by posting a notice to such effect on the Technology Site. Nothing herein shall be construed to prevent You, at Your option and expense, and subject to applicable law and the restrictions and responsibilities set forth in this License and any Supplements, from replacing Reference Code in Affected Materials with non-infringing code or independently negotiating, without compromising or prejudicing Original Contributor's position, to obtain the rights necessary to use Affected Materials as herein permitted.

3. Disclaimer. ORIGINAL CONTRIBUTOR'S LIABILITY TO YOU FOR ALL CLAIMS RELATING TO THIS LICENSE OR ANY SUPPLEMENT HERETO, WHETHER FOR BREACH OR TORT, IS LIMITED TO THE GREATER OF ONE THOUSAND DOLLARS (US$1000.00) OR THE FULL AMOUNT PAID BY YOU FOR THE

MATERIALS GIVING RISE TO THE CLAIM, IF ANY. IN NO EVENT WILL ORIGINAL CONTRIBUTOR BE LIABLE FOR ANY INDIRECT, PUNITIVE, SPECIAL, INCIDENTAL OR CONSEQUENTIAL DAMAGES IN CONNECTION WITH OR ARISING OUT OF THIS LICENSE (INCLUDING, WITHOUT LIMITATION, LOSS OF PROFITS, USE, DATA OR ECONOMIC ADVANTAGE OF ANY SORT), HOWEVER IT ARISES AND ON ANY THEORY OF LIABILITY (including negligence), WHETHER OR NOT ORIGINAL CONTRIBUTOR HAS BEEN ADVISED OF THE POSSIBILITY OF SUCH DAMAGE AND NOTWITH-STANDING FAILURE OF THE ESSENTIAL PURPOSE OF ANY REMEDY.

D. Termination.

You may terminate this License at any time by notifying Original Contributor in writing.

All Your rights will terminate under this License if You fail to comply with any of the material terms or conditions of this License and do not cure such failure in a reasonable period of time after becoming aware of such noncompliance.

If You institute patent litigation against a Community Member with respect to a patent applicable to Community Code, then any patent licenses or covenants granted by such Community Member to You under this License shall terminate as of the date such litigation is filed. In addition, if You institute patent litigation against any Community Member or Original Contributor alleging that Reference Code, Technology or Technology Specifications infringe Your patent(s), then the rights granted to You under Section III.A above will terminate.

Upon termination, You must discontinue all uses and distribution of Community Code, except that You may continue to use, reproduce, prepare derivative works of, display and perform Your Modifications, so long as the license grants and covenants of this license are not required to do so, for purposes other than to implement functionality designated in any portion of the Technology Specifications. Properly granted sublicenses to third parties will survive termination. Provisions which, by their nature, should remain in effect following termination survive.

E. Miscellaneous.

1. Trademark. You agree to comply with Original Contributors Trademark & Logo Usage Requirements, as modified from time to time, available at the Technology Site. Except as expressly provided in this License, You are granted no rights in or to any Sun, Jini, Jiro or Java trademarks now or hereafter used or licensed by Original Contributor (the "Sun Trademarks"). You agree not to (a) challenge Original Contributor's ownership or use of Sun Trademarks; (b) attempt to register any Sun Trademarks, or any mark or logo substantially similar thereto; or (c) incorporate any Sun Trademarks into Your own trademarks, product names, service marks, company names or domain names.

2. Integration and Assignment. Original Contributor may assign this Research Use License to another by written notification to the other party. This License represents the complete agreement of the parties concerning the subject matter hereof.

3. Severability. If any provision of this License is held unenforceable, such provision shall be reformed to the extent necessary to make it enforceable unless to do so would defeat the intent of the parties, in which case, this License shall terminate.

4. Governing Law. This License is governed by the laws of the United States and the State of California, as applied to contracts entered into and performed in California between California residents. The United Nations Convention on Contracts for the International Sale of Goods shall not apply. Nor shall any law or regulation which provides that a contract be construed against the drafter.

5. Dispute Resolution.

    a) Any dispute arising out of or relating to this License shall be finally settled by arbitration as set forth in this Section, except that either party may bring an action in a court of competent jurisdiction (which jurisdiction shall be exclusive), relative to any dispute relating to such party's intellectual property rights. Arbitration will be administered (i) by the American Arbitration Association (AAA), (ii) in accordance with the rules of the United Nations Commission on International Trade Law (UNCITRAL) (the "Rules") in effect at the time of arbitration, modified as set forth herein, and (iii) by an arbitrator described in Section 5.b who shall apply the governing laws required under Section V.E.4 above. Judgment upon the award rendered by the arbitrator may be entered in any court having jurisdiction to enforce such award. The arbitrator must not award damages in excess of or of a different type than those permitted by this License and any such award is void.

    b) All proceedings will be in English and conducted by a single arbitrator selected in accordance with the Rules who is fluent in English, familiar with technology matters pertinent in the dispute and is either a retired judge or practicing attorney having at least ten (10) years litigation experience. Venue for arbitration will be in San Francisco, California, unless the parties agree otherwise. Each party will be required to produce documents relied upon in the arbitration and to respond to no more than twenty-five single question interrogatories. All awards are payable in US dollars and may include for the prevailing party (i) pre-judgment interest, (ii) reasonable attorneys' fees incurred in connection with the arbitration, and (iii) reasonable costs and expenses incurred in enforcing the award.

6. U.S. Government. If this Software is being acquired by or on behalf of the U.S. Government or by a U.S. Government prime contractor or subcontractor (at any tier), the Government's rights in this Software and accompanying documentation shall be only as set forth in this license, in accordance with 48 CFR 227.7201 through 227.7202-4 (for Department of Defense acquisitions) and with 48 CFR 2.101 and 12.212 (for non-DoD acquisitions).

7. International Use.
    a) Covered Code is subject to US export control laws and may be subject to export or import regulations in other countries. Each party shall comply fully with all such laws and regulations and acknowledges its responsibility to obtain such licenses to export, re-export or import as may be required. You must pass through these obligations to all Your licensees.

    b) You must not distribute Reference Code or Technology Specifications into countries other than those listed on the Technology Site by Original Contributor, from time to time.

READ ALL THE TERMS OF THIS LICENSE CAREFULLY BEFORE ACCEPTING. IF YOU ARE AGREEING TO THIS LICENSE ON BEHALF OF A COMPANY, YOU REPRESENT THAT YOU ARE AUTHORIZED TO BIND THE COMPANY TO THE LICENSE.

WHETHER YOU ARE ACTING ON YOUR OWN BEHALF OR THAT OF A COMPANY, YOU MUST BE OF MAJORITY AGE AND OTHERWISE COMPETENT TO ENTER INTO CONTRACTS.

ATTACHMENT A-1
COMMUNITY MEMBER CERTIFICATE

You certify that You are a Licensee in good standing under the Sun Community Source License for the _____ Technology (fill in applicable Technology and Version) (the "License") and that You agree to use and distribute code, documentation and information You may obtain pursuant to this certification only in accordance with the terms and subject to the conditions of the License.

Signature:_____

Printed Name and Title:_____

Company: _____

ATTACHMENT A-2
STUDENT ACKNOWLEDGMENT

You acknowledge that this software and related documentation has been obtained by your educational institution subject to the Sun Community Source License (the "License"). You have been provided with access to the software and documentation for use only in connection with your course work as a matriculated student of your educational institution. Commercial use of the software and documentation is expressly prohibited.

THIS SOFTWARE AND RELATED DOCUMENTATION CONTAINS PROPRIETARY MATERIALS OF SUN MICROSYSTEMS, INC. PROTECTED BY VARIOUS INTELLEC-TUAL PROPERTY RIGHTS. YOUR USE OF THE SOFTWARE AND DOCUMENTATION IS LIMITED.

Signature:_____

Printed Name:_____

ATTACHMENT B (ADDITIONAL TERMS/RESPONSIBILITIES): NONE

COMMERCIAL USE SUPPLEMENT TO SUN COMMUNITY SOURCE CODE LICENSE GENERAL TERMS

I. PURPOSE AND EFFECT.

This Commercial Use Supplement General Terms ("CUSupp") is required for Commercial Use of Covered Code and, once signed by You and Original Contributor, is operative for all Technologies specified in all Technology Specific Attachment(s) hereto. The rights and responsibilities set forth in this CUSupp are additional to those in Your License.

II. DEFINITIONS.

"Commercial Use" means uses and distributions of Covered Code for any direct or indirect commercial or strategic gain or advantage.

"Compliant Implementation" means Covered Code that fully implements the Technology Specifications and complies with Sun's requirements.

"Compliance Materials" means the test programs, guides, documentation and other materials identified in the Technology-Specific Attachment(s) for use in establishing that Covered Code is a Compliant Implementation.

"Technology-Specific Attachment(s)" means an attachment or attachments to this CUSupp which contains terms and conditions specific to the Technology therein identified as well as the specifics of the Compliance Materials and requirements for such Technology.

III. COMMERCIAL USE RIGHTS.

A. Commercial Use. Subject to and conditioned upon Your compliance with the terms and conditions of Your Research Use license and the additional terms and conditions set forth in this CUSupp and associated Technology-Specific Attachment(s), including the provisions of Section IV, below, Original Contributor hereby adds to those rights enumerated under Section III.A.1 of the Research Use license the rights to, within the specified Field of Use denoted in the Technology Specific Attachment:

> e) use the Compliance Materials to determine whether Covered Code constitutes a Compliant Implementation;
>
> f) use, reproduce, display, perform and distribute internally source and object code copies of Compliant Implementations for Commercial Use;
>
> g) reproduce and distribute to third parties and Community Members through multiple tiers of distribution object code copies of Compliant Implementations for Commercial Use;
>
> h) reproduce and distribute the source code of Compliant Implementations to Community Members licensed for Commercial Use of the same Technology; and
>
> i) reproduce and distribute a copy of the Technology Specifications (which may be reformatted, but must remain substantively unchanged) with Compliant Implementations for Commercial Use.

B. Covenant. In addition, Original Contributor's covenant under Section III.A.2 is hereby expanded to include Your using, making, having made, selling, importing and distributing Compliant Implementations for Commercial Use insofar as permitted above.

IV. ADDITIONAL REQUIREMENTS AND COMMUNITY RESPONSIBILITIES.

As a condition to the Commercial Use rights granted above, You must comply with the following restrictions and community responsibilities (in addition to those in the License):

F. Certification. You may distribute source code of Compliant Implementations for Commercial Use only to Community Members from whom You have first obtained a certification of status in the form set forth in Attachment A-1. You must keep a copy of each such certificate and acknowledgment You obtain and provide a copy to Original Contributor, if requested.

G. Compliance Materials. Depending on the Technology licensed, Your access to and use of the Compliance Materials may be subject to additional requirements such as entering into a support agreement and trademark license. Such additional requirements, if any, are as set out in the Technology-Specific Attachment. You agree to comply fully with all such applicable requirements.

H. Compatibility. Only Compliant Implementations may be used and distributed for Commercial Use.

I. Commercial Distribution Requirement. You may distribute object code copies for Commercial Use as herein contemplated under a license agreement of Your choice which is consistent with Your rights and obligations under the License and this CUSupp. You may provide warranties, indemnities and/or other additional terms and conditions in Your license agreements, provided that it is clear that such additional terms and conditions are offered by You only. You hereby agree to hold each Community Member harmless and indemnify them against any liability arising in connection with such terms and conditions. You will pay all damages, costs and fees awarded by a court or arbitrator having jurisdiction over the matter or any settlement amount negotiated by You and attributable to such claim.

J. End User License Terms. You must include the following terms and conditions in end user license agreements accompanying copies of Compliant Implementations distributed for Commercial User hereunder:

1. Software contains copyrighted information of Sun Microsystems, Inc. and title is retained by Sun.

2. Use, duplication or disclosure by the United States government is subject to the restrictions set forth in the Rights in Technical Data and Computer Software clauses in DFARS 252.227-701(c)(1)(ii) and FAR 52.227-19(c)(2) as applicable.

K. Defense. Original Contributor will have the right, but not the obligation, to defend You, at Original Contributor's expense, in connection with a claim that Your Commercial Use of Reference Code is an infringement of a third party's intellectual property rights, in which case You agree to cooperate with Original Contributor and Original Contributor will pay all damages costs and fees awarded by a court or tribunal of competent jurisdiction, or such settlement amount negotiated by Original Contributor and attributable to such claim.

L. Notice of Breach or Infringement. Each party shall notify the other immediately in writing when it becomes aware of any breach or violation of the terms of this License, or when You become aware of any potential or actual infringement by a third party of the Technology or Sun's intellectual property rights therein.

M. Proprietary Rights Notices. You must not remove any copyright notices, trademark notices or other proprietary legends of Original Contributor or its suppliers contained on or in the Covered Code, Technology Specifications and Contributed Code Specifications.

N. Relationship. The relationship created is that of licensor and licensee only. You hereby waive the benefit of any law or regulation dealing with the establishment and regulation of franchises or agencies.

Agreed:

You   Original Contributor

By: _____   Sun Microsystems, Inc.

Name: _____   Name: _____

Title: _____   Title: _____

Date: _____   Date: _____

TECHNOLOGY SPECIFIC ATTACHMENT TO THE SUN COMMUNITY SOURCE LICENSE JINI TECHNOLOGY CORE PLATFORM
Version: 3.0/Jini TSA 1.0

1. Effect. This Technology Specific Attachment to the Commercial Use Supplement applies to the Jini Technology Core Platform as described on the Technology Site. The rights and responsibilities set forth in this Technology Specific Attachment are additional to those in Your License and the CUSupp. The term "License" hereinafter refers to the License, the CUSupp, and this Technology Specific Attachment.

2. Additional Requirements and Responsibilities. In addition to the requirements and responsibilities specified in the License, and as a condition to exercising the rights granted therein, You agree to the following additional requirements and responsibilities:

a) Distribution of Source Code. Source Code of a Compliant Implementation authorized for distribution for Commercial Use may be distributed only to another Commercial Use Licensee of the same Technology. You must include a prominent notice with every copy of Source Code of Covered Code that You distribute indicating that use is limited to Licensees in good standing and is subject to the terms and conditions of this License. You may not offer or impose any terms on any Source Code of Covered Code that alters the recipient's rights, requirements, and responsibilities under the recipient's License.

b) Upgraded Code. From time to time, Original Contributor may post Upgraded Code to the community web-server described at the Technology Site. Upgraded Code as used in this Section 2 means new versions of the Technology designated by Original Contributor as an upgrade to the Technology at the Technology Site. Wherever commercially and technically reasonable, You agree that each release by You of a product comprising or incorporating a Compliant Implementation will implement the most current Upgraded Code available no less than one hundred and twenty (120) days prior to Your Commercial Use of such Compliant Implementation. If you determine that it is not commercially or technically reasonable to incorporate Upgraded Code as contemplated, You are then not required to incorporate such Upgraded Code provided that, from the date one hundred twenty (120) days after such Upgraded Code is first made commercially available, You may not thereafter, for Commercial Use, distribute any new Modifications or Interfaces, alone or integrated with Covered Code or other code, unless and until such time as You incorporate the then-current Upgraded Code and pass the associated TCK. You may, however make Error Corrections and You may correct the adverse effect of a failure of Your Modifications and Interfaces to perform their functions. It is Original Contributor's intent to maintain compatibility between Covered Code and Upgraded Code.

c) Additional Services. If you provide any services, in the form of interfaces or otherwise, whose functions are substantially similar to those core services whose Interfaces are provided under this License (the "Standard Service Interfaces"), then You must also support the Standard Service Interfaces in Your product or technology. In addition, You must support Standard Service Interfaces associated with Upgraded Code in connection with Your Commercial Use of Compliant Implementations in the same manner as required for Upgraded Code under Section 2.b.

d) Branding. Compliant Implementations used for Commercial Use may, at Your option, be branded with the Technology compliance logo under a separate trademark license to be executed by You and Original Contributor concurrent with execution of this Technology Specific Attachment.

3. Support Programs.

a) Support to You. Technical support is not provided to You by Original Contributor under this License. You may obtain one or more support programs, if available, from Original Contributor relating to the Technology which are described on the Technology Site.

b) Customer Support. You are responsible for providing technical and maintenance support services to Your customers for Your products and services incorporating the Compliant Implementation.

4. Royalties and Payments.

Royalty per Unit $: None.

5. Compliance Materials; Use Restrictions.

Compliance Materials: Jini Technology Core Platform Compatibility Kit

a) The Compliance Materials for the Technology may be accessed at the Technology Site.

b) You are not authorized to create derivative works of the Compliance Materials or use the Compliance Materials to test any implementation of the Technology Specifications that are not Covered Code. You shall only use the Compliance Materials for purposes of verifying compatibility with the Technology Specifications. You must not publish your test results or make claims of comparative compatibility with respect to other implementations of the Technology Specifications. In consideration for the license grant in Section III.A of the CUSupp, You agree not to develop Your own tests which are intended to validate conformance with the Technology Specifications.

c) Notwithstanding subsection 6.b above, You may use and modify the Source Code of programming code contained in the Compliance Materials for the sole purpose of creating error corrections or modifications to the Compliance Materials to propose to Original Contributor for inclusion in the Compliance Materials. You may not use such modified code for any other purpose including, without limitation, in testing Covered Code pursuant to Section III.A. Any changes to the Compliance Materials which you propose to Original Contributor shall be subject to the license grant set forth in Section III.B.

6. Requirements for Determining Compliance.

a) Development Restrictions. A Compliant Implementation:

i) must fully comply with the Technology Specifications for the Technology to which this Technology Specific Attachment applies; and

ii) must not modify or extend the required public class or public interface declarations whose names begin with "java", "javax", "jini", "net.jini", "sun.hotjava", "COM.sun" or their equivalents in any subsequent class, interface and/ or package naming convention adopted by Original Contributor. It is specifically suggested that You name any new Java packages using the "Unique Package Naming Convention" as described in "The Java Language Specification" by James Gosling, Bill Joy, and Guy Steele, ISBN 0-201-63451-1, August 1996. Section 7.7 "Unique Package Names," on pages 125 and 126 of this specification says in part:

> You form a unique package name by first having (or belonging to an organization that has) an Internet domain name, such as "sun.com". You then reverse the name, component by component, to obtain, in this example, "com.sun" and use this as a prefix for your package names, using a convention developed within your organization to further administer package names.

b) Covered Code. All Covered Code must constitute a Compliant Implementation prior to any Commercial Use (other than pre-deployment testing), whether originating with You or acquired through a third party. Successful compatibility testing must be completed by You, or by a third party authorized by Original Contributor to conduct such tests, using the most current version of the applicable Compliance Materials available no less than one hundred and twenty (120) days prior to Your Commercial Use. If You make any further Modifications to any Covered Code previously determined to be a Compliant Implementation, You must retest the new Covered Code to ensure that it continues to be a Compliant Implementation. For this retest, You may use the same version of the Compliance Materials as used originally or, at your option, You may use a more current version of the Compliance Materials.

c) Test Results. Upon Original Contributor's written request, You agree to provide to Original Contributor or the third party test facility, if applicable, Your test results that demonstrate that Covered Code is a Compliant Implementation, and that Original Contributor may publish or otherwise distribute such test results.

Agreed:

You   Original Contributor

By: _____   Sun Microsystems, Inc.

Name: _____   Name: _____

Title: _____   Title: _____

Date: _____   Date: _____

Sun Industry Standards Source License (SISSL)

taken from: http://www.openoffice.org/licenses/sissl_license.html

Sun Industry Standards Source License
Version 1.1

1.0 DEFINITIONS

1.1 "Commercial Use" means distribution or otherwise making the Original Code available to a third party.

1.2 "Contributor Version" means the combination of the Original Code, and the Modifications made by that particular Contributor.

1.3 "Electronic Distribution Mechanism" means a mechanism generally accepted in the software development community for the electronic transfer of data.

1.4 "Executable" means Original Code in any form other than Source Code.

1.5 "Initial Developer" means the individual or entity identified as the Initial Developer in the Source Code notice required by **Exhibit A.**

1.6 "Larger Work" means a work which combines Original Code or portions thereof with code not governed by the terms of this License.

1.7 "License" means this document.

1.8 "Licensable" means having the right to grant, to the maximum extent possible, whether at the time of the initial grant or subsequently acquired, any and all of the rights conveyed herein.

1.9 "Modifications" means any addition to or deletion from the substance or structure of either the Original Code or any previous Modifications. A Modification is:

> A. Any addition to or deletion from the contents of a file containing Original Code or previous Modifications.
>
> B. Any new file that contains any part of the Original Code or previous Modifications.

1.10 "Original Code" means Source Code of computer software code which is described in the Source Code notice required by **Exhibit A** as Original Code.

1.11 "Patent Claims" means any patent claim(s), now owned or hereafter acquired, including without limitation, method, process, and apparatus claims, in any patent Licensable by grantor.

1.12 "Source Code" means the preferred form of the Original Code for making modifications to it, including all modules it contains, plus any associated interface definition files, or scripts used to control compilation and installation of an Executable.

1.13 "Standards" means the standards identified in **Exhibit B.**

1.14 "You" (or "Your") means an individual or a legal entity exercising rights under, and complying with all of the terms of, this License or a future version of this License issued under Section 6.1. For legal entities, "You" includes any entity which controls, is controlled by, or is under common control with You. For purposes of this definition, "control" means (a) the power, direct or indirect, to cause the direction or management of such entity, whether by contract or otherwise, or (b) ownership of more than fifty percent (50%) of the outstanding shares or beneficial ownership of such entity.

2.0 SOURCE CODE LICENSE

2.1 The Initial Developer Grant.

The Initial Developer hereby grants You a world-wide, royalty-free, non-exclusive license, subject to third party intellectual property claims:

(a) under intellectual property rights (other than patent or trademark) Licensable by Initial Developer to use, reproduce, modify, display, perform, sublicense and distribute the Original Code (or portions thereof) with or without Modifications, and/or as part of a Larger Work; and

(b) under Patents Claims infringed by the making, using or selling of Original Code, to make, have made, use, practice, sell, and offer for sale, and/or otherwise dispose of the Original Code (or portions thereof).

(c) the licenses granted in this Section 2.1(a) and (b) are effective on the date Initial Developer first distributes Original Code under the terms of this License.

(d) Notwithstanding Section 2.1(b) above, no patent license is granted: 1) for code that You delete from the Original Code; 2) separate from the Original Code; or 3) for infringements caused by: (i) the modification of the Original Code or (ii) the combination of the Original Code with other software or devices, including but not limited to Modifications.

3.0 DISTRIBUTION OBLIGATIONS

3.1 Application of License.

The Source Code version of Original Code may be distributed only under the terms of this License or a future version of this License released under Section 6.1, and You must include a copy of this License with every copy of the Source Code You distribute. You may not offer or impose any terms on any Source Code version that alters or restricts the applicable version of this License or the recipients' rights hereunder. Your license for shipment of the Contributor Version is conditioned upon Your full compliance with this Section. The Modifications which You create must comply with all requirements set out by the Standards body in effect one hundred twenty (120) days before You ship the Contributor Version. In the event that the Modifications do not meet such requirements, You agree to publish either (i) any deviation from the Standards protocol resulting from implementation of Your Modifications and a reference implementation of Your Modifications or (ii) Your Modifications in Source Code form, and to make any such deviation and reference implementation or Modifications available to all third parties under the same terms as this license on a royalty free basis within thirty (30) days of Your first customer shipment of Your Modifications.

3.2 Required Notices.

You must duplicate the notice in **Exhibit A** in each file of the Source Code. If it is not possible to put such notice in a particular Source Code file due to its structure, then You must include such notice in a location (such as a relevant directory) where a user would be likely to look for such a notice. If You created one or more Modification(s) You may add Your name as a Contributor to the notice described in **Exhibit A.** You must also duplicate this License in any documentation for the Source Code where You describe recipients' rights or ownership rights relating to Initial Code. You may choose to offer, and to charge a fee for, warranty, support, indemnity or liability obligations to one or more recipients of Your version of the Code. However, You may do so only on Your own behalf, and not on behalf of the Initial Developer. You must make it absolutely clear than any such warranty, support, indemnity or liability obligation is offered by You alone, and You hereby agree to indemnify the Initial Developer for any liability incurred by the Initial Developer as a result of warranty, support, indemnity or liability terms You offer.

3.3 Distribution of Executable Versions.
You may distribute Original Code in Executable and Source form only if the requirements of Sections 3.1 and 3.2 have been met for that Original Code, and if You include a notice stating that the Source Code version of the Original Code is available under the terms of this License. The notice must be conspicuously included in any notice in an Executable or Source versions, related documentation or collateral in which You describe recipients' rights relating to the Original Code. You may distribute the Executable and Source versions of Your version of the Code or ownership rights under a license of Your choice, which may contain terms different from this License, provided that You are in compliance with the terms of this License. If You distribute the Executable and Source versions under a different license You must make it absolutely clear that any terms which differ from this License are offered by You alone, not by the Initial Developer. You hereby agree to indemnify the Initial Developer for any liability incurred by the Initial Developer as a result of any such terms You offer.

3.4 Larger Works.
You may create a Larger Work by combining Original Code with other code not governed by the terms of this License and distribute the Larger Work as a single product. In such a case, You must make sure the requirements of this License are fulfilled for the Original Code.

4.0 INABILITY TO COMPLY DUE TO STATUTE OR REGULATION

If it is impossible for You to comply with any of the terms of this License with respect to some or all of the Original Code due to statute, judicial order, or regulation then You must: (a) comply with the terms of this License to the maximum extent possible; and (b) describe the limitations and the code they affect. Such description must be included in the LEGAL file described in Section 3.2 and must be included with all distributions of the Source Code. Except to the extent prohibited by statute or regulation, such description must be sufficiently detailed for a recipient of ordinary skill to be able to understand it.

5.0 APPLICATION OF THIS LICENSE

This License applies to code to which the Initial Developer has attached the notice in **Exhibit A** and to related Modifications as set out in Section 3.1.

6.0 VERSIONS OF THE LICENSE

6.1 New Versions.
Sun may publish revised and/or new versions of the License from time to time. Each version will be given a distinguishing version number.

6.2 Effect of New Versions.

Once Original Code has been published under a particular version of the License, You may always continue to use it under the terms of that version. You may also choose to use such Original Code under the terms of any subsequent version of the License published by Sun. No one other than Sun has the right to modify the terms applicable to Original Code.

7.0 DISCLAIMER OF WARRANTY

ORIGINAL CODE IS PROVIDED UNDER THIS LICENSE ON AN "AS IS" BASIS, WITHOUT WARRANTY OF ANY KIND, EITHER EXPRESSED OR IMPLIED, INCLUDING, WITHOUT LIMITATION, WARRANTIES THAT THE ORIGINAL CODE IS FREE OF DEFECTS, MERCHANTABLE, FIT FOR A PARTICULAR PURPOSE OR NON-INFRINGING. THE ENTIRE RISK AS TO THE QUALITY AND PERFORMANCE OF THE ORIGINAL CODE IS WITH YOU. SHOULD ANY ORIGINAL CODE PROVE DEFECTIVE IN ANY RESPECT, YOU (NOT THE INITIAL DEVELOPER) ASSUME THE COST OF ANY NECESSARY SERVICING, REPAIR OR CORRECTION. THIS DISCLAIMER OF WARRANTY CONSTITUTES AN ESSENTIAL PART OF THIS LICENSE. NO USE OF ANY ORIGINAL CODE IS AUTHORIZED HEREUNDER EXCEPT UNDER THIS DISCLAIMER.

8.0 TERMINATION

8.1 This License and the rights granted hereunder will terminate automatically if You fail to comply with terms herein and fail to cure such breach within 30 days of becoming aware of the breach. All sublicenses to the Original Code which are properly granted shall survive any termination of this License. Provisions which, by their nature, must remain in effect beyond the termination of this License shall survive.

8.2 In the event of termination under Section 8.1 above, all end user license agreements (excluding distributors and resellers) which have been validly granted by You or any distributor hereunder prior to termination shall survive termination.

9.0 LIMIT OF LIABILITY

UNDER NO CIRCUMSTANCES AND UNDER NO LEGAL THEORY, WHETHER TORT (INCLUDING NEGLIGENCE), CONTRACT, OR OTHERWISE, SHALL YOU, THE INITIAL DEVELOPER, ANY OTHER CONTRIBUTOR, OR ANY DISTRIBUTOR OF ORIGINAL CODE, OR ANY SUPPLIER OF ANY OF SUCH PARTIES, BE LIABLE TO ANY PERSON FOR ANY INDIRECT, SPECIAL, INCIDENTAL, OR CONSEQUENTIAL DAMAGES OF ANY CHARACTER INCLUDING, WITHOUT LIMITATION, DAMAGES FOR LOSS OF GOODWILL, WORK STOPPAGE, COMPUTER FAILURE OR MALFUNC-TION, OR ANY AND ALL OTHER COMMERCIAL DAMAGES OR LOSSES, EVEN IF SUCH PARTY SHALL HAVE BEEN INFORMED OF THE POSSIBILITY OF SUCH DAMAGES. THIS LIMITATION OF LIABILITY SHALL NOT APPLY TO LIABILITY FOR DEATH OR PERSONAL INJURY RESULTING FROM SUCH PARTY'S NEGLIGENCE TO THE EXTENT APPLICABLE LAW PROHIBITS SUCH LIMITATION. SOME JURISDIC-TIONS DO NOT ALLOW THE EXCLUSION OR LIMITATION OF INCIDENTAL OR

CONSEQUENTIAL DAMAGES, SO THIS EXCLUSION AND LIMITATION MAY NOT APPLY TO YOU.

10.0 U.S. GOVERNMENT END USERS

U.S. Government: If this Software is being acquired by or on behalf of the U.S. Government or by a U.S. Government prime contractor or subcontractor (at any tier), then the Government's rights in the Software and accompanying documentation shall be only as set forth in this license; this is in accordance with 48 C.F.R. 227.7201 through 227.7202-4 (for Department of Defense (DoD) acquisitions) and with 48 C.F.R. 2.101 and 12.212 (for non-DoD acquisitions).

11.0 MISCELLANEOUS

This License represents the complete agreement concerning subject matter hereof. If any provision of this License is held to be unenforceable, such provision shall be reformed only to the extent necessary to make it enforceable. This License shall be governed by California law provisions (except to the extent applicable law, if any, provides otherwise), excluding its conflict-of-law provisions. With respect to disputes in which at least one party is a citizen of, or an entity chartered or registered to do business in the United States of America, any litigation relating to this License shall be subject to the jurisdiction of the Federal Courts of the Northern District of California, with venue lying in Santa Clara County, California, with the losing party responsible for costs, including without limitation, court costs and reasonable attorneys' fees and expenses. The application of the United Nations Convention on Contracts for the International Sale of Goods is expressly excluded. Any law or regulation which provides that the language of a contract shall be construed against the drafter shall not apply to this License.

EXHIBIT A—Sun Standards License

The contents of this file are subject to the Sun Standards License Version 1.1 (the "License"); You may not use this file except in compliance with the License. You may obtain a copy of the License at _____.

Software distributed under the License is distributed on an "AS IS" basis, WITHOUT WARRANTY OF ANY KIND, either express or implied. See the License for the specific language governing rights and limitations under the License.

The Original Code is _____.

The Initial Developer of the Original Code is: **Sun Microsystems, Inc.**

Portions created by: _____

are Copyright (C): _____

All Rights Reserved.

Contributor(s): _____

EXHIBIT B—Standards

The Standard is defined as the following:

OpenOffice.org XML File Format Specification, located at http://xml.openoffice.org

OpenOffice.org Application Programming Interface Specification, located at http://api.openoffice.org

Sun Public Documentation License (PDL)

taken from: http://www.openoffice.org/licenses/PDL.html

PUBLIC DOCUMENTATION LICENSE
Version 1.0

1. DEFINITIONS

1.1. "Commercial Use" means distribution or otherwise making the Documentation available to a third party.

1.2. "Contributor" means a person or entity who creates or contributes to the creation of Modifications.

1.3. "Documentation" means the Original Documentation or Modifications or the combination of the Original Documentation and Modifications, in each case including portions thereof.

1.4. "Electronic Distribution Mechanism" means a mechanism generally accepted for the electronic transfer of data.

1.5. "Initial Writer" means the individual or entity identified as the Initial Writer in the notice required by the Appendix.

1.6. "Larger Work" means a work which combines Documentation or portions thereof with documentation or other writings not governed by the terms of this License.

1.7. "License" means this document.

1.8. "Modifications" means any addition to or deletion from the substance or structure of either the Original Documentation or any previous Modifications, such as a translation, abridgment, condensation, or any other form in which the Original Documentation or previous Modifications may be recast, transformed or adapted. A work consisting of editorial revisions, annotations, elaborations, and other modifications which, as a whole represent an original work of authorship, is a Modification. For example, when Documentation is released as a series of documents, a Modification is:

> A. Any addition to or deletion from the contents of the Original Documentation or previous Modifications.

> B. Any new documentation that contains any part of the Original Documentation or previous Modifications.

1.9. "Original Documentation" means documentation described as Original Documentation in the notice required by the **Appendix**, and which, at the time of its release under this License is not already Documentation governed by this License.

1.10. "Editable Form" means the preferred form of the Documentation for making Modifications to it. The Documentation can be in an electronic, compressed or archival form, provided the appropriate decompression or de-archiving software is widely available for no charge.

1.11. "You" (or "Your") means an individual or a legal entity exercising rights under, and complying with all of the terms of this License or a future version of this License issued under Section 5.0 ("Versions of the License"). For legal entities, "You" includes any entity which controls, is controlled by, or is under common control with You. For purposes of this definition, "control" means (a) the power, direct or indirect, to cause the direction or management of such entity, whether by contract or otherwise, or (b) ownership of more than fifty percent (50%) of the outstanding shares or beneficial ownership of such entity.

2. LICENSE GRANTS.

2.1. Initial Writer Grant.

The Initial Writer hereby grants You a world-wide, royalty-free, non-exclusive license to use, reproduce, prepare Modifications of, compile, publicly perform, publicly display, demonstrate, market, disclose and distribute the Documentation in any form, on any media or via any Electronic Distribution Mechanism or other method now known or later discovered, and to sublicense the foregoing rights to third parties through multiple tiers of sublicensees in accordance with the terms of this License.

The license rights granted in this Section 2.1 ("Initial Writer Grant") are effective on the date Initial Writer first distributes Original Documentation under the terms of this License.

2.2. Contributor Grant.

Each Contributor hereby grants You a world-wide, royalty-free, non-exclusive license to use, reproduce, prepare Modifications of, compile, publicly perform, publicly display, demonstrate, market, disclose and distribute the Documentation in any form, on any media or via any Electronic Distribution Mechanism or other method now known or later discovered, and to sublicense the foregoing rights to third parties through multiple tiers of sublicensees in accordance with the terms of this License.

The license rights granted in this Section 2.2 ("Contributor Grant") are effective on the date Contributor first makes Commercial Use of the Documentation.

3. DISTRIBUTION OBLIGATIONS.

3.1. Application of License.

The Modifications which You create or to which You contribute are governed by the terms of this License, including without limitation Section 2.2 ("Contributor Grant"). The Documentation may be distributed only under the terms of this License or a future version of this License released in accordance with Section 5.0 ("Versions of the License"), and You must include a copy of this License with every copy of the Documentation You distribute. You may not offer or impose any terms that alter or restrict the applicable version of this License or the recipients' rights hereunder. However, You may include an additional document offering the additional rights described in Section 3.5 ("Required Notices").

3.2. Availability of Documentation.

Any Modification which You create or to which You contribute must be made available publicly in Editable Form under the terms of this License via a fixed medium or an accepted Electronic Distribution Mechanism.

3.3. Description of Modifications.

All Documentation to which You contribute must identify the changes You made to create that Documentation and the date of any change. You must include a prominent statement that the Modification is derived, directly or indirectly, from Original Documentation provided by the Initial Writer and include the name of the Initial Writer in the Documentation or via an electronic link that describes the origin or ownership of the Documentation. The foregoing change documentation may be created by using an electronic program that automatically tracks changes to the Documentation, and such changes must be available publicly for at least five years following release of the changed Documentation.

3.4. Intellectual Property Matters.

Contributor represents that Contributor believes that Contributor's Modifications are Contributor's original creation(s) and/or Contributor has sufficient rights to grant the rights conveyed by this License.

3.5. Required Notices.

You must duplicate the notice in the **Appendix** in each file of the Documentation. If it is not possible to put such notice in a particular Documentation file due to its structure, then You must include such notice in a location (such as a relevant directory) where a reader would be likely to look for such a notice, for example, via a hyperlink in each file of the Documentation that takes the reader to a page that describes the origin and ownership of the Documentation. If You created one or more Modification(s) You may add your name as a Contributor to the notice described in the **Appendix.**

You must also duplicate this License in any Documentation file (or with a hyperlink in each file of the Documentation) where You describe recipients' rights or ownership rights.

You may choose to offer, and to charge a fee for, warranty, support, indemnity or liability obligations to one or more recipients of Documentation. However, You may do so only on Your own behalf, and not on behalf of the Initial Writer or any Contributor. You must make it absolutely clear than any such warranty, support, indemnity or liability obligation is offered by You alone, and You hereby agree to indemnify the Initial Writer and every Contributor for any liability incurred by the Initial Writer or such Contributor as a result of warranty, support, indemnity or liability terms You offer.

3.6. Larger Works.

You may create a Larger Work by combining Documentation with other documents not governed by the terms of this License and distribute the Larger Work as a single product. In such a case, You must make sure the requirements of this License are fulfilled for the Documentation.

4. APPLICATION OF THIS LICENSE.

This License applies to Documentation to which the Initial Writer has attached this License and the notice in the **Appendix.**

5. VERSIONS OF THE LICENSE.

5.1. New Versions.

Initial Writer may publish revised and/or new versions of the License from time to time. Each version will be given a distinguishing version number.

5.2. Effect of New Versions.

Once Documentation has been published under a particular version of the License, You may always continue to use it under the terms of that version. You may also choose to use such Documentation under the terms of any subsequent version of the License published by _____ *[Insert name of the foundation, company, Initial Writer, or whoever may modify this License]*. No one other than _____ *[Insert name of the foundation, company, Initial Writer, or whoever may modify this License]* has the right to modify the terms of this License. Filling in the name of the Initial Writer, Original Documentation or Contributor in the notice described in the **Appendix** shall not be deemed to be Modifications of this License.

6. DISCLAIMER OF WARRANTY.

DOCUMENTATION IS PROVIDED UNDER THIS LICENSE ON AN "AS IS" BASIS, WITHOUT WARRANTY OF ANY KIND, EITHER EXPRESSED OR IMPLIED, INCLUDING, WITHOUT LIMITATION, WARRANTIES THAT THE DOCUMENTATION IS FREE OF DEFECTS, MERCHANTABLE, FIT FOR A PARTICULAR PURPOSE OR NON-INFRINGING. THE ENTIRE RISK AS TO THE QUALITY, ACCURACY, AND PERFOR-MANCE OF THE DOCUMENTATION IS WITH YOU. SHOULD ANY DOCUMENTA-TION PROVE DEFECTIVE IN ANY RESPECT, YOU (NOT THE INITIAL WRITER OR ANY OTHER CONTRIBUTOR) ASSUME THE COST OF ANY NECESSARY SERVICING, REPAIR OR CORRECTION. THIS DISCLAIMER OF WARRANTY CONSTITUTES AN ESSENTIAL PART OF THIS LICENSE. NO USE OF ANY DOCUMENTATION IS AUTHORIZED HEREUNDER EXCEPT UNDER THIS DISCLAIMER.

7. TERMINATION.

This License and the rights granted hereunder will terminate automatically if You fail to comply with terms herein and fail to cure such breach within 30 days of becoming aware of the breach. All sublicenses to the Documentation which are properly granted shall survive any termination of this License. Provisions which, by their nature, must remain in effect beyond the termination of this License shall survive.

8. LIMITATION OF LIABILITY.

UNDER NO CIRCUMSTANCES AND UNDER NO LEGAL THEORY, WHETHER IN TORT (INCLUDING NEGLIGENCE), CONTRACT, OR OTHERWISE, SHALL THE INITIAL WRITER, ANY OTHER CONTRIBUTOR, OR ANY DISTRIBUTOR OF DOCUMENTATION, OR ANY SUPPLIER OF ANY OF SUCH PARTIES, BE LIABLE TO ANY PERSON FOR ANY DIRECT, INDIRECT, SPECIAL, INCIDENTAL, OR

CONSEQUENTIAL DAMAGES OF ANY CHARACTER INCLUDING, WITHOUT LIMITATION, DAMAGES FOR LOSS OF GOODWILL, WORK STOPPAGE, COMPUTER FAILURE OR MALFUNCTION, OR ANY AND ALL OTHER DAMAGES OR LOSSES ARISING OUT OF OR RELATING TO THE USE OF THE DOCUMENTATION, EVEN IF SUCH PARTY SHALL HAVE BEEN INFORMED OF THE POSSIBILITY OF SUCH DAMAGES.

9. U.S. GOVERNMENT END USERS.

If Documentation is being acquired by or on behalf of the U.S. Government or by a U.S. Government prime contractor or subcontractor (at any tier), then the Government's rights in Documentation will be only as set forth in this Agreement; this is in accordance with 48 CFR 227.7201 through 227.7202-4 (for Department of Defense (DOD) acquisitions) and with 48 CFR 2.101 and 12.212 (for non-DOD acquisitions).

10. MISCELLANEOUS.

This License represents the complete agreement concerning the subject matter hereof. If any provision of this License is held to be unenforceable, such provision shall be reformed only to the extent necessary to make it enforceable. This License shall be governed by California law, excluding its conflict-of-law provisions. With respect to disputes or any litigation relating to this License, the losing party is responsible for costs, including without limitation, court costs and reasonable attorneys' fees and expenses. The application of the United Nations Convention on Contracts for the International Sale of Goods is expressly excluded. Any law or regulation which provides that the language of a contract shall be construed against the drafter shall not apply to this License.

Appendix

Public Documentation License Notice

The contents of this Documentation are subject to the Public Documentation License Version 1.0 (the "License"); you may only use this Documentation if you comply with the terms of this License. A copy of the License is available at _____ *[Insert hyperlink]*.

The Original Documentation is _____. The Initial Writer of the Original Documentation is _____ Copyright (C)_____ *[Insert year(s)]*. All Rights Reserved. (Initial Writer contact(s):_____ *[Insert hyperlink/alias]*).

Contributor(s): _____.
Portions created by _____ are Copyright (C)_____ *[Insert year(s)]*. All Rights Reserved. (Contributor contact(s):_____ *[Insert hyperlink/alias]*).

NOTE: The text of this **Appendix** may differ slightly from the text of the notices in the files of the Original Documentation. You should use the text of this **Appendix** rather than the text found in the Original Documentation for Your Modifications.

APPENDIX C

Contributor Agreements

In this appendix are the full texts of the contributor agreements for several open-source projects. Included with each is a pointer to where it may be found.

Apache Contributor Agreement

Free Software Foundation Copyright Assignment Form

Mozilla Contributor Assignment

OpenOffice.org Contributor Assignment

Project JXTA Contributor Assignment

Apache Contributor Agreement

The Apache Software Foundation
Individual Contributor License Agreement V2.0
http://www.apache.org/licenses/

Thank you for your interest in The Apache Software Foundation (the "Foundation"). In order to clarify the intellectual property license granted with Contributions from any person or entity, the Foundation must have a Contributor License Agreement ("CLA") on file that has been signed by each Contributor, indicating agreement to the license terms below. This license is for your protection as a Contributor as well as the protection of the Foundation and its users; it does not change your rights to use your own Contributions for any other purpose.

If you have not already done so, please complete and send an original signed Agreement to The Apache Software Foundation, 1901 Munsey Drive, Forest Hill, MD 21050-2747, U.S.A. If necessary, you may send it by facsimile to the Foundation at +1-410-803-2258. Please read this document carefully before signing and keep a copy for your records.

Full name: _____   E-Mail:_____

Mailing Address: _____   Telephone:_____

_____   Facsimile:_____

_____   Country: _____

You accept and agree to the following terms and conditions for Your present and future Contributions submitted to the Foundation. In return, the Foundation shall not use Your Contributions in a way that is contrary to the public benefit or inconsistent with its nonprofit status and bylaws in effect at the time of the Contribution. Except for the license granted herein to the Foundation and recipients of software distributed by the Foundation, You reserve all right, title, and interest in and to Your Contributions.

1. **Definitions.** "You" (or "Your") shall mean the copyright owner or legal entity authorized by the copyright owner that is making this Agreement with the Foundation. For legal entities, the entity making a Contribution and all other entities that control, are controlled by, or are under common control with that entity are considered to be a single Contributor. For the purposes of this definition, "control" means (i) the power, direct or indirect, to cause the direction or management of such entity, whether by contract or otherwise, or (ii) ownership of fifty percent (50%) or more of the outstanding shares, or (iii) beneficial ownership of such entity.

"Contribution" shall mean any original work of authorship, including any modifications or additions to an existing work, that is intentionally submitted by You to the Foundation for inclusion in, or documentation of, any of the products owned or managed by the Foundation (the "Work"). For the purposes of this definition, "submitted" means any form of electronic, verbal, or written communication sent to the Foundation or its representatives, including but not limited to communication on electronic mailing lists, source code control systems, and issue tracking systems that are managed by, or on behalf of, the Foundation for the purpose of discussing and improving the Work, but excluding communication that is conspicuously marked or otherwise designated in writing by You as "Not a Contribution."

2. **Grant of Copyright License.** Subject to the terms and conditions of this Agreement, You hereby grant to the Foundation and to recipients of software distributed by the Foundation a perpetual, worldwide, non-exclusive, no-charge, royalty-free, irrevocable copyright license to reproduce, prepare derivative works of, publicly display, publicly perform, sublicense, and distribute Your Contributions and such derivative works.

3. **Grant of Patent License.** Subject to the terms and conditions of this Agreement, You hereby grant to the Foundation and to recipients of software distributed by the Foundation a perpetual, worldwide, non-exclusive, no-charge, royalty-free, irrevocable (except as stated in this section) patent license to make, have made, use, offer to sell, sell, import, and otherwise transfer the Work, where such license applies only to those patent claims licensable by You that are necessarily infringed by Your Contribution(s) alone or by combination of Your Contribution(s) with the Work to which such Contribution(s) was submitted. If any entity institutes patent litigation against You or any other entity (including a cross-claim or counterclaim in a lawsuit) alleging that your Contribution, or the Work to which you have contributed, constitutes direct or contributory patent infringement, then any patent licenses granted to that entity under this Agreement for that Contribution or Work shall terminate as of the date such litigation is filed.

4. You represent that you are legally entitled to grant the above license. If your employer(s) has rights to intellectual property that you create that includes your Contributions, you represent that you have received permission to make Contributions on behalf of that employer, that your employer has waived such rights for your Contributions to the Foundation, or that your employer has executed a separate Corporate CLA with the Foundation.

5. You represent that each of Your Contributions is Your original creation (see section 7 for submissions on behalf of others). You represent that Your

Contribution submissions include complete details of any third-party license or other restriction (including, but not limited to, related patents and trademarks) of which you are personally aware and which are associated with any part of Your Contributions.

6.   You are not expected to provide support for Your Contributions, except to the extent You desire to provide support. You may provide support for free, for a fee, or not at all. Unless required by applicable law or agreed to in writing, You provide Your Contributions on an "AS IS" BASIS, WITHOUT WARRANTIES OR CONDITIONS OF ANY KIND, either express or implied, including, without limitation, any warranties or conditions of TITLE, NON-INFRINGEMENT, MERCHANTABILITY, or FITNESS FOR A PARTICULAR PURPOSE.

7.   Should You wish to submit work that is not Your original creation, You may submit it to the Foundation separately from any Contribution, identifying the complete details of its source and of any license or other restriction (including, but not limited to, related patents, trademarks, and license agreements) of which you are personally aware, and conspicuously marking the work as "Submitted on behalf of a third-party: [named here]".

8.   You agree to notify the Foundation of any facts or circumstances of which you become aware that would make these representations inaccurate in any respect.

Please sign: _____ Date: _____

Free Software Foundation Copyright Assignment Form

from: http://ftp.xemacs.org/old-beta/FSF/assign.changes

(The following is sent in an email message to a potential contributor from a developer working on an FSF project. For more details see: http://www.gnu.org/prep/maintain/html_node/Legally-significant.html

The way to assign copyright to the Foundation is to sign an assignment contract. This is what legally makes the FSF the copyright holder so that we can register the copyright on the new version. I'm assuming that you wrote these changes yourself; if other people wrote parts, we may need papers from them.

If you are employed to do programming (even at a university), or have made an agreement with your employer or school saying it owns programs you write, then you and we need a signed piece of paper from your employer disclaiming rights to the program.

The disclaimer should be signed by a vice president or general manager of the company. If you can't get at them, anyone else authorized to license software produced there will do. Here is a sample wording:

> Digital Stimulation Corporation hereby disclaims all copyright interest in the changes and enhancements made by Hugh Heffner to the program "seduce," also including any future revisions of these changes and enhancements.

> Digital Stimulation Corporation affirms that it has no other intellectual property interest that would undermine this release, or the use of the Program, and will do nothing to undermine it in the future.

> <signature of Ty Coon>, 1 April 1987
> Ty Coon, President of Vice, Digital Stimulation Corp.

(If your employer says they do have an intellectual property claim that could conflict with the use of the program, then please put me in touch with a suitable representative of the company, so that we can negotiate what to do about it.)

IMPORTANT: When you talk to your employer, *no matter what instructions they have given you*, don't fail to show them the sample disclaimer above, or a disclaimer with the details filled in for your specific case. Companies are usually willing to sign a disclaimer without any fuss. If you make your request less specific, you may open Pandora's box and cause a long and unnecessary delay. Below is the assignment contract that we usually use. You would need to print it out, sign it, and snail it to:

Richard Stallman
545 Tech Sq rm 425
Cambridge, MA 02139
USA

Please try to print the whole first page below on a single piece of paper. If it doesn't fit on one printed page, put it on two sides of a single piece of paper.

Don't forget to put down the date when you sign! Spell out the month name— don't use a number for the month. Dates using a number for the month are ambiguous; 2/8/95 means one thing in the US and another in Europe.

Snail a copy of the employer's disclaimer as well.

Please send me email about what you decide to do. If you have any questions, or would like something to be changed, ask rms@gnu.org via email.

ASSIGNMENT

For good and valuable consideration, receipt of which I acknowledge, I, NAME OF PERSON, hereby transfer to the Free Software Foundation, Inc. (the "Foundation") my entire right, title, and interest (including all rights under copyright) in my changes and enhancements to the program NAME OF PROGRAM, subject to the conditions below. These changes and enhancements are herein called the "Work." The work hereby assigned shall also include any future revisions of these changes and enhancements hereafter made by me.

Upon thirty days' prior written notice, the Foundation agrees to grant me non-exclusive rights to use the Work (i.e. my changes and enhancements, not the program which I enhanced) as I see fit; (and the Foundation's rights shall otherwise continue unchanged).

For the purposes of this contract, a work "based on the Work" means any work that in whole or in part incorporates or is derived from all or part of the Work.

The Foundation promises that all distribution of the Work, or of any work "based on the Work," that takes place under the control of the Foundation or its assignees, shall be on terms that explicitly and perpetually permit anyone possessing a copy of the work to which the terms apply, and possessing accurate notice of these terms, to redistribute copies of the work to anyone on the same terms. These terms shall not restrict which members of the public copies may be distributed to. These terms shall not require a member of the public to pay any royalty to the Foundation or to anyone else for any permitted use of the work they apply to, or to communicate with the Foundation or its agents in any way either when redistribution is performed or on any other occasion.

The Foundation promises that any program "based on the Work" offered to the public by the Foundation or its assignees shall be offered in the form of machine-readable source code, in addition to any other forms of the Foundation's choosing. However, the Foundation is free to choose at its convenience the media of distribution for machine-readable source code.

The Foundation promises to give or send me, upon reasonable prior notice and payment of a fee no more than twenty times the cost of the necessary materials and postage, a copy of any or all of the works "based on the Work" that it offers to the public or that it has offered within the past six months, or that it distributed for the first time within the past six months. For works that are programs, the machine-readable source code shall be included. My request shall detail whether I wish to receive all such works or specific works. My choice of works to request may affect the cost and therefore the fee.

I hereby agree that if I have or acquire hereafter any patent or interface copyright or other intellectual property interest dominating the program enhanced by the Work (or use of that program), such dominating interest will not be used to undermine the effect of this assignment, i.e. the Foundation and the general public will be licensed to use, in that program and its derivative works, without royalty or limitation, the subject matter of the dominating interest. This license provision will be binding on my heirs, assignees, or other successors to the dominating interest, as well as on me.

I hereby represent and warrant that I am the sole copyright holder for the Work and that I have the right and power to enter into this contract. I hereby indemnify and hold harmless the Foundation, its officers, employees, and agents against any and all claims, actions or damages (including attorney's reasonable fees) asserted by or paid to any party on account of a breach or alleged breach of the foregoing warranty. I make no other express or implied warranty (including without limitation, in this disclaimer of warranty, any warranty of MERCHANT-ABILITY or FITNESS FOR A PARTICULAR PURPOSE).

Agreed: [signature]   Date: [Write the month with LETTERS]

For the Free Software Foundation,

Richard Stallman, President:

Please print the following as a separate page.

Please email a copy of the information on this page to fsf-records@gnu.ai. mit.edu, if you can, so that our clerk doesn't have to type it in. Use your full name as the subject line.

[For the copyright registration, what country are you a citizen of? What year were you born? Please write the information here; sending it separately (e.g. in a message) makes extra clerical work for us.]

[Please write your email address here.]

[Please write your snail address here, so we can snail a copy back to you.]

[Which files have you changed so far, and which new files have you written so far?]

Mozilla Contributor Assignment

taken from: http://www.mozilla.org/hacking/CVS-Contributor-Form.pdf

mozilla.org CVS Contributor Form
For Committing Code To The mozilla.org CVS Source Repository

In order to obtain the ability to commit changes to a mozilla.org CVS source repository and become a "Committer" you must indicate your agreement to the terms below by completing and signing this agreement and returning it to mozilla.org at the address specified at http://www.mozilla.org/hacking/form.html (the "Notification Address").

1. Contact Information

Name: _____

Employer Name:_____

(complete Employer Name if you are committing code to mozilla.org on behalf of your employer)

Email: _____

Phone Number:_____

Address:_____

If you are committing code on behalf of your employer, then you confirm that an appropriate person at the "Employer Name" above has authorized the inclusion of such code in the mozilla.org source repository under the terms of this agreement.

2. Treatment of Account. Committer's mozilla.org account username will be the email address (above) with the '@' character replaced by '%'. Committer will not allow anyone other than Committer to use this account or username to access a mozilla.org CVS repository or other mozilla.org systems. Should Committer become aware of any such use, Committer will immediately notify mozilla.org in the manner specified at http://www.mozilla.org/hacking/form.html; until such notice is received Committer will be presumed to have taken all actions made through Committer's account. Mozilla.org will have complete control and discretion over capabilities assigned to Committer's account, and may disable Committer's account for any reason at any time. Committer's name and account will be visible worldwide via the Internet.

3. License Terms. Code committed to the mozilla.org CVS source repository ("Committed Code") must be governed by the Netscape Public License ("NPL"),

Mozilla Public License ("MPL"), or another license acceptable to mozilla.org. Committer will verify that Committed Code contains the text of Exhibit A of the MPL or NPL, or another license acceptable to mozilla.org. Other licenses are not acceptable by mozilla.org until mozilla.org declares them to be acceptable in writing.

4. Committing Code Created by Others. Committer may check-in code to the mozilla.org CVS source repository that was not written by Committer, provided that:

> a) Committer identifies the author of such code through a comment in the CVS log that includes the name and email address of the author; and
> b) To the best of Committer's knowledge, such code complies with the terms of this agreement.

5. Cryptography. Committer understands that cryptographic code may be subject to government regulations with which mozilla.org and/or entities using Committed Code must comply. Any code which contains any of the items listed below must either be checked-in to a mozilla.org module explicitly identified as containing cryptography, or must not be checked-in until mozilla.org staff has been notified and has approved such contribution in writing.

> a) Cryptographic capabilities or features; or
> b) Calls to cryptographic features; or
> c) User interface elements which provide context relating to cryptography; or
> d) Code which may, under casual inspection, appear to be cryptographic.

6. Notices and Knowledge. Committer agrees that, to the best of his/her knowledge:

> a) For any committed Code using the NPL or the MPL, any notices required by Sections 3.3, 3.4, or Section 4 of the NPL or MPL are included in any Committed Code; and
> b) Committed Code does not violate the rights of any person or entity.

Signed: _____ Date: _____

Printed Name:_____

v. 2/01

OpenOffice.org Contributor Assignment

taken from: http://www.openoffice.org/licenses/jca.pdf

OpenOffice.org Open Source Project
Joint Copyright Assignment by Contributor
To Sun Microsystems, Inc. ("Sun")

Contact Information:

Full Name: _____ (the "Contributor")
e-mail: _____
Mailing Address: _____
_____

Telephone: _____
Facsimile: _____
Country: _____

1. Contributor owns, and has sufficient rights to contribute, all source code and related material intended to be compiled or integrated with the source code for the OpenOffice.org open source product (the "Contribution") which Contributor has ever delivered, and Sun has accepted, for incorporation into the technology made available under the OpenOffice.org open source project.

2. Contributor hereby assigns to Sun joint ownership in all worldwide common law and statutory rights associated with the copyrights, copyright application, copyright registration and moral rights in the Contribution to the extent allowable under applicable local laws and copyright conventions. Contributor agrees that this assignment may be submitted by Sun to register a copyright in the Contribution. Contributor retains the right to use the Contribution for Contributor's own purposes. This Joint Copyright Assignment supersedes and replaces all prior copyright assignments made by Contributor to Sun under the OpenOffice.org project.

3. Contributor is legally entitled to grant the above assignment and agrees not to provide any Contribution that violates any law or breaches any contract.

Signed: _____ Date: _____
Printed Name: _____
Please fax and then send a signed original of this assignment to:
Fax: +1-650-562-2629

Mail: Eric Renaud
        OpenOffice.org/Sun Microsystems
        4120 Network Circle, USCA12-105
        Santa Clara, CA 95054 USA

Project JXTA Contributor Assignment

taken from: http://www.jxta.org/jxta_contrib_agreement.PDF

Sun Project JXTA Software Contributor License Agreement
Version 15 March 2003

Thank you for your interest in Project JXTA (the "Project"). In order to clarify the intellectual property license granted with contributions of software from any person or entity to the Project (a "Contributor"), Sun requires that a Contributor License Agreement be on file that has been signed by each Contributor, indicating agreement to the license terms below. This license is for your protection as a Contributor of software to the Project and does not change your right to use your own contributions for any other purpose.

If you have not already done so, please complete this Agreement and send it by facsimile to the Project Office or send a photocopy by regular mail to:

By Fax:

JXTA Project Community Manager

c/o Lauren Zuravleff

(408) 276-6193

By Mail:

The JXTA Project Community Manager

c/o Lauren Zuravleff

Sun Microsystems, Inc.
Mail Stop USCA21-308
4210 Network Circle
Santa Clara, CA 95054
USA

Please read this document carefully before signing and keep the original for your records.

Your Full Name: _____   e-mail: _____

Mailing Address: _____   Telephone: _____

_____   Facsimile: _____

_____   Country: _____

JXTA.org User Name: _____

Contributor and Sun Microsystems, Inc. ("Sun") hereby accept and agree to the following terms and conditions:

1. "Contributions" means all past, present and future contributions of object code, source code and documentation to the Project, however submitted by

Contributor to the Project, excluding any submissions that are conspicuously marked or otherwise designated in writing by Contributor as "Not a Contribution."

2. Contributor hereby grants to Sun's Project JXTA, a world-wide, royalty-free, non-exclusive license:

(a) under Contributor's intellectual property rights (other than patent or trademark) Licensable by Contributor, for Sun and any third party developer of Project JXTA to use, reproduce, modify, display, perform, sublicense and distribute the Contributions created by such Contributor (or portions thereof) with or without modification; and

(b) under Contributor's patent claims infringed by the making, using, or selling of Contributions made by that Contributor either alone and/or in combination with other Contributions (or portions of such combination), to make, use, sell, offer for sale, have made, and/or otherwise dispose of: 1) Contributions made by that Contributor (or portions thereof); and 2) the combination of Contributions made by that Contributor with other software and hardware.

(c) the licenses granted in Sections 2(a) and 2(b) above are effective on the date Contributor delivers the Contributions to Sun's Project JXTA.

(d) notwithstanding Section 2(b) above, no patent license is granted: 1) for any code that a licensee has deleted from the Contribution; 2) separate from the Contribution; or 3) for infringements caused by: (i) third party modifications of a Contribution or (ii) the combination of Contributions with other software or other devices if such combination causes the infringement.

Except for the rights granted to Sun's Project JXTA in this paragraph, Contributor reserves all right, title and interest in and to your Contributions.

3. Contributor represents that Contributor is legally entitled to grant the above licenses. If Contributor's employer(s) have rights to intellectual property that Contributor creates, Contributor represents that Contributor has received permission to make the Contributions on behalf of that employer, or that Contributor's employer has waived such rights for Contributor's Contributions to the Project.

4. Contributor represents that, except as disclosed in Contributor's Contribution submission(s), each of Contributor's Contributions is Contributor's original creation. Contributor represents that Contributor's Contribution submission(s) include complete details of any license or other restriction (including, but not limited to, related patents and trademarks) associated with any part of Contributor's Contribution(s) (including a copy of any applicable license agreement). Contributor agrees to notify Sun of any facts or circumstances of

which Contributor becomes aware that would make Contributor's representations in this Agreement inaccurate in any respect.

5. Contributor is not expected to provide support for Contributor's Contributions, except to the extent Contributor desires to provide support. Contributor may provide support for free, for a fee, or not at all. Contributor's Contributions are provided as-is, with all faults defects and errors, and without warranty of any kind (either express or implied) including, without limitation, any implied warranty of merchantability and fitness for a particular purpose and any warranty of non-infringement.

Please sign: _____ Date: _____

APPENDIX D

Codename Spinnaker

The following article was originally published on XML.com.[1]

Codename Spinnaker

By Leigh Dodds
July 19, 2000

The Apache XML developer lists have seen some turmoil recently over a proposed plan to develop their next generation XML parser. However a phoenix may have been borne out of the ashes: this week we report on "Spinnaker," a.k.a. the Xerces Refactoring Initiative.

SPARRING OVER SPINNAKER

In a bold announcement on the general Apache developer list, James Davidson outlined his intention to start a project, code-named "Spinnaker," with some ambitious goals:

> Spinnaker is an attempt to create a next generation Apache XML Parser based on all the lessons learned from the current versions of Xerces and Crimson.

The announcement listed goals for the Spinnaker effort itself. Amongst these was the desire to produce a parser suitable for inclusion in the Java Development Kit, a goal that apparently had internal backing from Sun.

To say that the announcement was welcomed with less than open arms by some of the IBM developers would be an understatement:

> Looks like a "coup d'etat" to me.

---

1. http://www.xml.com/pub/a/2000/07/19/deviant/index.html. Copyright ©2000 O'Reilly & Associates, Inc. Reprinted with permission from O'Reilly & Associates, Inc.

377

This was the reaction of Arnaud Le Hors. Andy Clark, another IBM developer, questioned the wisdom of beginning such a project at the start of the weekend:

> *Is it possible that, in the future, we hear about submissions to the tree *before* everyone goes home on Friday? I want us all to work together on the future of the Xerces parser instead of being surprised by a new source tree over a weekend.*

These opening remarks set the tone for a heated debate, which threatened to turn into an IBM versus Sun squabble over who was playing fair by open source rules. Abrasive remarks were exchanged, with both sides quickly disavowing any corporate-lead motives, whilst questioning those of the other side. James Davidson believed the timing of his announcement was irrelevant:

> *This is open source, Apache style. People work whenever they work and that's the way this all works. Most Apache developers don't work on the main sources during the typical M-F 8-4 (local time) window. They work when they get time, or the muse is with them, or whatever. There are no limits, it's a 24/7 shop and to be blunt, conformance with a corporate schedule isn't part of the mandate.*

Arnaud Le Hors singled out the method of initiating the project for particular criticism:

> *The problem is not about Sun vs IBM. It is not about corporate vs individuals. Not about creating a new project. Not about working on week-ends. Not about questioning the current goals or implementation. The problem is about making decision on your own. Not communicating. Not consulting others in the project.*

Ironically, it seems that a lack of communication, along with a good deal of miscommunication, was the root cause of the argument. This is symptomatic of an internal divide within the Apache parser development community. Stefano Mazzocchi, in valiant attempts to defuse the situation, highlighted the cause of the divide:

> *...Tomcat, Xerces and Xalan didn't start as Apache projects and their development community was _imposed_ and did not emerge from the community of volunteers.*

Both Xerces and Crimson are "donations" to the Apache effort. However, these donations haven't been made into the arms of a waiting team of Apache volunteers. Both projects are still largely driven by development teams at IBM and Sun. Mazzocchi's key point is that simply providing a public CVS server does not make for a good open source project. If the development teams continue as they have done prior to opening the source (e.g., by having off-line design meetings), then there's little chance for a developer community to form around the project.

Mazzocchi suggested that the Tomcat developers have managed to make the transition from internally driven development to a full open source community, whereas the Xerces, Xalan, and Crimson teams have yet to achieve it. Rajiv Mordani further illustrated this point:

> . . .since most of you'll work in the same office there is a lot of things that happen in there that should be actually done on the mailing lists. I don't remember seeing a mail going out proposing the implementation of schemas for [example]. The only info that was sent out is that the repository will be a little unstable for the next few days as schema support is being added to Xerces so please use the tagged version of the workspace.

It would be wrong to single out just the IBM developers in this regard. It appears that the Sun team is as much at fault—although, as Brett McLaughin commented, it's the external perspective that matters:

> What I meant to focus on, and what we may have miscommunicated on, is the /perception/ of what is happening. . . The _perception_ . . .is what we have to fight in an open source project.

As tempers cooled, it quickly became apparent that the perception that neither team is interested in the other's software was incorrect. Once the rhetoric was laid aside, a lot of common ground was discovered. At that point the real work started.

To help push matters forward, Sam Ruby suggested that the project should be known as the Xerces Refactoring Initiative (XRI)—a name he described as "intentionally boring." Stefano Mazzocchi produced a "virtual press release" to explain the common purpose of the initiative:

> The Apache XML community started a "Refactoring Initiative" to create [a] next generation XML parser for Java. This will be known as "codename Spinnaker" (or simply spinnaker) and will be the collective design whiteboard where the worldwide Apache community of individuals will openly develop such [a] new XML parser. The final result of this RI will be determined when "final" status is reached and, as always, decided by the community.

TAKING THE INITIATIVE

Turf wars aside, what are the driving forces for XRI, and what are its goals?

In his opening announcement, James Davidson listed several perceived problems with Xerces. These included performance problems under HotSpot, and code complexity. Both of these appear to be the result of efforts put in by the Xerces team to optimize the parser for the Java 1.1 platform. While the efforts have clearly paid off, the optimizations do make the code harder to understand, and limit the ability of HotSpot to automatically optimize performance on Java 1.2 and 1.3 virtual machines.

Edwin Goei observed that code complexity is one reason why additional contributions haven't been made by the XML community:

> *The main objection I have to the current Xerces code is not about which VM it runs on, but on the ability for a developer to understand the code and make changes to it. I think one major reason there has not been more developer participation is because the code is difficult to understand ... I looked at two other parsers that I believe are easier to understand: Aelfred2 (not Apache) and Crimson/ProjectX... With Xerces it takes much more effort to understand the code and I prefer not to make changes to code I don't understand.*

This observation was echoed by Brett McLaughlin who suggested that developers are turning their efforts elsewhere:

> *I have lots of users on the JDOM lists who think Xerces is great, but are totally scared by the code—unfortunately, I can't blame them. They would rather spend their time working on JDOM, or something similar.*

The complexity of Xerces was one issue that wasn't disputed. Arnaud Le Hors explained that the IBM Xerces team had been considering a redesign all along:

> *The fact is that we're also interested in a new version of Xerces which is more modular. As a matter of fact, we've given it quite some thoughts already, and [have] even written down a first draft of a design document on it that we'll be happy to send out as input.*
>
> *We don't think the current model is perfect. We refer to it as "the star model." Basically every piece knows about the others and the flow of information is far from being linear. Instead, we're thinking of a pipeline model. Where every piece works as a box with an input and output stream working independently of the others. It will be hard to make this as efficient as the current parser. But this, among other things, would let one to easily plugin the validator or not.*

Once the common ground had been found, the requirements began to emerge thick and fast. Scott Boag described his vision of what the initiative would involve:

> *I think the point is to build/refactor a next generation, commercially viable, parser based on the current state of the art (including and especially Schema*

support), and the collected requirements. It is indeed pointless, in my opinion, to talk about "adapting" other code bases—what is going to occur is a mining operation from Xerces and Crimson. Anything that's open source with the right license is open to be mined for ideas...

Arved Sandstrom agreed that the search for ideas should be expanded to all parsers with available source and suitable licensing:

There's stuff that microparsers like nanoxml can contribute to the discussion. Python XML parsers (and there is more than one) are quite good. If we are talking James Clark, let's not forget expat; this is a very good parser and represents the core of the Perl XML processing family.

...I think there is potential here for making this project best-of-breed when it comes to showing that open-source can do process.

The project has now taken on a life of its own: differences seem to have been set aside (at least temporarily) to focus instead on the technology. Ed Staub has taken on the task of co-ordinating the collection and publication of the XRI requirements. The discussion has already thrown out some interesting ideas such as Grammar caching (avoiding reparsing of the same DTD multiple times), and compiling an XML Schema into a custom parser.

There's obviously a long road ahead for XRI/Spinnaker but it should yield some interesting results. Don't go looking for a Xerces 2 just yet, and don't despair, as Xerces 1 is not about to be abandoned: the IBM team is currently hard at work completing XML Schema support.

Perhaps the key benefit of this project, despite its rocky beginnings, is that the internal fragility of the Apache XML may be removed. With effort from both the Xerces and Crimson teams, as well as the wider developer community, we'll not only benefit from a next-generation parser, but also a more stable and collaborative process underpinning the development of a vital component in the XML infrastructure.

BIBLIOGRAPHY

Beck, Kent (1999). *Extreme Programming Explained: Embrace Change.* Boston: Addison-Wesley.

Blood, Rebecca (2002). *The Weblog Handbook: Practical Advice on Creating and Maintaining Your Blog.* Cambridge, MA: Perseus Publishing.

Boston Consulting Group Hacker Survey (2002). Available at: http://www.osdn. com/bcg/index.html

Brooks, Frederick P. (1995). *The Mythical Man-Month: Essays on Software Engineering.* Reading, MA: Addison-Wesley.

Chesbrough, Henry (2003). *Open Innovation: The New Imperative for Creating and Profiting from Technology.* Cambridge, MA: Harvard Business School Press.

DeMarco, Tom, and Timothy Lister (1999). *Peopleware: Productive Projects and Teams,* 2nd ed. New York: Dorset House.

DiBona, Chris, Sam Ockman, and Mark Stone (eds.) (1999). *Open Sources: Voices from the Open Source Revolution.* Sebastopol, CA: O'Reilly & Associates, Available at: http://www.oreilly.com/catalog/opensources/book/toc.html

Dinkelacker, Jamie, Pankaj K. Garg, Rob Miller, and Dean Nelson (2001). *Progressive Open Source.* Palo Alto: HP Laboratories. Available at: http:// www.hpl.hp.com/techreports/2001/HPL-2001-233.html

Dodds, Leigh (2000). "Codename Spinnaker."Available at: http://www.xml.com/ pub/a/2000/07/19/deviant/index.html

Fleury, Marc, and Julia Lindfors (2001). "Enabling Component Architecture with JML." Available at: http://www.onjava.com/pub/a/onjava/2001/02/01/ jmx.html

Florida, Richard (2002). *The Rise of the Creative Class.* New York: Basic Books.

FLOSS—Free/Libre Open Source Software: Survey and Study, Berlecon Research (2002). Available at: http://www.infonomics.nl/FLOSS/report

Fogel, Karl (1999). *Open Source Development with CVS.* Scottsdale, AZ: CoriolisOpen Press.

Freiberger, Paul, and Swaine Michael (2000). *Fire in the Valley*, 2nd ed. New York: McGraw-Hill.

Gabriel, Richard P. (1990). "Lisp: Good News, Bad News, How to Win Big." Keynote address given at the European Conference on the Practical Applications of Lisp, Cambridge University, Cambridge, England, March 1990. (Reprinted in AI Expert, June 1991, pp. 31–39; exccrpted in Simson Garfinkel, Daniel Weise, and Steven Strassman (1994), *The Unix-Haters Handbook*. San Mateo, CA: IDG Books.) Available at: http://dreamsongs.com/WorseIsBetter.html

Gabriel, Richard P., and Ron Goldman (2000). "Mob Software: The Erotic Life of Code." Invited talk given at the ACM Conference on Object-Oriented Programming, Systems, Languages, and Applications on October 19, 2000, in Minneapolis, Minnesota, USA. Available at http://www.dreamsongs.com/Essays.html

Gabriel, Richard P., and William N. Joy (1998). "Sun Community Source License Principles." Available at: http://www.sun.com/software/communitysource/principles.html

Gamma, Erich, and Kent Beck (2003). *Contributing to Eclipse: Principles, Patterns, and Plugins*. Boston: Addison-Wesley.

Gibbs, W. Wyatt (1994). "Software's Chronic Crisis." Scientific American 271, 3 (September): p.72–81.

Hall, Peter (2002). *Cities of Tomorrow: An Intellectual History of Urban Planning and Design in the Twentieth Century*. Malden, MA: Blackwell Publishers.

Hugo, Richard (1992). *The Triggering Town: Lectures and Essays on Poetry and Writing*. New York: W. W. Norton.

Kaplan, Robert, and David Norton (2002). *The Strategy-Focused Organization*. Cambridge, MA: Harvard Business School Press.

Kim, Amy Jo (2000). *Community Building on the Web*. Berkeley, CA: Peachpit Press.

Leuf, Bo, and Ward Cunningham (2001). *The Wiki Way: Collaboration and Sharing on the Internet*. Boston: Addison-Wesley.

Moffett, Charles S., Ruth Berson, Barbara Lee Williams, and Fronia E. Wissman (1989). *The New Painting, Impressionism, 1874–1886: An Exhibition Organized by the Fine Arts Museums of San Francisco with the National Gallery of Art, Washington*. Seattle: University of Washington Press.

Moody, Glyn (2001). *Rebel Code: Inside Linux and the Open Source Revolution*. Cambridge, MA: Perseus Publishing.

Open Source Software Challenge in 2001. (2001). Stanford University Graduate School of Business Case SM 85, Stanford, CA.

Petzinger, Tom (2000). *The New Pioneers: The Men and Women Who Are Transforming the Workplace and Marketplace*. New York: Simon & Schuster.

Preminger, Alex, T.V.F. Brogan (co-editors) (1993). *New Princeton Encyclopedia of Poetry and Poetics*. Ewing NJ: Princeton University Press.

Raymond, Eric (1999). *The Cathedral & the Bazaar*. Sebastopol, CA: O'Reilly & Associates. Original paper available at: http://www.catb.org/~esr/writings/cathedral-bazaar/

Rhodes, Richard (1995) *How to Write: Advice and Reflections*. New York: William Morrow & Co.

Shah, Sonali (2003). *Community-Based Innovation & Product Development: Findings from Open Source Software and Consumer Sporting Goods*, PhD diss., Massachusetts Institute of Technology.

Standish Group (1995). *The CHAOS Report (1994)*. Report of the Standish Group. Available at: http://www.standishgroup.com/sample_research/chaos_1994_1.php

Steele, Guy L., Jr. (1984). *Common Lisp: the Language*, 2nd ed. Bedford, MA: Digital Press.

Tellis, Gerard J., and Peter N. Golder (2002). *Will & Vision: How Latecomers Grow to Dominate Markets*. New York: McGraw-Hill.

Yates, JoAnne, and Wanda J. Orlikowski (1993a). "From Memo to Dialogue: Enacting Genres of Communications in Electronic Mail." MIT Sloan Working Paper #3525, Sloan School, MIT, Cambridge, MA.

Yates, JoAnne, and Wanda J. Orlikowski (1993b). "Knee-Jerk Anti-LOOPism and Other E-mail Phenomena: Oral, Written, and Electronic Patterns in Computer-Mediated Communication." MIT Sloan Working Paper #3578-93, Sloan School, MIT, Cambridge, MA.

INDEX

A

AbiWord project, 254
Acquisition and partnership, 96
ADA programming language, 120
Agile Manifesto, 40–42
Agile methodologies, 39–45
    defined, 39–40
    development principles, 40–42
    open source versus, 40, 42
    practices, 40
Aladdin Enterprises, 81
Allen, Paul, 279
Allman, Eric, 86
All-volunteer open source, 7
Amanuenses, 46
Ampex, 23
Announcements, 264
Apache, 31
    committers, 150
    governance, 42
    HTTP Server Project, 56, 162, 224
    Incubator project, 66, 67
    license, 116, 126, 127, 128, 286–289
    Portable Runtime, 56
    Project Management Committee, 235
    topos, 226
    web server, 18, 47
    XML Project, 258
Apache Software Foundation, 126, 151, 162, 204
    Apache license changes, 127
    committers rule, 239–240
    conflict resolution, 278
    Contributor Agreement, 362–364

entry path into, 66
governing board, 235
wiki, 243
work-in-progress effect, 67
Apache Software License, 116, 126, 127, 128, 286–289
    reasons to use, 190
Apple, 4
    Darwin project, 4, 5, 81
    Macintosh, 21
    open source projects, 4
    OS X, 4, 5, 81
Apprenticeships, 77
Approval process, 205–216
    business analysis, 207–208
    creating new subprojects, 268–269
    due diligence, 208
    EOL product, 215–216
    existing project participation, 211–212
    individuals, 212–214
    small project, 215–216
    source code release, 207–208
    stopping/lessening participation, 214–215
    third-party code use, 208–211
Archives, 145, 158, 166, 204, 262
ARPAnet, 3, 10, 46
Artistic License, 116, 125, 290–292
AspectJ, 59
AT&T, 19, 67, 251
Audience, targeting, 186, 229–230
Augmentation of Human Intellect project, 22
Augustin, Larry, 31